# Academic Podcasting and Mobile Assisted Language Learning:
## Applications and Outcomes

Betty Rose Facer
*Old Dominion University, Virginia*

Mohammed Abdous
*Old Dominion University, Virginia*

**INFORMATION SCIENCE REFERENCE**

Hershey · New York

| | |
|---|---|
| Senior Editorial Director: | Kristin Klinger |
| Director of Book Publications: | Julia Mosemann |
| Editorial Director: | Lindsay Johnston |
| Acquisitions Editor: | Erika Carter |
| Typesetter: | Casey Conapitski |
| Production Coordinator: | Jamie Snavely |
| Cover Design: | Nick Newcomer |

Published in the United States of America by
Information Science Reference (an imprint of IGI Global)
701 E. Chocolate Avenue
Hershey PA 17033
Tel: 717-533-8845
Fax: 717-533-8661
E-mail: cust@igi-global.com
Web site: http://www.igi-global.com

Library of Congress Cataloging-in-Publication Data

Academic podcasting and mobile assisted language learning : applications and outcomes / Betty Rose Facer and Mohammed Abdous, Editors.
     p. cm.
   Includes bibliographical references and index.
   ISBN 978-1-60960-141-6 (hardcover) -- ISBN 978-1-60960-143-0 (ebook)  1. Language and languages--Study and teaching--Computer network resources. 2. Language and languages--Computer-assisted instruction. 3.  Second language acquisition.  I. Facer, Betty Rose. II. Abdous, Mohammed.
   P53.285.A23 2011
   418'.00785--dc22
                          2010043163

British Cataloguing in Publication Data
A Cataloguing in Publication record for this book is available from the British Library.

All work contributed to this book is new, previously-unpublished material. The views expressed in this book are those of the authors, but not necessarily of the publisher.

# Table of Contents

**Foreword** ..................................................................................................................... xi

**Preface** .......................................................................................................................... xiii

**Acknowledgment** ......................................................................................................... xvi

### Section 1
### MALL and Language Acquisition

**Chapter 1**
Podcasting - Past, Present and Future: Applications of Academic Podcasting In and
Out of the Language Classroom ............................................................................................ 1
> *Lara Lomicka, University of South Carolina, USA*
> *Gillian Lord, University of Florida, USA*

**Chapter 2**
Four L2 Learning Objectives to Guide Podcast Design ...................................................... 21
> *Claudia Fernández, Knox College, USA*

**Chapter 3**
Going beyond Audio: Adding Multimedia to Podcasts for Foreign Language Education ................... 37
> *Tony Gonzalez, University of Georgia, USA*

**Chapter 4**
Getting Started: Academic Podcasting made Simple.......................................................... 54
> *Maria Elena Corbeil, The University of Texas at Brownsville/Texas Southmost College, USA*
> *Joseph Rene Corbeil, The University of Texas at Brownsville/Texas Southmost College, USA*

**Chapter 5**

Challenges of Adopting Web 2.0 and Mobile 2.0 for Language Learning .......................................... 70
*Su-Ling Hsueh, Defense Language Institute, USA*

**Section 2**
**Student Centered Projects**

**Chapter 6**

Mobile-Assisted Language Learning from the Student Perspective: Encouraging
Effective Language Learning Strategies Outside of the Classroom ....................................................... 93
*Daryl L. Beres, Mount Holyoke College, USA*

**Chapter 7**

Simulating Immersion: Podcasting in Spanish Teaching ...................................................................... 111
*Mario Daniel Martín, The Australian National University, Australia*
*Elizabeth Ann Beckmann, The Australian National University, Australia*

**Section 3**
**MALL and Study Abroad**

**Chapter 8**

iStudyAbroad ......................................................................................................................................... 133
*Kathryn Murphy-Judy, Virginia Commonwealth University, USA*

**Chapter 9**

Crossing Classroom Settings and Academic Disciplines while Crossing
Geographic Boundaries .......................................................................................................................... 147
*Giovanna Summerfield, Auburn University, USA*

**Section 4**
**MALL and ESL**

**Chapter 10**

A Case Study of Using Podcasts in ESL Modules for Hong Kong Pre-Service Teachers
and its Impact on their Attitudes toward Podcasting ............................................................................ 160
*Adrian Ting, Hong Kong Institute of Education, Hong Kong*

**Chapter 11**
Podcasts in Four Categories: Applications to Language Learning ....................................................... 176
*Ulugbek Nurmukhamedov, Northern Arizona University, USA*
*Randall Sadler, University of Illinois at Urbana-Champaign, USA*


**Afterword**.................................................................................................................................................... 196

**Compilation of References** ........................................................................................................................ 198

**About the Contributors** ............................................................................................................................. 216

**Index**............................................................................................................................................................ 221

# Detailed Table of Contents

**Foreword** ............................................................................................................................. xi

**Preface** .............................................................................................................................. xiii

**Acknowledgment** ............................................................................................................. xvi

### Section 1
### MALL and Language Acquisition

**Chapter 1**

Podcasting - Past, Present and Future: Applications of Academic Podcasting In and
Out of the Language Classroom .................................................................................................. 1
    *Lara Lomicka, University of South Carolina, USA*
    *Gillian Lord, University of Florida, USA*

This chapter provides the necessary and essential foundation for academic podcasting technology in the K-12 and higher education settings by providing a brief (yet comprehensive) history of relevant research into podcasting, by offering practical suggestions for its use, and by exploring the future trends in podcasting. Authors Lomicka and Lord skillfully draw upon the documented research in Second Language Acquisition (SLA) and discuss to the implementation of pedagogically sound practices that remain true to communicative and meaningful tasks. Their conclusion is that, considering its past and present, academic podcasting technology has a promising future in education.

**Chapter 2**

Four L2 Learning Objectives to Guide Podcast Design ............................................................ 21
    *Claudia Fernández, Knox College, USA*

Fernández identifies four learning objectives to consider when searching for or developing academic podcasting technology for second language acquisition. In her chapter, she stresses the importance of podcast design based on sound L2 acquisition theories and best teaching practices, stressing the creation of podcasts that are comprehensible and meaningful, and that effectively deal with authentic language and culture.

**Chapter 3**

Going beyond Audio: Adding Multimedia to Podcasts for Foreign Language Education .................. 37
*Tony Gonzalez, University of Georgia, USA*

A more technical approach to multimedia podcast production with a pedagogical basis is provided by Gonzalez in Chapter 3. The author discusses the textual and visual components for language learning, from the initial planning stages of a project to its final development, offering a comprehensive pros-and-cons approach for each strategy. In addition, Gonzalez provides important and necessary information related to copyright issues, free multimedia content, and Creative Commons.

**Chapter 4**

Getting Started: Academic Podcasting made Simple.......................................................................... 54
*Maria Elena Corbeil, The University of Texas at Brownsville/Texas Southmost College, USA*
*Joseph Rene Corbeil, The University of Texas at Brownsville/Texas Southmost College, USA*

A simple and straightforward guide to creating a podcast is the basis for Chapter 4. In this chapter, authors Corbeil and Corbeil explore the instructional, technological, and production factors involved in using academic podcasting technology. The authors offer script samples and suggestions, surveys and results, and reflections on lessons learned.

**Chapter 5**

Challenges of Adopting Web 2.0 and Mobile 2.0 for Language Learning ........................................... 70
*Su-Ling Hsueh, Defense Language Institute, USA*

Can students' burgeoning use of social networks contribute to their language learning? The author discusses various Web 2.0 applications and their potential applications and challenges, and explores the ways in which mobile technologies are assisting language learning.

## Section 2
## Student Centered Projects

**Chapter 6**

Mobile-Assisted Language Learning from the Student Perspective: Encouraging
Effective Language Learning Strategies Outside of the Classroom ...................................................... 93
*Daryl L. Beres, Mount Holyoke College, USA*

M-Learning (or mobile learning) in second language acquisition redirects the focus from the instructor to the learner. From this perspective, Beres investigates how students choose to integrate academic podcasting technology and MALL into their daily routines and how students perceive these technologies. Beres reports on the long-term research at her university concerning the use of m-learning strategies for language studies.

**Chapter 7**

Simulating Immersion: Podcasting in Spanish Teaching.................................................. 111
*Mario Daniel Martín, The Australian National University, Australia*
*Elizabeth Ann Beckmann, The Australian National University, Australia*

Based on careful planning and quality design, Martín and Beckmann explain the background, educational design, and outcomes of their academic podcasting technology experiences over a three-year period. They describe the successful simulated immersion experience and the ways in which the fully interactive engagement of their students has set their program apart from others.

## Section 3
## MALL and Study Abroad

**Chapter 8**

iStudyAbroad ................................................................................................................. 133
*Kathryn Murphy-Judy, Virginia Commonwealth University, USA*

The potential for m-learning during the study abroad experience is gaining popularity. Murphy-Judy discusses her own technology-enhanced study abroad program which combined the use of mobile devices for second language acquisition with well-planned Web 2.0 resources for local/on-site and long-distance communications. In her chapter, she addresses the advantages of connecting learners abroad to learners at home, using MALL technologies. From her experiences, she provides helpful suggestions for optimizing iStudy Abroad.

**Chapter 9**

Crossing Classroom Settings and Academic Disciplines while Crossing
Geographic Boundaries.................................................................................................. 147
*Giovanna Summerfield, Auburn University, USA*

This chapter examines the new technologically-tailored curriculum for study abroad in Italy for Auburn University students. Summerfield's instrumental case study reports on the implementation of iPods® abroad and their benefits as repositories of study materials and as tools for cultural involvement. Summerfield explains the ways in which the new generation of learners going abroad has the opportunity to become global citizens with an iBroad experience.

## Section 4
## MALL and ESL

**Chapter 10**

A Case Study of Using Podcasts in ESL Modules for Hong Kong Pre-Service Teachers
and its Impact on their Attitudes toward Podcasting ........................................................ 160
*Adrian Ting, Hong Kong Institute of Education, Hong Kong*

Academic podcasting technology in English as a Second Language (ESL) teaching and its potential benefits to ESL learners is examined in this case study conducted by Ting at a Hong Kong tertiary institute. The author reports on the instructional, informational, and developmental purposes of podcasts for pre-service teachers and on the changing attitudes of students and teachers concerning its use in language education.

**Chapter 11**
Podcasts in Four Categories: Applications to Language Learning .................................................... 176
*Ulugbek Nurmukhamedov, Northern Arizona University, USA*
*Randall Sadler, University of Illinois at Urbana-Champaign, USA*

Determining the best podcasts to use for English as a Second Language can be a daunting task. Authors Nurmukhamedov and Sadler provide a comprehensive analysis of academic podcasts by discrete category, carefully describing ESL-focused, general audience, and super-podcasts. Each category provides accessible examples, along with strengths and weaknesses.

**Afterword** .......................................................................................................... 196

**Compilation of References** ........................................................................... 198

**About the Contributors** ................................................................................ 216

**Index** .................................................................................................................. 221

# Foreword

The advent of the iPod in 2001 has resulted in explosive growth in the use of a variety of portable electronic devices (e.g., iPods and smartphones). The use of portable electronic devices in general may also represent one of the distinguishing characteristics of today's generation of students. It is difficult to walk across a college campus without seeing students equipped with earbuds and wires connected to some kind of portable electronic device. Since 2005, podcasting—in its simplest form, the distribution and downloading of digital media via the web—has experienced growth similar to that of iPods. Even a cursory review of websites listing podcasts reveals a vast spectrum of podcasts on almost every conceivable topic; some have been produced by commercial entities with professional recording equipment (e.g., news broadcasts or entertainment series), and others have been created by private individuals with hand-held video cameras (e.g., family events or personal travelogues). As the technology underlying podcasting evolves and becomes easier to use, it is expected that the development of podcasting materials will progress at an even more rapid pace.

Podcasting, along with blogs, wikis, and popular social-networking websites such as Facebook, Twitter, and YouTube, is often considered to be one of the integral elements of what is commonly called the Web 2.0. However, podcasting has the potential to significantly extend the reach of Web 2.0 activities because of the ease with which users can download podcasts on portable electronic devices connected to the internet. Within the context of education, podcasting also lends itself particularly well to the support of distance learning because, again, of the ease with which students can download and interact with course materials. As distance education continues to grow, whether in the form of completely online or partially online courses, podcasting seems destined to play an even greater role in students' learning in the future.

The use of educational podcasts on portable electronic devices has given rise to the notion of mobile learning, or m-learning. M-learning allows students, untethered from desktop computers, to use learning materials on different portable electronic devices and represents a new dimension in anytime/anywhere learning. Within the field of computer-assisted language learning (CALL), m-learning has come to constitute a new subfield, mobile assisted language learning (MALL; see Shield & Kukulska-Hulme, 2008) in which podcasting is the fundamental means of the delivery of language learning materials.

MALL is a relatively young discipline, and, because it is relatively young, basic questions about the use of language learning podcasts in MALL abound. Even the meaning of the term "podcasting" is not completely free of ambiguity. Early on, one of the essential features of podcasts was the use of procedures to notify podcast subscribers of the availability of new podcasts by means of a really simple syndication (RSS) feed. However, some developers now refer to podcasting as any distribution of downloadable digital materials with or without a notifying RSS feed.

Some of the other questions that remain to be addressed in empirical and systematic ways include the following: For which areas of second language acquisition is podcasting the most useful: listening, speaking, reading, or writing? How can podcasting advance the learning of culture? If learners' interaction with materials is an essential component in language learning, how can podcasting maximize this interactivity? Will students actually use podcasts on portable electronic devices for language learning purposes or will they continue to prefer playing podcasts for entertainment purposes? Will portable electronic devices be able to supplant desktop computers as the primary means of viewing language learning podcasts? As in distance education in general, can we assume that learners will be able to take responsibility for their learning in MALL? How does one actually go about making and distributing podcasts? What are the technical or logistical problems associated with their development? How can podcasting be integrated into other MALL instructional processes? How can the effectiveness of podcasts be evaluated?

The chapters in this volume address these and other questions. They take an honest look at the advantages and disadvantages of podcasting in MALL, underscoring the immense potential of podcasting and proposing solutions for the challenges involved in creating and distributing podcasts. As a whole, the volume bears witness to the progress that podcasting has made over the past 5 years and suggests future directions for podcasting as MALL matures as a discipline.

*Robert Fischer, Executive Director, CALICO*

**Robert Fischer** *is Professor of French and Chair of the Department of Modern Languages at Texas State University. He has served as the Executive Director of the Computer Assisted Language Instruction Consortium (CALICO) for 12 years. He has published, presented papers, and consulted widely in the field of computer-assisted language learning and has directed several grant-funded projects in the development and use of multimedia authoring tools for foreign language listening and reading comprehension.*

## REFERENCE

Shield, L., & Kukulska-Hulme, A. (Eds.). (2008). Mobile assisted language learning [Special issue]. ReCALL, 20(3).

# Preface

The use of Academic Podcasting Technology and Mobile Assisted Language Learning (MALL) is reshaping teaching and learning as it supports, expands, and enhances course content, learning activities, and teacher-learner interactions. The new wave of "enabled wifi" personal multimedia players is expanding learners' access and mobility and is providing opportunities for them to time-shift their learning activities.

Indeed, Mobile Assisted Language Learning (MALL) continues to gain popularity as it is becoming carefully and thoughtfully integrated into the foreign language curriculum, and as it provides learning tools to the "net generation" (Oblinger & Oblinger, 2005). For this new generation, which comprises students who have been encouraged to "to take control of what they learn" (Kukulska-Hulme & Shield, 2007), MALL (and particularly podcasting) is playing a key role in their learning as it provides them with instructional materials and low-cost tools which enable them to work toward developing and improving language proficiency. As an audio/video content delivery approach based on web syndication protocols, podcasting provides increased flexibility and portability of learning materials, while allowing students the ability to time-shift and multitask (Thorne & Payne, 2005). Syndication is the cornerstone of podcasting; by allowing subscription and notification, this XML-based protocol shifts audio/video file handling from a static and manual mode to a dynamic and automated mode.

"Academic Podcasting Technology" refers to the use of iPods and other MP3/MP4 players to disseminate audio and video programming over the Internet. "MALL" refers to any type of learning which is mediated by handheld devices, regardless of time or location. Their creative possibilities and their ease and popularity of use, as well as their overall cost effectiveness, make podcasting and MALL attractive, innovative, and pedagogically effective ways to improve and enhance foreign language education for both students and faculty. In fact, the integration of podcasting and MALL technologies (personal multimedia players, cell phones, and handheld devices) into the foreign language curriculum is commonplace in many secondary and higher education institutions, as these students are generally more accepting of these new technologies in other parts of their lives.

In this regard, current research has identified both pedagogically sound applications for these new technologies and important benefits to students from the use of these applications. For example, recent findings indicate that when instructors use podcasts for multiple instructional purposes (e.g., to critique student projects and exams, for student-centered video presentations, for student-paired interviews, to complete specific assignments or dictations, in roundtable discussions, or for guest lectures), students are more likely to use this technology in a new, academic setting, and to report academic benefits. Perhaps one of the most important benefits of podcasting, in addition to its ability to ease content distribution and to expand classroom time (Brien and Hegelheimer, 2007), is its potential "to foster a more seamless integration of in-class and out-of-class activity and materials" (p. 386).

## PURPOSE OF THE BOOK

Mobile devices are ubiquitous in the educational landscape. These devices, particularly the new power-ful and promising ones which offer rich multimedia experiences using a tactile interface, continue to penetrate into the field of education. To contribute to the effective integration of podcasting and MALL, the main purpose of this book is to provide an overview of ways to plan, design, produce, and integrate podcasting and MALL into language learning and acquisition. While this book attempts to provide effec-tive ways of using podcasting, it also aims at helping the reader understand the pedagogical, technical, and logistical issues associated with podcasting in particular, and with MALL in general.

By offering a compilation of best practices and recommended processes for planning, designing, and producing effective podcasts for second language learning and acquisition, this book approaches an audience that is broad enough to include all practitioners interested in using podcasts for language education. Faculty reading it will find a solid pedagogical framework that will help them to anchor their integration of podcasting and MALL into their teaching and learning activities. Similarly, librar-ians will find relevant references and practical case studies to share with members of their faculty who are interested in using podcasting as part of their curricula. Instructional designers and technologists will find planning and production steps for developing podcasts. However, while this book provides enough basic technical information to enable the production of podcasts, it should not be considered to be merely a technical reference book, as it offers pedagogical and philosophical underpinnings for the use of podcasting in enhancing and extending language learning. Finally, this book is also intended to assist researchers interested in exploring and advancing the field of MALL and its integration into language learning and acquisition.

## ORGANIZATION OF THE BOOK

This book is organized into four sections. The first section, which comprises five chapters, introduces MALL and language acquisition. In the first chapter, Lomicka and Lord offer a historical review of the uses of podcasting in K-12 and higher education language learning classrooms, while exploring cur-rent and potential pedagogical applications for academic podcasting. In the second chapter, Fernandez presents practical guidance for the design and production of pedagogically effective podcasts, with a focus on the importance of setting learning objectives. Following the same line of thinking, but writing from a more technical angle, Gonzalez, in the third chapter, describes several strategies to use in order to incorporate multimedia content into podcasts, and addresses the gray area of copyright. In the fourth chapter, Corbeil and Corbeil offer what they call a "simple guide for creating your first podcast." In the final chapter of this section, Hsueh draws attention to the usefulness of social networks' applications to language learning. The author discusses various Web 2.0 applications and their potential and challenges, while exploring the ways in which mobile technologies are assisting language learning.

In the second section, the focus of the book shifts to student-centered projects. In the first chapter, Beres refocuses the discussion to one from the student perspective and discusses the ways in which MALL is blurring the boundaries between students' personal and educational lives. In this regard, the author reminds us of the pressing need to "better understand our learners, their needs, and the contexts in which they study language." In the second chapter, Martín and Beckmann guide us through the implementation of a pedagogically-sound model for the effective use of academic podcasting in immersive-style language teaching. The authors describe the genesis, implementation, and evaluation of an innovative approach to the intensive use of academic podcasting in the teaching of Spanish to undergraduate students.

The third section describes the potential of podcasting's use to engage students during their study abroad experiences. In the first chapter, Murphy-Judy discusses ways in which podcasting can help students create a transnational community of practice that shares the wealth of experiential learning through carefully structured and planned activities. In the second chapter, Summerfield describes how podcasting can "engage students extensively in language- and culture-based tasks" while cultivating collaboration and creativity among students.

The final section focuses on the use of podcasting in teaching English as a Second Language (ESL). In the first chapter, Ting describes how podcasting can be used for instructional, informational, and developmental purposes for pre-service teachers. In addition to providing an insight into the attitudes of these prospective teachers toward podcasting in education and its future use in schools, the author reiterates previous research findings that have reported that podcasting not only is an "integrative and supplementary learning tool, but also as a powerful generator of knowledge, which encourages active learning." In the second chapter, Nurmukhamedov and Sadler attempt to assist language teachers in their search to find "useful and learner-friendly podcasts to supplement their language instruction." To this end, the authors categorize podcasting into four categories and offer practical suggestions that allow for the integration of podcasts into both in- and out-of-class activities.

As the convergence of hardware, telecommunication, and software infuse the educational landscape with more and more powerful mobile devices, we hope that this book will contribute to a better understanding and a stronger integration of these tools, particularly as they reconfigure traditional teaching and learning practices while extending both our and our students' cognitive abilities.

*Betty Rose Facer*
*Old Dominion University, Virginia*

*Mohammed Abdous*
*Old Dominion University, Virginia*

# Acknowledgment

We wish to thank our accomplished authors for their dedication to this book project. Their invaluable contributions have provided a rich and powerful volume of work on MALL and Academic Podcasting Technology. It was a pleasure working with them.

We also wish to express our deep gratitude to the Editorial Advisory Board and to the many dedicated reviewers for their thoughtful comments and suggestions that strengthened the overall project. In particular, we would like to acknowledge the contributions of Alison Schoew for proofreading the entire manuscript, and Elizabeth Gordon for meticulously reviewing all the chapters' references.

We would also like to recognize Joel Gamon at IGI Global. We are particularly grateful for his guidance, support, and encouragement.

A very special thanks to Robert Fischer and Peter Lafford for writing the Foreword and Afterword to this book. Your support and enthusiasm over the years has been an incredible gift. It is an honor to work with you.

Betty Rose Facer: *To my parents, Natalie and Bruce H. Facer, who always believed in me, my passion for languages, travel, literature, and so much more. They truly are an amazing and inspirational force in my life. They would be very proud.*

Mohammed Abdous: *My special thanks and gratitude to my parents who worked hard for my education. My heartfelt thanks to my wife for her ongoing support and unconditional love. My special thanks my daughters and son for their inspiration and love.*

*Betty Rose Facer*
*Old Dominion University, Virginia*

*Mohammed Abdous*
*Old Dominion University, Virginia*

# Section 1
# MALL and Language Acquisition

# Chapter 1

# Podcasting – Past, Present and Future:
## Applications of Academic Podcasting In and Out of the Language Classroom

**Lara Lomicka**
*University of South Carolina, USA*

**Gillian Lord**
*University of Florida, USA*

## ABSTRACT

*This chapter explores current and potential pedagogical applications of academic podcasting in K-12 and higher education language learning classrooms. In order to fulfill the purpose of the chapter, it is composed of three primary sections: (1) Where we've been - a review of published research on podcasting; (2) Where we are - an investigation of what current teachers and researchers are doing with podcasting in their language classes based on survey results; and (3) Where we're going - an assessment of future trends and applications. After reading the chapter, the reader should be eager to continue to explore the applications of academic podcasting in the language classroom.*

## INTRODUCTION

Among the first institutions in which instructors used podcasts in the language classroom was Osaka Jogakuin College in Japan, where iPods® were provided to students. Podcasts downloaded to the iPods consisted of audio learning aids designed to help with the learning of English (McCarty, 2005)[1]. Podcasting trends can now be found in different parts of the world; many universities and colleges are embarking on projects using podcasting and MP3 devices in innovative ways. The possibilities for podcasting, both in and out of the language classroom, are many and varied, ranging from areas such as pronunciation and listening to study abroad and peer review.

Since this chapter addresses where we've been, where we are now, and where we're going, it will shed light on current podcasting research which is specific to language teaching and learning, current projects and their uses in K-12 and

DOI: 10.4018/978-1-60960-141-6.ch001

higher education settings, ideas based on recent research, and current views of language learning and teaching. It will also consider ways in which podcasting might be used in the future to explore new trends in academia. The chapter also offers suggestions for implementation and for overcoming challenges, so that interested readers will be equipped with the knowledge and tools necessary to begin their own podcast project, research, and data collection.

## WHERE WE'VE BEEN: DOCUMENTED RESEARCH ON PODCASTING

The latest edition (3rd) of the *Oxford English Dictionary* defines podcasting as "a digital recording of a broadcast" that is typically "made available on the web for downloading to a computer or personal audio player" (Simpson, 2009). Podcasting is considered a Web 2.0 tool which can be used in ways that are dynamic, collaborative, and interactive. In fact, the dynamic nature of podcasting is linked with any audio or video file that listeners can download and play on a digital player (Barsky & Lindstrom, 2008). The use of audio in language learning itself is not particularly new or innovative; however, Web 2.0 tools take advantage of existing technologies or platforms and use them to do more and different tasks, as will be discussed in this chapter. While the use of audio in language learning is well documented, research on podcasting has only recently begun to appear in the literature. This section, in order to pave the way to where we are now, addresses the research that has already documented, including reports on previously implemented podcasting projects and some of the more empirical results of podcasting research.

## Theoretical Underpinnings

While much of the literature surrounding podcasting and language learning has focused on the technical aspects and practical examples of podcasting projects (e.g., Godwin-Jones, 2005; McCarty, 2005; McQuillan, 2006a; Stanley, 2006; Young, 2007; and below), few articles have considered the theoretical aspects of podcasting (McQuillan, 2006b; O'Bryan & Hegelheimer, 2007; Rosell-Aguilar, 2007). Blake (2008) argued that "[t]he technology is theoretically and methodologically neutral. But how technology is used—its particular culture of practice—is not neutral; it responds to what the practitioners understand or believe to be true about SLA" (p. 11).

Podcasting has several theoretical underpinnings in Second Language Acquisition (SLA) research, especially in the areas of input, output, and motivation. O'Bryan and Hegelheimer (2007) proposed that podcasting represents a rich source of input via audio, and potentially via video. This input can reinforce class instruction by offering an additional or alternative mode (rather than the traditional textbook or teacher) of input to students. Dervin (2006) suggested that podcasts can help to develop autonomous learning and motivation (see also Stanley, 2006). Motivation may be increased, speculated Stanley (2006), due to the fact that students are creating authentic content for a real audience and not just for a grade. In addition, Dervin (2006) underscored that students can, for example, take the initiative to ask questions of, interact with, and communicate with podcasters, thus providing opportunities for both autonomy and motivation. Output is also recognized as essential for second language learning. Swain and Lapkin (1995) suggested having students record and then listen to themselves as they edit their output; afterwards, students can go back, listen again, and revise as needed. This type of approach can be quite useful in podcasting as it is easy to record, re-record, and listen to various segments of a podcast. After students record podcasts, they can listen multiple times, edit their podcasts, and comment on their classmates' recordings (see also Lord, 2008; Meng, 2005).

With these theoretical considerations in mind, many scholars have touted the potential power of podcasting in education in general, and in language instruction in particular. The following subsections review these prophesied benefits and then discuss some of the empirical studies carried out so far in an effort to determine their validity.

## Podcasting's Potential

Many language-specific articles have addressed podcasting and have provided practical ideas for its use in the classroom (Fox, 2008; McQuillan, 2006; Schmidt, 2008; Sze, 2006; Young, 2007). Fox (2008) provided the idea of a talk radio podcast, which is set up like a talk show and allows students to listen, create, and publish podcasts. The particular podcast discussed by Fox, *Absolutely Intercultural,* offered a corresponding blog where information, or "show notes," about corresponding episodes were archived, and where listeners could communicate with the podcasters. Fox explained that users interacted with the available podcasts in several ways: by writing a text comment to the podcast blog, by submitting an audio comment, by recording an idea to include in the blog, by expressing an interest in producing a podcast edition, or by creating and publishing a podcast. Similarly, McQuillan (2006) discussed producing podcasting "shows" that provided interesting, comprehensible input to those at the intermediate or higher levels of proficiency in which students "record[ed] themselves and classmates for a classroom assignment and provide speech samples to the teacher for assessment" (p. 6). Sze (2006) offered a variety of ways in which podcasting could be used: Teachers can produce podcasts to assist their students and reach out beyond the four walls of the classroom, students can produce podcasts for other students, and inter-school podcasting projects can be set up which allow teachers at

different schools to organize projects that afford their students the ability to communicate and respond to each other.

In addition to podcast production and talk shows, podcasting has capitalized on authentic materials and has promoted listening comprehension (McBride, 2009; McQuillan, 2006; Schmidt, 2008; Sze, 2006). McBride (2009) underscored the importance of authentic listening materials and how they can easily be incorporated into podcasting projects (see also Schmidt, 2008; Stanley, 2006). She proposed that students, when listening to authentic podcasts, respond to a series of questions that target top-down listening skills. These questions can request information about the general topic, who the speakers might be, where the recording took place, or how the speakers felt when recording. She also suggested that students listen for key words by writing down the time that they heard the word used. Bottom-up skills can also be honed by engaging students in more detailed, careful, and repeated listening. Schmidt (2008) described a project in which students listened to podcast episodes two or three times per week and kept a listening journal to record comments or questions for each episode.

Other articles on podcasting have also addressed ways in which podcasts promote oral production. McQuillan (2006) highlighted several tasks that focus on producing oral work, such as using audio diaries or conducting interviews with native speakers. Sze (2006) proposed that speaking activities for student podcasts can help to develop pronunciation and intonation. He provided examples such as radio drama, radio plays, and English Language Teaching (ELT) rap (rap written with ELT purposes in mind). Similarly, Pettes Guikema (2009) examined the discourse of French language podcasts through authentic podcast transcripts. She exploited the linguistic, lexical, and cultural features of podcasts to demonstrate ways in which podcasts can be used in and out of the classroom. It is clear that podcasting has made its way into language classrooms, but questions still remain about its quantifiable benefits, for which we turn now to empirical research on the subject.

## Empirical Research

### General Gains and Benefits

As can be inferred from the above publications, a number of language educators have implemented podcasting projects into their teaching; however, research specific to podcasting remains a young but growing area. Abdous, Camarena, and Facer (2009) and Facer, Abdous, and Camarena (2009) reported on podcasting projects and indicated a positive reception by students, as well as a perceived increase in language skill acquisition. For example, Abdous et al. (2009) discussed using podcasts for multiple purposes, such as guest lectures, providing feedback on student work, paired interviews, student video presentations, and roundtable discussions. With a post-study design, they administered a survey to assess the effects of podcasts for instructional purposes on students' language skill acquisition and compared the effects of integrated (planned) vs. supplemental (unplanned) uses of podcasting. The 113 participants were from varying language backgrounds, and the administered tasks varied in each class (which the authors report as a limitation). Results indicated that student use of podcasts (as well as language skill acquisition) increased, and that students were more willing to report academic benefits. Similarly, Facer et al. (2009) shared initial results of a pilot study comparing the academic benefits of integrating podcasts into course content to using podcasts as supplemental tools. In a post-test design, 33 participants from two pilot classes completed a survey that examined their academic backgrounds, study habits, access to computers, podcasting experiences, and perceived usefulness of podcasting. The most common use of podcasts was to review course lessons. Students self-reported that the use of podcasts helped them to improve their language skills in all areas, but

especially with aural and oral skills and with building vocabulary. Results indicated that podcasting can offer greater benefits if it is used as more than merely a tool for reviewing course work.

Student enjoyment of podcasting projects has also been documented in the research (O'Bryan & Hegelheimer, 2006; Ducate & Lomicka, 2009a; Lys, 2008; and Sathe & Waltje, 2008). O'Bryan and Hegelheimer (2006) reported on the use of podcasts in a listening course (semester long, graduate, and undergraduate students (n=6) who listened to 14 podcasts). Their findings, based on surveys, interviews, and a teacher reflective journal, addressed attitudes, feelings about podcasts, and student needs. Results indicated that the podcasts were viewed very positively and that few technical problems occurred. Examining podcasting from a mobility standpoint, Ducate and Lomicka (2009a) investigated four different podcasting projects implemented in university-level language learning or teacher training courses. Each project made use of both input and output to promote speaking and listening comprehension. Findings suggested that the majority of participants enjoyed the podcasting assignments and felt that they benefited from them. However, results also point to the fact that many students chose convenience over mobility, since students preferred to listen to podcasts on their personal computers rather than updating their MP3 players (see also Lee, Miller, & Newnham, 2008). Ducate and Lomicka suggested that educators should carefully consider task design and how it may relate to mobility as part of the language learning process (see also Colpaert, 2004; Rosell-Aguilar, 2007; Young, 2007).

Positive student responses were also found by Lys (2008), who documented a study with 18 participants taking an advanced German class. Each student was encouraged to use an iPod Touch® to develop vocabulary and oral communication skills and to interact collaboratively. Specifically, students were asked to use the devices to view authentic target language video clips and websites, to comment, and to produce a report. Results indicate that students responded positively to the project. Finally, Sathe and Waltje (2008) discussed a project in which iPods® were distributed on loan to 120 U.S. university-level language students (in German, French, Spanish, ESL, or Linguistics). The iPods were used as mini-language labs (listening and recording) and students were asked to report on their use. The overall results were positive; students expressed perceived benefits from working with their iPods, and many felt that the iPod lab was more convenient than the traditional, physical, language lab.

## Linguistic Benefits

The number of studies that report on gains made by the use of podcasting to specific areas of language learning is scant. Amemiya, Hasegawa, Kaneko, Miyakoda, and Tsukahara (2007) reported on a study using a foreign word learning system with iPods, in which they examined the pronunciation and images of the vocabulary items (n = 10) with iPods versus with pen and paper. Results indicated that some of the iPod group's participants claimed that they continued to hear the pronunciation of the word even when not listening to the iPod. No immediate difference in the groups was found immediately following the experiment; however, after two weeks, the iPod participants retained the meaning of 40% of the English words by using the audio-oriented system, while only 27% of the word meanings were retained by the conventional paper-and-pencil group.

Both Lord (2008) and Ducate and Lomicka (2009b) reported on results from projects involving pronunciation and podcasting. In Lord's (2008) study, 19 students in an undergraduate phonetics class recorded tongue-twisters, short readings, and personal reflections using their own pronunciation. Lord used the Pronunciation Attitude Inventory (Elliott, 1995), in addition to scores from six oral tasks, and students were rated by three judges on overall pronunciation ability.

Both attitudes and pronunciation abilities were assessed pre-semester and post-semester; both were found to improve. Podcasts also remained available as references for students to revisit and work on individual pronunciation issues. Ducate and Lomicka (2009b) examined podcasting as a tool for honing pronunciation skills in intermediate language learning. The 22 students in Intermediate German and French courses prepared five scripted pronunciation recordings and produced three extemporaneous recordings. The study also included results from a pre- and post-survey based on Elliott's (1995) Pronunciation Attitude Inventory. Results suggested that students' pronunciation did not significantly improve in regard to accentedness or comprehensibility, but the podcast project was perceived positively by students, who reported that they appreciated the feedback provided and enjoyed the opportunities to be creative during extemporaneous podcasts.

Having examined where we have been by exploring the literature surrounding podcasting in language learning and its perceived benefits, its effects on listening and pronunciation, and its pedagogical uses in the classroom, we know that there is still much to be learned. As we move on to the next section and situate where we are now, it is our hope (as we discuss current projects and uses of podcasting) that we will come to a better sense of potential future directions for this technology.

## WHERE WE ARE NOW: DATA GATHERED FROM AN ONLINE SURVEY

In order to examine current views of podcasting, this section highlights a preliminary project from which data were gathered via a short online survey. The survey sought to answer the following general research questions:

- **RQ1:** Who uses podcasting in language classes?

- **RQ2:** Where is podcasting implemented in language education?
- **RQ3:** Why do language educators use podcasting?
- **RQ4:** How do language educators use podcasting?

## Task

The data presented here were gathered through an online anonymous survey administered through www.surveymonkey.com. Our goal in administering this survey was to gain a general overview as to the types of projects in which teachers are currently engaged; it was not in the scope of this project to collect and report quantitative data. Therefore, while they do not reflect a fully representative sample of all language teachers *per se*, the data reported are relevant to the current chapter and its goals.

The survey questions targeted teachers' reasons for using podcasting and their current uses of podcasting tools in their classes. (Please see the Appendix for a complete copy of the survey text and questions.) The overall goal of the survey was to obtain information from those who currently use podcasts in one way or another; therefore, we did not focus on whether the respondents did or did not use podcasts. The assumption was that, if they were answering the survey questions, it was because they had some experience with the tool.

## Participants

A weblink to the survey and the appropriate consent forms was distributed widely via various educational and language-related listservs, such as FLTeach, AAUSC, and CALICO's membership lists. A total of 37 responses were received. While this number is relatively low, it does represent the self-selected participants who chose to answer the questions because they wanted to share their work in podcasting. Further details regarding the

participants' backgrounds will be discussed in the Results section, below.

## Results

This section is divided into various subsections which address the primary questions that motivated the survey in the first place: who is using podcasting; when (or at what levels) they are doing so; why educators employ podcasting; and what specific kinds of projects they are developing.

## RQ1: Who uses Podcasting in Language Classes?

We wanted to gauge who is using podcasting. In other words, we wanted to know which teachers of what languages and what levels at what institutions were using the tool, and what grades were given. Based on the responses we received, it seems that podcasting appeals to almost everyone as a pedagogical tool of one sort or another. Of the teachers who responded, a variety of languages, levels, and institutions were represented. For example, we heard from teachers of several different languages, ranging from French and Spanish to German, Russian, Chinese, Arabic, Italian, Portuguese, ESL/EFL, Japanese, Hebrew, Hindi, Thai, and Vietnamese. We also heard from language technology specialists who work with multiple languages. While the vast majority of our respondents reported teaching at the college/university level, we did get responses from educators in elementary, middle, and high schools, and from both public and private institutions. It seems, though, that podcasting is enjoyed as an academic tool or activity for older (rather than younger) learners: over 90% of responders were teaching at the high school and college levels. Thus, we must keep in mind, as we continue to discuss these survey findings, that the reported projects were geared more toward learners in high school and in higher education. This fact is reinforced by respondents' answers to the survey question that asked for the average age of their learners: 50% indicated 19-23 year olds, and a quarter said 16-18 years, with the remaining fourth of the responses divided among the younger ages.

## RQ2: Where is Podcasting Implemented in Language Education?

Although the learners involved in the reported podcast projects tend to be older, our respondents indicated that podcasting is being used at all levels of language instruction: beginning, intermediate, and advanced, and in fairly equal numbers. Of course, there are a variety of tasks that can be employed at differing levels, since what is asked of the learner can be determined by language proficiency. These tasks will be discussed in the next subsections.

## RQ3: Why do Language Educators use Podcasting?

Perhaps the most important question we asked in our survey was *why* educators use podcasting. This was an open-ended question, yet answers tended to fall into three primary categories: for listening practice, for speaking practice, and for pronunciation practice. Of course, other reasons were given, as well. Table 1 presents the responses received and the frequency with which they were mentioned.

Respondents to this study viewed podcasting as a tool that can aid in developing both receptive and productive skills. Educators feel that it is useful for listening as well as for speaking practice. On the receptive end, podcasts provide unlimited access to authentic materials, as was discussed previously, and can greatly benefit students' listening comprehension skills (if used regularly and appropriately). On the productive end, if students create their own podcasts, the tool becomes an outlet for creativity, oral practice, pronunciation exercises, and personalization of the learning process. In this respect, our survey respondents seem to concur with previous studies, reviewed above (e.g., Ducate & Lomicka 2009b, Lord 2008), in their recognition of podcasting as a valuable tool for improving linguistic abilities.

At the same time, there is a multiplicity of additional motivations for incorporating podcasts into language classes, as can be seen from the variety of responses. Some educators seek to increase students' independence by making class materials available in podcast format, which allows students

*Table 1. Responses to the survey question asking about educators' goals in using podcasting*

| Reason given | # of times mentioned | % of mentions |
|---|---|---|
| Listening practice | 30 | 41.10% |
| Speaking practice/presentational skills | 17 | 23.29% |
| Pronunciation practice | 9 | 12.33% |
| Increase students' independence (learning outside of class, replace lectures, etc.) | 4 | 5.48% |
| Learn / be exposed to cultural information and authentic materials | 4 | 5.48% |
| Collaborate with peers or students at other institutions | 3 | 4.11% |
| Writing practice | 2 | 2.74% |
| Vocabulary learning | 2 | 2.74% |
| Other: Increased motivation; provide individual feedback; promote digital literacy; enhance class discussions | 1 each | 1.37% each |
| *TOTAL* | *73[2]* | *100%* |

to practice on their own, outside of class time. This approach takes advantage of the (possibly) mobile aspect of podcasting, in that it allows students to access course materials anytime and anywhere. Surprisingly few educators commented on the collaborative aspect of podcasting, although (as we have seen above) podcasting's potential for collaborations and group learning is enormous. Other cited motivations include increasing learner motivation and fostering digital literacy among students. Although previous research has not examined all of these facets (e.g., Ducate & Lomicka 2008a, Lys 2008, Sathew & Waltje 2008), our survey respondents do recognize the potential of podcasting in language education. The next section examines how these goals can be achieved through a variety of project types suggested by our respondents.

## RQ4: How Do Language Educators use Podcasting?

In this subsection, we examine the types of projects discussed by the survey respondents. As will become evident in this discussion, these projects mirror the uses discussed previously in the review of current research. This is not to say that these uses are not unique or interesting to their participants, but rather to point out that what we are reporting on now (in large part) resembles what we have reported already. (Future possible uses of podcasting that go beyond these traditional approaches are discussed in the next section.) A cursory examination of the survey responses provided reveals that project types tend to be divided in to two main trends: those which use existing target language podcasts and those for which teachers create their own podcast materials. Each will be discussed in turn.

## Using Existing Materials

A number of educators are taking advantage of the multitude of podcasts available in every lan-

guage by having students access these authentic materials as part of a project. Many educators rely on podcasts for providing authentic input to their students, and for this reason, they require students to subscribe to them. For example, in one kind of project, students choose podcasts based on their own interests and then engage in some kind of follow-up activity, such as blogging about their reactions to the content or creating their own podcast following that style. Another option that many educators are beginning to employ is the use of podcasts and sound files created by textbook companies or other language programs; while these are not specifically "authentic" materials (in the sense that they were not created by and for native speakers), they can provide several advantages to students, from mobility of learning to the reinforcement of vocabulary. At the same time, many have recognized their potential in creating podcasts, a task that allows either the teacher or the students (or both) to create and collaborate with the language.

## Teacher-Created Podcasts

Many teachers who responded to our survey indicated that they create their own podcasts and make them available for their students to access outside of class time. This practice takes advantage of the "anywhere, anytime" idea behind podcasting and encourages students to continue their learning beyond the confines of the classroom.

Some teachers create grammar lectures to supplement the textbook and make them available in podcast format to their students. Others record vocabulary and useful phrases for students to access on their own in an attempt to increase their vocabulary outside of class time. Yet others create podcasts which offer guides for pronunciation and vocabulary, to which students are encouraged to listen. These audio tools can all be created with visual supplements too, taking advantage of the latest technologies available to provide both audio and visual input in podcasts.

Other instructors are involved in more process-oriented activities related to podcasting. For example, some educators create podcasts as a means to provide an oral text to the students, and then ask accompanying comprehension questions for students to answer in writing. In this way, podcasting becomes a part of students' homework assignments and allows them to incorporate regular listening practice, as well. Similarly, one educator indicated that s/he uses podcasts to summarize recent class lectures and to provide students with comprehension or summary questions to be handed in. Again, these uses of podcasting serve primarily to enhance the classroom experience and to broaden it in time and space beyond the limits of the classroom.

## Student-Created Podcasts

The final type of podcast project reported in our survey was the creation of podcast projects by the students, themselves. There are a number of options presented in this category, all of which allow learners to create (and, often, to collaborate). For example, educators use podcasting to allow students to talk on any topic that interests them in order to practice their oral abilities, or to systematically respond to guided questions from the instructor. Many teachers also encourage students to comment on each other's work in these kinds of projects. Another option for podcasting is for students to use the recording capacities of the tool to practice their speaking and pronunciation. Some instructors have students read stories or dramatic performances (either by recognized authors or that the class has created for that purpose) aloud. These podcasts provide a performance outlet for the students, and give them another stage on which to perform. Other instructors have students perform their class presentations as a podcast.

From a more project-oriented perspective, educators have embraced the possibilities that podcasting offers to create longer-term projects. For example, one survey respondent indicated that his/her students create their own podcasts by reviewing books that they have read or films that they have watched. Others have had their students create genre-based podcasts, such as newscasts or sportscasts. In these projects, students express their own opinions while learning about the opinions of their classmates, as well. Similarly, another reported podcast project involves carrying out audio interviews with native speakers, which are then posted to a class podcast site. Such a project not only involves the cultural aspects of communication, but also gets students connected to a broader community of target-language speakers than they would otherwise be exposed to.

Clearly, the data presented in this section confirm that podcasting is "[…] well known, popular, and widely available […]" (Seitzinger, 2006, p. 1), and that it has been used in a variety of language classes and levels. Furthermore, educators have implemented podcasting in myriad ways – some of which are more traditional (recording lectures) and some of which are more collaborative (class presentations, projects). In gaining an idea as to where we are currently, we can better suggest ideas for where we are going and provide suggestions for potential uses of podcasting in language learning.

## WHERE WE'RE GOING: THE FUTURE OF PODCASTING

Our survey respondents overwhelmingly indicated their interest in continuing to explore podcasts and their use in language classes in the future. As can be seen in Figure 1, in response to the question of whether they will use podcasting again, the vast majority of respondents indicate that they will or maybe will incorporate another podcasting project in their classes. In fact, only one respondent indicated that s/he would not do so.

The question we must ask at this point, however, is *how* educators will expand the use of podcasting in the future. Since it is based on the current trends in language teaching and in tech-

*Figure 1. Percentage of survey responses indicating respondents' plans to use podcasting again in the future*

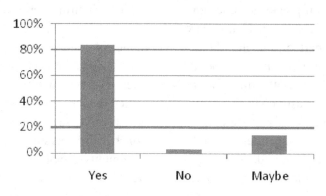

**Will you use podcasting again?**

nology-assisted language instruction, this section briefly outlines some podcasting trends that link schools, students, classes, and institutions. These are trends which we have identified as those likely to shape the future of podcasting in language teaching and learning.

First, projects could establish a focus on digital literacy, which Wikipedia defines as "the ability to locate, organize, understand, evaluate, and create information using digital technology." One example of a podcasting project focusing on digital literacy is documented as "Clubcasting" (Beilke, Stuve, & Williams-Hawkins, 2008). In this particular project, students worked with inner-city children to produce podcast episodes for a radio show, in order to promote digital literacy and multiculturalism. Goals for the project included increasing literacy skills in inner-city children; contributing to authentic identity constructions; and gaining acceptance from white teachers (see Beilke et al. 2008). This type of project could easily be adapted to language classes, especially among Hispanic or other language communities, who could benefit from digital literacy skills. Simultaneously, students would benefit from the contact with the community and from the

opportunities to use their target language in real communicative situations.

Second, projects could focus on community outreach through partnerships with local businesses, non-profits, and organizations. For example, Hartigan, Hill, Lewis-Faupel, and Springsteen (2006) discussed a project in which anthropology students produced podcasts in the form of audio guides for local museums. Language classes could provide a service to these organizations in translating material into the target language, thus allowing students to practice both language and digital skills while connecting with the community, at the same time.. Similarly, Bruce and Lin (2009) reported on a project based on an inquiry-learning model in which podcasting was used to foster personal growth and community engagement among a group of Mexican-American youth enrolled in an afterschool program. Learners worked with the Mexican-American students to produce audiovisual podcasts that served as mini-video productions. This kind of project can promote collaborative spaces that young people can use to learn "new media, enjoy creative expression, take action for community needs, and develop potential for civic engagement by serving their family, friends, and communities" (p. 230).

This type of community service project could easily be adapted to upper-level language classes. Language students could partner with institutions to produce target language audio campus guides, and upper-level language classes could establish connections with literature and history classes to work on projects for other community groups or institutions, such as local libraries and historical foundations.

Third, podcasting trends move educators beyond utilizing podcasts merely for practicing speaking or pronunciation and more toward the integration of skills and a focused use of mobility. Using podcasting in language classes could be framed with both a broader goal and a focus on multiple skills, simultaneously. Some applications are now ready to expand to speech-to-text conversion to access transcripts and search podcasts and use for reading/writing (podscope, 2007; Ramp, 2007). Also, more research is needed in the area of mobility, or time/place shifting. Lee, Miller, and Newnham (2008) reported that students did not tend to subscribe to podcasts or take advantage of the mobility offered, but rather followed traditional trends of downloading audio directly to their computers and listening to it on their computers. The authors concluded that one reason students do not download podcasts by subscribing may be due to "pre-established habits in the way they use the Internet and access web-based information" (p. 58). Perhaps projects should focus on providing students with reasons to subscribe, making subscription mandatory or necessary for completion of the associated tasks.

Finally, we can capitalize on others' experiences to empower our current students. One example of this trend can be found in podcasts from those who study abroad. Students who study abroad can provide podcasts or audio segments in the target language to share with students at the home institution (or elsewhere) or can provide podcasts discussing intercultural issues (example at http://www.absolutely-intercultural.com/?p=49). Students can also interview those who have studied

abroad, or can create a podcast about a place in which they would like to study abroad some day. The possibilities for these kinds of podcasts are endless, ranging from student reports to interviews and more. Such resources would benefit current as well as future students and would form a resource for students and faculty.

The podcasting uses proposed above, which are based on current practices and look toward the future, offer ample ideas for language teachers to make the most of podcasting tools as they design their curricula. However, the incorporation of podcasting is not without challenges, some of which have been discussed in previously published work while others have also come up in the responses to our survey. The following subsections address some of these challenges and offer possible solutions.

## Challenges

As we have seen, podcasting is being increasingly implemented in educational settings (Barsky & Lindstrom, 2008) and thus in the language classroom. We have also seen that educators are interested in continuing to do so. Nonetheless, we must carefully consider our goals in using this or any other tool. While "foreign language instruction has always had a close relationship with technology" (Simon, 2008, p. 6), researchers and educators have cautioned against using technology merely for technology's sake. Instead, as O'Bryan and Hegelheimer (2007) suggested, if educators decide to use podcasts, it is important to determine instructional goals. Rosell-Aguilar (2007, 2009) reminded educators to maintain an emphasis on pedagogy when implementing podcasting. Similarly, Simon (2008) suggested that while MP3 devices "might have an instructional potential, […] it is the educators who arrange and structure instructional events around it to make learning happen, not the instrument itself" (p. 6). Keeping instructional goals and an emphasis on pedagogy in mind, the success of podcasting (or lack thereof) depends on its use (Bush, 2008; McCloskey, 2007). This section takes a closer look at the challenges that educators face in designing podcasting projects for the language classroom and offers suggestions for overcoming those challenges. Thus, interested readers will be equipped with the knowledge and tools necessary to begin their own podcast project, research, and data collection.

Teachers face various hurdles when designing podcasts or when preparing to implement podcasting projects. For example, podcasting projects can be extremely time-consuming to create (Schmidt, 2008), and often require technological know-how that is beyond some teachers' comfort level. Students may require extra training and assistance with the technical competence for production of podcasts (Facer et al., 2009). Schmidt (2008) encouraged educators to provide students with guidance in the early stages of podcasting. Especially challenging is the creation of materials in languages encompassing unique or exotic fonts that are not common to all computing systems in this country; in this case, teachers need to seek creative solutions. In addition, administrative concerns (such as the blocking of certain sites or the disallowing of the use of podcasts in schools) can severely hinder an educator's efforts. A common theme among survey respondents was the issue of how to assess podcasts and how to assign grades for the projects. Additionally, many of these educators reported that they included student-generated podcasts in their classes as supplemental activities – either due to administrative or time limitations – and so it was difficult to get students to take them seriously if they were not rigidly graded.

Students also face challenges in classes in which podcasts are part of the curriculum. For example, not all students have access to the appropriate recording or playback equipment, and often the recordings that they make can be of poor quality. If students don't have portable listening devices – or if they don't want to use

their personal devices for academic endeavors – they may not be making the most of the podcasting potential (Ducate & Lomicka, 2009b). Since students are invariably busy, they often do not listen to podcasts for more than the required time, thus limiting the potential of the authentic input to aid in their comprehension and listening skills. Finally, many students are shy in front of a microphone or camera, or are reluctant to be as creative as they can be.

These challenges are not unique to any learning environment, but they can be particularly limiting in the context of podcasting. For this reason, the next subsection offers solutions to these challenges. These are offered in the hope that educators will be encouraged to try new tactics and to incorporate new podcast projects in their classes.

## Solutions

In proposing possible solutions to the challenges discussed above, survey respondents indicated that podcasting could be an in-class activity. First, from a technical standpoint, support could be on-demand and provided instantly if podcasting occurs as a part of class time. For educators (as well as for students), increased administrative support could be provided (Schmidt, 2008). Second, from a pedagogical point of view, educators should state objectives explicitly and integrate podcast tasks and projects into the curriculum, making certain to provide both a purpose and a rationale (Abdous et al., 2009; Herrington & Kervin, 2007; O'Bryan & Hegelheimer, 2007).

Further, Rosell-Aguilar (2009) noted that "[…] many podcasts created for educational purposes follow a behavioristic view of language learning and assume knowledge is acquired individually by a listen-and-repeat approach" (p. 23). Rather than limiting oneself to this type of approach, one could explore more interactive types of tasks for podcasts, such as group projects, native speaker interviews, radio shows, and a variety of student-generated podcasts, such as those discussed above. Educators could be encouraged to try student-generated podcasts, rather than (or in addition to) offering pre-created material. For student-generated podcasts, the focus could shift to collaboration, self-reflection (Seitzinger, 2006), and interactivity, through the use of, for example, audio or video responses, tweets, or blog comments. Rosell-Aguilar (2007) and Edirisingha, Rizzi, Nie, and Rothwell (2007) agreed that podcasting can be made more interactive by using Web 2.0 tools to provide opportunities to engage and collaborate with other learners, which can offer a discursive dimension to learning.

Regardless of the projects that educators create, in the end, the success of any podcasting endeavor depends on the goals and administration of the project. Below, we offer some practical ideas to consider when creating podcasting projects, using the word "PODCAST" as a mnemonic device. These suggestions come from the lessons learned in published work at large, as well as from the wisdom of our survey respondents, linked with our own experience and knowledge.

**P** = portability. Take advantage of the mobility offered by podcasting and MP3 players and make mobile learning a priority. Encourage students to access materials outside of class time and to make language learning a part of their daily lives.

**O** = originality. Use authentic materials that have already been created, but also encourage originality and creativity among learners in designing their own recordings and/or their own responses to podcasts they hear. The more that learners create with the language, the closer they will come to their communicative goals.

**D** = distribution. Remember that that podcasts can be widely distributed to potential audiences in order to promote authenticity, and that there are a number of available distribution options (e.g., in class, out of class, mobile, etc.) which teachers can explore.

**C** = collaboration. Take advantage of podcasting's potential to create communities of learners, and allow learners to interact with each other

and with native speakers. Keep this interaction in mind, as podcasting in the real world exists to generate discussion, commentary, reactions and responses. Our podcast projects should do the same thing, and student-created material should not exist in a vacuum.

**A** = authenticity. Podcasts should be used in academic contexts in the same kinds of ways that they are used in non-academic settings. Consider the authenticity of your podcast project, and use podcasting in class in the same way that you would use it in your everyday life. Make sure that it is relevant and interesting to students' lives and that its academic implementation mimics natural podcasting use.

**S** = sustainability. Create reusable projects that can be used semester after semester and can become self-sustaining, in the interest of maximizing your time and talents. Of course, projects can always be tweaked and modified as the course's goals or tools change, but creating self-sustaining projects will save time and energy.

**T** = technology. Prensky (2009) refers to our students' "digital wisdom" as an additional benefit of including technology-based tasks in our curricula. This digital wisdom is a "twofold concept, referring both to wisdom arising from the use of digital technology to access cognitive power beyond our innate capacity and to wisdom in the prudent use of technology to enhance our capabilities" (n.p.). As educators, we must keep in mind that the advantages of including podcasting projects go beyond the immediate goals of the project itself and help prepare our students to become active citizens in this increasingly technological world.

## CONCLUSION

Our goal in this chapter has been to provide the reader with a solid foundation in podcasting's past, present, and future. We have explored both previous research and current podcasting projects, and we have provided suggestions for incorporating podcasting into the language classroom. Pedagogically, there are myriad ways that podcasting can be incorporated into language learning tasks, but the emphasis should remain on the task rather than on the technological tool. Young (2007) offered suggestions as to how to make podcasting tasks both communicative and meaningful. Essentially, teachers need to keep in mind that these projects should be designed around sound pedagogy. Young (2007) underscored that we must use knowledge of SLA to design effective podcasting tasks in order to create activities that are "engaging, problem-solving and task-based, and that encourage authentic self expression for a purpose, are more appealing than listening to mechanical discrete-point verb conjugations or prefabricated audio files" (p. 45). Additionally, Colpaert (2004) reminded us to focus on the learner rather than the technology. He stressed the importance of developing the language learning environment before deciding on the role of mobile technologies.

Clearly, educators can benefit from learning what other scholars have done and from exploring the data that they have collected, as well as from understanding the projects in which our colleagues are currently involved. As the contents of this volume confirm, podcasting is a popular and productive tool with ample academic potential. Podcasting has enjoyed a fruitful past and is engaged in a productive and developing present. The future of podcasting is bright, especially for academic and educational purposes.

## REFERENCES

Abdous, M., Camarena, M. M., & Facer, B. R. (2009). MALL technology: Use of academic podcasting in the foreign language classroom. *ReCALL Journal*, *21*, 76–95. doi:10.1017/S0958344009000020

Amemiya, S., Hasegawa, K., Kaneko, K., Miyakoda, H., & Tsukahara, W. (2007). Development and evaluation of a foreign-word learning system by iPods. In *Proceedings of the Sixth IASTED International Conference on WEB-Based Education* (pp. 264-269). Chamonix, France.

Barsky, E., & Lindstrom, K. (2008). Podcasting the sciences: A practical overview. *Issues in Science and Technology Librarianship*. Retrieved August 4, 2009, from http://www.istl.org/08-fall/article7.html

Beilke, J., Stuve, M., & Williams-Hawkins, M. (2008). "Clubcasting": Educational uses of podcasting in multicultural settings. *Multicultural Education & Technology Journal*, *2*(2), 107–117. doi:10.1108/17504970810883379

Blake, R. J. (2008). *Brave new digital classroom: Technology and foreign language learning*. Washington, DC: Georgetown University Press.

Bruce, B., & Lin, C. C. (2009). Voices of youth: Podcasting as a means for inquiry-based community engagement. *E-learning*, *6*(2), 230–241. doi:10.2304/elea.2009.6.2.230

Bush, M. (2008). Computer-assisted language learning: From vision to reality? *CALICO Journal*, *25*, 443–470.

Colpaert, J. (2004). From courseware to coursewear? *Computer Assisted Language Learning*, *17*(3-4), 261–266. doi:10.1080/0958822042000319575

Dervin, F. (2006). Podcasting demystified, *Language Magazine*, 30-31. Retrieved August 4, 2009, from http://www.languagemagazine.com

Ducate, L., & Lomicka, L. (2009a). Podcasting in the language classroom: Inherently mobile or not? In Oxford, R., & Oxford, J. (Eds.), *Second language teaching and learning in the Net Generation* (pp. 113–128). Honolulu: University of Hawaii, National Foreign Language Resource Center.

Ducate, L., & Lomicka, L. (2009b). Podcasting: An effective tool for honing language students' pronunciation? *Language Learning & Technology, 13*(3), 66–86.

Edirisingha, P., Rizzi, C., Nie, M., & Rothwell, L. (2007). Podcasting to provide teaching and learning support for an undergraduate module on English language and communication. *Turkish Online Journal of Distance Education, 8*(3), Article 6.

Elliott, A. R. (1995). Foreign language phonology: Field independence, attitude, and the success of formal instruction in Spanish pronunciation. *Modern Language Journal, 79*, 530–542. doi:10.2307/330005

Facer, B., Abdous, M., & Camarena, M. (2009). The impact of academic podcasting on students: Learning outcomes and study habits. In R. de Cassia Veiga Marriott, & P. Lupion Torres (Eds.), *Handbook of Research on E-Learning Methodologies for Language Acquisition* (pp. 339-351). IRM Press: Cybertech Publishing.

Fox, A. (2008). Using podcasts in the EFL classroom. *TESL-EJ, 11*(4). Retrieved November 16, 2009, from http://tesl-ej.org/ej44/a4.html

Godwin-Jones, R. (2005). Skype and podcasting: Disruptive technologies for language learning. *Language Learning & Technology, 9*(3), 9–12.

Hartigan, T., Hill, J., Lewis-Faupel, S., & Springsteen, A. (2006). iPods and podcasting: Too cool for school? Retrieved November 30, 2009, from http://www.educause.edu/ir/library/pdf/NCP0664A.pdf

Herrington, J., & Kervin, L. (2007). Authentic learning supported by technology: Ten suggestions and cases of integration in classroom. *Educational Media International, 44*(3), 219–236. doi:10.1080/09523980701491666

Lee, M. J. W., Miller, C., & Newnham, L. (2008). Podcasting syndication services and university students: Why don't they subscribe? *The Internet and Higher Education, 12*, 53–59. doi:10.1016/j.iheduc.2008.10.001

Lord, G. (2008). Podcasting communities and second language pronunciation. *Foreign Language Annals, 41*, 364–379. doi:10.1111/j.1944-9720.2008.tb03297.x

Lys, F. (2008, March 18-22). *In touch with the iPod Touch.* Paper presented at CALICO 2008, University of San Francisco, San Francisco, CA.

McBride, K. (2009). Podcasts and second language learning: Promoting listening comprehension and intercultural competence. In Abraham, L. B., & Williams, L. (Eds.), *Electronic discourse in language learning and language teaching* (pp. 153–167). Amsterdam: John Benjamins.

McCarty, S. (2005). Spoken Internet to go: Popularization through podcasting. *JALT CALL, 1*(2), 67-74. Retrieved November 16, 2009, from http://www.waoe.org/president/podcasting_article.html

McCloskey, P. (2007, July 9). Consensus: Podcasting has no 'inherent' pedagogic value. Campus Technology. Retrieved November 4, 2009, from http://campustechnology.com/articles/49018

McQuillan, J. (2006). Language on the go: Tuning in to podcasting. *The International Journal of Foreign Language Teaching, 2*, 16–18.

Meng, P. (2005). Podcasting and vodcasting: A white paper. Retrieved November 16, 2009, from http://edmarketing.apple.com/adcinstitute/wp-content/Missouri_Podcasting_White_Paper.pdf

O'Bryan, A., & Hegelheimer, V. (2007). Integrating CALL into the classroom: The role of podcasting in an ESL listening strategies course. *ReCALL, 19*(2), 162–180. doi:10.1017/S0958344007000523

Pettes Guikema, J. (2009). Discourse analysis of podcasts in French: Implications for foreign language listening development. In Abraham, L. B., & Williams, L. (Eds.), *Electronic discourse in language learning and language teaching* (pp. 169–189). Amsterdam: John Benjamins.

*podscope.* (2007). Retrieved November 30, 2009, from http://podscope.com/

Prensky, M. (2009). H. sapiens digital: From digital immigrants and digital natives to digital wisdom. *INNOVATE Journal of Online Education, 5*(3). Retrieved November 16, 2009, from http://innovateonline.info/pdf/vol5_issue3/H._Sapiens_Digital-__From_Digital_Immigrants_and_Digital_Natives_to_Digital_Wisdom.pdf

*Ramp.* (2007). Retrieved November 30, 2009, from http://www.ramp.com/

Rosell-Aguilar, F. (2007). Top of the pods: In search of a podcasting 'podagogy' for language learning. *Computer Assisted Language Learning, 20*, 471–492. doi:10.1080/09588220701746047

Rosell-Aguilar, F. (2009). Podcasting for language learning: Re-examining the potential. In Lomicka, L., & Lord, G. (Eds.), *The next generation: Social networking and online collaboration in foreign language learning* (pp. 13–34). San Marcos, TX: CALICO.

Sathe, N., & Waltje, J. (2008). The iPod project: A mobile mini-lab. *Journal of the Research Centre for Educational Technology, 4*, 32–56.

Schmidt, J. (2008). Podcasting as a learning tool: German language and culture every day. *Unterrichtspraxis, 41*, 186–194. doi:10.1111/j.1756-1221.2008.00023.x

Seitzinger, J. (2006). Be constructive: Blogs, podcasts, and wikis as constructivist learning tools. *Learning Solutions*. July, 2006.

Simon, E. (2008). Foreign language faculty in the age of web 2.0. *EDUCAUSE Quarterly, 3*, 6–7.

Simpson, J. (Ed.). (2009). *Oxford English Dictionary* (3rd ed.). New York: Oxford University Press. Retrieved March 30, 2010, from http://dictionary.oed.com

Stanley, G. (2006). Podcasting: Audio on the internet comes of age. *TESL-EJ 9*(4), 1-7. http://tesl-ej.org/ej36/int.html

Swain, M., & Lapkin, S. (1995). Problems in output and the cognitive processes they generate: A step towards second language learning. *Applied Linguistics, 16*, 371–391. doi:10.1093/applin/16.3.371

Sze, P. M.-M. (2006). Developing students' listening and speaking skills through ELT podcasts. *Education Journal, 34*, 115–134.

The University of Wisconsin Language Institute Website. Retrieved November 16, 2009, from http://languageinstitute.wisc.edu/

Thorne, S. L., & Payne, J. S. (2005). Evolutionary trajectories, internet-mediated expression, and language education. *CALICO Journal, 22*(3), 371–397.

Young, D. J. (2007). iPods, MP3 players and podcasts for FL learning: Current practices and future considerations. *NECTFL Review, 60*, 39–49.

## KEY TERMS AND DEFINITIONS

**Mobile Assisted Language Learning:** MALL is an approach to language learning that is carried out or enhanced through use of mobile devices such as mobiles phones, MP3 players, or laptop computers. The primary focus of MALL is to allow students to access language learning materials, and to communicate with teachers or peers, at anytime, and from anywhere.

**MP3 Player:** This device is designed to play digital audio files, and can store, organize, and play back. It is also referred to as a portable media player.

**Podcast:** A podcast is a collection or series of digital media files that are released in episodes and downloaded through web syndication (ATOM or RSS).

## ENDNOTES

[1]    Other pioneering projects include those at Duke University and Middlebury College (cited in Thorne & Payne, 2005) and at the University of Wisconsin (The University of Wisconsin Language Institute Website, n.d.).

[2]    Note that the total number of reasons mentioned is greater than the number of respondents. This is because a number of respondents indicated multiple reasons for using podcasting, and each reason was recorded.

## APPENDIX: SURVEY

*Figure 2.*

**Exit this survey**

Podcasting in language teaching

1. What language(s) do you teach? (check all that apply)

*Figure 3.*

⌐ Arabic
⌐ Chinese
⌐ ESL
⌐ French
⌐ German
⌐ Italian
⌐ Portuguese
⌐ Russian
⌐ Spanish
Other (please specify)

2. At what kind of institution do you teach? (check all that apply)

*Figure 4.*

⌐ Elementary school
⌐ Middle school
⌐ High school
⌐ College/University
⌐ Public
⌐ Private

Other (please specify)

3. What level(s) of language do you teach? (check all that apply)

*Figure 5.*

   ⌐  Beginning

   ⌐  Intermediate

   ⌐  Advanced

Other (please specify)

4. What is the average age of the students you teach?

*Figure 6.*

   ☐  5-10

   ☐  11-15

   ☐  16-18

   ☐  19-23

   ☐  Over 23

Other (please specify)

5. What are the goals of your podcasting project? (i.e., to develop listening, to work on pronunciation, etc…)

6. Please provide a brief description of your project.

7. What challenges did you face/are you facing in the design and implementation of your project?

8. Do you plan to use podcasting in future projects?

*Figure 7.*

☐ Yes
☐ No
☐ Maybe

Comments? _____

9. What would you do differently for future projects?

```
┌──────────────────────────────────────────────────────────┐
│                                                          │
└──────────────────────────────────────────────────────────┘
```

10. May we contact you for further information regarding this or other podcast projects in which you've been involved?

*Figure 8.*

☐ No
☐ Yes

If yes, please provide an email address _____

# Chapter 2
# Four L2 Learning Objectives to Guide Podcast Design

**Claudia Fernández**
*Knox College, USA*

## ABSTRACT

*This chapter addresses the production of podcasts as second language (L2) instructional materials developed by language instructors. The author discusses the importance of having clear language learning objectives when creating podcasts. The clarity of the objectives will depend on the particular nature of these materials and will influence podcast design and outcomes. In an effort to contribute to the understanding of podcast design that effectively promotes L2 acquisition and development, the author proposes that podcasts - when used by students as listening tools - can help the L2 learner accomplish four main learning objectives: (1) language acquisition, (2) development of listening comprehension skills, (3) learning of explicit information about the L2 and (4) awareness of the target culture. As with any L2 learning materials (Mobile Assisted or not), podcast development should be based on what is known about L2 acquisition and best teaching practices (Rosell-Aguilar, 2007; 2009). Therefore, the author addresses some of the aspects of language learning and teaching that should be considered in order to create well-informed podcasts that aim at the four proposed learning objectives.*

## INTRODUCTION

Podcasts have had a very successful beginning as tools for learning, in particular for learning second languages. A number of scholars have recognized their potential as L2 learning tools (Godwin-Jones, 2005; McQuillan, 2006a; Thorne & Payne, 2005) and there has been recent increased interest in investigating their use and effectiveness (Abdous, Camarena & Facer, 2009; Bird-Soto & Rengel, 2009; Ducate & Lomicka, 2009; Lord, 2008; O'Bryan & Hegelheimer, 2007). This interest cannot be more evident than when we look at the enormous number of podcasts for L2 learning

DOI: 10.4018/978-1-60960-141-6.ch002

available on the internet. At the time of writing this chapter, there were more than 180 podcast series for foreign language learning featured on the iTunes® list only, with thousands of podcast episodes available across the series. However, as with any emerging technology, little is still known about podcasts, particularly about the effectiveness of their design, and the learning outcomes that can be expected after podcasts are used in an L2 setting. This scarcity of information, in part, has contributed to the poor podcast design, blurred learning objectives, and outdated methodologies that are present in many of the podcasts for language learning available on the internet (McQuillan, 2006b; Rosell-Aguilar, 2007).

Because podcasts enjoy such popularity and have such a large potential for the promotion of L2 learning in both the Computer Assisted Language Learning (CALL) and the emerging Mobile Assisted Language Learning (MALL) contexts, it has become very important to identify the elements which make a podcast effective. This issue is particularly relevant for academic podcasting and for the L2 teaching profession, in particular for L2 instructors who are either creating their own podcasts for their classes or who are looking for already-produced podcasts to complement their teaching. In this chapter, I address the importance of podcast design by (1) highlighting the importance of setting podcast objectives, (2) considering the nature of podcasts and (3) proposing four L2 learning objectives that can be achieved through listening to podcasts. I also offer some considerations gleaned from what we currently know about L2 acquisition and about best teaching practices that can inform podcast design, based on the four proposed learning objectives. It is hoped that this discussion will contribute to our understanding of podcast design and will help L2 instructors who are creating their own podcasts or looking for already-produced podcasts to encourage language learning.

## BACKGROUND

In an article published in 2007, Rosell-Aguilar called for a search for a podcasting pedagogy for L2 learning. He addressed the nature, the potential, the advantages and disadvantages of podcasts for language learning and concluded that materials developed for podcasting, based on their nature, fit with what we currently know about the way in which languages are learned. That is, podcasts have the potential to provide authentic materials, to be meaningful, to provide comprehensible input, and to promote a focus on target forms. However, in spite of their potential, Rosell-Aguilar particularly pointed out the poor quality of the design and the outdated teaching methodologies that were prevalent in most of the podcasts available on the internet at that time. He observed that "…having the technical know-how does not necessarily imply a pedagogic know-how" (p. 486). He concluded that a deeper look at the way in which materials are conceived is necessary and is called for the need for a better design, one based on theory and best teaching practices.

Other scholars have commented upon the same situation. McQuillan (2006b), for example, mentioned that, as with any emerging technology used for language learning purposes, there is always the chance of falling back to outdated methodologies. This is what he called the "old wine into new skins problem" (p. 18). He highlighted the promise of podcasting as a means of disseminating L2 listening materials, and pointed out the practice at that time: "…to replicate the often dull largely unsuccessful listening material that predominates the current market in the podcasting venue" (p. 18).

Although these observations were made a few years ago (when podcasting technologies were only beginning to emerge), at the time at which this paper was written, the situation had not changed much. Many of the podcasts for language learning available on the internet are still product-oriented. They ask the listener to listen and repeat, many times without providing the meaning of what is being repeated, with an aim at offering "natural" language. But they do not provide the listener with the type of input that is necessary to make the form-meaning connections essential for language acquisition to happen. In addition, the learning objectives are seldom explained and their relationship with the instruction is not always clear. This situation reveals that, although the potential for podcasts to have a positive impact upon L2 learning is recognized, it is not yet well-known how to design and develop podcasts that effectively make use of their potential.

One reason for this problem is the fact that anyone enthusiastic in foreign language instruction can create (and then post to the world) a series of podcasts. He or she does not need to show any expertise in the field of language teaching. However, there are other issues as well. Given the fact that podcasts are relatively a new trend in L2 instruction, there is little empirical data to confirm their potential benefits, and there is scarce information regarding standards or guidelines to produce effective podcasts that actually promote L2 development (Lord, 2008; Rosell-Aguilar, 2007). We certainly have more information on the effectiveness of podcasts for language learning than what we had a few years ago, as there are already a several studies that have shed light on a variety of podcasting issues (Rosell-Aguilar, 2009). However, there is still much more to investigate, especially in the area of podcast design and the way in which it is influenced by podcast affordances and L2 learning objectives.

## PODCAST DESIGN: FOUR LANGUAGE LEARNING OBJECTIVES

### The Nature of Podcasts

The design of podcasts for L2 learning is perhaps the feature that will have the most impact on de-

sired learning outcomes (Rosell-Aguilar, 2007). A well-designed podcast is conceptualized based on (1) the particular nature of these audio files, (2) the aspects of L2 learning for which they are potentially useful and (3) the particular L2 learning objectives sought to achieve. Once these three features are identified, it is necessary to consider relevant information about the way in which languages are learned and the ways in which the best L2 teaching practices can be incorporated in order to fulfill the intended learning objectives.

In order to identify the L2 learning aspects that MALL technologies can potentially affect, it is essential that we understand the nature of these materials. Rosell-Aguilar (2009) summarizes podcast characteristics as "…a series of regularly updated media files that can be played on a number of devices (portable and static) and are distributed over the internet via a subscription service" (p. 14). He highlights the features of *being part of a series* and *being automatically delivered through RSS subscription* as key to the nature of podcasts. These are the attributes that make podcasts different from any other type of audio file. The consideration of these characteristics will impact both the podcast design and the L2 learning aspects for which they can be potentially useful. For example, in terms of design, podcasts will need a specific format to guide both the listeners and the host(s); and in terms of L2 learning, podcasts may not be the most appropriate tools for the promotion of oral interaction or for the development of writing skills.

There are, however, some aspects of L2 learning for which podcasts can be potentially useful. Because podcasts are audio/video files, they can deliver hundreds of hours of language exposure. Therefore, podcasts are excellent sources of L2 input. This ability to be an excellent source of L2 input is a very powerful quality because, as we know from SLA theories and from empirical evidence, input is *essential* for language learning (Gass, 1997; Krashen, 1985; VanPatten, 2003). That is, without exposure to input, students will not acquire the morpho-syntactic (i.e., grammar) knowledge of the L2, its phonological features, its vocabulary, and/or its pragmatic use (to name a few linguistic components of the target language). No matter how many grammar and vocabulary rules are taught to students, or how much oral practice they engage in, learners will not develop an implicit linguistic system that allows them to use the language unless they are exposed to large amounts of comprehensible, meaning-bearing input. Because podcasts are audio files that belong to a series (and, thus, there can be hundreds of files) and because they are automatically delivered, learners can have access to the essential elements for L2 acquisition frequently, regularly, and automatically. Because of these features, podcasts can be one of the best tools for L2 acquisition and teaching.

Rosell-Aguilar (2007) and O'Bryan and Hegelheimer (2007) argued that the effectiveness of podcast design depends on its purpose. I want to propose that through listening to podcasts, students can achieve four L2 learning objectives: (1) L2 acquisition, (2) development of listening comprehension skills, (3) learning of explicit information about the L2, and (4) awareness of the target culture. In the following sections, I will expand on each of these objectives and I will address some of the aspects of language learning and teaching that should be considered in order to create well-informed podcasts that aim to achieve the four proposed learning objectives.

## Objective One: Podcasts for L2 Acquisition

If the main purpose of the podcasts is for learners to develop their implicit linguistic systems, then the podcasts, first and foremost, have to contain comprehensible, meaning-bearing input. Comprehensible input refers to language that learners are able to understand—if not word by word, then, at least enough to extract the general meaning of what they are listening to (Krashen, 1985). This feature is extremely important because acquisition occurs when learners connect the linguistic form

with its meaning (VanPatten, 2003). For example, that learning comes when an ESL or EFL learner hears the aural form /kaet/ and is able to assign the meaning (e.g., a domestic feline animal). If learners only perceive (i.e., notice) the linguistic forms, but are unable to connect meaning to them, then these forms will not be taken in; that is, they will not enter the learner's implicit linguistic system.

There are a number of ways in which aural texts for podcasts can be made comprehensible. One of them is by shortening their length and by slowing the pace of speech, especially by creating longer pauses between phrases and sentences to allow the listener time to process them (Blau, 1990). Rost (2006) suggests that elaboration (rather than simplification) of the aural texts also makes them more comprehensible because more context is provided from which learners can draw in order to come up with a mental representation of the unknown words or structures. In addition, he suggests that adding redundancy (i.e., various types of natural repetition, amplification, and paraphrasing) and transparency (i.e., overt signaling of topic saliency, logic chronological order of events, and a prevalent use of the here-and-now) improves listening comprehension. Another way to promote comprehension is by choosing topics that are known by the learners and that occur in contexts with which they are familiar. In this sense, students' knowledge of the world and experience, which Rumelhart (1980) called "schemata", will compensate for their limited linguistic knowledge and will help them fill in the blanks created by what is not understood.

A common teaching practice that aims at comprehension is to provide the meaning of key content words before approaching the task of listening. The rationale behind this practice is that not only do content words (i.e., nouns, verbs, and adjectives) carry the most meaning, but studies have shown a preference for learners to attend to these words when attempting to understand an aural text (Field, 2008a). An important factor to consider, noted by Field (2008b), is that knowing the meaning of the aural or written form in isolation will not necessarily ensure that learners will recognize that same form in connected speech, since words often deviate from their standard form when they are combined with others. A suggestion for podcast design is to introduce the meaning and the aural form of the content words before the listening of the main text of the podcast. The words can be both introduced in isolation and embedded in several sentences (including, perhaps, the sentences where they will actually appear in the main text of the podcast).

Another common way of promoting comprehension is to accompany the aural text of the podcasts with their corresponding script and with images, or with a video component. Such podcasts are referred to as "enhanced" [see Chapter 3, "Going beyond audio: Adding multimedia to podcasts for foreign language education" in this volume]. The learning advantages of supporting aural texts with visual aids are well-documented in the literature (Gruba, 2006; Guichon & McLornan, 2008; Mueller, 1980; Secules, Herron, & Tomasello, 1992), since images provide additional sources of information which facilitate comprehension. In addition to promoting language comprehension, enhanced podcasts can also reduce the need for enhanced explanation and elaboration (even, perhaps, explanations that need to be conveyed in the L1 for novice L2 students) and may be more appealing to the listeners.

In order to promote L2 acquisition, the input must not only be comprehensible, but it must also have a communicative intent (i.e., it must be "meaning-bearing" VanPatten, 2003) While podcasts can be formatted in a variety of genra (e.g., a description, a narration of a story, a set of instructions on how to do something, a movie review, a dialogue, a poem, etc.), their purpose should always be to convey a message to which learners attend. Chapelle (2005) clearly points out that the basic assumption of CALL pedagogy is that "learners should be working with texts and tasks that require them to attend to the meaning of

the language" (p. 747). It is important to mention here that although the conventional purpose of podcast listening is for the listeners' own pleasure, best teaching practices advise that learners should be asked to do something concrete with the input to which they are being exposed (Lee & VanPatten, 2003). In that sense, podcasts not only contain meaning-bearing input, but also give learners a reason to pay attention to the message for the meaning it conveys.

Research has suggested that providing comprehensible, meaning-bearing input -although essential for L2 acquisition - is not enough for learners to acquire certain linguistic forms, especially morpho-syntactic forms (Doughty & Williams, 1998; Swain & Lapkin, 1989). Because learners must attend to a number of linguistic features in the input (lexicon, phonology, grammar, etc.) when attending to a message, and because there is only so much attentional capacity available to process all this input, there will be certain forms that learners will miss (Field, 2008a; Just & Carpenter, 1992; VanPatten, 2003). This is more prevalent in beginning L2 learners; for them, simply attending to the message of the input (i.e., figuring out the meaning of content words) can use up most of their attentional resources and thus, they have no room to process other less meaningful forms such as morphological inflections, function words, certain phonological features, redundant forms, etc. Only when the effort to attend to content words is reduced do learners have spare attentional capacity to attend to other linguistic features of the L2. However, certain forms, because of their lack of salience or their minor contribution to the overall meaning of the message, are often not noticed by even the most advanced learners (Swain & Lapkin, 1989). In these cases, instructors can "enhance the input" (Sharwood-Smith, 1993). Input enhancement refers to the instructional techniques that attempt to make certain features of the input more noticeable. The rationale is that enhancing the input increases the chances that students will detect target forms, promoting their acquisition.

The relevant question for podcast design is: how can aural input be enhanced in a podcast?

There are several L2 teaching techniques that have been designed for classroom contexts but that can be adapted or can serve as a point of departure for MALL (in particular podcast design), in order to enhance the aural input. These techniques are input flood, aural enhancement, and explicitly drawing attention to form. Input flood (Kon, 2002 [cited in Chapelle, 2005]; Trahey & White, 1993) consists of including a number of instances of the target form in the input (either aural or written). For example, if the purpose is for learners to notice the third person singular present tense forms in English (i.e., she eat*s*, he goe*s*, etc.), the instructor would create or adapt a text that includes the use of more than the "normal" number of these forms. The rationale is that the frequency of the forms will make them more salient and thus, more noticeable for students. Aural enhancement (with its original counter-part: textual enhancement; see Leow, 2009) consists of including a change in tone or pitch every time the target form(s) appears in the aural text in an effort to draw students' attention to these specific forms. If the written script is made available to learners, it can also have some type of visual enhancement by highlighting the target forms (by using bold, color, or italic fonts, and by underlining words, etc.).

Another technique is explicitly drawing learners' attention to the grammatical or lexical forms that the instructor wishes the students to notice in the aural text. In the case of podcasts, the host may request that the listeners pay attention to the forms that they are about to hear (for example, to attend to the use of the French *passé composé* and the *imparfait* in the narration, or to note the way the speakers use the Spanish *usted* and *tú* forms to signal speakers' perceived social differences). It is important to note that such indication, if given before the main text in the podcast, can potentially prime students to notice the target forms (Ellis, Basturkmen & Loewen, 2001), but it may also encourage them to only focus on the forms instead of attending to the meaning of the text, diminishing its effectiveness for L2 acquisition. Therefore, it is important to design podcasts in a way that will promote that meaning is always the main focus of the listening. One way of doing this is by designing a podcast format in which learners listen to the main text twice during the same episode: the first time for learners to attend to its meaning (and ideally, the instructor can provide a task that encourages this), and a second time for them to focus on the form.

One example of podcasts used for language acquisition is the series called ESLpod, created by the Center for Educational Development (n.d.) for students of English as an L2. These podcasts provide comprehensible input through descriptions, narrations, and dialogues (conveyed at slower pace) and through elaboration on the meaning of the aural text. The input is also meaning-bearing, as each distinct podcast episode addresses a topic of general interest (e.g., how to buy produce, how to discuss social class, how to blow the whistle at work, etc.). The host draws attention to specific words and expressions in the explanation part of each episode by expanding and elaborating on their meanings. After the explanation portion, the main text is played again, offering learners the opportunity to comprehend the aural text better the second time, thus promoting acquisition.

In sum, podcasts for L2 acquisition should be comprehensible and meaningful and should offer some type of input-enhancement feature that facilitates the development of form-meaning connections in order to develop the implicit linguistic system.

## Objective Two: Podcasts for the Development of Listening Skills

If the purpose of the podcasts is for students to become expert listeners who are able to understand the meaning of the aural message effectively, then podcasts should provide ample practice in the application of the listening skills, strategies, and processes necessary to understand the message. That is, podcasts should prepare students to effectively deal with authentic spoken speech.

Mendelsohn (2006), Field (2008b), and others have claimed that, traditionally, teaching listening in the classroom has been a practice of *testing* listening. That is, students have traditionally been exposed to an aural text and then were asked comprehension questions. If comprehension was not achieved to the instructor's expectations, then the text was played again and again until some students finally figured out the answers, or until the instructor, defeated, provided the missing information. According to these authors, the rationale for this practice is that by repeatedly exposing learners to aural texts, they will - somehow and on their own - eventually acquire the skills and processes necessary to improve listening comprehension. These authors believe that a more effective approach is actually *teaching* listening (that is, training students on how to go about getting the meaning of the aural message). In this section, I will explain some of the different approaches to teaching listening and I will share some ways in which podcasts can be designed to achieve this objective.

A number of scholars have proposed different approaches to teaching listening by giving learners the "tools" to deal with connected speech effectively. Richards (1983), for example, suggested a skill-based approach. Because listening is not a monolithic phenomenon in which one single skill can be applied to solve all listening challenges, he compiled several lists of sub-skills in an effort to identify the elements that make up listening expertise. Some of these sub-skills refer to the ability to discriminate between distinctive sounds, to distinguish word boundaries, to detect key words, to recognize both major syntactic patterns, and to determine the communicative function of utterances. By identifying these skills, instructors can create or select materials that aim at practicing the use of these skills in order to make sense of what is being listened.

An approach using a strategy-based perspective proposed by Mendelsohn (2006) allows students to learn and practice strategies in order to better understand the aural text. Mendelsohn's listening strategies involve the identification of different linguistic, paralinguistic, and extralinguistic signals for learners to use in order to determine the content of the discourse they are listening to. Some of these strategies include forming hypotheses, predicting, and making inferences.

A third approach, proposed by Field (2008b), consists of identifying the listening processes that expert listeners employ when dealing with spoken discourse. Field (2008b) argues that L2 learners have developed listening processes in their first language for years, and thus are competent L1 listeners. Therefore, instruction, rather than teaching new L2 capabilities, should help learners adapt their existing listening processes in order to make them relevant to the different demands of the L2. He divides these processes into two categories: (1) decoding processes and (2) meaning-building processes. The decoding processes involve recognizing the L2 at various linguistic levels (e.g., the phoneme, syllable, word, syntactic, and intonation group levels). The meaning-building processes involve drawing from a range of contextual information necessary to arrive at a full understanding of the speaker's message.

All of these approaches have given instructors a framework with which they can implement listening instruction that goes beyond merely testing comprehension. Also - by identifying skills, strategies, or processes - the approaches encourage a developmental style to the teaching of listening, one which breaks the process into its component parts for localized practice. It is important to consider such approaches, and ways in which they can be implemented, when designing podcasts for the promotion of listening skills.

Regarding learners' use of strategies, it has been argued that aural texts pose different challenges for each listener; thus, each listener adopts strategies that best help him or her with comprehension. These strategies may be very different from the strategies of other listeners (White, 2006). Therefore, focusing the podcast on one strategy at a time may serve some learners, but not others, as not all listeners would find that particular strategy useful for their specific needs. Thus, instruction may involve aural texts to target the use of specific strategies with the purpose of familiarizing students with a range of strategies at the beginning, but eventually, students would have to figure out which strategy best serves their needs. Field (2008b) and others advocate for a listening/teaching session that involves a reflection phase which might help students take time to ponder the effectiveness of the strategies they used while listening to certain aural texts.

Regardless of the approach selected to teach listening (i.e., skill, strategies, or process-based), researchers seem to agree that listening instruction should be given in a piecemeal fashion (Al-jasser, 2008; Daly, 2006; Field, 2008b). That is, teachers might create a series of small-scale training exercises that focus on a certain strategy (e.g., predicting), skill (e.g., distinguishing word boundaries), or process (e.g., recognizing intonation) or that allows learners to individually select the strategies which they feel would be most appropriate. The key is to provide extensive practice in controlled conditions, and then ask learners to reflect and assess their performance. The rationale is that by practicing these skills, strategies, or processes in contrived conditions, students will eventually use them automatically (that is, accurately, fast, and effortlessly) every time they are exposed to real spoken language (Field, 2008b).

This piecemeal fashion of teaching listening makes podcasts the ideal tools for listening instruction. The instructor can design a podcast project that contains a series of episodes (i.e., micro-listening sessions), each targeting certain listening skills (or promoting learners to use their own choice of skills). Each episode can contain explicit explanation of what these skills are, and what their purpose is, along with an aural main text in which learners can practice applying them. After listening to the podcast, the learners can reflect upon and assess the ways in which applying the target skills helped them in the comprehension of the aural text. They can even share their reflections in class blogs, discussion boards, or in class. An entire listening program can be developed using a series of podcasts that can eventually give students the tools necessary to deal with spoken language effectively.

Research on listening skill-based programs through podcast listening is beginning to appear in the literature. One example is a study conducted by O'Bryan and Hegelheimer (2007), in which they implemented a podcast-based listening skills course for university students and found very positive results, especially in using those podcasts to explain, and then show through video, how to use certain skills when listening to a classroom lecture.

One consideration to keep in mind when designing podcasts for the development of listening skills is to make certain that students hear actual spoken language. Mendelsohn (2006) correctly points out that while this may sound obvious, that is often not the case. He reports that listening materials usually present learners with written language that has been recorded. He argues that such materials do not demonstrate many of the features that characterize spoken language. If our objective is for students to understand authentic language, then we should prepare them to deal with imperfect and incomplete sentences, false starts, vowel reduction, hesitations, and distortions of word boundaries, among other features of spoken language. Listening materials that only present written, contrived recorded language do not properly prepare students to deal with real, spontaneous connected speech because they do not offer the type of language to practice the skills necessary to understand actual spoken speech.

Including actual spoken language in the production of podcasts may pose a problem because of the copyright limitations incurred when using authentic samples of spoken language such as commercials, newscasts, and TV or radio programs. However, there are several options to keep in mind that would resolve the problem of providing learners with authentic language.

One option is for learners to start practicing with contrived, scripted aural texts that were created by the instructor and that are appropriate for the application of a targeted listening skill. That is, some instructors may choose to use samples of language that contain challenges to the listener and that would be likely, in natural conditions, given rise to the listening strategy (Field, 2008b), to aid in L2 listening. Once the learners have had ample practice applying a series of strategies with instructor-developed aural scripted texts, the instructor can assign learners to listen to some of the hundreds of commercially available podcasts (easily found in the iTunes® directory, for example) that are targeted at advanced or native-language audiences (not necessarily created merely for L2 instruction), that cover a variety of topics, and that are an excellent sources of authentic listening material.

Another option that can be used to solve the problem of providing authentic language is for the instructor to record samples of real speech. With the new mini-recorders that are available (for example, one that plugs directly to an mp3 player and records on it), it is easier than ever to record natural, unscripted speech in a variety of contexts, and in a variety of genra (i.e., an interview, a narration of a story, a description, or a dialogue), with different native or native-like speakers, that can be edited later and included in a podcast. It is true that this may represent more work than the instructor is willing to do, but it may be worth the effort.

A third option is provided by Tony Gonzalez in Chapter 3, "Going Beyond Audio: Adding multimedia to podcasts for foreign language education" in this volume. He describes ways in which instructors can find and use free multimedia

content to use in their podcasts. Another, perhaps easier, solution is for the host to record a text in which he or she describes something or someone, narrates a story, or conducts an interview in a spontaneous, natural way without a script (or much planning).

To summarize, podcasts that encourage the development of listening skills should actually prepare students to understand spoken language, rather than only to test student comprehension. Regardless of the approach, the choice, skills, strategies, or processes should be explained, and students should be given ample practice in applying the tools they need when being exposed to aural texts. Texts should contain actual spoken language, and they should contain challenges to the student that will require the use of their listening abilities.

## Objective Three: Podcasts for the Provision of Explicit Information about the L2

The objectives of these types of podcasts are not to provide input for language acquisition or to provide practice in applying listening skills in order for students to become better listeners. Rather, a podcast designed to provide explicit information (EI) gives information about the L2 and how it works. Some are used to provide learners with information about prescriptive grammar rules, about how the subjunctive works in Spanish, about how the system of case works in German, about the different tones in Chinese, about the article system in English, or about the meaning of "aspect" or common false cognates between English and Spanish (to name a few). In sum, these are podcasts that provide information about the L2 that is given to the learners in an explicit way.

It is important to note that EI, although beneficial, is not essential for L2 acquisition (VanPatten, 2003). That is, having an explicit knowledge about the rules of the L2 does not directly affect the development of an implicit linguistic system in the way that input does (Schwartz, 1993). However, there is both theoretical and empirical evidence that EI affects the rate of acquisition (Larsen-Freeman & Long, 1991), that it promotes noticing while attending to the input (Doughty & Williams,1998), and that it is helpful in monitoring language use, especially when the learner has time and is focused on the form (Williams, 2004).

In accomplishing the previously described two types of learning objectives (Objective 1: L2 acquisition and Objective 2: development of listening skills), the use of podcasts seem to be a clear fit. It is true that one may not see the purpose of creating podcasts to assist in the understanding of explicit information because such information is usually given in printed materials (i.e., textbooks and grammar practice books). However, there are several shortcomings to the EI provided in textbooks, especially in the information related to grammar. Katz and Blyth (2009) address what is, perhaps, one of the most common limitations. They mention that textbooks, in their effort to be "communicative", provide brief and concise grammar information that is often superficial, linguistically unsound, and incomplete. In many cases, this information does not reflect the actual use of grammar rules by native speakers in discourse, as was reported by O'Connor di Vito (1991) and Takenoya (1995). In addition, because of their printed nature, textbooks do not provide aural samples of language that illustrate linguistic rules (morpho-syntactic and pragmatic, for example), as was observed in a study conducted on six best-selling Spanish textbooks by Fernández (forthcoming). In all of these textbooks, the common way used to provide students with language data, in order to exemplify how grammar rules work, was through written and contrived examples at the sentence level. Therefore, it seems that podcasts can make up for the limitations that textbooks present, regarding the quality of the EI and the modality in which it is delivered.

A suggestion is to create podcasts that provide EI in a way that closely reflects actual language use by providing examples that illustrate this use. Such examples can be taken from authentic written and aural texts so that learners have the opportunity to analyze the target rule or structure as it is used (and said) in authentic materials. One popular series of podcasts which aims at the provision of explicit linguistic information is Grammar Girl (2009). In these podcasts, the host usually takes an example of language use from advertisements or from other authentic sources and uses it as a springboard to explain certain rules behind it, from a variety of linguistic perspectives. It is true that often language use is so subtle that even linguists have trouble coming up with an explicit account of the rules behind its use (and, in any case, it is doubtful that learners need the technical information of highly sophisticated linguistic phenomena in order to have a working knowledge of how the L2 works). It is also true that many instructors do not have the linguistic knowledge necessary to explain how certain forms are used in authentic communication and at the discourse level, as Katz and Blyth (2009) have pointed out. However, as a point of departure, it might be desirable for the instructor to identify the points in the textbook where the EI falls short, and to create a series of podcasts that complete such information (by clarifying or expanding on the topic), providing genuine examples where certain rules apply, which learners can experience in an aural way.

In sum, podcasts for the provision of EI about the L2 should reflect rules as they are actually used in both formal and informal contexts, and should provide learners with the opportunities to hear language in which the explained forms are used (for example, to complement traditional printed materials). In addition, instructors should be aware that podcasts that provide EI only may not be the ideal podcasts if the objective is helping the development of an implicit linguistic system.

## Objective Four: Podcasts for the Awareness of the Target Culture

Podcasts can also serve as materials with the purpose of teaching culture and as a way to promote cultural awareness and intercultural competence. As with podcasts for the provision of EI, the main objective of these materials is not necessarily language acquisition or the development of listening skills. Of course, if the cultural content of the podcast is given in the target language, students will be processing language for acquisition and may use listening strategies to better understand the message. However, the main objective of these podcasts is for students to learn a piece of information about the target culture(s) that promotes the analysis and reflection of its meaning. Given these objectives, the information does not even have to be conveyed in the target language. Of course, because language instruction should aim at providing learners with large amounts of input, it is desirable that cultural information be given in the target language as well, as another way of exposing learners to the L2; but, as in the case of beginning listeners, this may not be efficient if the listeners cannot understand the message. However, if the cultural information is conveyed in the target language, the aural text does not necessarily need to have input enhancement features, although it should be comprehensible to the audience. By the same token, the content does not necessarily have to aim at providing spoken discourse challenges that ask for learners to use listening comprehension strategies. The main purpose of these podcasts is to convey cultural information about the perspectives, products, and practices of the target culture(s) in a way that promotes cultural awareness.

One of the five C's in foreign language education, according to the National Standards for Foreign Language Education Project (NSFLEP, 1999) is *Cultures*. According to these standards, students should be able to "gain knowledge and understanding of other cultures" (p. 47). Based on an anthropological approach to representing culture, the standards are based on a cultural paradigm that includes the Three P's: *Perspectives, Practices,* and *Products*. Perspectives refer to the ideas, attitudes, beliefs, meanings, and values of a certain culture. Practices refer to the patterns of behavior of a society (such as ways of addressing one another, mealtime etiquette, and use of public spaces, for example). Products refer to concrete and abstract things created by members of the target culture (for example, a painting or a system of education). According to the standards, the products and the practices originate from the perspectives of the members of given culture.[1] The goals of the Cultures standards are for students to demonstrate an understanding of the relationship between the perspectives and products, as well as the relationship between the perspectives and the practices (NSFLEP, 1999).

Byram and Feng (2005) advocate for a constructivist approach, in which students' attitudes toward the target culture and their intercultural competence evolve over time as they observe, participate in, analyze, and reflect upon aspects of the target culture. In order for instructors to adopt this approach (and thus aim towards the goals of the Cultures standards), it is necessary to move beyond the facts-oriented approach in which culture is taught as bits and pieces of information that do not form an integral part of language learning. Byram and Feng (2005) noted that a facts-oriented approach may lead to the teaching of stereotypes, and Pulverness (2003) observed that unmediated information about the target culture may carry connotations that imply the "superiority" of the target culture.

The problem with the facts-oriented approach is that is does not provide learners with the meaning behind the facts about the target culture(s). After all, this knowledge is the first step towards a deeper understanding of aspects of the target culture(s), especially in those instructional settings (which are, often, the only L2 contexts that the students experience). The problem may lie in the type of cultural information offered, perhaps when it attempts to over-generalize practices or when it does not address the individual differences within a certain cultural community. More importantly, the problem lies with the restricted instruction of these facts, since this type of instruction often does not go beyond the factual information and does not promote a deeper understanding of the meanings of the facts. A very illustrative study where the instructor taught facts along with their relationship to the L2 perspectives was conducted by Herron, Dubreil, Corrie, and Cole (2002). The authors used video to promote cultural understanding, based on the National Standards. The instruction showed aspects of everyday life in French-speaking cultures through several video episodes, and went beyond just asking students for learned knowledge. The authors promoted analysis and reflection by asking students to make inferences about certain cultural situations, and by asking students to answer questions from the perspectives of the members of the target culture, based on the information conveyed in the videos.

Similar instructional approaches to the one proposed by Herron et al. (2002) (described above) are possible to apply to learning using podcasts. A podcast project can be developed and can form an integral part of the language teaching curriculum, allowing each episode to address a cultural aspect of the target culture that can serve as the springboard for further analysis in class, on blogs, or on discussion boards. In addition, these types of podcasts, since they are teacher-generated materials, can be designed in such as way as to elaborate, modify, challenge, or complement the cultural information provided in textbooks. Instructors can also convey cultural information in a way that can make it more relevant to their students' everyday lives by addressing the local practices of the target culture, commenting on the current social and artistic events of the community regarding the target culture, or focusing on the L2 cultural perspectives relevant to the particularities of the instructor's class. In this way, podcasts can complement and enhance the cultural component of the language class.

There are, perhaps, an infinite number of cultural topics that podcasts can address, in order to illustrate the practices and products of the target culture. The selection may be influenced by a variety of factors, including the instructor's knowledge of the target culture, the cognitive level of the listeners, the listeners' interests, and the relation of the topics to the language course in general. In that sense, finding a cultural topic may not pose a great problem. The problem may lie in choosing which approach to follow when presenting it in the podcast episode. An uncommon approach was described by Pulverness (2005), in which the cultural topics did not address the typical, but rather the idiosyncratic, practices of a culture. He proposed that this approach might break stereotypes and might promote a better understanding of the L2 culture. For example, the Japanese are known for their tidy and uncluttered houses. The instructor may know a Japanese person that does not mind having a messy space and might conduct a brief interview on her housekeeping perspective and include it in a podcast episode. Pulverness also suggests that topics that challenge learners beyond their level of comfort be included. Topics that confront the natural tendency to overgeneralize and that de-familiarize the familiar may promote the development of learners' cultural awareness.

Another example of a good use of podcasting to teach Culture is to create a series of podcasts that address the instructor's experiences in the target culture. Davies (2002) presented his "Teacher Biographies" in which he showed his personal cultural products (e.g., photos, bus tickets, magazines, etc.), narrated his experiences with the practices of the target culture, and shared his own reflection on the target culture's perspectives. He observed a very positive reaction from his students, who were asked to elaborate or comment on the aural or written texts in which he shared his "biographies." Although Davies (2002) did not create podcasts in his project, his ideas could very well be adapted to a podcast project and could achieve similar results.

In sum, podcasts for L2 culture learning should be designed so as to convey information about certain perspective, product, or practice of the target culture, but they should go beyond merely factual information by always being accompanied by activities or projects that promote the understanding of the relationships among these cultural components.

## CONCLUSION

This chapter addressed the need for better understanding of podcast design to effectively promote L2 learning. I proposed four possible objectives that podcasts for L2 learning can achieve. Because each objective was presented separately, the reader may be led to think that it is suggested that one single podcast episode should only have one single objective. Although there is nothing wrong with this perspective, it is certainly possible for one single podcast episode to aim at more than one of the four objectives addressed here, or for one podcast project to aim at addressing all four objectives (and even more) at once. To be sure, there is no reason to believe that a podcast for the learning of culture cannot deliver input for L2 acquisition, or that a podcast for L2 acquisition cannot include explicit information about a certain aspect of the L2. However, it is advisable to consider that to do it all in one single podcast episode may blur the objectives, affecting the design (and thus, the effectiveness) of the instruction. It is certainly valid to create efficient podcasts, as long as there is a clear idea of what aspects of language learning they are working to enhance. That is why I propose in this chapter that by identifying at least four learning objectives and then considering ways in which the L2 acquisition theories and best teaching practices suggest to accomplish them, instructors will be able to offer their students the best learning when looking for already-produced

podcasts or when creating their own podcasts for L2 learning and development.

## REFERENCES

Abdous, M., Camarena, M., & Facer, B. (2009). MALL Technology: Use of academic podcasting in the foreign language classroom. *ReCALL, 21,* 76–95. doi:10.1017/S0958344009000020

Al-jasser, F. (2008). The effect of teaching English phonotactics on the lexical segmentation of English as a foreign language. *System, 36,* 94–106. doi:10.1016/j.system.2007.12.002

Bird-Soto, N., & Rengel, P. (2009). Podcasting and the intermediate-level Spanish classroom. In Oxford, R., & Oxford, J. (Eds.), *Second language teaching and learning in the Net Generation* (pp. 101–109). Honolulu: University of Hawaii, National Foreign Language Resource Center.

Blau, E. (1990). The effect of syntax, speed, and pauses on listening comprehension. *TESOL Quarterly, 16,* 517–528. doi:10.2307/3586469

Byram, M., & Feng, A. (2005). Teaching and researching intercultural competence. In Hinkel, E. (Ed.), *Handbook of Research in Second Language Teaching and Learning* (pp. 911–930). Mahwah, NJ: Earlbaum.

Chapelle, C. (2005). Computer-assisted language learning. In Hinkel, E. (Ed.), *Handbook of Research in Second Language Teaching and Learning* (pp. 743–755). Mahwah, NJ: Earlbaum.

Daly, D. (2006, May). *Learner evaluation of a ten-session intensive listening programme.* Paper presented at BAAL/CUP conference. University of Warwik, UK.

Davies, A. (2002). Using teacher-generated biography as input material. *ELT Journal, 56,* 368–379. doi:10.1093/elt/56.4.368

Doughty, C., & Williams, J. (1998). *Focus on form in classroom second language acquisition.* Cambridge, UK: Cambridge University Press.

Ducate, L., & Lomicka, L. (2009). Podcasting: An effective tool for honing language students' pronunciation? *Language Learning & Technology, 13,* 66–86.

Ellis, R., Basturkmen, H., & Loewen, S. (2001). Preemptive focus on form in the ESL classroom. *TESOL Quarterly, 35,* 407–432. doi:10.2307/3588029

Fernández, C. (forthcoming). *Approaches to grammar instruction in teaching materials*: A study in current, beginning-level Spanish textbooks. *Hispania.*

Field, J. (2008a). Bricks or mortar: Which parts of the input does a second language listener rely on? *TESOL Quarterly, 42,* 411–431.

Field, J. (2008b). *Listening in the language classroom.* Cambridge, UK; New York: Cambridge University Press.

Gass, S. (1997). *Input, interaction, and the second language learner.* Mahwah, NJ: Lawrence Erlbaum Associates.

Geoghegan, M., & Klass, D. (2007). *Podcast solutions: The complete guide to audio and video podcasting* (2nd ed.). New York: Friendsof.

Godwin-Jones, R. (2005). Skype and podcasting: Disruptive technologies for language learning. *Language Learning & Technology, 9,* 9–12.

Grammar Girl. (2009). Retrieved on November 20, 2009 from http://grammar.quickanddirtytips.com/

Gruba, P. (2006). Playing the video-text: A media-literacy perspective on video-mediated L2 listening. *Language Learning & Technology, 10,* 77–92.

Guichon, N., & McLornan, S. (2008). The effects of multimodality on L2 learners: Implications for CALL resource design. *System, 36,* 85–93. doi:10.1016/j.system.2007.11.005

Herron, C., Dubreil, B., Corrie, C., & Cole, S. P. (2002). A classroom investigation: Can video improve intermediate-level french language students' ability to learn about a foreign culture? *Modern Language Journal, 86,* 36–53. doi:10.1111/1540-4781.00135

Just, M., & Carpenter, M. A. (1992). A capacity theory of comprehension: Individual differences in working memory. *Psychological Review, 99,* 122–149. doi:10.1037/0033-295X.99.1.122

Katz, S., & Blyth, C. (2009). What is grammar? In Katz, S., & Blyth, C. (Eds.), *AAUSC 2008 Volume, Conceptions of L2 grammar: Theoretical approaches and their application in the L2 classroom* (pp. 2–14). Boston, MA: Heinle Cengage Learning.

Krashen, S. (1985). *The input hypothesis.* London: Longman.

Larsen-Freeman, D., & Long, M. (1991). *An introduction to second language acquisition research.* New York: Longman.

Lee, J., & VanPatten, B. (2003). *Making communicative language teaching happen.* New York: McGraw-Hill.

Leow, R. P. (2009). Input enhancement and L2 grammatical development: What the research reveals. In Katz, S., & Blyth, C. (Eds.), *AAUSC 2008 Volume, Conceptions of L2 grammar: Theoretical approaches and their application in the L2 classroom* (pp. 16–34). Boston, MA: Heinle Cengage Learning.

Lord, G. (2008). Podcasting communities and second language pronunciation. *Foreign Language Annals, 41,* 364–379. doi:10.1111/j.1944-9720.2008.tb03297.x

McQuillan, J. (2006a). *iPod in Education: The potential for language acquisition.* One in a series of iPod in education white papers. Cupertino, CA: Apple Inc.

McQuillan, J. (2006b). Language on the go: Tuning into podcasting. *The International Journal of Foreign Language Teaching, 2,* 16–18.

Mendelsohn, D. J. (2006). Learning how to listen using learning strategies. In Usó-Juan, E., & Martínez-Flor, A. (Eds.), *Current trends in the development and teaching of the four language skills* (pp. 75–89). Berlin: Mouton de Gruyter. doi:10.1515/9783110197778.2.75

Mueller, G. A. (1980). Visual contextual cues and listening comprehension: An experiment. *Modern Language Journal, 64*(3), 335–340. doi:10.2307/324500

National Standards in Foreign Language Education Project (NSFLEP). (1999). *National Standards for foreign language learning: Preparing for the 21st century.* Lawrence, KS: Allen Pres.

O'Bryan, A., & Hegelheimer, V. (2007). Integrating CALL into the language classroom: The role of podcasting in an ESL listening strategies course. *ReCALL, 19,* 162–180. doi:10.1017/S0958344007000523

O'Connor di Vito, N. (1991). Incorporating native speaker norms in second language teaching materials. *Applied Linguistics, 12,* 383–395. doi:10.1093/applin/12.4.383

Pulverness, A. (2003). Materials for cultural awareness. In Tomlinson, B. (Ed.), *Developing materials for language teaching* (pp. 426–438). London: Continuum.

Richards, J. C. (1983). Listening comprehension: Approach, design, procedure. *TESOL Quarterly, 17,* 219–239. doi:10.2307/3586651

Rosell-Aguilar. F. (2009). Podcasting for language learning: Re-examining the potential. In L. Lomicka and G. Lord (Eds.), *The next generation: Social networking and online collaboration in foreign language learning* (pp. 13-34). San Mateo, TX: CALICO.

Rosell-Aguilar, F. (2007). Top of the Pods –In search of a podcasting "podagogy" for language learning. *Computer Assisted Language Learning, 5,* 471–492. doi:10.1080/09588220701746047

Rost, M. (2006). Areas of research that influence L2 listening instruction. In Usó-Juan, E., & Martínez-Flor, A. (Eds.), *Current trends in the development and teaching of the four language skills* (pp. 47–74). Berlin: Mouton de Gruyter. doi:10.1515/9783110197778.2.47

Rumelhart, D. (1980). Schemata: The building blocks of cognition. In Spiro, R., Bruce, B., & Brewer, W. (Eds.), *Theoretical issues in reading comprehension* (pp. 33–35). Hillsdale, NJ: Earlbaum.

Schwartz, B. D. (1993). On explicit and negative data affecting competence and linguistic behavior. *Studies in Second Language Acquisition, 15,* 147–163. doi:10.1017/S0272263100011931

Secules, T., Herron, C., & Tomasello, M. (1992). The effect of video context on foreign language learning. *Modern Language Journal, 76,* 480–490. doi:10.2307/330049

Sharwood-Smith, M. (1993). Input enhancement in instructed SLA: Theoretical bases. *Studies in Second Language Acquisition, 15,* 165–179. doi:10.1017/S0272263100011943

Shrum, J., & Glisan, E. (2005). *Teacher's handbook: Contextualized language instruction.* Boston, MA: Thomson-Heinle.

Swain, M., & Lapkin, S. (1989). Canadian immersion and adult second language teaching –What's the connection. *Modern Language Journal, 73,* 150–159. doi:10.2307/326570

Takenoya, M. (1995). Acquisition of pragmatic rules: The gap between what the language textbooks present and how learners perform. In Haggstrom, M. A., Morgan, L. Z., & Wieczorek, J. A. (Eds.), *The foreign language classroom: Bridging theory and practice* (pp. 149–164). New York: Garland.

The Center for Educational Development. Retrieved April 21, 2010 from http://www.eslpod.com/website/index_new.html

Thorne, S. L., & Payne, J. S. (2005). Evolutionary trajectories, internet mediated expression, and language education. *CALICO Journal, 22,* 371–397.

Trahey, M., & White, L. (1993). Positive evidence and preemption in the second language classroom. *Studies in Second Language Acquisition, 15,* 181–204. doi:10.1017/S0272263100011955

VanPatten, B. (2003). *From input to output: A teacher's guide to second language acquisition.* New York: McGraw-Hill.

White, G. (2006). Teaching listening: Time for a change in methodology. In Usó-Juan, E., & Martínez-Flor, A. (Eds.), *Current trends in the development and teaching of the four language skills* (pp. 111–135). Berlin: Mouton de Gruyter. doi:10.1515/9783110197778.2.111

Williams, J. (2004). *Teaching writing in second and foreign language classrooms.* New York: McGraw-Hill.

## KEY TERMS AND DEFINITIONS

**Aural Text:** The aural text is the podcast text that is usually scripted and contains instructional content (see also Main text).

**Episode:** An episode is a separate podcast that is part of a series.

**Format:** The format is the way the podcast program is structured. A basic podcast usually has a beginning, middle, and end type of format. Content is organized based on the format, and the format can serve a template for subsequent podcast episodes.

**Host:** The host is the person who conducts the program in each podcast episode. This person can be the language instructor, but it does not necessarily have to be. The instructor can be the producer behind the podcast series, allowing someone with a different voice to be the host. Many podcasts for language learning feature more than one voice.

**Implicit Linguistic System:** The implicit linguistic system is the learners' linguistic system; it exists outside of awareness.

**Main Text:** The main text is the part of the podcast episode that contains instructional content. This part does not include greetings, farewells, or copyright information, for example.

**Podcast Project:** A podcast project is a plan that consists of a series of podcasts connected through a common theme, objectives or other characteristics (e.g., that form part of a beginning L2 course).

## ENDNOTE

[1]   Shrum and Glisan (2005) note that the products and practices are not always easily identifiable with the perspectives; sometimes, the perspective has lost its historical significance and is no longer accepted by the contemporary culture.

# Chapter 3

# Going beyond Audio:
## Adding Multimedia to Podcasts for Foreign Language Education

**Tony Gonzalez**
*University of Georgia, USA*

## ABSTRACT

*Podcasting presents exciting new opportunities for delivering pedagogical content, but, for effective learning, teaching second languages and their associated cultural aspects often demands the use of textual and visual components. The flexible nature of distributing information via RSS feeds allows for a variety of approaches to delivering multimedia content. This chapter begins with a discussion of some important questions that must be asked at the planning stages of any multimedia podcasting project, followed by several strategies for incorporating multimedia content into podcasts, including situations where each strategy might be appropriate and some of the pros and cons of each approach. Also discussed are some issues related to copyright, and some ways that educators can legally obtain free content to use in their podcasts. The chapter closes with a look at some unanswered questions related to the use of multimedia content in second language education.*

## INTRODUCTION

When Apple released the first line of iPods® in 2001, the devices represented, for most users, a way to conveniently store their libraries of music and audio books. The first iPods capable of displaying video were not introduced until 2005, and the interim four years created a strong association between iPods and audio content delivery.

Currently, however, video display technology is available across most of the iPod product line, and multimedia podcasts can also be viewed, not only on other media players such as Microsoft's Zune® and Sony's Walkman®, but also on a variety of other popular devices such as the Sony PlayStation Portable® and high-end cellular phones. With the 2010 release of the Apple iPad® and similar tablet devices from a number of other companies, the trend towards multimedia consumption in portable formats seems likely to accelerate over the coming

DOI: 10.4018/978-1-60960-141-6.ch003

years. Not only is compatible playback hardware now more widespread, but so is access to broadband delivery—not only via wireless networks in homes and on campuses, but increasingly through 3G and 4G cellular networks—making it much easier for students to download the large files that multimedia content requires. Furthermore, the cost per megabyte of hard drives and solid state storage media has continued to plummet, making it easier for broadcasters and users to serve and store those files.

Things have become easier, not only for multimedia podcast consumers, but also for content creators. Many new computers now come with built-in microphones, video cameras, and multimedia development software, making them ready for basic content development "out of the box." For more advanced projects, sound and video editing software that would have cost thousands of dollars just a decade ago can now be had for hundreds (or less).

Now that many of the barriers related to creating and using multimedia podcasts are disappearing, podcasts are rapidly becoming the learning content vehicle of choice for many language educators. The value added by incorporating multimedia content into pedagogical materials is clear. From the learner's perspective, an audio-only podcast could be compared to a class taught in the dark. Adding visual elements to your podcast turns on the lights.

Use of multimedia is not a "silver bullet," however, and as is the case when designing any form of pedagogical device, a clear understanding of your goals for instruction, as well as an awareness of the strengths and weaknesses of this new media, is vital. In this chapter, I will examine some of the benefits of incorporating multimedia elements into your podcast, consider some of the drawbacks of using multimedia, and share some techniques for maximizing your use of multimedia for podcasting in second language education. I will also discuss considerations im-

portant when planning your multimedia podcast, including target population, time and financial costs, and technical issues. After reading this chapter, I hope that you will have some concrete ideas about what kind of multimedia podcasting project will best fit the needs of both your students and your skill and resource base. I hope to offer a starting point for you, as you begin to develop your multimedia podcasting project. I also hope to offer you a basic understanding of some important issues related to copyright as applied to developing multimedia podcasts, and some sources for legally obtaining third party content that you can use for development.

## BACKGROUND

Multimedia has long been used in second language education, with its history going as far back as the 1960s (Jung, 1997). Its effectiveness has also been demonstrated, leading to the development of listening skills and speaking skills, as well to as an improved understanding of cultural contexts, while at the same time increasing learner motivation and decreasing anxiety (White, Easton, & Anderson, 2000). Multimedia can be also be used in language education as a method for addressing cognitive styles and for aiding in cognitive organization of pedagogical content (Toma, 2000).

Despite its relatively short history, the effectiveness of podcasting in higher education is well documented. Fernandez, Simo, and Sallan (2009), for example, showed that students found podcasting to be an excellent supplement to traditional course resources, and showed that the incorporation of podcasts into higher education courses increased students' feelings of contact with teachers and increased student motivation. Multimedia podcasts were found to be particularly effective, as the inclusion of multimedia content is a method of addressing multiple learning styles.

Incorporating multimedia into podcasts also serves some very practical roles. Just as using textual or visual materials in classroom teaching can aid instructors by giving learners a point of focus and reference, such materials can play a similar role as an accompaniment to verbal instruction in digitally distributed materials (Jamet, Gavota, & Quaireau, 2008). Well designed content can, for example, reduce the need for students to take notes, reducing cognitive load and allowing them to better concentrate on *understanding* instructional content, rather than *recording* it.

In the next section, we will examine some specific options for incorporating multimedia into podcasts for second language education, but first, we must discuss some of the limitations of using this new technology that should be kept in mind as you plan your content development. First, podcasting is inherently a one-to-many information delivery method. While the use of a variety of instructional strategies incorporating podcasting can help increase student involvement (Abdous, Camarena, & Facer, 2009), designing for specific learning goals can be more difficult. In the next section, we will see how multimedia podcasting can be used as a bridge to other course features that allow for instructor-learner and learner-learner interaction, but the broadcasting nature of podcasting alone does not allow for interaction with instructors or with other learners. Furthermore, lack of content interactivity makes some important language learning features (such as immediate corrective feedback) difficult. Likewise, there is a need to learn navigation and other features that are important to computer-aided language learning design (Gimeno, 2002). For this reason, multimedia podcasts for second language education should be viewed as a method for supplementing, rather than replacing, course content (Parson, Reddy, Wood, & Senior, 2009). Finally, the loss of learner-instructor interaction means that potential sources of student confusion must be carefully considered and planned for, when developing multimedia content; consequently, developing content for multimedia podcasts can be somewhat more difficult than planning for classroom instruction.

The specifics of how you design the *content* of your podcast are highly dependent upon factors such as course focus, learner level, and goals for instruction, so the basis for planning course content should follow good general instructional design practices, rather than media-specific approaches. The remainder of this chapter, therefore, focuses instead on the *form of delivery* of multimedia podcasts in second language education, as that topic allows us to recommend specific strategies that can be applied across a wide variety of situational contexts, regardless of the details of the instructional content.

## STRATEGIES FOR INCORPORATING MULTIMEDIA

### Initial Planning

Before discussing specific strategies for developing multimedia podcasts, we will discuss some initial concerns that you will need to consider in the initial planning stages of your project.

First, it is vital that you have a clear idea of the goals of your podcast *before* you begin content development. Do you want to provide periodic updates related to your course in a highly time-sensitive fashion? If so, the additional time required for multimedia development might prevent you from releasing new materials quickly enough, especially if you have a tight schedule yourself, so your class might benefit more from audio-only delivery (due to its lower associated time costs). Will your podcasts mainly contain *new* content information, or will they be a *review* or *synthesis* of previously learned information? In the case of the former, you will need to be careful to design your multimedia content in a manner that emphasizes the clarity of information delivery, in order to minimize the chance of student confusion. In the latter case, you may want to intentionally use target learning content in ambiguous ways, to reflect how learners will likely see the language features being used in a real world setting. Review and synthesis study is also an excellent opportunity to introduce cultural aspects to the course, showing learners how the language they are studying is used in varying cultural contexts.

It is also important to keep your target learners' context in mind while developing podcasts. Some important questions to ask include: do your target learners have sufficient technological skill to understand how to access your podcasts, and to display multimedia content in web browsers or via a podcast aggregator? If not, are you able to develop tutorials and devote class time to teach them how? Do all of your students have access to a computer and an Internet connection? If not, can you arrange for alternate media delivery methods, such as copying files onto a distributable CD-ROM or placing them on language laboratory computers? Does your delivery method work with most popular browsers, even those that may be one or two versions older than the latest release? Do any of your students have any other special needs that might preclude them from using the podcasts, and if so, how might you address those needs?

Also, do not forget to consider your own resources and working environment. Will you have enough time to develop all of the content your project requires before it must be delivered to students? Are there any technical skills that you will need to develop before you can begin, such as learning about how to manage RSS feeds, how to use sound and video editing software, or how to handle other technical issues? Do you have adequate access to required resources, such as microphones, video cameras, software, media content, and hosting? Remembering that the files produced for multimedia-enriched podcasts can be many times larger than audio-only files, will you have adequate disk storage and bandwidth allotments to handle the amount of data? Does your

school have any policies related to instructional material design and distribution that need to be kept in mind as you build and release your podcast?

Finally, developing multimedia content can be both expensive and time consuming. When developing multimedia projects, therefore, it is often advantageous to incorporate media such as graphics, sounds, music, and video that others have developed. Multimedia content released under a Creative Commons or other free license (see the "Finding and using free multimedia content" section, below) can be a treasure trove of useful resources, but its use comes with specific limitations on how you are allowed to distribute podcasts. When you create any podcast, you are producing a creative work, and you are therefore entering the murky world of copyright law. It is in your best interest to read up on some of the legal issues related to podcasting, especially those related to copyright, and to check with your school's legal department for information related to legal issues, such as who owns the copyright to materials developed for school courses, the use of the school's name and logo in the materials you develop, and other potential legal landmines.

Once you have firm goals in mind for podcast development, are confident that you have the skills required for production, have confirmed or secured the necessary resources to produce your podcast, and have read up on the legal issues that are involved, you are finally ready to begin development. The first step in development is deciding what form your multimedia podcast should take. You have several options for content presentation, each with its own set of advantages and disadvantages, so you should carefully consider each for your podcasting projects on a case-by-case basis, aiming to select the option that best fits your goals and environment. The options presented are developing "enhanced" podcasts, static image video production and full video production. Each option is discussed in detail in the following sections.

## Option 1: "Enhanced" Podcasts (Audio with Images, Markers, and Links, Created on Macintosh Systems)

AAC (Advanced Audio Coding) is an audio file format designed as the successor to the MP3 format, and, as such, it delivers better sound quality than MP3 files. While the format is an open standard, it was first popularized by Apple in 2003 when it became the "native" format for the iTunes Music Store® and the iPod, and later the iPhone® and iPod Touch® devices. In recent years, numerous other devices (such as the Sony Walkman, Sony PSP®, Nintendo DSi®, Microsoft Zune, Creative Zen®, and many high-end cellular phones) have expanded support for this format as well, and, for many applications, it appears that AAC will eventually replace MP3 as the de facto standard for audio files.

Not only do AAC files provide better sound quality than MP3 files, but they can also be used to create enhanced podcasts, podcasts that contain additional non-audio features such as chapter markers, embedded hyperlinks that direct viewers to an external URL, and, perhaps most importantly,

the ability to add graphics that can be displayed at specified times during audio playback. This last feature allows a podcast to be turned into something resembling a slideshow presentation with accompanying audio.

The ability to display text and images on-screen to illustrate the content of your narration can be of enormous benefit to any educational podcast. This is particularly true for those used in second language education. Doing so allows you, for example, to show the written form of unfamiliar words so that orthography can be taught alongside the pronunciation and syntax, to present vocabulary words along with culturally authentic images, to visually illustrate complex grammatical constructs, and even to help maintain student focus through the presentation of stimulating visuals. Furthermore, creating and editing still images is generally easier than working with video, and errors discovered late in the production process can more easily be corrected before public release.

Another subtle advantage to using enhanced podcasts is the ability to place hyperlinks directly into your video content. This can be an aid to overcoming one of the inherent weaknesses of

*Figure 1. An enhanced podcast displaying an accompanying graphic (lower left) and named chapter markers (menu)*

podcasting as a medium for instructional content: its lack of interactivity. Links to external resources can add value to your podcast by giving learners immediate access (1) to additional information related to the content, (2) to online applications that allow learners to practice the language skills they are studying, and (3) to contact points such as email forms or messaging boards, aiding communication with the instructor or with other learners.

A major drawback to creating enhanced podcasts, however, is a loss in platform flexibility for both podcast consumers and creators. Because the AAC file format and enhanced podcasts were first commercially promoted by Apple and were widely distributed to Apple products (iPods) via an Apple service (iTunes), it comes as no surprise that the world of enhanced podcasts is somewhat Mac-centric. At the time of this writing, while numerous devices can play the audio portion of AAC files, the only portable media players (PMPs) which support enhanced podcast features are iPods and the Microsoft Zune. (Note that, since AAC files can still be played with enhanced features using most web browsers and many standalone applications, *portability* may be hindered, but *usability* will not.)

The more serious drawback for many podcast developers is that (at the time of this writing), creating enhanced podcasts is far easier on a Macintosh® than on a Windows® PC. In fact, the author is aware of podcast creators who bought Macintosh computers solely to create enhanced podcasts. If you do not have access to a Macintosh computer, the lack of authoring tools on the Windows platform may be reason enough to prevent you from creating enhanced podcasts.

All new Macintosh computers come bundled with iLife®, a suite of media creation, editing, and management applications. The iLife package is also available as a standalone product. One component of this package is GarageBand®, a multitrack music and audio editor that supports the creation of enhanced podcasts. To incorporate images into your podcast, you simply drag the image into the

"podcast" track, then click and drag the edges of the image bubble to adjust the length of time that you want the image to be shown.

Of course, you will need to create the images that you want to show during your podcast. The dimensions of those images should be 300×300 pixels (the "native" size of enhanced podcast graphics), and they can be saved in most common graphics file formats (PNG, JPEG, GIF). One recommended way to create the images for your podcast is as follows:

1. Using presentation software such as Keynote® or PowerPoint®, create a 300×300 pixel custom-sized presentation.
2. Create slides within the presentation software to accompany the audio narration in the same way that you would to accompany an in-person presentation.
3. Export your presentation's slides as JPG or PNG image files.
4. Import the images into GarageBand one by one at the appropriate location in your audio narrative, as shown in Figure 2.

Exporting the GarageBand file in AAC format will automatically result in an enhanced podcast source file, ready for upload and distribution. See Nardo (2009) for a more detailed description of how to create enhanced podcasts using Garage-Band.

## Advantages

- GarageBand allows the use of still images in your podcast, supplying a visual component to support your narrative.
- It allows the use of chapter markers for easy navigation between named sections of your podcast.
- It also allows you to add hyperlinks to other online materials at specific points in your podcast.

*Figure 2. Creating an enhanced podcast in GarageBand. The top pane shows audio tracks along with a synchronized enhanced podcast track. Images are added by dragging and dropping image files into the podcast track. Chapter markers and external URLs can be associated with imported images in the bottom pane.*

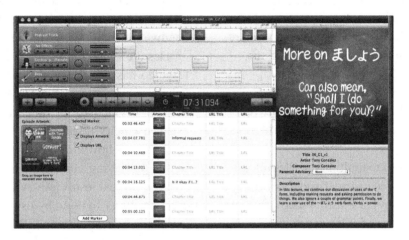

- It is compatible with a wide range of iPods, including older devices that cannot play video.
- It offers better sound quality than MP3 files (in most cases).
- No special hardware is required, beyond what is needed to record the audio portion of the podcasts.
- File sizes are much smaller than video-based podcasts (and, depending on the number of images shown, not much larger than audio-only podcasts), reducing storage and bandwidth requirements for producers, as well as download times for users.

## Disadvantages

- Unlike MP3 files, AAC enhanced podcasts cannot be played with graphics on many personal media players. Users who do not have an iPod, iPhone, iPod Touch, or Microsoft Zune device may need to view your podcast on their computer using iTunes, or in a web browser using a QuickTime®-compatible plug-in.

- If your project must support the widest possible range of PMPs, you may need to create a separate audio-only MP3 version of your podcast and distribute those episodes without enhanced features in an alternate RSS feed.
- Creating enhanced podcasts might be a complex task if you are not using a Macintosh computer.

## Recommended Usage Scenarios

While there is some loss of podcast portability and flexibility in selection of authoring tools, considering the numerous advantages to this form of delivery, this method may present the best way to "get your feet wet" with multimedia podcast development. Some situations in which enhanced podcasting might provide the optimal solution include:

- Situations in which you want multimedia content but have limited time, money, or other resources.
- Podcasts in which you want to include contextual external links to other supple-

mentary material, especially material that you cannot directly include in your podcast due to copyright, length, or other considerations.

- Podcasts that would benefit from visual representations of content, but do not require animation or video presentations.

## Option 2: Static Image Video Production (Audio with Still Images on Windows or Macintosh Systems

"Static video" refers to multimedia files released in a full motion video format such as MPEG4 (.mp4, .m4v, or .mov) or Flash® Video (.flv), but composed of a series of still images in the same manner as an enhanced podcast. This approach allows you to avoid some of the limitations of enhanced podcasts (at the expense of introducing some new ones).

One advantage is that, unlike enhanced podcast AAC files, MPEG4 video files can be played on almost all PMPs, potentially expanding your portable audience. On the other hand, some computers will not come with support for playing MPEG4 videos preinstalled into their default browsers, so some users may have trouble viewing your videos, especially if they are using language laboratory computers that don't have the necessary plug-ins installed in their browser applications and will not allow software updates. Using the Flash Video format improves compatibility with personal computers (the default browser applications on all computers come with Flash support preinstalled), but Flash is supported by few portable devices and cannot be distributed through iTunes or iTunesU. Before using a video format, therefore, you will need to think carefully about how learners will be viewing your podcast. If you expect that some students will be viewing your podcast on portable devices and some from within web browsers on their PC, then you may need to create two RSS feed items for each podcast episode: one delivering a Flash Video version for viewing on PCs, and one delivering an MPEG4 version for viewing on iPods and other portable devices. Note also that video files will usually be significantly larger than same-length MP3 or AAC files, increasing costs related to disk storage, bandwidth, and download times.

Despite such complications, however, going to video has some clear advantages over using enhanced podcasts. For one, even relatively low resolution videos offer much more screen real estate in which you can display your content, (One soon realizes how limiting a 300×300 screen can be for displaying complex information or long passages of text, especially while keeping learner accessibility in mind by using large fonts that can easily be read on small PMP screens.) There is also a wider variety of tools available for video production. Free or bundled software include iMovie® on OS X, Movie Maker® for Windows XP®, and Windows Live Movie Maker® for Vista® or Windows 7®. High-end products with advanced features include Adobe Premiere Pro® (Windows, OS X) and Final Cut Studio® (OS X). Due to the wide variety of available video editing tools and their very different user interfaces, specific examples of creating static image videos are beyond the scope of this chapter. Links to tutorials for iMovie, Movie Maker, and Windows Live Movie Maker are listed in the "Tutorials, references, and technical resources" section of this chapter, and many more can easily be found through an Internet search. Copley (2007), for example, describes one method of easily creating a static image video using MovieMaker.

For some still image projects, video editing software has a significant advantage over enhanced podcast development software such as GarageBand. Most video editing software has features for easily adding subtitles to your project during the final stages of production. In some applications, using subtitles can be a powerful aid to second language comprehension, especially for intermediate learners (Seufert, Schutze, & Brunken, 2009; Taylor, 2005), and ease of cap-

*Table 1. A comparison of usage variables for file formats that can be used in static image video production*

| AAC | MPEG4 | Flash Video |
|---|---|---|
| Limited PMP support (iPod, iPhone, iPad, Zune) | Wide PMP support (practically all PMPs) | Very limited PMP support |
| Web browser playback requires plug-in (often not pre-installed) | Web browser playback requires plug-in (usually pre-installed) | Required plug-in pre-installed on all modern web browsers |
| Small file size for static image videos | Large file size for static image videos | Small file size for static image videos |

tioning with video editing software may be an important consideration when trying to decide between an enhanced podcast or a static image video approach. With some work, static images can be used to add captions to enhanced podcasts, but in the author's experience, the results are often not satisfactory—many portable devices have relatively slow processors working under low power consumption conditions to conserve battery life, and the result is a delay before image displays (while the device works to decompress the image). As a result, precise timing of image display cannot be relied upon. While the timing of caption display may look fine when the video is viewed on a personal computer, the lag may be excessive on PMPs.

## Advantages

- MPEG4 video files can be played on a wide variety of PMPs.
- They allow for larger images than enhanced podcasts (640×480 pixels is recommended).
- They are easier to plan and create than scripted full motion video.
- Creating video files is easier than creating enhanced podcasts on a Windows-based PC.

## Disadvantages

- They require significantly larger file sizes as compared to AAC enhanced podcasts.

- They may require creating multiple formats to ensure maximum compatibility among viewers.

## Recommended Usage Scenarios

- These can be used in situations in which full motion video is not required, but you do not have access to resources for enhanced podcast production.
- They are also best used in situations in which produced podcasts must be playable on the widest possible variety of PMPs

## Option 3: Incorporating Full Motion Video Production

Incorporating full motion video can create a powerful impression in learners, and video has many significant advantages over static content. One advantage is that moving images create a strong attention draw, aiding in maintaining your learners' focus. Video is also an excellent way to capture the nonverbal aspects of human communication that are difficult or impossible to capture in text or in static image representations, such as body language and facial expressions. Animated displays of instructional materials can also have beneficial effects over static presentations (Hoffler & Leutner, 2007).

Whereas, in static video production. your primary source of content will be computer-generated static images, with full motion video production you will primarily use digitally captured footage from a video camera. From a technical standpoint, many of the issues related to full motion video production, such as selection of file format and editing software, will be similar to the case of static video production. The more significant difference lies in the wide range of complexity that full motion video production can entail.

At one end of the spectrum, these projects can be simpler to produce than static video productions. For example, if your goal for your podcasts is simply to make classroom lectures available to distance learners, then videotaping your lectures and transferring them to your computer is very simple, and the resulting file can be published to your RSS feed with minimal editing. Many laptop computers now come with built-in cameras that allow you to capture video footage directly to your computer without even the need for transfer from an external device. Those cameras can be an excellent tool for creating a "headshot" video that mainly shows you speaking directly to the camera. At the other end of the spectrum, advanced projects such as acted-out scenes demonstrating language usage in context may call for extensive planning, scripting, filming, and editing. Creating high quality productions can become very complex and resource intensive, and producing even a ten-minute video can easily require many hours of work. Somewhere in between are hybrid approaches that combine short full motion video clips with static images used to reinforce presented content. This can be an excellent way to combine the advantages of full motion video while keeping project complexity manageable. Another hybrid approach is to use sources of authentic video materials, rather than creating your own videos. Avoiding copyright restrictions can be a challenge with this approach, however. Some potential solutions are discussed in the following section.

## Advantages

- This method can capture culturally specific nonverbal cues such as body language

that cannot be easily expressed in other formats.
- It can provide a strong aid to focus for learner attention.
- Video is the easiest way to capture the entirety of classroom content for projects aimed at including distance learners in a mixed access course.

## Disadvantages

- Video composition, editing, and other production skills represent the steepest learning curves for podcast producers.
- This is the most resource intensive solution, requiring specialty equipment such as video cameras.
- Large file sizes will result in increased storage demands and bandwidth costs for you and increased download times for your viewers.

## Recommended Usage Scenarios

- This is a good way to make classroom lectures and activities available for viewing or review on the Internet.
- This method can be used for contextual learning scenarios that rely on nonverbal or situational content.

### Option 5: Using Supplementary Materials as File Attachments

While the discussion above has pertained primarily to multimedia in its traditional sense—video, animations, and the like—text is an important form of media, too, and one that in many cases will be the easiest for your audience to make practical use of. A text accompaniment to podcasts can be a vital learning tool for students, and this strategy is unique in that in can be combined with the other multimedia deliver options discussed in the previous sections. If your podcast will be available to learners with whom you do not have direct contact (and thus are unable to supply, directly, with supplementary materials), there are few cases where a language learning podcast would not be enhanced by the inclusion of supplementary materials, especially if the podcast introduces new learning content.

Supplementary materials can be delivered in the same way that your podcast's audio or video file are: through an RSS feed. The only difference is that the item will not contain a podcast such as an audio or video file like those discussed above, but instead a text or image file. For example, you may want to attach a self assessment tool for podcast users to assess their content comprehension after listening to or viewing your podcast. Other suggestions for types of supplementary materials, such as audio transcripts, vocabulary lists, and optional materials, are given in the "Recommended usage scenarios" section, below.

Note that while some podcast feed publishing software (WordPress®, for example) allows publishers to create a single feed item with multiple enclosures (for example, a podcast along with an accompanying PDF file), many popular RSS feed readers, including Google Reader® and Internet Explorer 7®, do not support multiple attachments in a single feed item—the second and subsequent attachments will be ignored by those readers and therefore difficult or impossible for users to obtain. Supplementary files should therefore be delivered as separate RSS feed items, creating a potential source of confusion for learners who locate one item but not the other. To prevent this, you should include explicit links between associated materials, for example a link to an accompanying PDF file from the podcast, and a link to the podcast from the feed containing the PDF file.

Note that while any file type can be attached to your feed items, some RSS aggregators may ignore uncommon or application-specific file types as a way to reduce the risk of spreading viruses. To ensure that your file will be delivered, therefore, you should limit supplementary materials to .txt

(text only), .rtf (formatted text), or .pdf (Portable Document Format) file formats. You should only use application-specific file formats (including Microsoft Word® .doc and .docx files) when you have a specific (and unavoidable) reason why other file formats do not fulfill your needs.

## Advantages

- Supplementary materials can greatly reduce the need for note taking, lowering the listener's cognitive load and allowing them to focus on the content of your podcast.
- Supplemental files can be created using applications that you probably have at hand, such as word processing or presentation applications. You will not need to buy expensive software or learn how to use a new application.
- Creating supplemental files usually does not require special hardware (though depending on your project, you may occasionally want to have access to a scanner).
- Creating supplemental files is not environmentally sensitive—you will not need to find a quiet room for recording as you do when making narrative podcasts, for example.

## Disadvantages

- Because many RSS feed readers will block file attachments other than text, RTF, and PDF files, unless you know exactly how your subscribers will be obtaining your podcasts, and know that their access method will allow for other formats, you may have a limited selection of file formats that you can use. If you need to distribute other file formats, hosting those files on a web server and supplying podcast users with a download link may be a more appropriate method of file distribution.

• Supplementary files should be delivered as separate RSS feed items, creating a potential source of confusion for learners should they obtain the podcast but not the accompanying file, or vice versa. To avoid this, you need to be careful about providing users with guidance for steps to take to obtain all related files.

## Recommended Usage Scenarios

Both audio-only and multimedia-rich podcasts for second language learning will often benefit from an accompanying text-based component. Some situations where you might want to create separate text files associated with your podcast include:

• Creating a supplementary vocabulary list that presents words that are used in your podcast but are not covered in students' textbooks or elsewhere in the class.
• Supplying transcripts to accompany podcasts of conversations or other examples of spoken target language, allowing students to check words and phrases that they cannot understand on the audio. Supplying audio transcripts is also a good way to address the needs of individuals with disabilities that prevent them from learning based on audio content alone.
• Giving listeners a summary page of newly introduced grammar and syntax for later reference or review.
• As a method of delivering optional materials that are peripherally related to the content of your podcast, but which may cause confusion or be distracting if they are included in the main presentation in the podcast.
• Providing students with review exercises so that they can practice what they learned in the podcast immediately after exposure, thus reinforcing target skills.

## Finding and Using Free Multimedia Content

Developing multimedia podcasts relies, of course, on the use of multimedia content. However, creating multimedia content, especially video and music, can be very time consuming and resource intensive, so it is often convenient to use materials developed by others. Using external resources can also be an excellent way of incorporating authentic materials into language education, exposing learners to cultural aspects of the language taught.

Language educators have long used videos, music, artwork, and other artistic works in classroom teaching. In a traditional classroom environment, use of copyrighted materials is, in most cases, covered under the "fair use" doctrine of U.S. copyright law, which means that explicit permission to use copyrighted materials is not required. Fair use is not applicable, however, to the use of copyrighted materials in a publicly distributed podcast, and even the use of copyrighted materials in a podcast intended for limited distribution (only to those students registered for a particular course, for example) is potentially dangerous, given the ease of copying and disseminating multimedia files. Under current U.S. law, all creative works are automatically assigned copyright protection, even if the creator does not specifically claim such rights through legal means, such as by making a statement of copyright ownership within the work. The result is that you cannot safely use *any* creative work in your podcast unless you have created the work yourself, or have the express permission of the copyright holder. Luckily, over the past several years, it has become increasingly easy to sidestep the issue of copyright by instead using multimedia materials that were released under alternative "free" licenses.

The most popular free licenses for multimedia materials are the Creative Commons (CC) licenses, developed by the nonprofit Creative Commons Corporation. The CC's licenses allow for the reuse and distribution of creative works under a number of licensor-specified conditions. The conditions of the license state whether the licensed material can be used in commercial products, whether the licensed materials can be edited to create derivative works, and whether derivative works must themselves be released under a free license. For example, a work released under a CC "Attribution" license requires only that the source of the material be credited, but allows for use of the material in commercial products, and allows for derivative works to be created from the material. A work released under a CC "Attribution-No Derivative Works" license allows use of the material in unmodified form only. An "Attribution-Share Alike" license permits free use of materials in unaltered form, or in a modified form if you, in turn, will allow others to make modifications to and reuse your materials (all articles on Wikipedia, for example, are released under this form of CC license). In 2008, an estimated 130 million creative works were available for reuse under a CC license, and the number of newly released CC-licensed works is increasing at an exponential rate ("History—Creative Commons," n.d.).

You can find CC-licensed materials from a number of sources. The Creative Commons website has a search engine (http://search.creativecommons.org/) that allows you to search for images, videos, and music from several popular sources. The popular photo sharing website Flickr® also has options in its advanced search page (http://www.flickr.com/search/advanced/) that allow you to search for CC-licensed photos. This allows you to, for example, search not only for photographs of houses, but of houses typical of countries in which the language you teach is spoken.

Another method of finding usable multimedia content is to look for materials produced by individuals who can easily be contacted to obtain permission for use. For example, if you are looking for music to use in a podcast, you might want to look at websites that host music for sale from independent artists, and contact those artists directly to request permission to use a specific song or clip.

You will probably find that most artists are happy to get the exposure, and to help teach their native language. (The author has contacted several bands who host music on the website CDBaby.com, and to date has never been denied permission for the use of a music clip in his podcasts.)

## FUTURE RESEARCH DIRECTIONS

While research has shown that podcasting can be an effective means of increasing student motivation and interest, there is still not enough research related to the use of multimedia podcasts and efficacy of target skill development (Lazzari, 2008; Mandernach, 2009). In particular, research is needed to establish guidelines for pedagogical content delivery for use by specific learner types and in specific contexts, since, in many cases, best practices may not jibe with common-sense thinking. For example, Plass, Chun, Mayer, and Leutner (2003) indicated that multimedia-based education might be most effective when learners are given a choice between visual and verbal modes of instruction, and that (in some cases) the simultaneous presentation of both modes can hinder learning. Supplying such choice within a single podcast episode is technically challenging, however -- so future research that closely examines the relationships between content delivery mode, learner type, and pedagogical goals is called for.

An important area for investigation from a design standpoint is examining ways in which podcasting can best be combined with other forms of digital content delivery to create synergistic effects between them. Boulos, Maramba, and Wheeler (2006) gave examples of combining podcasts with wikis and blogs as a method of developing an educational context that allows for more interactivity and learner reflection. Some studies have suggested that the portability aspects of podcasts are not as important as might be assumed, with most students preferring to view podcasts on their home computers during time set aside for study rather than on portable devices while away from their normal study environment (Evans, 2008). Confirmation of such findings across a broad range of student types, particularly from those engaged in foreign language learning, would have strong implications for the optimal format for multimedia podcast delivery.

## CONCLUSION

A successful multimedia podcasting project will always begin with a careful assessment of your goals and a realistic survey of your current (and needed) skill set and resource base. This should be complemented by an understanding of the needs and abilities of your target learner audience. That information will direct you towards selecting the most appropriate strategy for multimedia podcast development.

New modes of Internet-based information delivery arise, metamorphose, and blend into new forms very rapidly. Barriers to the cost and complexity of multimedia content development and distribution continue to fall, and, inevitably, new technologies will continue to deliver new possibilities. Over the next few years, for example, the new HTML 5 specifications will allow for easy audio and video content presentation on web sites without the need for third-party plug-ins, and additional scripting features may allow for easier implementation of interactive multimedia. At the same time, market penetration of smart phones with advanced network capabilities will increase, as will the proliferation of low-cost "netbook" and tablet devices, blurring the distinction between "portable device" and "personal computer." This context of constant change means that optimal solutions for digitally delivered instructional media, too, will continue to change in the future. The most important skill for practitioners of podcasting, therefore, is perhaps not proficiency with any particular type of content development, but rather flexibility in finding optimal ways of

incorporating new technologies as they become available.

## REFERENCES

Abdous, M., Camarena, M. M., & Facer, B. R. (2009). MALL technology: Use of academic podcasting in the foreign language classroom. *ReCALL*, *21*(01), 76–95. .doi:10.1017/S0958344009000020

Boulos, M., Maramba, I., & Wheeler, S. (2006). Wikis, blogs and podcasts: A new generation of web-based tools for virtual collaborative clinical practice and education. *BMC Medical Education*, *6*(41). doi:.doi:10.1186/1472-6920-6-41

Copley, J. (2007). Audio and video podcasts of lectures for campus-based students: Production and evaluation of student use. *Innovations in Education and Teaching International*, *44*(4), 387–399. doi:10.1080/14703290701602805

Evans, C. (2008). The effectiveness of m-learning in the form of podcast revision lectures in higher education. *Computers & Education*, *50*, 491–498. doi:10.1016/j.compedu.2007.09.016

Fernandez, V., Simo, P., & Sallan, J. M. (2009). Podcasting: A new technological tool to facilitate good practice in higher education. *Computers & Education*, *53*(2), 385–392. .doi:10.1016/j.compedu.2009.02.014

Gimeno, A. (2002). Principles in CALL software design and implementation. *International Journal of English Studies*, *2*(1), 109–128.

History—Creative Commons. (n.d.). Retrieved November 30, 2009, from http://creativecommons.org/about/history/

Hoffler, T. N., & Leutner, D. (2007). Instructional animation versus static pictures: A meta-analysis. *Learning and Instruction*, *17*(6), 722–738. doi:10.1016/j.learninstruc.2007.09.013

Jamet, E., Gavota, M., & Quaireau, C. (2008). Attention guiding in multimedia learning. *Learning and Instruction*, 18(2), 135–145. doi:10.1016/j.learninstruc.2007.01.011

Jung, U. (1997). *Encyclopedia of language and education, Volume 4: Second language education* (G.R. Tucker & D. Corson, eds.). Springer.

Lazzari, M. (2008). Creative use of podcasting in higher education and its effect on competitive agency. *Computers & Education*, 52(1), 27–34. doi:10.1016/j.compedu.2008.06.002

Mandernach, B. J. (2009). Effect of instructor-personalized multimedia in the online classroom. *International Review of Research in Open and Distance Learning*, 10(3).

Parson, V., Reddy, P., Wood, J., & Senior, C. (2009). Educating an "iPod" generation: Undergraduate attitudes, experiences and understanding of vodcast and podcast use. *Learning, Media and Technology*, 34(3), 215–228. doi:10.1080/17439880903141497

Plass, J. L., Chun, D. M., Mayer, R. E., & Leutner, D. (2003). Cognitive load in reading a foreign language text with multimedia aids and the influence of verbal and spatial abilities. *Computers in Human Behavior*, 19(2), 221–243. .doi:10.1016/S0747-5632(02)00015-8

Seufert, T., Schutze, M., & Brunken, R. (2009). Memory characteristics and modality in multimedia learning: An aptitude-treatment-interaction study. *Learning and Instruction*, 19(1), 28–42. doi:10.1016/j.learninstruc.2008.01.002

Taylor, G. (2005). Perceived processing strategies of students watching captioned video. *Foreign Language Annals*, 38(3), 422–427. doi:10.1111/j.1944-9720.2005.tb02228.x

Toma, T. (2000). Cognition and courseware design by teachers: The concept of multimediatizing. *Society for Information Technology & Teacher Education International Conference: Proceedings of SITE 2000*, 1-3.

White, C., Easton, P., & Anderson, C. (2000). Students' perceived value of video in a multimedia language course. *Educational Media International*, 37(3), 167–175. doi:10.1080/09523980050184736

## ADDITIONAL READING

Adobe Premiere Pro tutorials. (n.d.) http://www.mediacollege.com/adobe/premiere/pro/

Apple—iMovie tutorials. (n.d.) http://www.apple.com/ilife/tutorials/#imovie

Bartholome, T., & Bromme, R. (2009). Coherence formation when learning from text and pictures: What kind of support for whom? *Journal of Educational Psychology*, 101(2), 282–293. doi:10.1037/a0014312

Brown, A., & Green, T. D. (2008). Video podcasting in perspective: The history, technology, aesthetics, and instructional uses of a new medium. *Journal of Educational Technology Systems*, 36(1), 3–17. doi:10.2190/ET.36.1.b

Cann, A. J. (2007). Podcasting is dead. Long live video! *Bioscience. Education Journal*, 10.

ccLearn website. (n.d.) http://learn.creativecommons.org/

Chen, I., Chang, C., & Lee, Y. (2009). Applications of cognitive load theory to multimedia-based foreign language learning: An overview. *Educational Technology Magazine*, 49(1), 34–39.

Creative Commons website. (n.d.) http://creativecommons.org/

Fair use guidelines for educational multimedia. (n.d.) http://www.adec.edu/admin/papers/fair10-17.html

Geoghegan, M. (2007). *Podcast solutions: the complete guide to audio and video podcasting* (2nd ed.). Berkeley, CA: Friends of Ed.

Harrington, R., & Weiser, M. (2008). *Producing video podcasts: A guide for media professionals*. Focal Press.

Jones, L. C. (2009). Supporting student differences in listening comprehension and vocabulary learning with multimedia annotations. *CALICO Journal*, *26*(2), 267–289.

Kim, D., & Gilman, D. A. (2008). Effects of text, audio, and graphic aids in multimedia instruction for vocabulary learning. *Journal of Educational Technology & Society*, *11*(3), 114–126.

Liu, S., Liao, H., & Pratt, J. A. (2009). Impact of media richness and flow on e-learning technology acceptance. *Computers & Education*, *52*(3), 599–607. doi:10.1016/j.compedu.2008.11.002

Mayer, R. E. (2001). *Multimedia learning*. Cambridge, UK: Cambridge University Press.

Mayer, R. E. (Ed.). (2005). *The Cambridge handbook of multimedia learning*. New York: Cambridge University Press.

Mayer, R. E. (2008). Applying the science of learning: Evidence-based principles for the design of multimedia instruction. *The American Psychologist*, *63*(8), 760–769. doi:10.1037/0003-066X.63.8.760

Nardo, R. (2009). See! Hear! Enhanced podcasting with GarageBand. *General Music Today*, *23*(1), 27–30. doi:10.1177/1048371309342578

Price, A., Gay, P., Searle, T., & Brissenden, G. (2007). A history and informal assessment of the "Slacker Astronomy" podcast. *Astronomy Education Review*, *5*(1), 53–69. doi:10.3847/AER2006004

Ratcliffe, M., & Mack, S. (2007). *Podcasting Bible* (1st ed.). Wiley.

Read, B. (2007). How to podcast campus lectures. *The Chronicle of Higher Education*, *53*(21), A32.

Rosell-Aguilar, F. (2007). Top of the pods—In search of a podcasting "podagogy" for language learning. *Computer Assisted Language Learning*, *20*(5), 471–492. doi:10.1080/09588220701746047

Stiller, K. D., Freitag, A., Zinnbauer, P., & Freitag, C. (2009). How pacing of multimedia instructions can influence modality effects: A case of superiority of visual texts. *Australasian Journal of Educational Technology*, *25*(2), 184–203.

Sun, P., & Cheng, H. K. (2007). The design of instructional multimedia in e-learning: A media richness theory-based approach. *Computers & Education*, *49*(3), 662–676. doi:10.1016/j.compedu.2005.11.016

Using Windows Movie Maker 2 to present still photos. (n.d.) http://www.microsoft.com/windowsxp/using/moviemaker/expert/northrup_02december02.mspx

Webmaster Toolkit—Listing of file extensions and their associated MIME types. (n.d.) http://www.webmaster-toolkit.com/mime-types.shtml

Windows Live Movie Maker tutorials. (n.d.) http://www.intowindows.com/windows-live-movie-maker-wlmm-tutorials/

Xarj.net. What video format to use for your podcast. (n.d.) http://www.xarj.net/2008/what-video-format-to-use-for-your-podcast/

## KEY TERMS AND DEFINITIONS

**Chapter Marker:** A bookmark placed within an extended podcast, allowing for quick navigation among named sections using popup menus, etc.

**Creative Commons Licenses:** A set of licenses for creative works, used in place of copyright to allow free reuse, redistribution, and modification of the licensed materials under specific conditions.

**Derivative Work:** A creative work created using another person's work as a major element. For example, a translation of a podcast from its original language to another would be the creation of a derivative work.

**Enhanced Podcast:** A form of multimedia podcast that incorporates static graphic images to accompany recorded audio. Enhanced podcasts also allow for easy navigation between named sections within a podcast, as well as the incorporation of hyperlinks to web-based external resources.

**Fair Use:** A doctrine of U.S. copyright law that grants automatic legal use of copyrighted materials without permission from the rights holder for specific, limited purposes. In an educational context, fair use often allows educators to use copyrighted materials for classroom instructional purposes, within limitations (this doctrine will likely *not* apply to digital reproductions within a publicly available podcast, however).

**GarageBand:** A component of iLife (Apple Inc.'s suite of multimedia development tools that comes bundled with its computer products) that allows for easy recording and editing of audio content, as well as enhanced podcast creation. A good tool for creating audio-only or enhanced podcasts under OS X.

**Portable Media Player (PMP):** An small, battery-powered electronic device capable of playing digital audio and video files, and displaying image files. Examples include video-capable iPods, iPhones, the Microsoft Zune, Creative Zen, and most recent Sony Walkman products.

**Smart Phone:** A cellular phone with advanced features beyond telephony, usually including the ability to run custom applications and access web pages and other information via the Internet. Common examples include the Apple iPhone, the RIM Blackberry®, and cell phones using the Android OS®.

**Windows Live Movie Maker:** A free software application from Microsoft for Windows Vista and Windows 7 that allows for easy video editing and export. A good tool for creating video-based podcasts on Windows.

# Chapter 4
# Getting Started:
## Academic Podcasting made Simple

**Maria Elena Corbeil**
*The University of Texas at Brownsville/Texas Southmost College, USA*

**Joseph Rene Corbeil**
*The University of Texas at Brownsville/Texas Southmost College, USA*

## ABSTRACT

*Podcasting is an excellent way to engage students and to supplement the instructional materials used in face-to-face and online courses and in Mobile-Assisted Language Learning programs. A well-produced weekly podcast can enhance course content, learning activities, and student-teacher interactions, while enabling students to take their learning materials with them wherever they go, thus reinforcing and supporting language acquisition. While there are many resources that delineate how to create a podcast, few address the instructional, technological, and production factors that must be considered for the effective use of podcasting in instruction. This chapter includes a brief review of the literature that addresses the use of podcasts in language learning programs, and offers a simple guide for creating your first podcast, lessons learned, and the results of a student survey on the use of podcasts.*

## INTRODUCTION

During his 45-minute commute to work, Marcos is listening to a weekly podcast used in his upper-level course in technology education and corporate training. As a second-language learner, he appreciates the convenience and instructional support that the podcast offers. Although Marcos has mastered conversational English, he still struggles with his academic language skills. Using podcasts, his professor reviews key terms and concepts, and offers examples of their real-life applications. For several days, Marcos has been struggling to understand an upcoming project's requirements, but the podcast clarifies the assignment and sparks an idea for the training module that he needs to develop. He is excited because it is actually a project he can employ in his new position as technology trainer at the local hospital. He knows exactly what he's going to do!

During the spring of 2009, Marcos was enrolled in an upper-level, fully online class in

DOI: 10.4018/978-1-60960-141-6.ch004

which a weekly podcast was produced. The online course was offered as part of an innovative program designed to seamlessly transfer students with technical associate degrees into a bachelor's degree program. The podcasts were developed to engage students in critical reflection and to provide examples and authentic applications of the weekly topics and underlying concepts addressed in class. Since the instructor's class was over 90% Hispanic, with more than half of the students being second language learners, the podcasts had the added benefit of assisting those students to better comprehend the reading materials.

Marcos, and other students for whom English is not their primary language, can benefit from the use of podcasts. Podcasts can help second-language learners transfer concepts from academic isolation to socially and professionally meaningful contexts (Lee & Chan, 2007; Thorne & Scott Payne, 2005). After listening to the weekly topics discussed and expanded upon by the professor, Marcos is reassured that he now fully understands the readings. Students can listen to the podcasts as often as necessary and at their convenience, even on the commute to work, thereby allowing them to take advantage of normally unproductive time. Through podcasts, instructors can provide a valuable Mobile-Assisted Language Learning (MALL) resource for their second language learners, while enhancing the curriculum for all students.

This chapter provides an overview of the use of podcasts to enhance language learning, a guide to creating your first podcast, the results of a student survey, lessons learned during the first-year podcasting experience, and future directions.

## BACKGROUND

A podcast is a digital audio file which is created to be easily published on the Internet and downloaded to a computer or mobile device, such as an MP3 player, iPod®, or cell phone. According to eMar-keter (2009), the emergence of social networking and mobile technologies has set the stage for the exponential growth in the use and popularity of podcasting. "eMarketer projects that growth will continue at least through 2013, when there will be 37.6 million people downloading podcasts on a monthly basis, more than double the 2008 figure of 17.4 million" (para. 5). Currently, podcasting has replaced cassette recordings, and soon it may even replace compact discs. As an increasingly "popular, traditional media" (eMarketer, para. 9), podcasts are quickly becoming the preferred audio resource for business people, educators, and students, especially for mobile-assisted language learning (MALL).

Although podcasts are a recent phenomenon, the uses and benefits of audio for language acquisition are well established. Edirisingha, Rizzi, and Rothwell (2007, p. 89) cited research that dates back to 1984, when Durbridge noted that "learners respond to sound," such as "understanding spoken language, analysing music, listening in on conversations, being 'talked through' tasks… hearing facts, discussions and opinions from experts in their field;" and "being encouraged by the voice of somebody they know and respect." The integration of audio also helps learners work through course content and develop pronunciation skills by affording them the opportunity to listen to the recorded resources as often as necessary and at their convenience.

In particular, podcasts' current popularity elucidates the added benefits that they offer which are an improvement over those of former audio resources. They are, for example, easy to create, publish, and access (Rosell-Aguilar, 2007; Ractham & Zhang, 2006; Schlosser & Burmeister, 2006). Unlike tape cassettes or CDs, William and McMinn (2008), noted that "student produced podcasts have the potential for a world-wide audience, giving students purpose and motivation to create a better product" (p. 212). Although language learners may not speak the target language, more and more do speak the language of technology. They are adept at using social networking tools in their personal and professional lives to create and publish (in multimedia format) class work that includes communicating in text, chat, video, and audio in their native language. Consequently, podcasts can be instrumental in helping to resolve one of the biggest challenges faced by second/foreign language instructors: the limited class time available for learners to acquire and practice the complex linguistic and socio-linguistic skills required for language proficiency (William & McMinn, 2008). William and McMinn's research revealed that a student-produced podcast "increases a student's time allocated to language learning, and, while doing so, provides a meaningful experience that is motivating, stimulating and useful for a language learner" (p. 212). Therefore, the use of podcasts in mobile-assisted language learning can be motivating and meaningful because learners are both the consumers and creators (Pettit & Kukulska-Hulme, 2006) of online language-learning content.

In addition, the vast availability of podcasts through free, online sources such as iTunesU® affords language learners increased control and access to authentic input from sources around the world. According to Kukulska-Hulme (2006), "mobile learning promises to deliver closer integration of language learning with everyday communication needs and cultural experiences" (p. 119). This helps increase student perception of community in face-to-face, hybrid, and online mobile-assisted language learning courses. "The use of audio provides a high-touch learning material that builds a connection between instructor and students—and among students," noted Schlosser and Burmeister (2006, para. 6). The perceived connections established between the students and the instructor (teacher immediacy), and among learners (social presence) are important contributors to both learning outcomes and students' learning experiences. Feelings of connectedness and community are further enhanced when instructors are visibly present in their courses through the use of myriad instructional strategies and technologies,

such as podcasts. It is no surprise, then, that according to Edirisingha et al. (2007), "academics from many areas of education are showing interest in podcasting for education and the first results of research in this field point towards the benefits to learners" (p. 89). For instructors, podcasting supports different language learning approaches (Rosell-Aguilar, 2007), including collaborative and social networking activities (Ractham & Zhang, 2006), to engage students, especially those who have grown up with gaming, mobile devices, and social networking technologies (Robinson & Dodd, 2006).

In summary, podcasts are here to stay. Since they are easy to create, publish, and use, podcasts are quickly becoming the preferred tool for audio delivery. They engage language learners with the content, with the instructor, and with each other.

## CREATING YOUR FIRST PODCAST

Podcasts are actually very easy to produce. All you need is a computer, a microphone, and the podcast software. Two excellent and easy-to-use podcasting programs are Audacity® (for PC and Apple® computers) and Garage Band® (for Apple computers). If your laptop or computer comes with a built-in camera, it may also have a built-in microphone. However, investing in an inexpensive headset with a microphone will help reduce background noise and will improve the quality of the recording. The microphone need not be expensive, but obviously, the better the microphone, the better the recording. A USB headpiece with earphones and a microphone is comfortable for recording hands-free, and produces a fairly good quality audio recording. After you have downloaded the software and purchased the headset microphone, you are ready to create your first podcast by following the steps below:

1. *Write the script.* A typewritten, 1.5 to 2-page, single-spaced script is equivalent to a five-

minute podcast. We recommend reading the script aloud several times before recording your podcast. In order to assist second language learners, you can also provide a link to the script so they can read along while they listen to the podcast. Below, you will find a sample of a podcast script and corresponding discussion question.

Welcome to this Week's Podcast!

*Have you ever taken a class and immediately recognized that the teacher was an expert in his field, but that he did not have the skills to transmit that knowledge to you? Have you ever wondered why it is so difficult to teach another person something that we do so well and that comes naturally to us? Let's consider the following story:*

*An efficiency expert concluded his lecture with a note of caution. He said, "You don't want to try these techniques at home." "Why not?" asked someone in the audience. The expert explained, "I watched my wife's routine for making breakfast for years. She made lots of trips between the refrigerator, the stove, the table, and the cabinets, often carrying a single item at a time. One day I asked her, 'Honey, why don't you try carrying several things at once?'" The person in the audience asked, "So, did she try it your way? Did it save time?" The expert replied, "Actually, yes. It used to take her 20 minutes to make breakfast. Now, I do it in seven" (CleverComedy.com, 2009).*

*This week's lesson will help us learn the difference between the way an expert (such as the teacher and trainer in our example above) and a novice, process information. We will also better understand our role as trainers, the challenges faced with experts, and how the two types of knowledge interact in learning situations.*

*Let's take a moment to think about our day. As we meet with different people, we switch from being the expert learner to being the novice learner. Perhaps we run into a new employee and teach him or her an office procedure (here, we are the expert learners). We continue down the hall and meet up with our boss, who shows us the revised protocols for admitting patients (now, we are the novice learners).*

*When we are the experts, according to Stolovitch and Keeps (2003), we have learned the skills "over time and with practice," (p. 33), so we process most of our experience in the form of procedural knowledge. In other words, we know the procedures or steps for doing something, like driving, by instinct. On the other hand, declarative knowledge "allows us to name, explain, and talk about something" (p. 32).*

*In order to teach something effectively, we must be able to transform what we know how to do (procedural knowledge) into an explanation of how to do it (declarative knowledge). In turn, novice learners must take the declarative knowledge (everything we are explaining) and reconstruct it into procedural knowledge, so that they can do what we are able to do (Stolovitch & Keeps, 2003).*

*Now, you might be asking yourself, "I can see how that applies to me as a current or future trainer, but are there any real-life applications to this?"*

*The answer is yes. I invite you to do some Internet research on declarative and procedural knowledge; you will find a wealth of applications.*

*For example, in the article entitled, "The Future is Already Happening: Training Aeronautical*

*Skills in Virtual Environments," David O'Hare (2001), Associate Professor of Psychology at the University of Otago, details how research on declarative and procedural knowledge is helping him and his team develop virtual flight simulation programs for pilots. O'Hare noted that even with the advent of the computer, the way pilots fly planes has not changed much, so the way in which they are trained has remained consistent over the past 20 years. Interestingly, O'Hare and other researchers at the Cognitive Ergonomics and Human Decision Making Lab at the University of Otago, in partnership with NASA and the Federal Aviation Administration, began their development of virtual training programs for pilots by studying the distinction between declarative and procedural knowledge.*

*O'Hare (2001) noted, to train pilots, (and I quote):*

*Knowledge about lift and drag, lapse rates, and dewpoints...can be found in textbooks. Acquiring this knowledge can be done with book, video or PC, but it all involves the acquisition of declarative knowledge. In contrast, procedural skills are the abilities to fly a crosswind approach or to plot a navigational track etc. Procedural skills develop when declarative knowledge is put into practice. Sometimes, expert performers lose access to the original declarative knowledge altogether – they can perform the skill with ease but cannot explain how or why (para. 3). (End quote)*

*As you read this week's chapter, please reflect upon the impact of both procedural and declarative knowledge on your role as a trainer, as well as on the ways that the key ingredients for learning presented in this week's lesson will influence your training decisions.*

*Please join me next time, when we explore the role of memory and motivation in adult learning.*

### DISCUSSION QUESTION

*For this week's discussion question, briefly summarize the purpose of the training you are developing for the project in this course. Describe how a novice learner and an expert learner would approach your training topic in terms of procedural and declarative knowledge. Please specify 1-2 adjustments you will make in your training to account for learner differences in ability, prior knowledge, and motivation.*

2. ***Record the podcast.*** Have the script and podcast software open side-by-side on your computer monitor. On the podcast software, click the "record" button and begin your audio narration by speaking clearly and slowly, using a natural, conversational tone. Do not worry about rough spots. If you make a mistake, do not stop recording; just stop talking for a few seconds and then re-state the passage. The space with silence will allow you to locate the error and edit it out later. When you finish recording, save your podcast.

3. ***Edit the podcast.*** With the podcast software editing tools, it is easy to cut out mistakes, long pauses, breaths, and background noises. The podcast software allows you to zoom in on the recorded track so that the waveform of your recorded narration is visible (please see Figure 1). This will help you to locate the silent spaces you inserted between those sections where you made errors and find the re-recorded portions of your podcast. As you play back your audio track, stop the recording at the beginning of the section you want to edit. Highlight that section and delete it. Now, place the cursor slightly before the re-recorded section and press "play" to

*Figure 1. Screen shot guide for recording and editing the podcast*

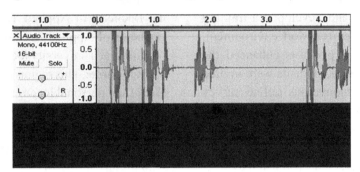

hear it. You can also remove deep breaths and awkward pauses by editing them out or replacing them with silence. Remember to save your work regularly.

4. ***Add a background music track.*** A music soundtrack as a lead-in and fade-out contributes to a more professional production. Select a royalty-free, instrumental track that establishes the appropriate tone for your podcast. The music should be appropriate for the topic or course and should not be too fast paced, so as to not distract the students from the narration. For the beginning of the podcast, begin the music track at an appropriate volume and reduce it as soon as the narration begins. If the music is not distracting, allow it to run softly in the background during the narration. This helps to mask background noises like shuffling papers or the air conditioner turning on and off. As you reach the end of the podcast, slowly increase the volume of the music track for a strong ending.

5. ***Convert the recording into the appropriate format.*** In order for a podcast to be accessible, it must be saved in a format that is compatible with most web browsers and multimedia players. The most common format is MP3. Different podcast software programs provide different ways to select the correct format.

6. ***Publish the podcast.*** In order for others to access your podcast, you will need to upload it to a hosting service, such as Apple's iTunes University®, TeacherTube®, or YouTube®. Once uploaded, the podcast's URL can be added to a web page or included in the body of an email message. If you have a web server account, you can also FTP (file transfer protocol) the podcast to the server and provide the link to the students through the course discussion board, calendar, or other course components. You can also create an RSS (Real Simple Syndication) feed that includes the podcast title, description, and hyperlink. Post the RSS link to your course web site to allow students to subscribe to the podcast.

## GAUGING STUDENTS' PERCEPTIONS: PODCASTING SURVEY AND RESULTS

A weekly podcast was implemented in two sections of a fully online, upper-level course held at a public, four-year university during the 2009 spring and fall semesters. The course addressed technology training methods and strategies in corporate and education environments. Through the study and application of adult learning and training principles and methods, students assessed adult learners' needs and developed a training module for use in their current work environment.

To determine if the podcasts enhanced the online learner experience, students were invited to participate in an anonymous online survey during the final week of class. The survey asked the following questions:

1. How many podcasts did you listen to?
2. Did the podcasts help to improve your academic performance in the course?
3. Did the podcasts help you to better understand the subject matter?
4. Did the podcasts help to make the instructor more real?
5. Did the podcasts positively affect your motivation in the course?
6. Did the podcasts provide real-life examples of the concepts or topics addressed in the course?

The podcasts provided an introduction and overview to the weekly topics. They were tied to the class discussion questions and projects, and included helpful tips and examples to encourage students to think critically about the issues addressed in the course. Scripts were written and then were rehearsed several times before the podcasts were recorded, in order to generate a natural-sounding audio narration. The podcasts were limited to five minutes, based on field trials and input received from students in prior classes. The recordings were then edited to remove mistakes and to clean up background noises, and an instrumental track was added as a lead-in and fade-out to produce a more polished, professional production. The finished podcasts were uploaded to a web server and were made accessible to students by 8:00 AM every Monday morning via hyperlinks posted to the Course Calendar and Announcements pages of the Learning Management System. The weekly announcements were also automatically emailed to students at the beginning of the week.

Students taking the course were enrolled in the Bachelor of Applied Technology (BAT) or Bachelor of Applied Arts and Science (BAAS) programs at a university located along the Texas-Mexico border. This region's Hispanic population (86%) and personal income levels (which are below state averages), have been increasing steadily over the past years (Window on State Government, 2010). The University is an open-access institution with a high rate of first-generation students and second language learners. Students who require additional support to achieve college-readiness enroll in developmental courses—usually in Math and English—before they can take college-level courses.

Of the 82 students enrolled in the two courses, 57 participated in the survey, for an overall response rate of 70%. Of the survey participants, 61.4% (35) were female, while 38.6% (22) were male. Of the respondents, 91.2% (52) of students self-identified as Hispanic with the remaining 8.8% (5) of students identifying themselves as being of White, Non-Hispanic ethnicity. Students who responded to the survey ranged in age from 25 to 60, with a median age range of 26–35 years. The demographics of the participants closely mirrored the demographics of the institution.

A summary of the results is presented in Figures 2 to 7 on the following pages.

In order to determine students' podcast listening habits, students were asked to indicate how many podcasts they listened to during the course of the semester. Of the respondents, 29% (17 students) responded that they had listened to all of the podcasts; 11% (six students) listened to between seven and nine podcasts; 26% (15 students) listened to between four and six podcasts; 32% (18 students) listened to between one and three podcasts; and 2% (one student) did not listen to any of the podcasts during the semester. Although listening to the weekly podcasts was not a course requirement, 67% (38 out of 57 students) tuned in to at least half of the podcasts.

*Figure 2. Podcast Survey Results for Question 1: How many podcasts did you listen to? (N = 57)*

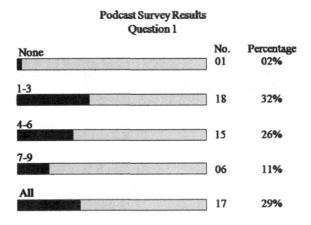

In Question 2, students were asked whether or not they thought podcasts had an impact on their academic performance in the course. A significant majority, 93% (53 students), indicated that podcasts did have a positive impact on their performance, while 7% (four students) responded to the contrary.

In Question 3, students were asked if the weekly podcasts helped them to better understand the subject matter. Of the respondents, 95% (54 students) indicated that the podcasts did help them to better understand the subject matter. Only 5% (three students) felt that the podcasts made no difference.

In order to determine the effect of the weekly podcasts on teacher immediacy in online courses, students were asked in Question 4 if they felt that the podcasts made the instructor appear more real.

Once again, an overwhelming majority, 95% (54 students), indicated that the podcasts added a human dimension to the online instructor. Only 5% (three students) disagreed with this statement.

In order to assess the motivational effects of the weekly podcasts on online learners, students were asked if they felt that the podcasts positively contributed to increased motivation in the course. Of the respondents, 82% (47 students) indicated that the podcasts did positively affect their motivation, while 18% (10 students) responded that they had not.

In order to determine the transferability of the topics addressed in class to real-world applications, students were asked in Question 6 if they felt that the podcasts provided authentic examples in real-world contexts. Of the respondents, 95% (54 students) responded that the podcasts did

*Figure 3. Podcast Survey Results for Question 2: Did the podcasts help to improve your academic performance in the course? (N = 57)*

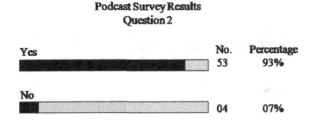

*Figure 4. Podcast Survey Results for Question 3: Did the podcasts help you to better understand the subject matter? (N = 57)*

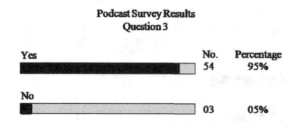

*Figure 5. Podcast Survey Results for Question 4: Did the podcasts help to make the instructor more real? (N = 57)*

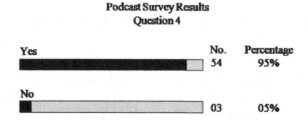

provide authentic examples of real-world applications, while 5% (three students) thought that the podcasts did not.

In addition to the six questions presented above, students were also given the opportunity to provide feedback through an open-ended question that asked: What is your opinion regarding the use of weekly podcasts in an online course? Although one student expressed finding little value in the podcasts, generally, students' perceptions of the use of podcasts in their courses were positive. Some students noted:

*"I enjoyed all of the podcasts and learned a lot from them. I wish that all of my professors had done them. Thank you for providing this valuable resource."*

*Figure 6. Podcast Survey Results for Question 5: Did the podcasts positively affect your motivation in the course? (N = 57)*

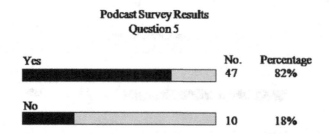

*Figure 7. Podcast Survey Results for Question 6: Did the podcasts provide real-life examples of the concepts or topics addressed in the course? (N = 57)*

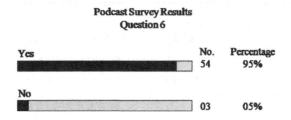

"*As an online student I believe podcasts supplement the information in the book and help clarify instructions that are not explained that well in the course… I can always play them again if I did not understand a topic.*"

"*Being a second language learner, the podcasts help me to understand the topics better. Sometimes the chapters did not make a lot of sense. Hearing the podcast helped to reinforce the readings.*"

"*Being an online learner, I think podcasts are a great idea. It is always nice to hear your instructor's voice, as opposed to only reading the instructor's messages and comments in the class discussion forums.*"

"*When I see instructors taking the time to work on a weekly podcast, it tells me they care about their students. So far, I had taken 9 online courses and only 3 instructors have used podcasts.*"

"*The quality of the podcasts and the enthusiasm portrayed by the instructor through the podcasts motivated me and got me excited to dive into each lesson. The podcasts made the "online" experience a little more real. They are great!!!*"

"*Podcasts provide another often needed auditory stimulus further enhancing the learning experience. I am a learner who learns better by listening.*"

Based on the survey results, a majority (67%) of students indicated that they listened to at least half of the podcasts. This percentage is much higher than that found in previous courses in which the podcasts were offered with less regularity and were much longer in length. Through trial and error over the past several semesters, the instructors learned to create podcasts of decreasing lengths in order to determine the ideal duration for maximizing student participation. Hour-long, lecture-based podcasts had an extremely low listening rate (less than 10%). Participation increased slightly (18%) when the podcasts dealt with test reviews and invited guest speakers (21%). The increased rate of listening to these podcasts indicated that students would be willing to listen to a podcast if they felt that the information would be helpful or interesting. However, several students complained that the podcasts were too long. Based on this feedback, the podcasts were shortened to 5 minutes and the topics became more focused and concise.

Another factor that improved the listening rate for the course podcasts was setting a more regular time for the release of the podcasts. In previous courses, podcasts took longer to produce and were not posted at regular intervals. Instead, they were posted as they were completed, often with no reliable frequency. Consequently, students did not know when to expect the podcasts, so they did not get accustomed to looking for them, and the listening rate, again, was less than 10%. As the podcasts became easier to produce, and as the instructors learned from student feedback what was working, podcasts were posted with greater reliability and frequency, and student participation steadily increased.

This increase in the listening rate for the course podcasts correlated positively with students' overall perceptions regarding the benefits of the podcasts in their learning. For example, 95% of students indicated that the podcasts used in the course helped them to better understand the subject matter. In addition, 93% of students felt that the podcasts had a positive impact on their performance, both on the course projects and in their understanding of the class discussion questions. Indeed, overall student performance in this course, in which podcasts were used with greater frequency and by more students, was slightly better than student performance in previous courses, in which podcasts were used with less frequency and by fewer students. Future research will examine in greater detail the relationship between student podcast use and academic achievement.

In summary, students' generally positive responses to the survey support the continued use of podcasts in this online course. Overall, students reported that the podcasts positively impacted their academic performance and motivation. Likewise, students overwhelmingly agreed that the weekly podcasts helped them to better understand the subject matter and provided them with examples of applications in real-world contexts. With regard to the asynchronous nature of this distance education course, students reported that the weekly podcasts made the instructor appear more present and real to the members of the class. The results of this preliminary study support expanding the use of this instructor's podcasts to other courses.

## LESSONS LEARNED

We have learned several important lessons during the time that we have been producing and using podcasts in our courses. Below are six instructional and/or logistical factors to keep in mind when producing podcasts for your courses.

1.  ***Create content that students actually want to listen to.*** In order for students to use an instructional resource, they must find value in it. Value can come in the form of perceived benefits, such as information that can help boost academic achievement and/or professional development. Instead of repeating content from the text, an introductory podcast can supplement the course content. For example, a podcast that summarizes the content of a test and provides tips on how to respond to questions would be perceived as extremely beneficial, and students would gladly take advantage of such a resource. A podcast can also have value if it communicates motivational and inspirational messages that help set the context for a topic or concept. Personal stories, experiences, cultural anecdotes, or relevant jokes about an upcoming topic can also help put students in a receptive frame of mind for learning.

2.  ***Keep your podcasts short.*** Conciseness is essential to producing a well-received podcast. Although consensus regarding student preferences of podcast length varies (Hew, 2008), Rossell-Aguilar (2007) noted that, on average, students listen to 5-20 minutes of downloaded podcasts. Based on student feedback and data collected from our survey, short podcasts (approximately five minutes in length) resulted in the highest listening rate. If the topic is complex and requires more time to cover, divide it into two or more podcasts. When you are writing the script for your first podcast, remember that

a five-minute podcast is approximately 1.5 to 2, single-spaced typed pages.

3. *Produce polished, professional-sounding podcasts.* There are several ways to make a podcast sound more professional. You do not need to invest a lot of money to produce a professional podcast. However, you will have to invest time to develop and rehearse a script, record and edit the podcast, add music, and publish the final product. You will also want to ensure that you do not sound like you are reading from a script. Your first five-minute podcast may take several hours to record, but as you gain experience, you should be able to produce a podcast in less than one hour (after the script has been written).

4. *Make the podcasts easily accessible.* Students will be less inclined to use any instructional resource if they have to search for it. Place a link or RSS feed to your podcasts in several locations within your course to make them easily accessible. For example, your podcasts can be posted to the announcements page, on the course schedule/calendar, and within the individual instructional modules. The podcasts can also be uploaded to a site to which students can subscribe, in order to have them automatically downloaded to their iPods® and MP3 players. The more accessible the podcasts are to your students, the more inclined they will be to listen to them.

5. *Maintain a consistent schedule for publishing your podcasts.* If you intend to produce a weekly podcast, it is beneficial to publish it on the same day each week. If you are inconsistent in your posting of podcasts, students will not establish a routine for listening to them. It is also more effective to release the podcasts individually, as opposed to releasing them all at the same time. This helps to engage students in the course (as

they return each week to listen to the latest podcast that has been published).

6. *Make your podcasts fun—and have fun producing them.* If it is evident that you are having fun producing your podcasts, students will keep coming back to the course to listen to them. How can we make our podcasts fun? Each week, look for timely articles that address current issues to establish a context for critical reflection of the weekly topics. It is also important to have an idea of the students' fields of study and to select examples from those professions. At first, we were nervous about producing our podcasts, but soon we came to enjoy the search for interesting resources and anecdotes, and even for appropriate jokes. If your podcasts reflect your passion for your subject matter and your mastery of your areas of expertise, your students will appreciate your hard work and enthusiasm for your discipline. This can, in turn, motivate them to want to learn more.

## FUTURE DIRECTIONS

Advancements in mobile technologies such as podcasting will continue to impact language learning. "The implications of mobile learning are far-reaching, and its potential effect on education profound. The next few years will see a period of rapid growth for mobile learning, with evolutionary rather than revolutionary changes" (Corbeil & Valdés-Corbeil, 2007, p. 57). The authors of the Horizon Report (The New Media Consortium & EDUCAUSE Learning Initiative, 2008), noted that these changes pose some of the most significant challenges facing educators today and raise the question of how to keep up with the pace of new advancements in learning. They added, "as the gap grows between new scholarship and old, leadership and innovation are needed at all levels of the academy—from students to faculty to staff and administrative leadership" (p. 5). Over the following years, the following six technology trends identified in the 2008 Horizon Report will have implications for research and implementation of academic podcasting in second language learning. For example: (1) Grassroots video. An inexpensive video camera and editing/publishing software is all that is required to add video to a podcast that can enhance language acquisition through the use of visual cues and authentic linguistic models; (2) Collaborative webs. Collaborative webs are online networking and collaboration tools that are already easily available and will afford instructors and students the opportunity to not only view course content and resources, but to collaborate on developing them; (3) Mobile broadband. The improved availability of high-speed Internet will greatly expand the use of podcasts and Mobile-Assisted Language Learning resources; (4) Data mashups. These tools merge information from multiple sources, such as online chats, databases, and microblogs, into one, convenient location. This allows for the convergence of tools and content for richer and more authentic learning experiences; (5) Collective intelligence-data. This refers to data that are collected in a shared online location and are editable by all users. A collective intelligence means that potentially, all user-created tools, including podcasts, can be readily accessible; and (6) Social operating systems. These are the "next generation of social networking systems" (p. 26). The educational potential of these social networking systems for mobile-assisted language learning lies in their ability to easily promote the connection and networking of people and resources.

## CONCLUSION

As the uses of academic podcasting are further explored, learners will benefit from the increased variety and flexibility for learning and reinforcement of their language skills. Meng (2005) noted, "the greatest opportunities for these technologies are in the ways they will be used that have not

yet been imagined" (p. 10). Initially, instructors may be intimidated by the thought of creating their first podcast because they may have no idea where to start. Therefore, we hope that this chapter will inspire others to try podcasting to enrich their courses and language learning programs. With practice and a few easily-accessible tools, producing podcasts can be a fun and productive process for instructors and students.

## REFERENCES

Comedy, C. com. (2009). Efficiency expert joke. Retrieved from http://www.clevercomedy.com/joke/j3795j14.html

Corbeil, J. R., & Valdés-Corbeil, M. E. (2007). Are you ready for mobile learning? *EDUCAUSE Quarterly, 30*(2), 51–58.

Edirisingha, P., Rizzi, C., & Rothwell, L. (2007). Podcasting to provide teaching and learning support for an undergraduate module on English language communication. *Turkish Online Journal of Distance Education, 8*(3), 87–107.

eMarketer. (2009, March 4). *Podcasting goes mainstream.* Retrieved from http://www.emarketer.com/Article.aspx?R=1006937

Hew, K. F. (2008). Use of audio podcast in K-12 and higher education: A review of research topics and methodologies. *Educational Technology Research and Development.*

Kukulska-Hulme, A. (2006). Mobile language learning now and in the future (pp. 119-134). Retrieved from http://www.groupe-compas.net/wp-content/uploads/2009/08/kukulska-hulme.pdf

Lee, M. J. W., & Chan, A. (2007). Reducing the effects of isolation and promoting inclusivity for distance learners through podcasting. *Turkish Online Journal of Distance Education, 8*(1). Retrieved from http://tojde.anadolu.edu.tr/tojde25/pdf/article_7.pdf

Meng, P. (2005). Podcasting and vodcasting: A white paper. IAT Services, University of Missouri (pp. 1-13). Retrieved from http://www.tfaoi.com/cm/3cm/3cm310.pdf

O'Hare, D. (2001). The future is already happening: Training aeronautical skills in virtual environments. Pacific Wings Magazine. Retrieved from http://psy.otago.ac.nz/cogerg/The%20Future%20is%20Already %20Happening.pdf

Pettit, J., & Kukulska-Hulme, A. (2006). Going with the grain: Mobile devices in practice. In *Proceedings of the 23rd Annual Ascilite Conference* (pp. 647-656). Retrieved from http://www.ascilite.org.au/conferences/sydney06/proceeding/pdf_papers/p91.pdf

Ractham, P., & Zhang, X. (2006). Podcasting in academia: A new knowledge management paradigm within academic settings. In K. Keiser et al. (Eds.), *Proceedings of the 44th Annual Computer Personnel Research Conference (ACM SIGMIS/CPR) 2006.* (pp. 314-317). New York.

Robinson, J. L., & Dodd, J. E. (2006). Case study: Use of handheld computers by university communications students. *MERLOT Journal of Online Learning and Teaching, 2*(1), 49–61.

Rosell-Aguilar, F. (2007). Top of the pods: In search of a podcasting "podagogy" for language learning. *Computer Assisted Language Learning, 20*(5), 471–492. doi:10.1080/09588220701746047

Schlosser, C. A., & Burmeister, M. L. (2006). *Audio in online courses: Beyond podcasting.* Retrieved from http://www.nova.edu/~burmeist/audio_online.html

Stolovitch, H. D., & Keeps, E. J. (2003). *Telling ain't training.* Alexandria, VA: ASTD.

The New Media Consortium & EDUCAUSE Learning Initiative. (2008). *Horizon report.* Retrieved from http://www.nmc.org/pdf/2008-Horizon-Report.pdf

Thorne, S. L., & Scott Payne, J. R. (2005). Evolutionary trajectories, internet-mediated expression, and language education. *CALICO Journal, 22*(3), 371–397.

William, S., & McMinn, J. (2008). *Podcasting possibilities: Increasing time and motivation in the language classroom.* European Institute for E-Learning (EIfEL) (pp. 212-215). Retrieved from http://www.eife-l.org/publications/proceedings/ilf08/contributions/improving-quality-of-learning-with-technologies/McMinn.pdf

Window on State Government. (2010). *Texas in focus: South Texas demographics.* Retrieved from http://www.window.state.tx.us/specialrpt/tif/southtexas/demographics.html

## ADDITIONAL READING

Abdous, M., Camarena, M., & Facer, B. (2009). Mall technology: Use of academic podcasting in the foreign language classroom. *ReCALL, 21,* 76–95. doi:10.1017/S0958344009000020

Acquaro, P., & Fadjo, C. (2008). Near-time podcasting: Using iTunes U to increase academic content distribution. In K. McFerrin et al., (Eds.), *Proceedings of Society for Information Technology & Teacher Education International Conference 2008* (pp. 2492-2496). Chesapeake, VA: AACE.

Anzai, Y. (2007). Empowering English learning utilizing podcasts. In T. Bastiaens & S. Carliner (Eds.), *Proceedings of World Conference on E-Learning in Corporate, Government, Healthcare, and Higher Education 2007* (pp. 10-15). Chesapeake, VA: AACE.

Bausch, S., & Han, L. (2006). Podcasting gains an important foothold among U.S. adult online population. *Nielsen/NetRatings.* Retrieved from: http://www.nielsen-netratings.com/pr/pr_060712.pdf

BBC. (2005, July 7). *Podcasting set for huge growth*. Retrieved from http://news.bbc.co.uk/1/hi/technology/4658995.stm

Cambell, G. (2005). There's something in the air: Podcasting in education. *EDUCAUSE Review, 40*(6), 32–47.

Cebeci, Z., & Tekdal, M. (2006). Using podcasts as audio learning objects. *Interdisciplinary Journal of Knowledge and Learning Objects, 2*, 47–57.

Chinnery, G. M. (2006). Going to the mall: Mobile assisted language learning. *Language Learning & Technology, 10*(1). Retrieved from http://llt.msu.edu/vol10num1/pdf/emerging.pdf.

Davi, A., Frydenberg, M., & Gulati, G. J. (2007). Blogging across the disciplines: Integrating technology to enhance liberal learning. *Merlot Journal of Online Learning and Teaching, 3*(3). Retrieved from http://jolt.merlot.org/vol3no3/frydenberg.htm

De Freitas, S., & Neumann, T. (2009). Pedagogic strategies supporting the use of synchronous audiographic conferencing: A review of the literature. *British Journal of Educational Technology, 40*(6), 980–998. doi:10.1111/j.1467-8535.2008.00887.x

Ducate, L., & Lomicka, L. (2009). Podcasting: An effective tool for honing language students' pronunciation. *Language Learning & Technology, 13*(3). Retrieved from http://llt.msu.edu/vol13num3/ducatelomicka.pdf.

Hoffert, B. (2009). Speak easy. *Library Journal, 134*(12), 22–25.

Howard, C. (2007). *m-Learning: The latest trends, development and real-world applications*. Oakland, CA: Bersin Associates.

Kukulska-Hulme, A., & Shield, L. (2008). An overview of mobile assisted language learning: From content delivery to supported collaboration and interaction. *ReCALL, 20*, 271–289. doi:10.1017/S0958344008000335

McLoughlin, C., & Lee, M. J. (2007). Listen and learn: A systematic review of the evidence that podcasting supports learning in higher education. In C. Montgomerie & J. Seale (Eds.), *Proceedings of World Conference on Educational Multimedia, Hypermedia and Telecommunications 2007* (pp. 1669-1677). Chesapeake, VA: AACE.

Motteram, G., & Sharma, P. (2009). Blending learning in a web 2.0 world. *International Journal of Emerging Technologies & Society, 7*(2), 83–96.

O'Brien, A., & Hegelheimer, V. (2007). Integrating CALL into the classroom: The role of podcasting in an ESL listening strategies course. *ReCALL, 19*, 162–180. .doi:10.1017/S0958344007000523

Pownell, D. (2004). iListen, iLearn, iPod: Life-long learning with mobile audio. In C. Crawford et al. (Eds.), *Proceedings of Society for Information Technology and Teacher Education International Conference 2004* (pp. 1830-1831). Chesapeake, VA: AACE.

Robin, R. (2007). Learner-based listening and technological authenticity. *Language Learning & Technology, 11*, 109–115.

Sharples, M. (2000). The design of personal mobile technologies for lifelong learning. *Computers & Education, 34*, 177–193. doi:10.1016/S0360-1315(99)00044-5

Shim, J. E., Shropshire, J., Parks, S., & Cambell, N. (2007). Podcasting for e-learning, communication, and delivery. *Industrial Management & Data Systems, 107*(4), 587–600. doi:10.1108/02635570710740715

Thorne, S. L. (2008). Mediating technologies and second language learning. In Leu, D., Coiro, J., Lankshear, C., & Knobel, M. (eds.), *Handbook of Research on New Literacies*. Mahwah, NJ: Lawrence Erlbaum. Retrieved from http://language.la.psu.edu/~thorne/Thorne_HandbookNewLiteracies_proofs.pdf

Vandergrift, L. (2004). Listening to learn or learning to listen? *Annual Review of Applied Linguistics*, *24*, 3–25. doi:10.1017/S0267190504000017

Woods, R., & Keeler, J. (2001). The effect of instructor's use of audio e-mail messages on student participation in and perceptions of online learning: A preliminary case study. *Open Learning*, *16*(3), 263–278. doi:10.1080/02680510120084977

## KEY TERMS AND DEFINITIONS

**Audacity:** This is a free, open source, digital audio recorder and editor available for Windows, Macintosh, and Linux operating systems. Because it is free and distributed under the GNU General Public License, it is a popular recorder and editor among podcasters.

**MP3:** An acronym for MPEG Audio Layer 3, MP3 is a popular file format used to transfer compressed audio files via the Internet to portable digital players, cell phones, laptops, and personal computers for storage and playback. MP3 is the preferred audio format for delivering podcasts.

**Podcast:** Created from the words "pod" after the popular iPod digital music player and "broadcast," a podcast is an audio recording, broadcast over the Internet and made available for download from a web site for playback on a portable digital player or computer.

**Social Presence:** The awareness of the presence of others in a computer-mediated environment is referred to as social presence. Social presence research suggests that a relationship exists between student learning outcomes and the amount of connection that students feel with their peers and instructors, especially in distance education courses in which participants do not physically meet.

**Teacher Immediacy:** Theoretically grounded in interpersonal communication research, teacher immediacy describes the way in which students perceive the distance between themselves and their instructors. In distance education environments, teacher immediacy is regularly associated with social presence and generally refers to how present or accessible the teacher is to his or her remote students.

# Chapter 5
# Challenges of Adopting Web 2.0 and Mobile 2.0 for Language Learning

**Su-Ling Hsueh**
*Defense Language Institute, USA*

## ABSTRACT

*Podcasts, blogs, and wikis are the best-liked Web 2.0 services used by language teachers for homework assignments or special projects. Although these services sound promising, the potential challenges to their use should not be overlooked. This chapter discusses challenges, including economic aspects, technical support and training, pedagogy and teachers' roles, and feedback and evaluation. Suggestions are also provided to resolve the concerns. Detailed introductions of podcasts, wikis, blogs, Web 2.0, and Mobile 2.0 are presented, along with analysis of geographic users' learning styles and characteristics. Mobile technology to assist language learning is also explored.*

## INTRODUCTION

Web 2.0 (i.e. Facebook®, YouTube®, Twitter®, etc.) has become a universal phenomenon and is eclipsing the one-way (regular) information distribution website. Web 2.0 allows "users to connect with one another" ("Web 3.0 and beyond," 2007, para. 10). Its two-way interaction and participation capabilities make Web 2.0 ideal for language teaching and learning in the classroom and beyond. According to Jon Stewart, Nielsen's research director for technology and research, the fastest-growing activities on the World Wide Web are social networking, news checking, and searching (Stewart, 2009). Interactive features, versatile web applications, easily created web pages, and constant improvement have made Web 2.0 into a vital part of Web society. Among all Web 2.0 services, podcasts, blogs, and wikis are the most popular learning and instruction tools.

Another recent phenomenon is the rise of handheld devices. Mobile devices and smartphones are in use around the world, especially in Asian countries. Smartphones, which are mobile phones with operating systems, afford both computer-like features and versatile functionalities (e.g.,

DOI: 10.4018/978-1-60960-141-6.ch005

emails, internet, etc.). They are mini-computers that can be easily carried in a pocket. Smartphone users can access a variety of applications and can network anywhere, anytime. The new term, Mobile 2.0, has been created to represent "Web 2.0 on mobile handsets" (Wang & Heffernan, 2009, p. 472). Mobile 2.0 enables mobile learning through Web 2.0 social networking, interaction, and collaboration in mobile devices. Pieri and Diamantini (2009) defined mobile learning as "a modality of distribution of any learning content with portable devices such as the personal digital assistant (PDA), tablet PC, e-book, and mobile phones" (p. 184). Mobile learning, both formal and informal, has experienced swift growth.

Accompanied by 4G or Wireless Broadband Access (i.e. WiMAX) technologies, the newest mobile phone networks allow faster data transmission, thereby affording user access to radio, GPS, camera, TV programs, websites, and email at any time and place. Mobile technology has rapidly progressed, especially in Asian countries such as Japan and China (Wang & Heffernan, 2009). Wang and Heffernan (2009) noted that Mobile 2.0 focuses more on user-led services than PC Web 2.0, which makes m-learning more personal and spontaneous. With the swift development of mobile technology, users may expect to see more user- and learner-friendly devices which will become necessities for daily life and learning. But while mobile technology is spreading widely and academic podcasts can be accessed at any time, are users around the world ready to use mobile devices to assist learning? This chapter discusses user characteristics, pedagogical approaches, mobile technology, and potential future developments. The chapter will

- provide an in-depth description of podcasts, along with wikis and blogs. Mobile 2.0 will then be discussed, along with introduction of portable and mobile devices (e.g., smartphones, tablet PCs, etc.) which

can be utilized for podcasts, blogs, and wikis.

- analyze geographic users' characteristics, culture, lifestyles, learning habits, and behaviors, versus the features and functionality of Web 2.0 and Mobile 2.0. An overview of the challenges of integrating learners, instructors, and the cutting-edge tools/web environments will be included.

- present approaches for overcoming the pedagogical impacts and economic challenges which may arise, despite the promise and popularity of Mobile 2.0.

- preview the future development of Web 2.0 and Mobile 2.0 technologies to their full potential.

## WEB 2.0 AND MOBILE 2.0

The amount of literature regarding the use of Web 2.0 and Mobile (Web) 2.0 to support formal and informal learning has rapidly increased. With the emerging popularity of Web 2.0, teachers, scholars, and students increasingly use these tools for learning and researching a variety of subjects. "Web 2.0 doesn't have a hard boundary, but rather, a gravitational core" (O'Reilly, 2005, p. 1). The web became a platform which allowed for user participation and control of data (O'Reilly). Syndication of Web 2.0 (e.g., blog, wiki, Flickr®, Delicious®, podcast, etc.) transmits data sufficiently and brings current information to users. However, the most successful feature of Web 2.0 is its social networking, which provides interaction and collaboration (O'Reilly). O'Reilly mentioned that Google® was the pioneer by using the web as a platform and providing a powerful database with free service. Web 2.0 is a medium -- a gravitational core, as O'Reilly stated -- which not only provides service to core users but also reaches many more potential users through the creation and the active participation of primary users.

Gilmore (2004) noted that, in the world of Web 2.0, audience participants play a role as information providers, and they are website creators or designers, as well. In fact, users are considered co-developers (O'Reilly, 2005). The collaborative and collective knowledge of Web 2.0 has enabled the inception of a more powerful database with resourceful information. Websites (i.e. podcasts and blogs) can become dynamic with constant updates through Really Simple Syndication (RSS) function. Furthermore, Mobile 2.0 "has changed both the way we live our lives and the learning styles we employ" (Wang & Heffernan, 2009, p. 483). For example, Mobile 2.0 serves as a portable entertainment center which provides the newest movies, music, and games, as well as network access to any websites. Jaokar (2006, para. 2) stated that "Mobile Web 2.0 extends the principle of 'Harnessing Collective Intelligence' to restricted devices [mobile devices]." This means that people carrying mobile devices are no longer merely consumers, but are active participants acting as reporters (Jaokar). Users' intelligence input and interaction generate more participation. Mobile 2.0 also provides the most up-to-date mobile accessible Web 2.0 services and information (e.g., podcasts, RSS feeds, Flickr/ShoZu®, maps, videos, etc.) through Wi-Fi networks (Waele, 2006).

The development of technological tools has also progressed rapidly, and often beyond conventional expectations. Mobile 2.0 involves "the extension of Web 2.0 to mobile devices" (Wang & Heffernan, p. 475), thereby embracing the more interactive functions and user-friendly features which enhance user interest and motivation. At a certain point, it becomes no longer practical to rely upon older technologies, and the focal point for language institutions turns to the ways in which learners and instructors can make use of the new tools to advance second language learning. Therefore, it is crucial to look into the attributes and impacts of the new tools that are available.

Web 2.0, as collaborationware, has been adopted in teaching several disciplines. Godwin-Jones observed that blogs, wikis, and RSS feeds provided powerful online collaboration for language learners and teachers in 2003. Nowadays, blogs, wikis and podcasts appear to be three extremely popular instructional Web 2.0 resources. They are the platforms and powerful database systems for storing all of the instructional content, collaboration logs, participants' individual portfolios, and so forth. Boulos, Maramba, and Wheele (2006, para. 22) stated that "Perhaps the two main big advantages of wikis, blogs and podcasts are their ease of use and the availability of many Open Source/free or low-cost software and hosting options to run them." The following is an introduction to podcast, blog, and wiki-assisted language learning.

## Podcasts

Podcasting is a term derived from "iPod®" and "broadcasting" (Chinnery, 2006). Podcasts require RSS (really simple syndication) feeds to distribute audio episodes/content to a users' podcatcher (e.g., iTunes®), which serves as the application which captures and downloads audio feeds (files) to music players ("Podcast," n.d.). "When audio content is delivered to a media player, it is referred to as podcasting" (Viswanathan, 2009, p. 226).

Podcasts have been widely used in many disciplines and academic fields since Apple first launched iPod products. There are many free and paid podcasting websites which offer constantly updated episodes to assist language learning (e.g., ChinesePod, iMandarin, dailyfrenchpod, RussianPod101, JapanesePod101, etc.). Gruba, Clark, Ng, and Wells (2009) classified recorded podcast listening materials into two categories: (1) purposely built to meet the specific needs of learners, and (2) unedited authentic materials designed for native language speakers and retrieved from mass media sources.

The diversity of podcasting materials allows beginners to listen to episodes repeatedly, an advantageous feature for language learners. As Stevick (1989) suggested, language learning requires "lots of listening before speaking" and "t[ying] language to some coherent reality" (p.147). Harris and Park (2008) summarized three advantages of academic podcasts: (1) an emphasis on critical information to augment teaching materials, (2) satisfaction of ownership acknowledgement needs, and (3) facilitation of repeated learning. Additional advantages of podcasting include the fact that episodes/programs are available at any time and place, at the learner's own pace, and at the learner's own convenience (Viswanathan, 2009).

"In the context of language learning, podcasts are most often used to teach listening skills" (Gruba et al., 2009, p. 402). Listening is a critical element for the successful learning of a foreign language, since "listening competence is universally larger than speaking competence" (Brown, 2001). Feyten (1991) demonstrated, through an experiment, that listening ability and foreign language acquisition are closely correlated. It is clear that listening plays an active role in the language acquisition process (Rost 2001; Feyten, 1991).

Rost (2001) stated that listening is still considered a mysterious "black box," and the best approach is "more practice." He advocated that more attention be paid to the "strategy development" designed to demystify the listening process. However, listening skill, which is often treated as the least important skill in the classroom, should really be considered the fundamental skill in second language learning because it is essential for understanding and comprehending the target language (Elkhafaifi 2005). Johnson (2001) stated that the process of learning starts with declarative knowledge (the process of *proceduralization)*, which includes listening and reading. That is to say, language learning starts with listening and reading (declarative knowledge).

Once students receive enough declarative knowledge, they can start producing what they've learned. Stevick (1989) echoed that students need to "repeatedly listen to and produce the same material with a native speaker" (1989, p.148).

Podcasts appear to be an ideal means for recording the interviews or discussions with native or non-native speakers that are often assigned for homework. Moreover, podcast episodes can also serve as an impetus for interclass exchanges. For example, Thorne and Payne (2005) proposed that students produce podcasts regarding their personal interests on a weekly or biweekly basis as an impetus for interclass or intercultural exchanges.

Through the process of creation, learners and instructors can have more interaction. Students' speaking abilities and motivation can be enhanced. According to Huann and Thaong (2006), "the publishing phase of podcasting serves to motivate students to improve on their own performances" (p. 8). That is because "when students are aware that their audio artifacts will be made available to an audience, this provides the intrinsic push for them to reflect on their initial audio recordings and improve on their oral performance during the content creation phase" (Huann & Thong, p. 8). Students have indicated that podcasts are helpful for understanding and retaining course content (McCombs & Liu, 2007), and students have expressed positive views about podcasts and assimilation of podcast episodes (Nathan & Chan, 2007).

Dale (2007) proposed that strategies for effective podcasting should take learning and technical issues into consideration. While learning issues include the engagement and guidance of learners, technical issues encompass technical and training support (Dale, 2007). Podcasting using effective pedagogical approaches can enhance learner self-regulation, active and self-directed learning, and learner-generated content (McLoughlin & Lee, 2007). Ediristingha, Rizzi, Nie, and Rothwell (2007) listed "three features of podcasts that supported learning in their study: a) learner choice and flexibility offered by podcasts; b) conversational and discussion style content of podcasts that offered perspectives and advice from peers and tutors, and an unconventional, different way of learning bringing a sense of informality to formal learning" (p. 96).

As to recording devices, instructors and learners do not need to worry about suffering from an insufficient hardware supply. Smartphone (mobile) devices, iPods (with voice recorders), and MP3 recorders are handy tools for recording content for podcasts at any time. Vincent (2009) stated that the iPod Touch® can be made into a little podcast studio, with its earbuds that have a built-in mic to record audio podcasts in classrooms where computers are scarce. Even though students can easily access and update programs by using mobile devices or desktop and laptop computers, the process of creating a podcast can be time consuming. For instance, "[a] 4-6 minute enhanced podcast can take approximately 2-3 hours to go through production to subscription phases as per the podcasting process" (Dale, 2007, p. 55).

## Blogs

The blog is a feedback system (Gilmore, 2004) which provides an environment for project-based learning (Godwin-Jones, 2003). According to Mattison (2003), blogs, or weblogs, are chronological online journals written mainly by individuals. They allow students' journals, reflections, and assignments to be categorized. Learners can subscribe to blogs (similar to podcast subscriptions) through RSS feeds. Thus, learners can always access the most up-to-date information. Godwin-Jones believed that "blogs are well suited to serve as on-line personal journals for students, particularly since they normally enable uploading and linking of files. Language learners could use a personal blog, linked to a course, as an electronic portfolio, showing development over time" (p. 13). Blogs are constituted not just with written texts, hyperlinks, and pictures, but also with voice recordings and video clips. An audioblog is a blog that includes voice recordings. "Audioblogs inherited the self-reflective nature of blogs, hence audioblogs tend to be reflective voice journals of bloggers who choose

to use their voice for self-expression" (Huann & Thong, 2006, p. 4). Audioblogging can facilitate students' listening and speaking ability, and the comments feature of blogs can provides interactive feedback between instructors and students.

Four potential benefits of blogs are (1) enhancement of learner motivation; (2) authenticity as a communicative medium; (3) a communicative and interactive medium; 4) enhancement of literacy (Carney, 2009). Carney (2009) mentioned that blog sites have more integration with multimedia and can blend with other social networking sites. Further, "weblogs provide an excellent opportunity for educators to advance literacy through storytelling and dialogue. Storytelling and literacy are the foundation of language development, and more so, the foundation of learning" (Huffaker, 2005, p. 96). The blog is an ideal medium to represent academic writing and post-process methods which enable learners to reflect upon their self-expression, and to rationalize and analyze (Murray, Hourigan, & Jeanneau, 2007). Murray et al. found that instructors are helped by having an academically-valid assessment framework to provide effective feedback through the two methods facilitated by the blog approach.

Instructors can also use blogs as tools for helping students prepare professional portfolios. For example, an advanced English writing instructor can assign students to compose their resumés as blogs. The resumés, then, can be shared with the public and the class. As the course proceeds, individual writing assignments will gradually accumulate until each student's portfolio is completed. Students can also subscribe to classmates' blogs. Through blog interaction, students with lower language level proficiency can read articles or listen to audio files of students with higher proficiency levels. Students can learn not only from instructors, but also classmates. This mutual learning experience can serve to enhance even more interactions among students.

## Wikis

A wiki is a collaboration website that allows users to create and edit content easily on a central page (location). Wiki use is often compared with blogging, but there is a slight difference between the two. Blogs are organized chronologically, whereas wikis are structured by content (Godwin-Jones, 2003). Godwin-Jones acknowledged that wikis are intensely collaborative and ideal for a "community of practice" (COP). Wikis enable instructors to create interactive activities for their students, and to present course information such as resources, external links, project information, and frequently asked questions (Schwartz, Clark, Cossarin, & Rudolph, 2003).

Duffy and Bruns (2006) listed some educational uses of wikis, including but not limited to developing research projects, adding summaries, building a collaborative annotated bibliography, creating a linked network of resources, presenting map concepts, sharing reflections, and using the wiki as a knowledge base (as cited in Parker & Chao, 2007). Additionally, Naomi, Raitman, and Zhou (2004) praised wikis as fully editable websites that facilitate collaboration by allowing users to read and add content, which then can be traced back for assessment. At Deakin University, "wikis were used successfully to enable hundreds of students to participate in a collaborative icebreaker exercise" (Augar, Raitman, & Zhou, 2004, para. 21).

Language instructors can design collective writing projects requiring exploration, in-depth research, and numerous modifications. For example, wiki topics can include a biography of a historical figure, an explanation of US foreign policy, an overview of economic crisis, etc. Wikis can also be used for debate assignment; students can contribute their opinions on pros or cons of the debate topic. At the end of the course, the wikis become a reference library with a great deal of subject-matter content and information.

## Portable and Mobile Devices

Most language learners use school desktop computers or personal devices to access online course assignments. iPhones® or smartphones are excellent personal portable devices for allowing language learners to complete homework assignments at any time and at any place. They are suitable for short assignments or for activities which do not require extensive composition or labor-intensive typing/input (e.g., multiple choice questions or instant messaging). At the beginning of the course, instructors can verify the types of devices possessed by students. For example, some school districts provide each student with a laptop computer (or tablet PC), which can make it easy to integrate podcasts, blogs, and wikis into language classrooms. Students can respond to homework assignments without the difficulties associated with finding technical equipment.

A teacher in a school without sufficient technical equipment may want to survey the kinds of technical equipment available in labs, libraries, or students' residences. Of course, if every student has a smartphone, accessing podcasts will be easy. However, if they do not, achieving equitable and ubiquitous learning will be a challenge. If teachers insist upon incorporating podcasting in or out of class, they can suggest that their students use (or purchase) certain devices. Of course, the prices and features of the individual gear used to achieve learning objectives needs to be carefully evaluated beforehand. Computer labs with recording devices and software are typically sufficient for podcast projects; however, the number of projects may need to be reduced, since most labs have set schedules and are not available at any time (or in sync with the students' availabilities). The more technical equipment that students can easily access, the more podcast episodes or blogs that their instructors can request. The following information for the reader's reference is provided regarding apparatuses which can be utilized for podcasts, blogs, and wikis.

The iPod is a popular and affordable hand-held device for accessing podcasts and audio files. Prices are quite affordable for a majority of users. However, iPods still need to rely on computers to upload and download sound or video files. Smartphones (e.g., iPhones) and iPod Touches have surpassed iPods with operating system software which allows users to access wikis, blogs, websites, and numerous applications. These smartphones don't need to depend on computers for file transferring.

The current Smartphone market has become very competitive, with many manufacturers, such as Apple, Motorola, and Nokia, offering products. More applications for Smartphone have been developed to attract additional consumers. Due to the rapid growth of Smartphone hardware and software, the market has become an intense commercial battlefield. Applications for iPhones and other smartphones have become more user-friendly to meet consumers' needs. Many instructors and learners have immediately grasped this great opportunity and have begun to utilize smartphones to support learning. According to Clough, Jones, McAndrew, and Scanlon (2009), most PDA and Smartphone users utilize the devices to take notes or note recording for informal learning.

Regular portable equipment for podcasts includes laptop or notebook computers. Currently, netbooks and iPads® are less expensive than regular MacBooks® or laptop computers. The contemporary displays of an iPad and a netbook are generally 9.7 and 10.1 inches, respectively. Most netbooks weigh 2.1-2.9 pounds, while iPads weigh 1.5-1.6 pounds. Brand names include Apple, HP, Asus, Toshiba, Lenovo, etc. Netbooks and iPads are portable and easily carried anywhere. They are mini-computers which use regular operating systems and software programs. Users can employ these two kinds of devices to access any website, word processor, and other software programs.

Tablet PCs are usually priced much higher than regular notebooks and netbooks. Popular brands include Fujitsu, Lenovo, HP, and Panasonic, among others. Tablet PCs allow users to write on the screen and to save hand-written notes. They may be suitable for language learners seeking to practice writing Far Eastern language characters. Tablet PCs typically use operating systems and software programs similar to those used for desktop and laptop computers. OneNote®, Windows Journal®, and Sticky Notes® are tablet PC-specific programs that let users create hand-written notes at any time.

## Geographic Characteristics (East Meets West)

A study by Purdie and Hattie (1996) showed that Japanese students attached more importance to the use of memorization in learning than did Western students. In a study of cross-cultural differences in online learning motivation, Lim (2004) found that Korean students scored significantly higher for learner control than did American students. In contrast, American students had significantly higher motivation regarding course relevancy, course interest, reinforcement, and self-efficacy (Lim). Lim stated that the result indicating that Korean students favor the control of their own learning processes may have been influenced by their orientation toward more effort attributions and performance goals. This particular tendency of Asian students could relate to the fact that Asians are increasingly involved in creating, and interacting in, Web 2.0 environments. According to a study from McCann University, more Asians create blogs, upload videos (YouTube), and join social networks (Facebook and MySpace®) than do Americans and Western Europeans (Digital Inspiration, 2008).

According to Park (2006), "in general, Asian American students tend to be passive and non-verbal [in the classroom] and rarely initiate class discussions until they are called on" (p. 78). But with respect to learning styles, Chinese and Korean students are more prone to be competitive and individualistic (Park). Park reported that Chinese and Korean students favor individual learning and the four basic perceptual learning styles (kinesthetic, tactile, visual, auditory), but do not prefer group learning, as the Anglo-American students do. In addition, Asian American students generally have higher academic achievement because they spend more time doing homework, attending out-of-school classes, and responding to higher educational expectations from parents (Peng & Wright, 1994).

As to the lifestyles related to consumer behavior and culture, Mooij (2004) stated that the Chinese tend to be situation-centered and obliged to be sensitive to their environment; in contrast, Americans are more likely to be individual-centered, expecting their environment to be sensitive to them (p. 184). Yanai asserted that "Japanese people are extremely interested in how different they are from each other, but hate to be very different" (cited in Mooij, p. 164). According to Mooij, people in individualistic cultures (e.g., western countries) emphasize the need for self-expression; while people in collectivistic cultures (e.g., Asia, South America, and Africa) are fundamentally interdependent and focus on the social adjustment. That is to say, "Ego boosting, performance, and showing-off are integrated aspects of North American self" (Mooij, p.104). Mooij further stated that "self-esteem is not necessarily the cause of behavior; behavior can be the cause of self-esteem. Because different cultural behavioral practices lead to self-esteem, the content of self-esteem can vary across cultures" (p. 164). In different cultural contexts, people behave differently to express certain emotional feelings (Mooij).

In order to compare Asian and Western technology consumers, Epsilon conducted research in April, 2009 on over 4000 consumer respondents in select countries in North America, Asia Pacific, and Europe (Guy, 2009). The Epsilon research showed that 32% of the Asians use a PDA or a Smartphone for emailing purposes, compared to the Europeans at 7% and the Americans at 9%

(Guy). Also, Asians are adapting to social networking. According to Guy's article in August 2009, the Epsilon research revealed that Asians are steadily adapting to social networks for communicating (8%) compared to the Europeans (5%) and the North Americans (4%). The Asian lifestyle (that of a collectivistic culture) may be one factor which contributes to the higher usage of Web 2.0 in Asian countries.

A study conducted by Vavoula in 2005 showed that in the UK, 51% of everyday adult learning took place at home and in the office; 21% occurred outside the office (in the workplace), 5% outdoors; 2% in a friend's house; 6% at places of leisure; 14% in other locations; and 1% on transport (as cited in Sharples, Taylor, & Vavoula, 2005). Young (n.d., para. 1) reported that "the penetration rates for the U.S. cell phone market are greater than 75%, and in Western Europe, Japan and Hong Kong penetration has already exceeded 100% (multiple cell phones per subscriber)." It is speculated that the percentage of adult learning during transportation may be higher (with assistance of mobile phones) in Asian, especially in Japan, Hong Kong, China, Taiwan, and in the countries in which large populations use public transportation.

From the aforementioned literature, one can perceive that learners in different cultures behave differently. The high percentage of smartphone use in Asian countries makes it easy for learners to retrieve and respond to podcasts, blogs, and wikis. Language instructors can request that users complete more language drills or activities to enhance memorization of vocabulary and grammar points, including small projects to report and record their experiences, surroundings, or situations. This activity is especially likely to occur during commuting. Many podcast episodes can include quizzes. Blogging and podcasting are ideal for providing online social networking environments that enable Asian students to interact with classmates at any time. Creating individual podcast episodes with ranking schemes can motivate learners to produce higher quality content.

Since Western countries do not have the same high usage of mobile devices, Western language teachers should make efforts to prepare one or two sophisticated but meaningful podcast projects. These need to take more than three weeks to develop, and should require group work cooperation. The complete project can be recognized or shared with the public. For example, the podcast project can be related to improving the ability of students to report on significant events of their school.

Finally, even though language instructors often design course activities based on learning styles commonly associated with geographic characteristics, they must not fall into the trap of cultural stereotyping. Teachers must take into account the individuality and uniqueness of each learner. Geographic characteristics can only provide references and guidance as a starting point, but not absolute answers to questions concerning learning styles. Each learner is unique and behaves differently, so teachers should observe these differences in order to adopt suitable instructional approaches and online homework (podcast) assignments. Language teachers should survey students' learning styles (i.e. group or individual; audio or visual) at the beginning of each course.

## CHALLENGES AND SOLUTIONS

Web 2.0 and Mobile 2.0 have become the terms that enterprises use to attract more users/consumers. Because of the increasing use of Web 2.0 and Mobile 2.0 tools, service providers (commercial enterprises) have become known and have gained sufficient profit to be able to provide better tools and services to customers. Because of this kind of close connection between consumers and providers, users can benefit from competition among commercial providers. Podcasts, blogs, and wikis encompass user-friendly and participatory platforms. Language learners and teachers

become frequent users because individualized and interactive instructional environments are developed. Instructors and learners no longer need to worry about writing complicated programming languages or codes (e.g., Javascript®, html, xml, php, etc.). Users are content contributors, developers, and managers. This kind of user-friendly phenomenon can greatly reduce the workload of language instructors, who can easily search (Google) and choose suitable Web 2.0/Mobile 2.0 tools for specific disciplines. This global, consumer-led market has already proven to be of benefit to consumers all over the world.

However, while consumers are eagerly catching the new waves of technology trends, there are several issues of social media to consider, for language teachers: the economic aspects, technical support and training, pedagogy and teachers' roles, and feedback and evaluation.

## Economic Aspects

Most Web 2.0 and Mobile 2.0 commercial products are dominated by service providers who gain profit by accumulating more users. Even though many Web 2.0 sites (learning environments) are free to access, quite a few of them require memberships in order to utilize the comprehensive functions or features of web pages and tools. Nevertheless, creating or procuring an institute- or college-wide (custom-made) Web 2.0 environment can be costly. Moreover, setting up network or wireless infrastructures can also be pricey, requiring an institution to utilize the services of commercial network providers and/or hire in-house technicians to set up internal network servers and connections. Institutes and schools should be careful to examine the proposal for their complete technology-enhanced setup.

As to hardware equipment, desktop and laptop computers are expensive. Mobile devices are less costly. However, "[t]he cost-effectiveness of mobile learning is important" (Leung & Chan, 2003, p. 79). The iPod Touch and iPhones can be affordable, for most academic institutions. iPod Touch can utilize a school-wide wireless network, but it cannot access that network in a non-wireless environment. Learning applications previously loaded onto an iPod Touch can be accessed ubiquitously. Vincent (2009) stated his favorite handheld device is the iPod Touch, which (at the time of writing) had over 85,000 applications. The iPhone can also download thousands of applications and appears to be an ideal learning tool that allows access to the Internet at any time and place. However, additional derivative monthly expenses for iPhones include service fees for unlimited texting and voice service (Cassavoy, n.d.). And more costs can be expected when newer versions of the devices come along. Apple updates portable media devices approximately once every one or two years. The devices can rapidly become obsolete, or can require updates. The cost can result in financial burden to parents, students, and schools. To remedy this, Ramasubbu and Wilcox (2009, para.12) suggested that "schools can also negotiate favorably priced voice plans that are affordable to parents and the total cost of ownership to the school should only include the cost of the device itself, the learning management system implementation and the network infrastructure on campus." By suggesting this, they are attempting to make "smartphones a competitive one-to-one learning solution" (Ramasubbu & Wilcox, para. 13). Newer technologies are definitely not a cheap lunch. This has become a great challenge that each educational institution will increasingly encounter.

Schools or districts can negotiate with manufacturers for a special educational price. For example, one-to-one computing (a computer for every student) has been initiated by many companies (such as Apple Computer, Microsoft, and Dell). Of course, school administration needs to be involved, in order to obtain better deals and adequate support. Manufacturers may also be willing to produce more equipment with less capacity and functionality, but which can perform required, education-related tasks. If the schools can make

the equipment available, teachers' willingness to introduce podcasts in language class will be enhanced. If students can use the same equipment and software, it will be easy for language instructors to design lesson plans and assign homework. In order to successfully implement podcasting to enhance language proficiency, it is suggested that every student have one device. The thought in doing this is that ubiquitous learning can provide more students with more opportunities to practice the language.

## Technical Support and Training

Newer technologies usually require additional training and technical support. Approximately 78% of the people between the ages of 18-34 in the United States have access to high-speed Internet service (Articlet, 2009). Twenty-two percent of American students don't have internet service, and are unable to access the internet at home. The percentage of iPhone or iPod Touch users is even lower, according the data in 2009. This figure can increase, and is expected to do so. To incorporate technology both in and out of the classrooms, school administrators will need to prepare budgets or workarounds for the cost issue. In addition, comprehensive training on the newest technologies should be provided, both to faculty and to students. On-site technicians may be needed, to troubleshoot device problems. Duke University's first-year experience report declared that the success of an iPod program (or podcast) can be highly affected by the lack of technical and administrative support (Blaisdell, 2006). Gruba et al. (2009) noted that the lack of technical support can thwart efforts to integrate podcasting into the classroom. Troubleshooting of technological problems can be time-consuming and crucial, but when technology does not work, it brings stress and setbacks to both teachers and students. Any unsolved technological problems can hinder the progress of classes. Bringing in technicians or technology specialists to assist faculty members may alleviate the stress. For example, the Defense Language Institute Foreign Language Center (DLIFLC) made efforts to address this barrier by employing more contract (on-site) technicians to troubleshoot all of the aspects of the technical problems involved in the implementation of iPod- and tablet PC-aided language learning. The scope of potential technical difficulties keeps expanding as new technologies come along.

Students and teachers should be properly trained to use podcasts, wikis, and blogs. In a 2007 study, Edirisingha, Rizzi, Nie, and Rothwell surmised that students' lack of familiarity with technologies such as podcasts can be a reason for the low level of students listening to podcasts. Unfamiliarity with newer technologies can frighten learners and teachers. Since a new technology is similar to a new language, it can take a certain amount of time for users to acquire a basic comfort level. In addition, teachers should be trained in how to integrate pedagogy, content, and technology in order to present effective instructional environments. Working with technology can increase a teacher's workload, especially in the time-consuming process of becoming familiar with basic and advanced features of new technological tools. In this case, the school administration can organize more hands-on technology training workshops or showcases. Follow-up and on-site support to teachers after the workshop appears to be needed, because more questions and concerns almost always arise when users are applying newly-learned knowledge in an educational context. If it is possible, successful execution awards can be arranged to encourage faculty to employ technologies learned in the workshops.

Even though schools are filled with technologically savvy students nowadays, non-technologically savvy students should be considered, too. Language teachers can invite technology savvy students to serve as volunteers to provide assistance to technical novices. Facilitation or mini-training should be also made available for students; an orientation or preliminary technology training for students should be provided when the new technology is introduced. Most universities have a specific technology center with technology specialists or technicians. Students may visit technicians when they encounter any technological problems. Another issue of concern is that "students' language proficiency does not necessarily parallel their familiarity and proficiency with technology (Sturm, Kennell, McBride, & Kelly, 2009, p. 379). In other words, some students can be adept at technology but poor at academic achievement. It is important to keep in mind that technology should not be used for technology's sake. So, setting objectives for how learners will achieve and produce becomes critical.

## Pedagogy and Teachers' Roles

conducted a 2004 experimental study and found that a technology-based activity is more effective than a paper-based activity for constructing words from syllables. In their study, Zurita and Nussbaumw observed that students performed better and achieved higher test score improvement with the assistance of technology-based activities run by handheld devices (smartphones). The study confirmed that e-learning and m-learning can produce positive learning results. Sharples, Taylor, and Vavoula (2005) believed that current learning can be reconciled by using both technology and knowledge as instruments for prolific inquisition in a dynamic and mutually-supportive connection.

Project-based learning (PjBL) is "the use of classroom projects, intended to bring about deep learning, where students use technology and inquiry to engage with issues and questions that are relevant to their lives. These classroom projects are used to assess student's subject matter competence compared to traditional testing" ("Project-based learning," n.d., para. 1). PjBL is quite suitable to be adapted for podcasts, wikis, and blogs. As to instructional procedures, Liu et al. (2003) suggested that teachers guide students through the six following pedagogical phases in wireless learning environment: (1) preparing before the class, (2) introducing guidelines, (3) designing the topic and planning projects, (4) implementing group projects, (5) presenting and evaluating the ready-prepared peer-evaluation checklist on the mobile device, and (6) revising, sharing, and grading.

Web learning and mobile learning involve the organization of information and require distribution, since "knowledge management includes the capability to collect, archive, manage, evaluate, and distribute information across the learning community" (Leung & Chan, 2003, p. 79). Leung and Chan emphasized that there was central human interaction component needed to make knowledge management successful in e-learning and m-learning environments. They declared that "it is shortsighted to think mobile learning will substitute traditional classroom-based learning" (Leung & Chan, p. 80). They noted that people can interact with each other and develop contacts in face-to-face classrooms; in contrast, students in mobile learning environments spend more time processing information. But it is hoped that learners will "use technology as a tool for creative expression" (Thorne & Payne, 2005).

Pedagogical goals in the podcasting learning environment ought to use learners' input to keep the focus on application and production. It is essential that learner creation is encouraged. Instructors' workloads may be increased (because more time and effort is often required to design courses in a more versatile, collaborative, and meta-cognitive fashion). In Blaisdell's 2006 article, one professor stated that he would not continue to integrate iPods into his teaching because the administration did not recognize the workload implications, which can include three to four times more course preparation time. Gruba et al. (2009) echoed the notion that the most daunting barrier to integrating podcasting into courses is insufficient time. They surmised that the situation might be alleviated by reducing teaching hours, by implementing support and materials sharing among colleagues, and by reducing the complexity of learning activities. If a reduction in teaching hours is impracticable, recognition and rewards can be good methods for motivating change. Another suggestion is to address the additional course preparation workload caused by technology use by modifying faculty performance evaluation standards (Blaisdell). For example, technology use is recognized and included in the DLIFLC faculty evaluation standards. Furthermore, credits given toward promotion, increase of salary, and tenure can also be considered (Blaisdell).

Podcasting is primarily used for listening comprehension in second language learning because of the huge variety of free podcasts with authentic materials that are accessible. Podcasting is also widely deployed to teach oral communication. The combination of listening and speaking training, using podcasts, can benefit language learners.

However, one must not forget the importance of teaching students the best strategies for listening and speaking. The purpose of strategy is to be "goal-oriented" (Rost, 2002). Ducate and Lomicka (2009) recommended that the output approach—listening to and editing one's recordings, commenting on others' podcasts, and receiving feedback—is quite helpful in podcasting. To enhance learners' verbal language proficiency, instructors can incorporate awareness-raising training to elicit longer discourse. Nakatani (2005) found that students receiving strategy training engaged in longer utterances and significantly improved their oral proficiency, in comparison to students without strategy training. The strategy training utilized by Nakatani included strategies for both achievement (i.e. help-seeking, modified interaction, modified output, time-gaining, maintenance, and self-solving) and reduction (i.e. message abandonment, first-language-based, etc.). "Learners need to learn to recognize and analyze specific linguistic and sociolinguistic cues in order to comprehend and integrate input into their schemata" (Nakatani, p.87).

Five successful listening ability strategies for second language learners include: "(a) predicting information or ideas prior to listening, (b) making inferences from incomplete information based on prior knowledge, (c) monitoring one's own listening processes, (d) attempting to clarify areas of confusion, and (e) responding to what one has understood (Rost, 2002, p. 155). Meanwhile, teachers can instigate a purposeful listening approach by preparing comprehensive questions when podcast episodes are introduced to students. Rost (1991) suggested that learners' listening ability develops by focusing on meanings—with active attitudes and specific goals oriented from well-designed comprehensive questions. The use of comprehensive questions can encourage students to listen selectively and purposefully, instead of merely offering an unfocused review of listening materials in a single cursory session.

Since academic podcasts are already widely implemented in speaking practices (i.e. interviewing native speakers, recording personal reflections, reporting on specific subjects, etc.), instructors can encourage learners to design comprehension questions for their assigned podcast episodes. Thus, the students can interact with each other and can respond to each other's projects. However, language teachers should take heed of possible stress caused for their students by time-consuming assignments or by expectations at different proficiency levels. It is not uncommon for a class to consist of students with different proficiency levels. Listener performance is worst when students don't pay attention or when they are undergoing a lot of stress (Rost, 1991). Reiterating note-taking strategies or using materials that students have heard before can sometimes be helpful as students attempt to reduce stress and mental noise, as stated by Burgess and Head (2005). Moreover, Elkhafaifi (2005) noted that students perform better if question-previewing activities are presented before listening and if they are given repeated exposure to the same listening passages.

As to the content of podcast episodes, Stephen Krashen's input hypothesis principle can provide guidance. The input hypothesis principle, emphasizing acquisition, is based on the $i + 1$ level, that is, on teaching vocabulary, syntax, and so forth slightly above the learners' current level and thereby exposing learners to comprehensive input (Schütz, 2005; Rost, 2001). Several online language learning podcasts (i.e. ChinesePod, RussianPod101, etc.) provide basic, intermediate, and advanced listening materials for different proficiency levels. They can be utilized as supplemental language-enhanced materials to prepare students for higher level (i+1) activity. The more that students are exposed to materials which are slightly higher than their proficiency, the more vocabulary and grammatical patterns they learn. For a membership fee, commercial podcasts also provide PDF transcripts along with vocabulary lists and grammatical patterns of listening materials. By this means, language learners can enhance not only their listening skills, but also their reading ability. As Andrew (2008) stated, producing video podcasts is very time-consuming. By using supplemental commercial podcasts, language instructors can save time, since they don't have to produce their own podcast episodes. To customize the work, language instructors can arrange speaking assignments or projects based on reflection or analysis of certain podcast episodes. Incorporation of blogs or wikis with podcasts is highly recommended, in order to sufficiently elicit the learners' four language skills (reading, listening, speaking, and writing).

During the training process, it is common for some students to feel frustrated and to lose their motivation. Yet "motivation can lead to success; but success can also lead to motivation" (Johnson, 2001, p. 132). In order to assist students' success, it is crucial to keep students motivated. To maintain and protect motivation, teachers should foster learners' autonomy by using technology-based approaches with a facilitating style of instruction (Dörnyei, 2001). Podcasts can easily be subscribed to, and students can work with them on their computers or mobile devices. Students can also post their speaking assignments at any time. Podcasts not only can advance students' listening and speaking proficiency levels, but can also help them to maintain motivation. Although technology can motivate learners and promote autonomy, use of technology for teacher scaffolding and student progress monitoring toward autonomy are even more crucial uses of technology (Murray, 2005; Rüschoff & Ritter, 2001). Rüschoff and Ritter stated that the best learning results can be achieved if authentic materials and tasks are used. Rifkin (2005) suggested that an "immersion learning experience" might be a key to shatter the "ceiling effect" observed in some traditional classroom settings. Podcasts in any subject, category, and language are sufficient online, which makes it easy for language learners to immerse themselves in an exclusive target language environment. Nevertheless, podcasts should be thoughtfully incorporated into an existing curriculum, or podcasts can worsen a program (Blaisdell, 2006). For instance, Gruba et al. (2009) successfully blended podcasts as self-study and supplementary materials into curriculum situations that were relatively well-resourced and were flexible (instead of fixed). Podcasts can also be used as preview materials; if used in this way, class time for lecture can be reduced and more time can be allowed for content discussion and interactions among students and teachers (McCombs & Liu, 2007).

It is suggested that instructors spend enough time to perform quality assurance and to monitor the quality of students' contributions to podcast episodes. Teachers should also recognize that they are the course designers and information organizers who oversee the display and the structure of the interface (platform). Without question, teachers must constantly ensure that no copyright-prohibited items or postings are made to blogs, wikis, or podcast episodes, whether in the public or the private domain. Instructors may also have to play the role of the technology assistant who facilitates and guides students to be familiar with the new learning delivery methods.

## Feedback and Evaluation

Before deciding upon feedback and evaluation criteria, teachers should consider their pedagogical goals. They should ask themselves which is more important: the end product? Or the processes of developing learners' skills and knowledge? In other words, will the assessment be formative or summative? According to Garrison and Ehringhaus (2007), "formative assessment is part of instructional process…[it] informs both teachers and students about student understanding at a point when timely adjustments can be made" (p.1). Conversely, "summative assessment is done at the end of a course and provides information about the students' overall achievement" (Graves, 2000, p. 208). In podcast learning environments, the evaluation is primarily related to formative assessment and feedback. Learners' participation and their contributions to the content development play an important part in helping teachers to evaluate the progress of their students. Of course, (online) summative assessment can also be offered, to determine students' absorption and comprehension regarding the content being discussed.

In second language learning with podcasts, evaluating the students' progress toward language proficiency can be crucial. Evaluation standards and criteria should be determined prior to the giving of any assignments. Instructors should cautiously prepare standards for every blogging, wiki, or podcast episode. To be specific, they should focus on what specific language structures, forms, or vocabulary can best be used in connection with certain topics. Instructors should determine if the form of language or the flow of paragraphs is a focus. This list of requirements (perhaps even a developed rubric) for every posting or product should be detailed. As it is being developed, teachers can contemplate an effective feedback and correction system in order to rectify incorrect use of language forms. In language learning, the fossilized use of incorrect grammar or vocabulary has been criticized as a communicative approach. But communicative and collaborative approaches, along with other interactive learning approaches, are often adopted in an online learning environment. The possible fossilization can be found in podcast, blog, or wiki sites which have not undergone peer-review or instructors' in-time correction.

For podcast listening assignments, it is easier to assess students' listening comprehension ability by using multi-choice or open-ended questions online or in the classroom. For speaking assignments, teachers should prepare self- and peer-review checklists to help students accomplish the required podcast oral speaking assignments. The self-checklist can include the must-be-completed items or can elaborate upon the steps required to finish a task. This is to elicit best performance and to ensure that students produce podcast episodes with required content and quality. The peer-review checklist should require students to evaluate vocabulary, grammar, fluency, pronunciation, and delivery. Peer-review provides a chance for students to reflect on vocabulary and grammar usage. It also can be time-efficient and can require less instructor effort for grammar and vocabulary correction. After a period of time, instructors can easily notice the patterns of common errors and can discuss correct usage. Then, it will be easy for instructors to educate the class about the correct language usage. While peer-review is being conducted, teachers can spend an efficient time focusing on providing feedback concerning flow of paragraphs and offering holistic feedback to students' writing, audio-recording, and other projects.

Setting up specific rubrics for podcasting projects is necessary, and Gruba et al. (2009) agreed that measurement of progress is desired. The Center for Advanced Research on Language Acquisition (n.d.) listed several kinds of rubrics for second language assessment: (1) generic, (2) task-specific, (3) holistic, (4) analytic, (5) primary trait, and (6) multiple trait rubrics. For podcast projects, task-specific rubrics should be considered. "Task-specific rubrics are used with particular tasks, and their criteria and descriptors reflect specific features of the elicited performance" (Center for Advanced Research on Language Acquisition, n.d. para. 8). For example, if the podcast assignment requires learners to describe their unforgettable traveling experience, the rubric should include the use of past tense, form of delivery (narration), length and organization of content, etc. Standards for scoring criteria need to be noticeably listed in the table. The rubrics can provide guidance to help students to execute a desirable performance.

Holistic evaluation is also ideal to evaluate podcast episodes. Teachers can make judgments by "forming an overall impression of a performance and matching it to the best fit from among the descriptions on the scale" (Center for Advanced Research on Language Acquisition, n.d. para. 1). The advantage of the holistic evaluation is to focus on what students *can do* instead of what they *cannot do*. Each group of holistic rubrics contains several levels of performance. For example, the standard for an "A" performance for oral assessment can be set as "makes minimal errors, uses rich and varied vocabulary, speaks with excellent pronunciation, speaks smoothly without stopping, uses a variety of sentence structures" (Blaz, n.d.). Many sample rubrics can be found on the internet; therefore, language instructors need not feel compelled to develop tailor-made evaluation rubrics (criteria).

## FUTURE RESEARCH DIRECTIONS

Technology innovation has progressed at a rapid speed, and many business and academic disciplines have been greatly influenced and have benefited from these innovations. Web 2.0 and Mobile 2.0 have really become the new terms to describe a phenomenon in which users become participants in several websites and experience lifestyle changes.

The World Wide Web has become a virtual place for social connection and activities. Researchers have begun to document and experiment with ways in which the newer technologies have changed the ways in which we learn, live, and experience our lives. For example, teacher-centered instruction is being replaced by the learner-centered and self-regulated learning styles needed in online learning environments.

Future research directions will have to embrace the continuously developing technological products (e.g., 4G, WiMax broadband wireless data access, and Web 3.0) and associate them with pedagogy and content for education. WiMax is much better and faster than 3G, and it is claimed that 50% of the geography in Japan will be covered by WiMax by 2010 (Tiwari, 2010). Future wireless networks will likely be able to support large file downloading and a wide variety of online activities. Web 3.0 is a semantic and powerful web which uses artificial intelligence to provide guidance as it responds to users' searches ("Web 3.0 and beyond," 2007, para. 1). "Web 3.0 is about giving the internet itself a brain" ("Web 3.0 and beyond," para. 8). While commercial technology developers and providers offer newer technologies to enhance human life, educational practitioners and researchers should take heed of newer technologies to improve learning and teaching. New studies should be conducted to evaluate the effectiveness of the newer technologies in order to understand the ways that they change the way we teach and learn.

Moreover, the newer technologies will continue to generate consumer expectation and satisfaction. Mobile technology makes network connection possible anywhere. Future research can consider students' achievements and performance as assisted by mobile technology. If possible, experts teaching with podcasts and mobile technology should be studied. Furthermore, researchers should inquire into how mobile technology changes the way in which students learn (meta-cognitive and higher-order thinking) and the ways in which instructors teach.

Researches can be conducted to evaluate the amount of time that teachers invest in the creation of podcasting learning environments versus resultant student achievements in various educational contexts. Evaluation and assessment criteria are different in various educational systems and institutions. For example, high school administrators face pressure to keep students' Scholastic Aptitude Test (SAT) scores high; universities might focus more on students' production, creation, and publications. Podcasts, wikis, and blogs should be suitable tools for eliciting improvement of student ability with respect to listening, reading, writing, and speaking. Researchers can investigate students' contributions through podcasts, blogs, and wikis versus test scores to indicate students' progress in language proficiency.

## CONCLUSION

The world is intertwined and closely connected through Web 2.0 social networking web sites, which enable users around the world to learn and interact in a variety of ways. The boundaries and limitations for information, knowledge, and life sharing are rapidly disappearing. Due to the promising advertising profit, industries will continue to invest in more advanced and versatile products (web sites) which can assist learning, entertainment (games and activities), and commercial marketing. Interrelated Web 2.0 platforms and Mobile 2.0 applications will continue to develop to meet the demand of the market. Wireless networks will continue to expand, until network access is provided anywhere and anytime. Learning is and will continue to be ubiquitous, with diminishing limitations. The consumer-led and learner-directed environments will continue to direct development in both industries and academia. The online (network) enterprise will attract more participants, will generate more profit, and will develop more user-friendly products. This kind of mutually-beneficial cycle is likely to result in closer global interaction.

There is no doubt that the newer technologies are moving forward toward interfaces that are more user-friendly, with a higher adaptability to fit individual needs. New technologies also realize individuality and personalization. Language educators can take advantage of this new movement, utilizing these new technologies to economically and smoothly help their students to reach higher levels of language proficiency. Following the escalating wave of technology inventions, one must carefully screen suitable technologies and overcome challenges for instructional purposes. Newer technology, social network connections with native speakers, and the ownership of blogs and podcasts can motivate language learners. But at the same time, these new technologies can overwhelm some learners. When one is exposed to too much information at one time, he or she can lose focus. The teacher's role must be to direct students toward educational objectives by providing detailed criteria and course guidelines, and disseminating them to students before they waste undue time on dead ends or indulge in irrelevant online games, entertainments, or information.

It is also expected that the future development of mobile technology will entail the inception of more powerful applications. Easily used and versatile web applications will make it convenient for users to create personalized and interesting activities. With the prevalence of 3G and other wireless access, Mobile 2.0 is likely to continue to grow at a rapid rate. And it is expected that the number of challenges associated with adopting new technologies will continue to arise; however, new solutions for effective adoption are also likely to be developed, in order to overcome obstacles.

In summary, this chapter is not meant to discourage use of technology in teaching. The purpose of raising any concern is to provide suggestions to overcome challenges. At the same time, edu-

cators should not naïvely assume that students' performance will automatically improve if new technologies are utilized. Oppenheimer (2003) cautioned educators that misapplied technologies can actually cause deterioration in student academic achievement. Educators must understand the technologies that they use, because students lean on instructor expertise when technical problems are encountered. For example, if students can't successfully upload podcast episodes, teachers should be the first to be consulted, in order to find ways to resolve the problem and keep their students' learning on-track.

The learning objectives for student achievement and pedagogy remain the same, even though technology is progressing rapidly. Academic podcasting is merely a different and convenient form of delivering sound and video files, hopefully within the context of a sound basic pedagogical scheme. Through RSS feeds and user-friendly interfaces, students and teachers can have easy access to course content. But the pedagogical goals involved in language learning should remain the preeminent priority.

# REFERENCES

Andrew, M. (2008). Student evaluation of video podcasts to augment live lectures in pharmaceutical microbiology. In *Proceedings of the 3rd International Blended Learning Conference: Enhancing the student experience* (pp. 272-282). Hertfordshire, 18-19 April. http://hlsweb.dmu.ac.uk/staff/mhea/blu/Andrew_BLU_conference_paper.pdf

Articlet. (2009, August 4). *Over 57 percent of American homes have access to high-speed internet service*. Retrieved August 28, 2009, from http://articlet.com/article791.html

Augar, N., Raitman, R., & Zhou, W. (2004). Teaching and learning online with wikis. In R. Atkinson, C. McBeath, D. Jonas-Dwyer & R. Phillips (Eds.), *Beyond the comfort zone: Proceedings of the 21st ASCILITE Conference* (pp. 95-104). Perth, 5-8 December. http://www.ascilite.org.au/conferences/perth04/procs/augar.html

Blaisdell, M. (2006, February 28). *Special double feature! Academic MP3s: Is it iTime yet?* Retrieved March 20, 2010 from Campus Technology website: http://campustechnology.com/articles/2006/02/special-double-feature-academic-mp3s--is-it-itime-yet.aspx

Blaz, B. (n.d.). *Steps in creating authentic and performance-based assessment tasks.* Retrieved March 20, 2010 from NC Standard Course of Study website: http://www.ncpublicschools.org/curriculum/secondlanguages/resources/orallanguages/05tools?&print=true

Boulos, M., Maramba, I., & Wheeler, S. (2006). Wikis, blogs and podcasts: A new generation of web-based tools for virtual collaborative clinical practice and education. *BMC Medical Education.* Retrieved from http://www.biomedcentral.com/1472-6920/6/41# doi. .doi:10.1186/1472-6920-6-41

Brown, D. (2001). *Teaching by principles: An interactive approach to language pedagogy* (2nd ed.). New York: Addison Wesley Longman.

Burgess, S., & Head, K. (2005). *How to teach for exams.* Essex, UK: Pearson Education Ltd.

Carney, N. (2009). Blogging in foreign language education. In Thomas, M. (Ed.), *Web 2.0 and second language learning* (pp. 292–312). Hershey, PA: Information Science Reference.

Cassavoy, L. (n.d.). *How much does an iPhone cost to buy and use.* Retrieved August 28, 2009, from About website: http://smartphones.about.com/od/smartphonebasics/f/iphone_cost.htm

Center for Advanced Research on Language Acquisition. (n.d.). *Process: Types of rubrics.* Retrieved March 20, 2010, from University of Minnesota website: http://www.carla.umn.edu/assessment/VAC/Evaluation/p_6.html

Chinnery, G. (2006). Emerging technologies going to the MALL: Mobile assisted language learning. *Language Learning & Technology, 10*(1), 9-16. Retrieved October 18, 2009, from http://llt.msu.edu/vol10num1/emerging/

Clough, G., Jones, A., McAndrew, G., & Scanlon, E. (2009). Inform learning evidence in online communities of mobile device enthusiasts. In M. Alley (Ed.), *Mobile learning: Transforming the delivery of education and training* (pp. 99-112). Edmonton, AG: Au Press.

Dale, C. (2007). Strategies for using podcasting to support student learning. *Journal of Hospitality, Leisure, Sport and Tourism Education, 6*(1), 49–57. .doi:10.3794/johlste.61.155

Digital Inspiration. (2008, April 24). *Social media survey highlights differences between US and Asia.* Retrieved October 22, 2009, from http://www.labnol.org/internet/blogging/social-media-survey-highlights-differences-between-us-and-asia/3065/

Dörnyei, Z. (2001). *Motivational strategies in the language classroom.* Cambridge, UK: Cambridge University Press. doi:10.1017/CBO9780511667343

Ducate, L., & Lomicka, L. (2009). Podcasting: An effective tool for honing language students' pronunciation? *Language Learning & Technology, 13*(3), 66–86. Retrieved from http://llt.msu.edu/vol13num3/ducatelomicka.pdf.

Duffy, P., & Bruns, A. (2006). The use of blogs, wikis and RSS in education: A conversation of possibilities. In *Proceedings of the Online Learning and Teaching Conference 2006.* Retrieved from https://olt.qut.edu.au/udf/OLT2006/gen/static/papers/Duffy_OLT2006_paper.pdf

Edirisingha, P., Rizzi, C., Nie, M., & Rothwell, L. (2007). Podcasting to provide teaching and learning support for an undergraduate module on English language and communication. *Turkish Online Journal of Distance Education, 8*(3), 87–107.

Elkhafaifi, H. (2005). The effect of prelistening activities on listening comprehension in Arabic learners. *Foreign Language Annals, 38*(4), 505–513. doi:10.1111/j.1944-9720.2005.tb02517.x

Feyten, C. (1991). The power of listening: An overlooked dimension in language acquisition. *Modern Language Journal, 75,* 173–180. doi:10.2307/328825

Garrison, C., & Ehringhaus, M. (2007). Formative and summative assessments in the classroom. Retrieved from http://www.nmsa.org/Publications/WebExclusive/Assessment/tabid/1120/Default.aspx

Gilmore, D. (2004). *We the media: Grassroots journalism by the people, for the people.* Sebastopol, CA: O'Reilly Media, Inc.

Godwin-Jones, R. (2003). Emerging technologies: Blogs and wikis environments for on-line collaboration. *Language Learning & Technology, 7*(2), 12–16.

Graves, K. (2000). *Designing language courses: A guide for teachers.* New York: Heinle & Heinle Thomson Learning.

Gruba, P., Clark, C., Ng, K., & Wells, M. (2009). Blending technologies in second language courses: A reflexive enquiry. In *Same places, different spaces. Proceedings ascilite Auckland 2009.* http://www.ascilite.org.au/conferences/auckland09/procs/gruba.pdf

Guy, T. (2009, August). *Research shows Asians use PDA/Smartphone for online communication more than Americans/Europeans.* Retrieved October 22, 2009, from Bloggersbase website: http://www.bloggersbase.com/internet/research-shows-asians-use-pdasmartphone-for-online-communication-than-americanseuropeans/

Harris, H., & Park, S. (2008). Education usages of podcasting. *British Journal of Educational Technology, 39*(3), 548–551. .doi:10.1111/j.1467-8535.2007.00788.x

Huann, T. Y., & Thong, M. K. (2006). *Audioblogging and podcasting in education.* Retrieved October 18, 2009, from Education Ministry: Government of Singapore website: http://iresearch.edumall.sg/iresearch/slot/u110/litreviews/audioblogg_podcast.pdf

Huffaker, D. (2005). The educated blogger: Using weblogs to promote literacy in the classroom. *AACE Journal, 13*(2), 91–98.

Jaokar, A. (2006). *Ajit Jaokar's mobile Web 2.0 blog: What is "Mobile Web 2.0"?* Retrieved October 18, 2009, from Web2journal website: http://web2.sys-con.com/node/251673

Johnson, K. (2001). *An introduction to foreign language learning and teaching.* London: Pearson Education Limited.

Leung, C., & Chan, Y. (2003). Mobile learning: A new paradigm in electronic learning. In *Proceeding of 3rd IEEE International Conference on Advanced Learning Technology* (pp. 76-80).

Lim, D. H. (2004). Cross cultural differences in online learning motivation. *Educational Media International, 41*(2), 163–175. doi:10.1080/09523980410001685784

Liu, T. C., Wang, H. Y., Liang, J. K., Chan, T. W., Ko, H. W., & Yang, J. C. (2003). Wireless and mobile technologies to enhance teaching and learning. *Journal of Computer Assisted Learning, 19,* 371–382. doi:10.1046/j.0266-4909.2003.00038.x

Mattison, D. (2003). Quickiwiki, swiki, twiki, zwiki and the plone wars: Wiki as a PIM and collaborative content tool. *Searcher, 11*(4), 32–48.

McCombs, S., & Liu, Y. (2007). The efficacy of podcasting technology in instructional delivery. *International Journal of Technology in Teaching and Learning, 3*(2), 123–134.

McLoughlin, C., & Lee, M. (2007). Listen and learn: A systematic review of the evidence that podcasting supports learning in higher education. In C. Montgomerie & J. Seale (Eds.), *Proceedings of World Conference on Educational Multimedia, Hypermedia and Telecommunications 2007* (pp. 1669-1677). Chesapeake, VA: AACE.

*Mobile phone adoption in developing countries.* (n.d.). Retrieved November 25, 2009, from wikiinvest website: http://www.wikinvest.com/concept/Mobile_Phone_Adoption_in_Developing_Countries

Mooij, M. K. (2004). *Consumer behavior and culture: Consequences for global marketing and advertising.* Thousand Oaks, CA: Sage Publications Inc.

Murray, D. (2005). Technologies for second language. *Annual Review of Applied Linguistics, 25,* 188–201. doi:10.1017/S0267190505000103

Murray, L., Hourigan, T., & Jeanneau, C. (2007). Blog writing integration for academic language learning purposes: Towards an assessment framework. *IBÉRICA, 14,* 9–32.

Nakatani, Y. (2005). The effects of awareness-raising training on oral communication strategy use. *Modern Language Journal, 89,* 76–91. doi:10.1111/j.0026-7902.2005.00266.x

Nathan, P., & Chan, A. (2007). Engaging undergraduates with podcasting in a business subject. In *ICT: Providing choices for learners and learning. Proceedings ascilite Singapore 2007.* Retrieved from http://www.ascilite.org.au/conferences/singapore07/procs/nathan.pdf

O'Reilly, T. (2005). *What is Web 2.0: Design patterns and business models for the next generation of software.* Retrieved September 28, 2009, from O'Reilly Media website: http://oreilly.com/web2/archive/what-is-web-20.html

Oppenheimer, T. (2003). *The flickering mind.* New York: Random House.

Park, C. (2006). Learning style preferences of Asian American (Chinese, Filipino, Korean, and Vietnamese) students in secondary schools. In Park, C., Endo, R., & Goodwin, A. L. (Eds.), *Asian and Pacific American education: Learning, socialization, and identity* (pp. 77–97). Scottsdale, AZ: Information Age Publishing.

Parker, K., & Chao, J. (2007). Wiki as a teaching tool, interdisciplinary. *Journal of Knowledge and Learning Objects, 3,* 57–72.

Peng, S. S., & Wright, D. (1994). Explanation of academic achievement of Asian American students. *The Journal of Educational Research, 87*(6), 346–352. doi:10.1080/00220671.1994.9941265

Phifer, L. (2009, August 10). *3G.* Retrieved October 18, 2009, from Search Telecom website: http://searchtelecom.techtarget.com/sDefinition/0,sid103_gci214486,00.html

Pieri, M., & Diamantini, D. (2009). From e-learning to mobile learning: New opportunities. In M. Alley (Ed.), *Mobile learning: Transforming the delivery of education and training* (pp. 99-112). Edmonton, AG: Au Press.

*Podcast.* (n.d.). Retrieved October 28, 2009, from PC Magazine Encyclopedia website: http://www.pcmag.com/encyclopedia_term/0,2542,t=podcast&i=49433,00.asp

Project-based learning. (n.d.). In *Wikipedia.* Retrieved November 27, 2009, from http://en.wikipedia.org/wiki/Project-based_learning

Purdie, N., & Hattie, J. (1996). Cultural differences in the use of strategies for self-regulated learning. *American Educational Research Journal, 33*(4), 845–871.

Ramasubbu, S., & Wilcox, B. (2009, January 8). *Mobile learning in classrooms of the future.* Retrieved November 25, 2009, from Converge website: http://www.convergemag.com/edtech/Mobile-Learning-in-Classrooms-of-the-Future.html.

Rifkin, B. (2005). A ceiling effect in traditional classroom foreign language instruction: Data from Russian. *Modern Language Journal, 89*, 3–18. doi:10.1111/j.0026-7902.2005.00262.x

Rost, M. (1991). *Listening in action.* Englewood Cliffs, NJ: Prentice Hall International (UK) Ltd.

Rost, M. (2001). Listening. In Ronald, R., & Nunan, D. (Eds.), *Guide to teaching English to speakers of other languages* (pp. 7–13). Cambridge, UK: Cambridge University Press. doi:10.1017/CBO9780511667206.002

Rost, M. (2002). *Teaching and researching listening.* Essex, UK: Pearson Education Ltd.

Rüschoff, B., & Ritter, M. (2001). Technology-enhanced language learning: Construction of knowledge and template-based learning in the foreign language classroom. *Computer Assisted Language Learning, 14*, 219–232. doi:10.1076/call.14.3.219.5789

Schütz, R. (2005). *Stephen Krashen's theory of second language acquisition.* Retrieved March 12, 2010, from http://perso.univ-lyon2.fr/~giled/050801Stephen%20Krashen's%20Theory.htm

Schwartz, L., Sharon Clark, S., Cossarin, M., & Rudolph, J. (2003). Educational wikis: Features and selection criteria. *Language Learning & Technology, 7*(2), 12–16.

Sharples, M., Taylor, J., & Vavoula, G. (2005). Towards a theory of mobile learning. Paper presented at *mLearn* 2005, Capetown South Africa. Retrieved from http://www.mlearn.org.za/CD/papers/Sharples- Theory of Mobile.pdf

Stevick, E. W. (1989). *Success with Foreign Languages: Seven who achieved it and what worked for them.* New York: Prentice Hall.

Sturm, M., Kennell, T., McBride, R., & Kelly, M. (2009). The pedagogical implications of Web 2.0. In Thomas, M. (Ed.), *Web 2.0 and second language learning* (pp. 367–384). Hershey, PA: Information Science Reference.

Swartz, J. (2009, October 21). *Marketers salivating over smartphone potential.* Retrieved October 31, 2009, from USA Today website: http://www.usatoday.com/tech/news/2009-10-20-social-network-smartphone_N.htm

Thorne, S. L., & Payne, S. J. (2005). Evolutionary trajectories, internet mediated expression, and language education. *CALICO Journal, 22*(3), 371–397. Retrieved from http://language.la.psu.edu/~thorne/thorne_payne_calico2005.pdf.

Tiwari, B. (2010, March 2). *Exciting time for WiMAX and LTE in Japan.* Retrieved March 12, 2010, from WiMax 360 website: http://wimax-community.ning.com/profiles/blogs/exciting-time-for-wimax-and

Vincent, T. (2009, October 6). *Create it in your hand, share it with the world.* Retrieved November 25, 2009, from Learning in Hand website: http://learninginhand.com/blog/2009/10/create-it-in-your-hand-share-it-with.html

Viswanathan, R. (2009). Using mobile technology and podcasts to teach soft skills. In Thomas, M. (Ed.), *Web 2.0 and second language learning* (pp. 223–235). Hershey, PA: Information Science Reference.

Waele, R. D. (2006). *Understanding Mobile 2.0.* Retrieved October 18, 2009, from Read Write Web website: http://www.readwriteweb.com/archives/understanding_mobile_2.php

Wang, S., & Heffernan, N. (2009). Mobile 2.0 and mobile language learning. In Thomas, M. (Ed.), *Web 2.0 and second language learning* (pp. 472–490). Hershey, PA: Information Science Reference.

*Web 3.0 and beyond: The next 20 years of the internet.* (2007, October 24). Retrieved March 12, 2010, from Times Online website: http://technology.timesonline.co.uk/tol/news/tech_and_web/the_web/article2726190.ece

*What is WiMax?* (n.d.). Retrieved November 27, 2009, from WiMax website: http://www.wimax.com/education

Young, J. (n.d.). *Mobile Phone Adoption in Developing Countries.* Retrieved March 12, 2010, from Wikinvest website: http://www.wikinvest.com/concept/Mobile_Phone_Adoption_in_Developing_Countries

Zurita, G., & Nussbaumw, M. (2004). A constructivist mobile learning environment supported by a wireless handheld network. *Journal of Computer Assisted Learning, 20,* 235–243. doi:10.1111/j.1365-2729.2004.00089.x

## KEY TERMS AND DEFINITIONS

**3G/4G:** 3G is "the third generation of mobile telephony (that is, cellular) technology to facilitate growth, increase bandwidth, and support more diverse applications. 3G can support mobile multimedia applications and deliver packet-switched data with better spectral efficiency, at far greater speeds" (Phifer, 2009, para. 1). 4G is the fourth generation of cellular wireless standards. It entails higher data transfer speeds than 3G.

**Community of Practice (COP):** A COP is an informal network which allows small groups of people to work together and share knowledge and experience through wide-ranging communication. The purpose of a COP is to enhance understanding and extensive knowledge of certain aspects and disciplines.

**WiMax:** WiMax is also called broadband wireless access, and is also known as IEEE 802.16. WiMax can provide a wider range of broadband wireless access than WiFi/802.11. "WiMAX is a second-generation protocol that allows for more efficient bandwidth use, interference avoidance, and is intended to allow higher data rates over longer distances" ("What is WiMax?" n.d., para. 3).

# Section 2
# Student Centered Projects

# Chapter 6

# Mobile–Assisted Language Learning from the Student Perspective:
## Encouraging Effective Language Learning Strategies Outside of the Classroom

**Daryl L. Beres**
*Mount Holyoke College, USA*

## ABSTRACT

*This chapter seeks to refocus the conversation about mobile-assisted language learning (MALL) from the instructor's perspective to the student's. I argue that mobile "teaching" does not need to be located within a course, but that we are "m-teaching" whenever we encourage or enable learners to use mobile devices "to facilitate, support, enhance and extend ... [their] learning" (Attewell, Savill-Smith, & Douch, 2009, p. 1). This chapter will explore important concerns related to this definition, including conceptions of learning, blurred boundaries between personal and educational lives, the affordances and limitations of mobile devices, and learner autonomy. A look at the m-learning research literature will show students' perceptions of MALL running the gamut from skeptics to believers. Finally, the chapter reports on the long-term investigation of learner beliefs and practices of MALL which is underway at Mount Holyoke College, and offers five initial conclusions.*

## INTRODUCTION

Mobile devices are ubiquitous in today's society, and college-aged students are adept at using them, for certain purposes. Rarely will college students be parted from their cell phones, and impressive is the speed at which they can text. Although students may carry their iPhones® at all times,

comfortably texting friends, playing games, and posting profile updates, will they explore the iTunes® application directory for language learning "apps" (applications)? And if they do, will they select apps that they can effectively integrate into their language-learning processes? Do they understand, beyond a general familiarity, what podcasts are and why they might be useful? And if they have subscribed to podcasts in the target language, will they utilize them in a manner that

DOI: 10.4018/978-1-60960-141-6.ch006

will be successful in advancing their language proficiency?

Second language teachers and researchers have lauded the potential of mobile-assisted language learning (MALL). Smart phones and MP3 players can become language learning tools, allowing students to easily and immediately access materials from a variety of sources and to engage with those materials where and when they please. Mobile devices are highly portable; are designed to work with text, images, audio, and video; are able to connect with other devices and with the Internet; and can function as miniature computers, running software applications and storing data, but costing much less. These characteristics afford a range of learning strategies known to be effective for language acquisition: breaking larger study activities into smaller chunks distributed over time (Chinnery, 2006), differentiation and individualization of instruction (Huizenga, Admiraal, Akkerman, & ten Dam, 2009), and allowing learners to study at their own pace (Cooney & Keogh, 2007). In essence, mobile devices allow us to extend language learning outside of the classroom in new ways, "freeing our students from their usual language lab assignment routine" (Sathe & Waltje, 2008, p. 32).

In response to the concern that "a new generation of pupils is largely being educated with old paradigms and methods" (Huizenga et al., 2009, p. 332), researchers have begun to investigate m-learning (mobile-learning) in general and MALL in particular. This growing body of literature largely reflects the teacher's perspective, building an empirical basis by which to answer questions such as: how can I effectively integrate m-learning activities into the design of my language course? Without denying the importance of this work, the present chapter will attempt to re-focus the conversation on the opposite side of the teaching-learning partnership. While m-learning can be seen as a supplement to the traditional classroom or as a medium for distance-education, we will look at the ways in which students choose to integrate MALL into their daily lives and study routines:

"The challenge lies in using mobile technologies well, both as an enhancer in the classroom and to bridge arenas that are usually referred to as separate—such as school and free time" (Mifsud, 2003, p. 103).

This chapter will survey the current literature on academic podcasting technology and MALL, asking what is known about how students perceive these technologies and how students choose to incorporate MALL in their personal process of learning a second language. It will also report initial results of an investigation underway at Mount Holyoke College, which seeks to answer the following questions:

1.  What MALL strategies do students find most effective for language learning?
2.  Why do students prefer these strategies?
3.  What support can a language resource center and language faculty provide to result in a greater number of students effectively applying MALL strategies?

## DEFINITIONS

M-learning can be defined as "the exploitation of ubiquitous handheld technologies, together with wireless and mobile phone networks, to facilitate, support, enhance and extend the reach of teaching and learning" (Attewell et al., 2009, p. 1). One of the touted benefits of m-learning is that it allows learning any time and anywhere, implying an exclusion of the times and locations in which learning has traditionally taken place. Indeed, much of the research investigating m-learning has been situated within distance- or blended-learning environments, in which the teachers and students may not have frequent (or any) face-to-face contact. This chapter will not follow a strict definition requiring the learner to be mobile. Instead, exploring Attewell et al.'s definition, the goal is to question how mobile devices can "facilitate, support, enhance and extend the reach of … learning" into students' lives outside of the classroom.

The accepted terminology of "m-learning" (but only rarely "m-teaching" or "m-instruction") puts the focus on the learners, perhaps assuming that these "handheld technologies" will largely be in the learners' hands (Kukulska-Hulme & Traxler, 2005). Nonetheless, much of the current research literature discusses m-learning as it is designed and structured by teachers. Having evolved beyond the nascency of show-and-tell-type "here is a new technology I'm using" reports, a current trend in the m-learning literature is a call for more careful instructional design, based on proven principles of effective pedagogy (e.g., Chinnery, 2006). More appropriate design will avoid translating less-than-optimal practices from the traditional classroom to a new mobile format: "Effective use of new technology requires an evaluation of current pedagogy and a move towards interactive and collaborative teaching and learning activities" (Maltby & Mackie, 2009, p. 50). Nonetheless, Kukulska-Hulme and Traxler (2005) offer a broader definition of "m-teaching" as simply the "facilitation and support of mobile learning" (p. 25), which we have found useful in framing our work. In other words, "m-teaching" is not limited to developing and integrating mobile activities, assignments, or assessments into a course curriculum. Instead, we are engaging in "m-teaching" when we encourage or enable learners to apply mobile strategies to achieve their personal learning goals, whether it be acing the traditional pen-and-paper vocabulary quiz or gradually moving closer to a native-like accent.

Working within this conception of "m-teaching," our question then becomes: how can we effectively support m-learning? A first step toward accomplishing this end is to better understand our learners. Beliefs about teaching typically can be characterized by a continuum from "content transmission" (the metaphor of the student as a sausage skin to be stuffed with knowledge) to "facilitating understanding" (the metaphor of the student as an oyster to be coaxed open revealing the pearl within). On the end toward content transmission, teachers may take a didactic approach to m-learning, focusing on mobile access to content and resources. A more discursive approach, taking advantage of the capabilities of mobile devices for communication and interaction (Kukulska-Hulme & Traxler, 2005), may appeal to teachers on the opposite end of the spectrum. Similarly, we should consider the conceptions of teaching and learning espoused by our students; at the college level, they are likely to have been influenced by the classrooms in which they have been immersed through their educational career. Although we may believe that "the skills of constructing and exploring knowledge, conversing and collaborating with peers, and the ability to control one's own learning are fundamental requirements of effective learning" (Sharples, 2003, p. 7), our students may feel more comfortable with a much more didactic approach.

An additional consideration is the inherent blurring of lines between our students' personal and educational lives that an m-learning approach can entail. Learners' reactions to this intrusion can be expected to vary with personality and learning style: "There is always a possibility that mobile phone users will see any educationally motivated use of this technology as an unwanted incursion into their own personal, social space, and as a result, would strongly reject this kind of usage" (Levy & Kennedy, 2005, p. 76). This seems to be a unique development in m-learning, as mobile devices are felt to be more private than previous technologies, such as desktop computers (Kukulska-Hulme & Traxler, 2005).

Finally, we must examine the capabilities and constraints of the mobile technologies that we hope learners will exploit. In the realm of language learning, some devices or m-learning strategies may apply particularly well to one domain of language acquisition or another. For example, Levy and Kennedy (2005) studied text messaging for vocabulary learning because the medium of texting afforded spaced (as opposed to massed) repetition, a proven technique from memory research. However, the affordances resulting from the characteristics of a device will also tend to bias learners toward certain modes of use, which may or may not be an ideal match for their learning styles or goals (Luckin et al., 2005). We need to be sure that these implicit affordances are made visible, so that decisions about use are rightly based upon learning goals and learner needs. Clearly, these considerations will be closely intertwined with understanding students' beliefs: "It is students' perception of their environment rather than its objective reality that impacts learning" (Willis, 1993, as cited in Maltby & Mackie, 2009, p. 51). Thus we must be aware not only of the objective capabilities of the mobile devices in question, but also of our students' subjective perception of how the devices might support their learning (Kukulska-Hulme & Traxler, 2005).

## STUDENT PERCEPTIONS OF MALL

### The Skeptics

Although the potential of m-learning appeals to many educators and researchers, it is not always clear whether students share these views. For example, during the 2004-2005 academic year, Duke University achieved fame for its "iPod® First-Year Experience," in which over 1600 entering students were given an iPod and over 40 courses were reported to have integrated some academic use of the devices (Belanger, 2005b). Students provided positive feedback about the project, with 85% rating the project 5 or higher on a scale of 1-10, but many commented that they liked the iPods for personal reasons (Belanger, 2005a). The program evaluation noted that 75% of the students reported some academic use of their iPod, and about 50% of these were not enrolled in a course which formally integrated the iPods (Belanger, 2005b). However, "us[ing] at least 1

feature of the iPod" (p. 2) for their studies is not a particularly stringent metric for a year-long project in which students were given free devices. The open-ended comments from students run the gamut from very positive to very negative:

*The Duke iPod experiment was unsuccessful in my opinion... I don't even know what they thought we were going to use the iPods for. That's not to say that I'm not very appreciative of my iPod, because I definitely am. I think iPods are amazing, just not for school-related work. (Belanger, 2005a, p. 19)*

*At the beginning, it was hard to see just how I was going to use the iPod, but I quickly found it becoming an attachment to my body. (p. 23)*

*It can serve beneficial academic purposes for those who chose to use it that way. (p. 20)*

These comments portray an interesting range of student perceptions, from a seeming unwillingness to consider educational uses for what was originally intended to be an entertainment device to a recognition that m-learning (as any form of learning) requires a certain amount of self-direction and responsibility on the part of the learner. Similarly, Sathe and Waltje (2008), using iPods as a portable language lab, reported that 75% of the students "enjoyed" making recordings (p. 45); 91% indicated that they "benefited" from the iPods (p. 51), but only 57% agreed that the iPod had helped them to learn the target language. The student comments revealed a number of skeptics in that group as well: "I thought that using the iPod was ridiculous. It took more time to explain how to use it than it would have taken to complete the exams orally in class," and "The iPods were nice... but in a time when the university is hurting for money, I'm going to need a more substantial use for a $250 gadget" (p. 54). Luckin, Brewster, Pearce, Siddons-Corby, and du Boulay

(2003) challenged students in their "Interactive Learning Environments" course to design and evaluate learning experiences for each other using Internet-capable PDAs. The students were almost evenly divided on whether or not they "saw a clear educational use for the device" (p. 90).

One source of negative perceptions may stem from frustrations with usability or technical problems. Luckin et al. (2003) reported user complaints about small screen sizes, crashing, and data loss. Problems with connectivity and Internet service providers are also common (Attewell et al., 2009). In addition, educators may think of their students as so-called "digital natives" (Prensky, 2001) but need to realize that the students may not have previously used their mobile devices in these particular ways (Attewell et al., 2009). Two studies in which instructors provided electronic feedback yielded opposite perceptions of usability and value. In one, students were initially concerned that downloading feedback by podcast would be difficult, but afterward, over 60% reported that it was easy to do, and almost all perceived the audio commentary to be of higher quality than the written feedback they customarily received (France & Wheeler, 2007). In another survey, over half the learners indicated that they preferred face-to-face feedback and that electronic feedback methods should be employed only as a supplement (Attewell et al., 2009). Clearly, we cannot assume that our students will be convinced of the utility of m-learning, raising a further question: To what extent should we proselytize and to what extent should we respect this diversity in conceptions and styles of learning?

On the other hand, student skepticism may stem from the same concerns that researchers (e.g., Kukulska-Hulme & Traxler, 2005; Reynolds & Bennett, 2008; Sathe & Waltje, 2008) have raised regarding the underlying pedagogical models applied to m-learning projects. For example, Attewell et al. (2009) described how learners reacted when paper-based worksheets were hastily converted to a mobile format: "Learners quickly recognised this and ... identified they didn't find this useful" (p. 45). If teachers are being "[led] towards outmoded, didactic approaches to delivery" (Reynolds & Bennett, 2008), it may be difficult for students to envision more effective applications of mobile technologies. Frustrated or unimpressed with the parameters of m-learning assignments in the classroom, students may not feel motivated to personally exploit m-learning strategies outside of class.

## The Believers

Much of the current literature in m-learning relies on student surveys or self reports as the major outcome measures. Frequently, students' reactions are gauged in terms of "motivation," "interest," or "enjoyment," and there is considerable evidence suggesting that m-learning strategies often have positive effects on these constructs. In "MoLeNET," the largest-scale m-learning project reported to date (involving, in its first year, over 10,000 learners in 32 projects across the UK), 91% of students surveyed agreed that m-learning helped them to learn, 93% that it made learning more interesting, and 84% that they would like to engage in more m-learning in the future. All of the MoLeNET projects investigating student motivation reported at least some positive impact, although some additionally indicated some neutral or negative effects. For example, at one location, the teachers reported a positive impact on their students' motivation, but the students' survey responses indicated the opposite: 22% felt the impact was positive, 44% felt no difference, and 33% felt m-learning had a negative effect on their motivation (Attewell et al., 2009).

Two recent studies investigating the use of mobile phones for language study also reported positive impacts on learners. In a five-week pilot study of Irish language acquisition at a secondary school in Ireland, learners used an interactive voice response system to record themselves speaking and received a text message with an Irish word or phrase each day; additionally, they participated in weekly web-based text chats with their peers, using desktop computers. 67% of the students reported that the activities helped them to progress in their Irish language skills, 95% enjoyed using the technology, and 93% recommended that the project be extended to other learners (Cooney & Keogh, 2007). Levy and Kennedy (2005) sent text messages at regular intervals between class sessions to the learners in a third-year college Italian class (18 students). Almost all of the students reported that they liked receiving the text messages; the lone dissenter did not care to use mobile phones for any purpose, including language learning.

Other studies have described podcasting as a strategy for m-learning. Reynolds and Bennett (2008) gauged students' attitude toward class podcasts by analyzing the content of messages which students posted to a class discussion board, finding 52% positive, 29% negative, and 19% neutral. Some negative comments were directed toward one episode, which was characterized as "slow and monotone" (p. 3), suggesting that students' reactions to the medium may have been tempered by the quality of the delivery. The posts were additionally analyzed for evidence of learning using the levels from Bloom's taxonomy; this analysis found no significant difference between podcast and text-based materials, but students did tend to omit information more often when responding to the text-based readings as compared to the material they heard through podcasts. Bennett, Maniar, Clark, and King (2008) studied pre- and post-lecture podcasts used as a supplement to face-to-face courses. They concluded that the podcasts were "not extensively used" (p. 7) as 56% of students listened to one or more, but only 14% listened to at least half of the available episodes. Those students who did listen reported that the podcasts were useful to help their understanding (51%), to provide a summary (44%), and to allow them to catch up if falling behind (40%). Only

5% reported that the podcast was not useful in helping them to understand the course material.

As the research in m-learning comes of age, more studies are incorporating outcome measures beyond surveys and self-reports. Thornton and Houser (2005) compared the effectiveness of delivering content via email to students' mobile phones with providing identical content online and on paper. Short "mini-lessons" in vocabulary were sent via email three times per day to 44 students in English language classes in Japan. Students using the email-to-mobile phone method showed significantly greater gains on the pre- and post-test measures than did students receiving either the web-based or paper delivery. 93% of the students found this teaching method to be valuable; 89% indicated that they would like to continue. The researchers concluded that the "push" aspect of the mobile delivery was particularly effective for vocabulary, as it "prodded [students] to study more often" (p. 223).

Lord (2008) used student-recorded podcasts to focus on pronunciation in her undergraduate Spanish phonetics class, exploring the effect of this strategy on students' attitude toward pronunciation as well as on their pronunciation proficiency. A pre- and post-semester attitude inventory revealed that overall, participants held significantly more positive attitudes towards pronunciation after participating in the podcasts. In addition, an evaluation of the students' pronunciation demonstrated significant improvement overall from the first to last recordings (although not every individual showed a positive change). On average, students reported enjoying the project, becoming more aware of their own pronunciation, learning a lot about their pronunciation abilities, being able to generalize that learning to their daily use of Spanish, and most strongly, believing that the instructor should continue the assignments with future classes.

Abdous, Camarena, and Facer (2009) compared the use of podcasts that were tightly integrated into a variety of course activities to supplemental podcasts, where class lectures and/or discussions were recorded and made available to students for review. In the integrated condition, only 28% of students reported that they never accessed the podcasted material and 8% reported using the podcasts several times per week; the remaining students' use ranged from once or twice a week to once or twice a semester. With the supplemental group, 55% never used the podcasts and no students reported using them as often as several times per week. In addition, the students in the integrated courses reported more positive effects of podcasts on their study habits and greater impact on their language acquisition, leading the researchers to conclude, "On the basis of student perceptions, podcasting can effectively promote the acquisition of a number of different language skills if instructors adapt and use the technology for a variety of instructional purposes" (p. 89).

Lord's (2008) and Abdous et al.'s (2009) studies both point to what may be a complicated interdependence between learner perception and the effectiveness of MALL strategies. In Lord (2008), did the learners perceive podcasting as effective because of some value intrinsic to the activity design? Or rather, did the activities become successful because of the students' positive attitude and willingness to engage? Abdous et al. (2009) found that even the students in the supplemental condition reported being more likely to enroll in a future language course if it had a podcast available, suggesting that they perceived some benefit even when the podcasts were not tightly integrated. If integration is argued to be more pedagogically sound, does this result lend support for the influence of students' apperception of value on their experienced reality of effectiveness? Should we provide materials or resources that our students perceive as effective even when they may not match our beliefs about pedagogical best practices? Further research will be needed to tease out these intertwined effects.

## The Issue of Autonomy

The conclusion of Abdous et al. (2009) that instructors must integrate podcasts into their courses in a variety of ways in order for students to perceive them as effective may suggest an underlying assumption that the responsibility for learning lies with the teacher. In the context of college language teaching, this scope of thinking makes sense: the goal is for students to complete their current course successfully, having gained enough skill and maintained enough interest to progress to the next level. Yet what happens if we take a broader view? How can we encourage and support our students in the goals of becoming competent, proficient, or even fluent speakers of the language? How can mobile technologies extend learning beyond the time period during which the student is attending a language course into the remainder of his or her life?

Learner autonomy is often defined as the ability to manage one's own learning without support from a teacher, but Blin (2004) suggests moving from that early conception to a richer definition that takes into account both student and teacher roles:

*Autonomy is both independence and interdependence. Independence entails taking responsibility for one's own learning, setting objectives, and making informed pedagogical decisions based on some form of self-evaluation. However, learners exercise their independence within a specific sociocultural context where interdependence, through socialisation and the nature of their interaction with peers and teachers, will impact on the levels of control they exercise and develop. (p. 378)*

M-learning is often assumed to be a means through which learner autonomy can be developed since learners are able to choose when and where they want to engage in study. For example, Cooney and Keogh (2007) asserted that in their project, "the students' abilities to learn autonomously were enhanced -- the technologies facilitated learning at any time, in any place and at the students' own pace" (p. 4). Without specific data leading to this conclusion, the assumption seemed to be that, given the option to make choices and to direct their own learning, students will naturally grow in the ability to do so successfully. Maltby and Mackie (2009) did not find this to be the case. In their study of student use of virtual learning environments, the researchers hypothesized that if at-risk students could be identified, early intervention would help them to develop more productive study habits. However, they found that students tended to develop regular patterns of behavior very early in the academic year, and interventions were not successful in changing them. Previous research has identified four key factors likely to constrain the development of learner autonomy through technology: learners' lack of technical competence, learners' lack of interest, learners' disinclination to be autonomous, and poor interaction among learners (Jones, 2001). Teachers may need to negotiate a fine line between intervening to cultivate autonomy in learners and maintaining distance to allow autonomy to flourish (Maltby & Mackie, 2009).

Sathe and Waltje (2008) began to explore how the iPods they loaned to students for the short-term might potentially have longer-term impacts on study habits. Sixty-seven percent reported feeling motivated to spend more time on their listening and speaking exercises when using the iPod, and 77% agreed that they would "use the iPod on a regular basis" if they had the opportunity to do so (p. 48). However, the researchers cautioned that the novelty of the iPod, characterized as a "sexy" device, was certainly a factor and questioned, "Would these numbers keep up when the iPod became an everyday tool and the magic wore off?" (p. 43). One study that did provide some evidence for the role of m-learning in developing autonomy involved younger (sixth-grade) students, who were given handheld devices to use during the school day and at home. Mifsud (2004) observed that the students made use of the devices throughout

their daily lives although the uses tended to fall into different categories depending on the context (school vs. home). In the classroom, the devices became "an integral part of the daily flow of school and classroom activities"; although the teacher made some suggestions, in general, she was able to "let go" of the control, and students were able to successfully make their own choices of how to use the devices to support their activities (p. 102).

## RESEARCH UNDERWAY

### Background

In the Language Resource Center (LRC) at Mount Holyoke College, a private, four-year, liberal arts college in the northeastern region of the United States, a long-term initiative to study learner perceptions and the use of MALL is underway. Following our mission "to promote innovation and collaboration in the teaching and learning of languages across the campus," we work closely with faculty to explore new teaching strategies, but as a resource center, we also have a unique interest in what our many learners, across a wide range of languages, do outside of the classroom.

A 2008 survey completed by 349 out of the 717 students currently enrolled in foreign language classes (a 49% response rate) revealed that over 85% of our students owned one or more MP3 players, cell phones with MP3 capability, and/or smart phones. However, of these, only about 32% reported using their mobile devices for language learning. Even more discouragingly, only 22% of all respondents felt that the LRC should provide more support to students for using MP3 players for language study. These data cautioned us that despite the initial research suggesting a close fit between MALL and the preferred learning styles of the present generation of college students, perhaps the situation is not so clear. In our student population, at a private, four-year college, it seemed that only a small minority of students were currently using MALL strategies, and further, the majority seemed unconvinced that they should consider adding MALL strategies to their study repertoire.

In a more positive note, 92 of the 97 students already using MALL also answered an open-ended question asking them to describe how they used their MP3 players to support their language learning. An analysis of their responses revealed eight common resources utilized. By far the most popular was listening to music in the target language, mentioned in 60% (n=58) of the students' responses. Twenty-seven percent (n=26) mentioned downloading and/or subscribing to podcasts, including both language learning podcasts and authentic materials produced for native speakers, such as podcasts of news broadcasts; 25% (n=26) described using other audio designed for language learners (e.g., textbook audio exercises, etc.). The other resource types were mentioned in only 5% or fewer of the responses and included watching TV shows or other video, listening to audiobooks, accessing the Internet, communicating with other learners, and changing the device operating system to the target language.

The open-ended responses also gave some initial insights into the students' beliefs about how m-learning might be applied in the process of language acquisition. Eight students specifically referenced the benefits of MALL for improving their pronunciation or becoming more familiar with phonology of the target language, e.g., "Even if I don't understand the songs, it helps to practice listening to the language" or "I've found that my ability to speak Spanish at a faster pace and with less of an American accent has greatly improved simply by drilling the songs and mimicking the sounds of the artist singing." Using MALL to support vocabulary development was mentioned in six student responses, such as "[I] play vocabulary lists between classes." Five students referred to improving comprehension of the target language: "[I] try to translate what the lyrics mean as practice." Finally, three student responses included grammar, e.g., "[I] reflect how it connects to grammar/themes from class."

In addition, students' responses supported a number of the advantages cited in the research literature: "I listen while I do other things," "I can use it anywhere, anytime," "[I] listen to it continuously," or "I listen … over and over again." Interestingly, some of the students who had not yet used their MP3 players for language learning also indicated that at times, they felt that mobile devices could benefit their studies, but they were unsuccessful in pursuing these strategies on their own: "To learn vocabulary, I cut up index cards … and this takes forever. I was just thinking the other day if there was anyway to get it on an MP3 player so that when I am on the bus or walking around I could be practicing," or "I tried to use it to download pronunciation … in French but I couldn't find anything."

## A Case Study in Japanese Learning

Although they were discouraging since they showed so few students taking advantage of the capabilities of their MP3 players to support their language learning, the survey results did indicate some appreciation of MALL, suggesting that other students might similarly benefit from m-learning strategies if they were provided more guidance and support. Building on the results of this formative assessment, we embarked upon a long-term project seeking to better understand our learners' perceptions and attitudes toward MALL and to investigate how we might best encourage students to more fully exploit the mobile devices already in their pockets. In the first year, the Japanese language course sequence was chosen as a case study, for a number of reasons: Japanese, at our college, is a relatively small department, giving a manageably sized cohort; it is perceived as a challenging language by many students, suggesting that they might especially benefit from new learning strategies; one of the areas of struggle is the Japanese writing system, and the capabilities of Apple's iPod Touch® are particularly suited to "kanji" study, as characters drawn by hand onto the screen can be recognized by the operating system; and numerous apps have been developed for Japanese language study.

The first semester focused on collecting further data regarding students' perceptions, beliefs, and usage of MALL. The students in the first-year classes were encouraged to use their own mobile devices while the second- and third-year Japanese students were loaned an iPod Touch, to observe how they might apply this specific device to their studies. In all of the Japanese courses, the faculty allocated one class period so that LRC staff could orient students to resources available to them. All of the students completed an initial survey at the beginning of the year and a follow-up survey at the close of the first semester. Students from the second- and third-year classes were additionally invited to participate in an interview, the analysis of which was underway at the time of this writing. In subsequent semesters, acting upon these data, additional resources and support will be provided, anticipated to fit learners' interests, styles, and needs.

The initial survey was completed by 44 students, including 28 at the 100-level, 10 at the 200-level and six at the 300-level. Due to course attrition, 38 students participated in the post-semester survey, down to 23 at the 100-level, 10 at the 200-level and five at the 300-level. The students ranged in age from 18 to 29 years old, with the majority being between 18 and 20.

## The Initial Survey

This sample showed an even higher rate of MP3 player ownership than in the previous survey across languages: 93% of the students studying Japanese reported owning some type of MP3-capable device. The most common type was a video-capable iPod (54%), followed by an iPhone or iPod Touch (29%). Fifteen to twenty percent reported owning a non-video capable iPod, another brand of non-video capable MP3 player, or an MP3-capable cell phone. Less than 10% owned a non-Apple brand of video-capable MP3 player or smart phone. In addition, the results confirmed that these devices were part of the typical student's everyday life: 83% indicated that they used their MP3 player "every day" or "several times per week," and 61% carry their MP3 players with them "always" or on "most days." Perhaps corresponding to the higher rate of MP3 player ownership in this group, there was also a somewhat higher rate of experience with MALL. At the beginning of the project, 39% of the students reported that they had tried using their MP3 player to support their language learning, and 12% indicated that they did so regularly.

The initial survey also gave some useful insights into students' preferred strategies for MALL, and uncovered some of the reasons why they had not explored m-learning for their language studies. Figure 1 shows that the most common use (95% of the students who had tried MALL) and by far the strategy practiced most regularly (76% regularly + 19% occasionally) was listening to music in the target language. Watching videos and listening to dialogues or other materials for learners were both used by 71% of the students, although watching videos saw much more regular use. Other types of audio, including listening to audiobooks and subscribing to podcasts, were used by about 50% of these students. Finally, only about 38% had tried using software for their mobile devices specifically designed for language learning, but interestingly, these apps were used more regularly (19%) than the previously mentioned "other audio" (less than 15%).

Overall, students' responses as to why they did not engage in MALL were encouraging to the project goals. Of the 20 students who had never tried using their MP3 player to help them with language learning, only three reported that they did not think it would be useful. The most frequently chosen reason was "I never thought of using it" (9 students), followed by "I don't know

*Figure 1. Students' preferred MALL strategies (the percentage of students indicating they used these strategies regularly and/or occasionally out of the total number of students' who had tried MALL)*

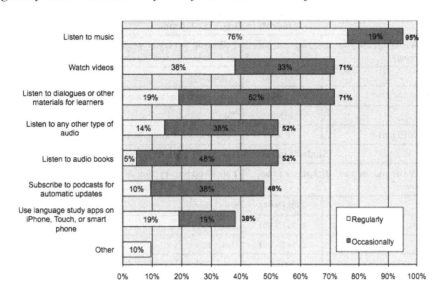

how to use it" (6), and "I've thought of it, but haven't done it yet" (3). This differs somewhat from Abdous et al. (2009), who found that the most common reasons for non-use were lack of time and the perception that it would not be helpful (although the researchers speculated that students underreported the impact of their limited technical skills).

## After One Semester

Based on their responses to the beginning- and end-of-semester surveys, our first-year Japanese students consistently maintained their previous patterns of using or not using MALL strategies (see Table 1). In other words, although students told us that they hadn't used MALL in the past because it hadn't occurred to them, simply raising their awareness through a survey about MALL and a one-hour orientation to available resources was not sufficient to effect any change in their habits. On the other hand, the second- and third-year students began with more experience using MALL, and their responses suggested further increase over the semester, perhaps (not surprisingly) since they

were loaned iPod Touches and probably enjoyed the novelty of the devices and felt some obligation to make use of them. Similar to Bennett et al. (2008), all of our students reported making extensive use of online resources, although only a small percentage loaded materials onto mobile devices. Eighty-seven percent indicated they had listened to the textbook audio online; 73% had watched the textbook video online; only 13% had downloaded these to their computers; another 13% had made use of a "Subscribe in iTunes" link to receive the audio in podcast format.

In addition, we wanted to explore some of the underlying attitudes and beliefs that might affect students' decisions regarding MALL (Figure 2). The highest and most consistent level of agreement was to the importance of listening to the target language in order become acquainted with the sound system. Students also agreed that they'd like to have access to more authentic audio and video materials in the target language. Although not many students reported making use of MALL strategies, nonetheless on average they agreed that it would be useful to be able to study with a portable device whenever they had a few minutes

*Table 1. Reported use of MALL by students in first-year and second-/third-year Japanese classes, on beginning- and end-of-semester surveys*

| Students in First-Year Japanese | | | |
|---|---|---|---|
| **Initial Survey:***How often do you use your MP3 player to help you with language learning?* | | **Follow-up Survey:***How often did you use your MP3 player this semester to help you learn Japanese?* | |
| "I use it regularly." | 4% (N=1) | "Frequently." | 5% (N=1) |
| "I've tried using it." | 37% (N=10) | "Occasionally or at least once." | 32% (N=7) |
| "I never have." | 59% (N=16) | "No." | 59% (N=13) |
| Total students owning MP3 player | N=27 | Total students owning MP3 player | N=22 |
| Students in Second- and Third-Year Japanese | | | |
| **Initial Survey:***How often do you use your MP3 player to help you with language learning?* | | **Follow-up Survey:***How many days per week did you typically use your iPod Touch for language study?* | |
| "I use it regularly." | 29% (N=4) | 5 to 7 days | 20% (N=3) |
| "I've tried using it." | 43% (N=6) | 2 to 4 days | 73% (N=11) |
| "I never have." | 29% (N=4) | 0 or 1 day | 0 |
| Total students owning MP3 player | N=14 | Total students loaned iPod Touch | N=15 |

free. On average, students disagreed with the statement that it would not be helpful to listen to target language audio while doing something else, suggesting that the multi-tasking advantage of MALL might appeal to them; on the other hand, these answers showed the largest amount of variation, reflecting the influence of individual learning styles. Surprisingly, students on average also disagreed that they did not have time for additional language study beyond their coursework; however, this statement showed a high level of variation. Finally, the strongest disagreement was with the idea that listening is not useful if you're not able to fully understand the language used.

*Figure 2. Student attitudes and beliefs in relation to MALL, expressed as average level of agreement and standard deviation on a five-point Likert scale*

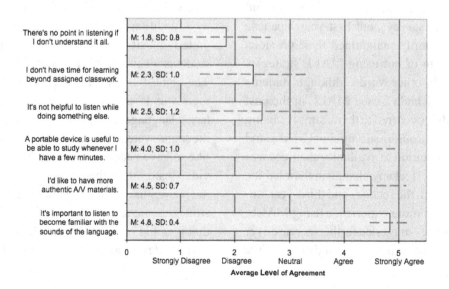

Following Young's (2007) call for more data on the types of materials or activities that students would like to use with an MP3 player, the follow-up survey incorporated her suggestions. Figure 3 shows students' average level of interest in 20 proposed activity or resource material types, including the standard deviations and modes for each set of responses to indicate the sizable variation among students' opinions. The option that generated the most interest and by far the least disagreement among students was "TV shows." Eight other possibilities averaged relatively high levels of interest and also were most commonly rated 5 ("very interested"). These included other types of authentic materials such as music, music videos, and educational programming; pronunciation, grammar, and vocabulary explanations or exercises; practice/drill games and interactive games or challenges with classmates. Although Young posited that "activities that are engaging, problem-solving, and task-based, and that encourage authentic self expression for a purpose, are more appealing than listening to mechanical discrete-point verb conjugations

or prefabricated audio files" (p. 45), our students' responses did not always agree -- many of their preferred activities would fall within the rubric of "mechanical," and many of Young's proposed activities providing authentic purposes for communication generated lower ratings of interest.

## DISCUSSION AND FUTURE DIRECTIONS

One semester into our initiative to better understand students' use and perceptions of MALL, what have we learned?

*Our students recognize that language learning is an endeavor that extends beyond the physical and temporal reaches of the classroom, and they are willing to undertake it.*

Despite their heavy academic loads, the majority of our students (63%) disagreed with the assumption that they would not have time for language learning beyond the assigned work for

*Figure 3. Students' interest in proposed MALL activities and materials, expressed as average level of interest, standard deviation and mode on a five-point rating scale*

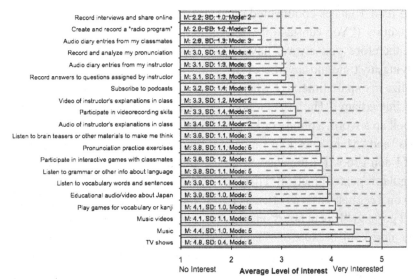

their language course. Although we had expected this statement to generate a high level of agreement, only 18% of the students agreed, and no one expressed strong agreement. This attitude is demonstrated in a comment from an upper-level student: "I have been swamped this semester... Next semester, I hope I will [have time to devote to it]... I want to use it more!" While in reality, their busy schedules may not allow them much time, they attempt to do what they can to reach their language learning goals: "During J-Term, however," (when the student would not be taking classes) "I intend to learn how to better use Smart.fm, etc., to put things like vocab flashcards on my iPod."

*Our students share (at least some of) our beliefs about the utility of MALL, but these perceptions and the resulting usage of MALL will vary greatly among learners.*

Of the students who had not previously tried MALL, only 15% reported that they felt it would not be useful. In the formative survey comments, students described using music on their MP3 players to immerse themselves in the target language and experiencing benefits from audio materials for their target language pronunciation, grammar, vocabulary, and comprehension. Different students using the iPod Touches commented on convenience, portability ("You can take it with you everywhere, therefore you always have a study tool"), studying any time and anywhere ("It enabled me to utilize my spare time, like when I was on [the bus]"), immediacy ("The best function is being able to look up a word, a phrase or kanji right there in class" and "Many questions I have I'd soon forget if I don't look for the answer at that moment"), regular, repeated practice ("I listen to textbook audio on a regular basis as often as I need to wherever I go" and "I spent hours on that app and remember more kanji because of it"), and increased interest ("Other applications made the Japanese learning process more enjoyable and

interesting" and "Great learning tool. I love it"). In reaction to the assertion that it is not helpful to listen while doing something else (such as working out), on average students disagreed, but there was a high level of variation among their responses.

Recent research in m-learning has moved beyond reliance on self-report and has begun to measure student learning gains. This is a step in the right direction, but we further need to analyze how the various characteristics of a learning strategy may contribute to the resulting benefits (Huizenga et al., 2009). For example, Bennett et al. (2008) point out that "the properties of a podcast (i.e., a regularly updated series of episodes that can be listened to on a portable MP3 player) that were initially put forward as reasons why podcasting may be an effective way of helping students to learn actually appear to be relatively unimportant when using a podcast to enhance face-to-face campus-based courses" (p. 8). Instead, the benefit may lie in the multimedia format. In their study of text-messaging for vocabulary acquisition, Thornton and Houser (2005) hypothesized that shorter messages would prove more effective. However, comparing long and short conditions experimentally, they found no significant difference in learning, leading to the conclusion that the success of the approach must result from regularly-spaced repetition.

*Our Students Need and Want our Help and Guidance*

The majority of our students had not previously tried MALL because they either had never thought of it or didn't know how to do so. Others had thought of it, but just hadn't tried yet, suggesting that encouragement might be in order. One student requested, "There should be another workshop so that we can learn more 'tricks'." In the literature also, there is consensus that m-learning requires intensive support for both teachers and learners (Attewell et al., 2009; Kukulska-Hulme & Traxler, 2005; Luckin et al., 2003; Sathe & Waltje, 2008).

After completing the follow-up survey, another student commented, "I wish I had been instructed to find audio or video resources." Although the students had been informed in their orientation that they were free to put any files that they'd like onto their iPods, and many students did so, this student seemed to want more direction. As our students move through our language programs and proceed into the "rest of their lives," the concept of autonomy will be important to engendering lifelong language learners. Mobile technologies, in and of themselves, will not automatically foster autonomy, but we believe that we should seek methods of m-teaching, in the sense of facilitating and supporting m-learning, that do. As an initial example, Luckin et al. (2005) explored an activity design that involved small groups of students working with mobile devices to collect scientific data in the field, each accompanied by a "facilitator." Her analysis demonstrated that the facilitator played a key role in scaffolding the groups' inquiry and use of the technology.

*Our students' conceptions about effective learning strategies may not necessarily match our conceptions about effective instructional design, and we need to explore both.*

As Young (2007) reminds us, "Most SLA/FLL/ Applied Linguists would strongly discourage using these technologies for memorizing dialogs or rote practice of verb conjugations. These promote mechanical and short-term solutions to a complex and long-term process" (p. 60). Nonetheless, many of our students indicated strong interest in that very type of activity. One student emphasized that she was "very interested" in "listening to a recording of Japanese vocabulary words and example sentences" by marking "!!" next to her rating. In response to "watching a video recording of my teachers' explanations from class," another student added "yes!" in the margin. But just as our learners are diverse, so too are their interests. Yet another student emphasized her interest in target

language jokes and added her own suggestion: "I think it might be fun to connect with students in class via a web service like Twitter®."

Ferdig (2007) asserts, "We need more research to not only examine the use of technologies, but the education of the users of those technologies" (p. 60). We need to understand our students' conceptions of learning, reflect on our own beliefs, and when there is a mismatch with what the research literature supports as effective language learning strategies, we need to help our students become aware of it. The research called for above, analyzing the design characteristics that contribute to the success of MALL, will inform us in this pursuit. This research should additionally explore how student perception influences m-learning success and vice versa.

*As we move toward our goal of becoming successful m-teachers, we need to better understand our learners, their needs, and the contexts in which they study language, and then ground our efforts to facilitate and support in learner-centered design principles.*

Kukulska-Hulme and Traxler (2005) offer the following question for future research: "What kinds of learning, learners, subjects and situations can mobile learning support most effectively?" (p. 29) We suggest that this inquiry begin with the learners: Who are our students? How do they conceive of the process of learning? In what contexts are they learning, toward what goals? What do they perceive to be their needs? Armed with this understanding and drawing upon evidence from the growing body of research connecting m-learning techniques with learning results, we can guide our learners toward MALL strategies that will suit them individually:

*A differentiated approach, in terms of both pedagogy and the technology used, is required, tailored to needs of specific individual learners or groups and their particular context, to maximise the benefits of mobile learning. (Attewell et. al, 2009, p. 4)*

This approach should be learner-centered; involving students in a "mutual construction of learning activities" may help to scaffold the learners in becoming autonomous in their application of MALL (Luckin et al., 2003, p. 8). Danielsson, Hedestig, Juslin, and Orre (2003) suggest a method of sharing and discussing possible use scenarios with groups of students which proved beneficial to their learners: "They could reflect on their present performance, benefits and problems connected to their strategies to achieve knowledge, and they had the opportunity to shape new ways of performance jointly" (p. 52). For the educators, this process helps bring to light previously unrecognized personal uses of technology crossing into the educational environment. Kadyte (2003) outlines a framework of three overlapping contexts within which m-learning may take place: personal mobile, learning community, and cultural. Luckin et al. (2005) apply a model of context as an "ecology of resources"; this analysis can "enable us to use mobile technology effectively to help learners (and teachers, peers, and parents) to adapt the resource they find within a particular context to best support their learning needs" (p. 3).

## CONCLUSION

This chapter has attempted to refocus the conversation about m-learning onto the students. Although the term "m-learning" might suggest an inherent emphasis on the learner, in fact much of the current research assumes that MALL will occur within the scope of a language course, a cultural context which may put primary responsibility for learning on the teacher. As a Language Resource Center, however, we have a unique interest in learning outside of the classroom as well. Applying Kukulska-Hulme and Traxler's (2005) definition, we argue that we are engag-

ing in "m-teaching" whenever we encourage or enable learners to use their mobile devices "to facilitate, support, enhance and extend ... [their] learning" (Attewell et al., 2009, p. 1). Important concerns in this endeavor include understanding students' conceptions of learning, considering how m-learning blurs the boundaries between students' personal and educational lives, and making visible the affordances of various mobile devices which will tend to bias the ways in which we use them.

A look at the growing research on m-learning demonstrated that students, in their perceptions of MALL, run the gamut from skeptics to believers. Learner skepticism may have grown out of frustrations with technology or might be influenced by negative perceptions of the pedagogical models through which MALL has been applied their courses. Conversely, positive attitudes may lead to (and/or result from) more successful learning. Effective m-teaching will require us to grapple with questions such as these: To what extent should we attempt to shape learners' beliefs and perceptions of their needs? And how can m-learning be applied to foster increased autonomy, engendering successful lifelong language learning?

Finally, the chapter reported on long-term research underway in the Language Resource Center at Mount Holyoke College, which seeks first to better understand learners' current beliefs and practices in relation to MALL, with the future goal of encouraging more learners to apply m-learning strategies to their language studies. Although this initiative has just begun, five initial conclusions were discussed:

- Our students recognize that language learning is an endeavor that extends beyond the physical and temporal reaches of the classroom, and they are willing to undertake it.
- Our students share (at least some of) our beliefs about the utility of MALL, but these perceptions and their resulting usage will vary greatly among learners.

- Our students need and want our help and guidance.
- Our students' conceptions about effective learning strategies may not necessarily match our conceptions about effective instructional design, and we need to explore both.
- As we move toward our goal of becoming successful m-teachers, we need to better understand our learners, their needs, and the contexts in which they study language, and then ground our efforts to facilitate and support in learner-centered design principles.

# REFERENCES

Abdous, M., Camarena, M., & Facer, B. (2009). MALL technology: Use of academic podcasting in the foreign language classroom. *ReCALL*, *21*(1), 76–95. doi:10.1017/S0958344009000020

Attewell, J., Savill-Smith, C., & Douch, R. (2009). *The impact of mobile learning: Examining what it means for teaching and learning*. Retrieved December 21, 2009, from http://www.lsnlearning.org.uk

Belanger, Y. (2005a, March). *Duke iPod initiative project evaluation update*. Retrieved December 21, 2009, from Duke University Web site: http://cit.duke.edu/pdf/reports/ITAC_iPod_eval_March05.pdf

Belanger, Y. (2005b, June). *Duke University iPod first year experience final evaluation report*. Retrieved December 21, 2009, from Duke University Web site: http://cit.duke.edu/pdf/ipod_initiative_04_05.pdf

Bennett, E., Maniar, N., Clark, R., & King, T. (2008). Using supplementary podcasts to enhance campus-based courses: Students' perceptions and usage. *Learning Technology Newsletter*, *10*(3), 6–9.

Blin, F. (2004). CALL and the development of learner autonomy: Towards an activity-theoretical perspective. *ReCALL*, *16*(2), 377–395. doi:10.1017/S0958344004000928

Chinnery, G. (2006). Going to the MALL: Mobile assisted language learning. *Language Learning & Technology*, *10*(1), 9.

Cooney, G., & Keogh, K. (2007). *Use of mobile phones for language learning and assessment for learning, a pilot project*. Retrieved December 21, 2009 from http://www.learnosity.com/files/learnosity-use-of-mobile-phones-for-language-learning-and-assessment-for-learning.pdf

Danielsson, K., Hedestig, U., Juslin, M., & Orre, C. (2003). Participatory design in development of mobile learning environments. In J. Attewell, & C. Savill-Smith (Eds), *Learning with mobile devices: Research and development* (pp. 47-53). MLEARN 2003: Learning with Mobile Devices; London, UK, May 19-20, 2003.

Ferdig, R. E., Coutts, J., DiPietro, J., Lok, B., & Davis, N. (2007). Innovative technologies for multicultural education needs. *Multicultural Education & Technology Journal*, *1*(1), 47–63. doi:10.1108/17504970710745201

France, D., & Wheeler, A. (2007). Reflections on using podcasting for student feedback. *Planet*, *18*, 10–11.

Huizenga, J., Admiraal, W., Akkerman, S., & ten Dam, G. (2009). Mobile game-based learning in secondary education: Engagement, motivation and learning in a mobile city game. *Journal of Computer Assisted Learning*, *25*(4), 332–344. doi:10.1111/j.1365-2729.2009.00316.x

Jones, Jeremy. (2001). CALL and the Teacher's Role in Promoting Learner Autonomy. *CALL-EJ Online 3*(1).

Kadyte, V. (2003). Learning can happen anywhere: A mobile system for language learning. In J. Attewell, & C. Savill-Smith (Eds.), *Learning with mobile devices: Research and development* (pp. 73-78). MLEARN 2003: Learning with Mobile Devices; London, UK, May 19-20, 2003.

Kukulska-Hulme, A., & Traxler, J. (2005). Mobile teaching and learning. In Kukulska-Hulme, A., & Traxler, J. (Eds.), *Mobile learning: A handbook for educators and trainers* (pp. 25–44). New York: Routledge.

Levy, M., & Kennedy, C. (2005). Learning Italian via mobile SMS. In Kukulska-Hulme, A., & Traxler, J. (Eds.), *Mobile learning: A handbook for educators and trainers* (pp. 76–83). New York: Routledge.

Lord, G. (2008). Podcasting communities and second language pronunciation. *Foreign Language Annals*, *41*(2), 364–379. doi:10.1111/j.1944-9720.2008.tb03297.x

Luckin, R., Brewster, D., Pearce, R. S., & du Boulay, B. (2003). SMILE: The creation of space for interaction through technology. In J. Attewell, & C. Savill-Smith (Eds), *Learning with mobile devices: Research and development* (pp. 87-93). MLEARN 2003: Learning with Mobile Devices; London, UK, May 19-20, 2003.

Luckin, R., du Boulay, B., Smith, H., Underwood, J., Fitzpatrick, G., & Holmberg, J. (2005). Using mobile technology to create flexible learning contexts. *Journal of Interactive Media in Education*, *22*, 1–21.

Maltby, A., & Mackie, S. (2009). Virtual learning environments—Help or hindrance for the "disengaged" student? *ALT-J: Research in Learning Technology*, *17*(1), 49–62.

Mifsud, L. (2003). Learning 2go: Making reality of the scenarios? In J. Attewell, & C. Savill-Smith (Eds.), *Learning with mobile devices: Research and development* (pp. 99-104). MLEARN 2003: Learning with Mobile Devices; London, May 19-20, 2003.

Prensky, M. (2001). Digital Natives, Digital Immigrants: A New Way to Look At Ourselves and Our Kids. *Horizon*, *9*(5), 1–6. doi:10.1108/10748120110424816

Reynolds, C., & Bennett, L. (2008, July). A social constructivist approach to the use of podcasts. *ALT Newsletter*, (July). Retrieved from http://newsweaver.co.uk/alt/e_article001142653.cfm

Sathe, N., & Waltje, J. (2008). The iPod project: A mobile mini-lab. *Journal of the Research Center for Educational Technology*, *4*(2), 32–56.

Sharples, M. (2003). Disruptive devices: Mobile technology for conversational learning. *International Journal of Continuing Engineering Education and Lifelong Learning*, *12*(5/6), 504–520. doi:10.1504/IJCEELL.2002.002148

Thornton, P., & Houser, C. (2005). Using mobile phones in English education in Japan. *Journal of Computer Assisted Learning*, *21*, 217–228. doi:10.1111/j.1365-2729.2005.00129.x

Young, D. (2007). iPods, MP3 players and podcasts for FL learning: Current practices and future considerations. *The NECTFL Review*, *60*, 39–49.

# Chapter 7
# Simulating Immersion:
## Podcasting in Spanish Teaching

**Mario Daniel Martín**
*The Australian National University, Australia*

**Elizabeth Ann Beckmann**
*The Australian National University, Australia*

## ABSTRACT

*This chapter describes the genesis, implementation, and evaluation of an innovative approach to the intensive use of Academic Podcasting Technology (APT) in the teaching of Spanish to undergraduates at the Australian National University from 2007 to 2009. Students became active users and producers of Spanish language podcasts in a simulated immersion environment. Integrating APT into the educational design of two thematic courses created authentic and engaging socio-cultural contexts for language use while meeting students' needs for resource accessibility and mobility. Pioneering and exciting in its conception and outcomes, this approach has received very positive feedback from students, and provides a pedagogically-sound model for the effective use of APT in immersive-style language teaching.*

## INTRODUCTION

A question of significant relevance to language lecturers is how to provide students with a comprehensively immersive experience within the context of a typical campus-bound program. In the Spanish program at The Australian National University (ANU), our answer has been to engage students using the opportunities offered by Mobile Assisted Language Learning (MALL), and specifically using academic podcasting technology (APT), in ways that have allowed the construction of contemporaneous real and virtual immersive language experiences for our students. This chapter describes the genesis and rationale of our approach to creating a simulated immersion experience in a specific course delivered annually from 2006 to 2009. In reporting on the ways in which we used action research to monitor and evaluate the

DOI: 10.4018/978-1-60960-141-6.ch007

teaching and learning outcomes from year to year, we show the importance of being responsive to feedback (the latter illustrated in this chapter by italicized quotes from our students) and of being committed to an improvement cycle. We also describe our findings in relation to a longitudinal view of the outcomes of APT integration, and show the benefits of using APT to simulate an immersive language environment.

## Using CALL and MALL in Teaching Spanish

Despite the well-recognized potential for Computer Assisted Language Learning (CALL), it is rare for the findings of sophisticated language-related research to be applied to the development of software. In the context of Spanish, for example, this appears to be because of a lack of necessary specialist intellectual resources; the high cost for both publishers and consumers of "technologically sophisticated and culturally authentic language learning programs"; and the inability of educational institutions to provide the necessary high-end hardware or to meet expensive licensing costs (e.g. Lafford, Lafford, & Sykes, 2007).

With these kinds of inhibitions slowing the development of the highest-quality CALL, it is not surprising that many authors are acknowledging MALL technologies, especially MP3 devices and APT, as the most exciting recent advances in language teaching (e.g. Godwin-Jones, 2005; Lafford & Lafford, 2005; Murphy, 2008; Abdous, Camarena & Facer, 2009; this volume). Its portability and accessibility opportunities alone make podcasting technology very attractive to language teachers. This has been even more true since Apple's 2005 release of the iTunes® software, which enables easy subscription to Really Simple Syndication (RSS) feeds.

However, Thomas (2008) reports that this technology appears often to be used simply to enhance the digital accessibility of material previously available in language labs, without any specific purpose or new educational objective. Even where podcasts are integrated into course content, this often occurs as one-way communication from the teacher: student production of podcasts is generally found only in technology-focused courses, such as new media and education (Lee & Chan, 2007; Lazzari, 2009). Potentially more expressive uses of APT are certainly being reported, especially in English as a Second Language teaching. There are examples of such use in language teaching in the United States of America (Gilgen, 2005; Cain, 2007) and in the United Kingdom (Jobbings, 2005), but in general it seems that APT remains underutilized (Thorne & Payne, 2005; Lazzari, 2009).

In Australia, the adoption of APT has been quite slow. Although there have been several positive and enthusiastic assessments of the potential of podcasting for language learning (e.g. Laing, Wootton, & Irons, 2006; Australian Learning and Teaching Council, 2009), there appear to be few examples of hands-on implementation. In late 2006, at the time this project was being designed, an extensive review of Australian-focused journals found no reports of university language courses in which course materials were composed exclusively of audio materials, or in which podcast production was integrated into educational design. As we were moving into very new territory, therefore, we recognized that there would be a significant amount of trial and error involved in introducing APT into ANU's Spanish program, and that we would have to incorporate evaluation accordingly.

## TEACHING SPANISH AT THE ANU

Spanish is a major international language, rich in literature and significant in international affairs and trade. As the national language of 22 countries -- including Spain, most countries of Central and South America, and Equatorial Guinea -- and with more than 400 million speakers worldwide,

Spanish is close to parity with English as the most spoken language in the world (after Mandarin Chinese). Spanish is also becoming increasingly important as a second language in the USA, which has 34 million citizens speaking Spanish at home (U.S. Census Bureau, 2009). Millions across the world learn Spanish as a second language, and more people study Spanish in U.S. institutions of higher education (in 2006 there were 823,000 such students of Spanish) than all other modern languages combined (Furman, Goldberg & Lusin, 2007). In the Australian context, Spanish is a vibrant community language with more than 98,000 speakers (Australian Bureau of Statistics, 2008). Nineteen Australian universities offer degree-level programs in Spanish. These programs attract not only people seeking to specialize in the language or to maintain a connection with their heritage, but also those wishing to complement studies in other disciplines, such as international relations, international business, European studies, sociology, political science, history, or development studies.

The ANU has had its own Spanish degree program since 2005 (previously having offered a program in cooperation with another university). Undergraduate students work through *Beginner*, *Continuing*, *Intermediate,* and *Advanced Levels* (or start at the appropriate level as determined by a placement test), typically over three years. As the university is located in the nation's capital, Canberra, learning opportunities are enhanced by proximity to the Spanish and Latin American diplomatic missions, and students are also able to go on exchange programs to universities in Spanish-speaking countries.

## A Focus on Skills

The program seeks specifically to develop students' communication skills to sufficiently high levels of proficiency to allow them to function linguistically in a natural, spontaneous, and efficient way in a Spanish-speaking environment. To this end, the program concentrates on developing students' Spanish listening and speaking skills throughout the program. In first- and second-year classes, the immersive experience is fostered by a high frequency of face-to-face contact, and a focus on multiple practical and self-checking language writing exercises combined with numerous speaking, listening, and reading opportunities. This approach ensures that all language skills are given equal emphasis, and allows these skills to develop in a balanced, more natural fashion over the duration of the program. Students appreciate the benefits of this kind of immersion:

*I started Spanish at the ANU as a first year with no knowledge whatsoever of the language. Although it was incredibly intimidating that ONLY Spanish was spoken from day one ... I am truly grateful. .... I am now completing 4th year Spanish ... and I can honestly testify that I wake up every morning looking forward to speaking Spanish.*

## A Focus on Plurality, Inclusivity, and Enabling Technology

As Spanish is a pluricentric language, with a wide variety of accents and local colloquial expressions, we have a deliberate policy of rotating tutors in the first year so that each student is continually exposed to accents from different Hispanic backgrounds. Promoting equity of culture, pronunciation, and accent is very important when dealing with a post-colonial language spoken in many countries and in many different socio-political contexts. This approach is much-praised by students:

*It has been incredibly valuable to have a variety of accents from different countries every day of the week ... This helped me A LOT when I went to South America, as I had some idea of what to expect in every country.*

*There is something special and different in every Latin country and each different nationality you come into contact with gives you a different insight into the language. I know that without the help of the many different Spanish teachers I had at ANU over the years, I never would have been as prepared as I was for the one year I spent on exchange in Colombia.*

A distinctive feature of ANU's Spanish program (and of author Mario Daniel Martín's teaching style and previous teaching experiences) is the combination of traditional communicative-based language learning with technology-enabled modules. Using both synchronous and asynchronous learning opportunities allows responsive interaction with instructors (either face-to-face or virtually), to provide rapid feedback or responses to questions. This in turn gives students flexibility in deciding the pace and timing of their learning. Unlike many Spanish programs in other universities, therefore, the ANU program does not rely on textbooks to determine its curriculum, even in first- and second-year compulsory courses. Rather, we focus on authentic audiovisual material from a wide variety of sources to help students develop a level of familiarity with speech in the mass media that changes them from language *learners* to language *users*.

## A Focus on Cultural Themes

By the *Intermediate Level*, students' listening and speaking skills need extension well beyond the basics. However, students' interest in the language alone may start to wane, especially when their primary interest for learning Spanish is to support another area of study. Moreover, our teaching aim is to provide students with both the linguistic and the cultural understanding necessary for them to interact effectively with Spanish native speakers. At the *Intermediate* and *Advanced Levels*, therefore, the program offers two parallel, thematic courses -- *Current Affairs in the Spanish-Speaking World* (SPAN3100) and *The Spanish-Speaking World through its Songs* (SPAN3101) -- to complement the "pure" language approach. Although language and culture are integrated into the program throughout, these thematic courses provide a stronger framework for intellectual engagement, not only with the Spanish language, but also with the many cultures that have arisen among speakers of that language in the past centuries.

For example, the *Songs* course allows students to explore significant political, social, and artistic issues in the Spanish-speaking world through its rich heritage of musical culture. Classic genres—such as the tango, the bolero, and the Spanish copla—are contrasted with their derived contemporary music genres, and with Spanish and Latin American responses to the rock, punk, and hip-hop movements. Students examine the social and cultural background of the societies that gave rise to such genres, and focus on significant political events that were reflected in music of the time, such as the Cuban revolution, the fall of Allende's Chile or the return to democracy in Spain after the Franco regime.

Initially, the thematic courses were traditionally structured as teacher-controlled, text-based learning environments. Audio resources were provided first as audio files presented in a classical language lab setting on campus and then as audio/MP3 CDs which students could copy. Since 2006, the files have been available as downloadable or streamed files through the university's virtual learning environment (VLE; more commonly known in Australia as a learning management system, or LMS), which is accessible both on- and off-campus. A course collection of readings, with articles on music genres or current affairs from the Spanish-speaking press, complemented the audios in classes and exams.

## A New Focus on Simulated Immersion: The 2006 Experience

Australia is home to many multicultural communities with strong ties to both European and Asian culture and languages. Yet, as Martín (2005) has shown, historical and cultural constraints mean that the investment in non-English language programs by Australian universities is generally lower than that of universities in the other countries in the Organisation for Economic Co-operation and Development (OECD). The result has been a decrease in class time devoted to language learning and a reduction in immersion teaching (Read, 1996). Although university and government funding supports international student exchange programs (e.g. Australian Government, 2008, 2009), relatively few students take up opportunities to immerse themselves in another language environment. Moreover, those that do are often poorly prepared culturally and linguistically for the immersion experience, often taking refuge in English-speaking enclaves. Students therefore stand to gain significantly from teaching strategies that simulate an immersion environment.

The thematic courses provided a particular opportunity for innovative teaching, since they offered educational technologies that could be used to simulate the characteristics of language learning immersion. Although their feedback showed that students had been stimulated and motivated by the 2005 thematic courses, it seemed that the teaching strategies had done little to extend students' aural and oral competencies. A decision was thus made to trial a stronger simulated immersion approach. From 2006, *Songs* was presented as a full-length course in its own right (as opposed to being simply a module in the *Intermediate Level* language course) with listening and speaking requirements becoming dominant through an emphasis on audio material as the primary learning sources. As an outcome of an action research model put in place to provide input into an improvement cycle approach, the *Songs* course, from 2006 to 2009, has seen an evolution in the way in which these audio resources are delivered, and in how the students use them. The consequent impact on student learning has been distinctly positive in the longer term, but lessons have been learned along the way.

From the start, the emphasis was placed on students having to listen to audio files (from 38 to 106 minutes in duration). In 2006, the focus was on providing web-streamed, CD, and MP3 options. At least two radio programs about each identified music genre and artist, as well as the songs to be analyzed in the final course examination. These were presented as either a single CD with MP3 files, or as a set of audio CDs, as well as via 24/7-access language laboratories. Each resource was clearly coded as either compulsory or optional. Students were asked to listen to the radio programs before the corresponding lecture class, and to summarize their content during tutorial classes. Lectures were recorded and made available via the LMS (both streamed and as MP3 files) and in the language laboratory, together with pdf files containing the lyrics of the songs analyzed in the lecture.

Notably, the primary issue in delivering the material in these ways was the clear divide that developed in the student cohort between those who owned an MP3 portable listening device (e.g. iPod®) -- who were able to download material and listen when and where it suited them -- and those who did not, who could only access materials through the audio CDs, the streaming server, or the language labs. Even though the language labs also seemed to offer flexible learning opportunities, it became apparent in the tutorials that the MP3-owners were better prepared and keener to participate, simply because they had been able to access the relevant songs and radio program more easily and more often.

This experience, and feedback from the 2006 cohort, demonstrated that both mobility and accessibility were important factors in students' learning options. Adequate preparation and study of audio resources meant having time and the opportunity to sit for many hours in a language lab on campus or at a computer off-campus. Yet the reality of life for many students (other courses, commuting, part-time or even full-time work, family commitments, etc.) meant that this kind of commitment often just could not happen. Those students with MP3 players, conversely, reported being able to use many otherwise uncommitted times (downtime between classes on campus, commuting on public transport, housework, certain kinds of paid work, etc.) to listen repeatedly to the songs and the radio programs. As most of the songs were just a few minutes long, but needed multiple auditions in order for complex or concise lyrics to be understood, students found the accessibility offered by a readily available MP3 player to be very convenient. Notably, the students who did not have MP3 players often asked for more material to be provided on CDs, which they could play in generic audio systems, again trying to improve their options to be able to listen to the resource material repeatedly and when it suited them.

The 2006 experience thus clearly showed that although the language learning and motivational benefits of an audio-based course were obvious in students' marks and feedback, there was significant variation in students' capacities to use the audio resources effectively. This in turn provoked considerations of equity, as—obviously quite unintentionally—students without MP3 players were being disadvantaged. In late 2006, therefore, internal university funding was sought, and gained, to run a pilot project that would address this issue by specifically incorporating MALL, and especially APT, in the teaching of *Songs*. The aim was to support educational goals and enhance student motivation by using APT, while retaining the existing emphasis on self-directed learning, and including group projects to promote reflection, cooperation, group accountability, and teamwork.

## Evaluating the Change

As with any educational innovation, we wanted not only to test the effectiveness of using APT from its introduction, but especially to use any evaluative data to improve the courses further. Like Zuber-Skerritt (1992), we believe that action research is a "more effective way of improving [higher education] learning and teaching practice" (p. 10). Similarly, we agree that one must analyze data from multiple sources -- such as experienced teachers, users, peers, and technical experts -- to triangulate conclusions about the outcomes of a specific educational technology innovation (Alexander, McKenzie & Geissinger, 1998). While circumstantial and some qualitative evidence suggests that using APT does impact student learning, many authors are calling for more research, noting the paucity of empirical data on the nature of that impact (Beldarrain, 2006; French, 2006; Huntsberger & Stavitsky, 2006).

We therefore sought a variety of both formative and summative evaluation inputs, and used these to drive an action research cycle (Kemmis & McTaggart, 1988), as a way of "thinking systematically about what happens in teaching practice, implementing action where improvements are considered possible and monitoring and evaluating the effects of the action for continuing future improvement" (Zuber-Skerritt, 1992, p. 16). This meant that, although APT has been the central focus of both thematic courses taught annually since 2007, each iteration has been differently structured in the light of feedback from previous courses. University-standardized course evaluation feedback was collected from participating students in 2006 (without APT), in 2007, 2008, and 2009 (all with APT, progressively developed). Specialist educational technologists and designers were also invited to comment, both formally and informally, on the APT innovations at various times. In addition, a lecturer peer support and review process was ongoing, as the 2007 internal innovations grant also funded a video podcasting (vodcasting) project in the university's Japanese program.

## EMBEDDING APT IN SPANISH TEACHING IN 2007

### Making the Resources Available

The need to improve mobility and accessibility opportunities in the thematic courses suggested that the highly portable MP3 players would be the best technology to introduce immediately, especially as, by early 2007, there were already many thousands of podcasts available in Spanish, as well as much material available either in MP3 format or in a format suitable for conversion. In addition, some MP3 players (such as iPods) offered the opportunity to include text files as well as audio files, which would allow incorporation of the kinds of support materials, such as written lyrics, that the 2006 students had suggested as potentially useful.

Although we knew that some students would have their own MP3 players, equity of access was paramount, so the internal grant was used to purchase a set of iPod Nano® (2GB) players, which were available on loan to all students enrolled in the thematic courses. Each iPod came with a pre-loaded database of relevant podcasts, carefully selected by the course lecturer. This iPod essentially became each student's portable learning space for the duration of the course. In the *Songs* course, the preloaded material included recordings of individual songs, their lyrics, and podcast radio programs about Spanish songs, singers, and music movements. The *Current Affairs* resources included both contemporary and historic radio programs and other audio material on the principal social, political, economic, and cultural issues of Latin American and Spanish societies. Additional material could be uploaded by students during the semester, either from the

course database on the LMS or syndicated from publicly available podcasts on the internet.

The attention paid to ensuring familiarity with the variety of Spanish accents in the program as a whole was also carefully addressed as audio sources were being selected. Podcasts were thus chosen not solely for their content but also for their provenance and linguistic challenges. For example, the class and tutorial devoted to the New Chilean Song Movement used material sourced from a variety of sources, so that students had to negotiate, linguistically and intellectually, not only the complex content, but also the different accents of interviewee and interviewer respectively (Table 1).

### Educational Design: The Primacy of Audio

In developing the 2007 pilot project, the approach was very much geared around the view, well expressed subsequently by Deal (2007), that "podcasting [has no] inherent value… it is only valuable inasmuch as it helps … reach … educational goals, by facilitating thoughtful, engaging learning activities that are designed to work in support of those goals." All courses in ANU's Spanish program are designed according to a model of constructive alignment (Biggs, 1999; 2003), and so the introduction of APT, and the educational opportunities thus afforded, informed not only learning outcomes and learning activities but also course assessment aligned with those activities.

Two major innovations in course design were introduced into the 2007 *Songs* course. First, the audio resources (that is, the songs and radio programs to which students had to listen before lectures and tutorials) became the *sole* course resources. In other words, readings as support texts were completely omitted, and the database of radio programs was expanded. This database was available to students both in the loaned iPods and as podcasts through the VLE. Only the first

*Table 1. The podcast database section for the New Chilean Song Movement as an example of the range of accents presented through the podcast resources*

| Audio Resource (Podcast Radio Program) | Interviewer(s) / Presenter(s) | Interviewee(s) | Item Listening time (minutes, seconds) | Cumulative Listening Time (hours, minutes, seconds) |
|---|---|---|---|---|
| 1a. *Semblanza de Salvador Allende* (La Matinal, Radio Netherlands) | Chilean / Spaniard | | 05:07 | 00:05:07 |
| 1b. *Entrevista a Victor Jara* (América canta así, Lima) | Peruvian | Chilean | 07:25 | 00:12:32 |
| 2. *Inti Illimani* (Cuando el Canto es Poesía, Segunda Serie, Radio Netherlands) | Cuban | Chilean | 47:55 | 01:00:27 |
| 3. Song to be analysed in tutorial (*La muerte no va conmigo*, Inti Illimani) | | | 02:16 | 01:02:43 |
| 4a. *La nueva canción chilena* (Cuando el Canto es Poesía, Primera Serie, Radio Netherlands) | Spaniard | Chilean / Argentinean | 28:54 | 01:31:37 |
| 4b. *Víctor Jara* (Especiales UFM, Radio Universidad del Estado de Morelos) | Mexican | Chilean | 49:25 | 02:21:02 |
| 5a. *Salvador Allende* (Documentos, Radio Nacional de España) | Spaniard | Chilean / Ecuadorean / Bolivian | 55:01 | 03:16:03 |
| 5b. *Canto cautivo. Los campos de prisioneros chilenos* (Series, BBC) | Colombian | Chilean | 25:14 | 03:41:17 |

weeks of audio were pre-loaded on the iPods, so those students who needed help were shown how to download the subsequent weeks' MP3 files from the VLE into the loaned iPods, and how to create their own playlists. Students who owned an MP3 player could borrow MP3 CDs and could create the weekly playlists themselves. The two examination sources were made available exclusively through the course virtual learning environment (VLE) for students to download.

Although this all sounds simple enough, valuable lessons were learned. For example, we discovered that some students simply would not admit to having problems with the iPods until they found themselves in trouble. One case of note involved an international student scheduled to make an oral presentation in a tutorial class. The task was to summarize the radio programs assigned for that week. A few minutes into the presentation, it became clear she had not listened to the required sources, so the teacher had to lead the discussion instead. Subsequent gentle probing showed that

the student was previously inexperienced with MP3 players, and had not known how to recharge the iPod. However, since she considered herself a member of the "digital native" generation (Brown, 2000; Prensky, 2001), she had not wanted to lose "technological face" by asking a fellow student or the lecturer to help.

## Educational Design: Creating Podcasts

Perhaps most taxing for the students -- and the aspect that made APT markedly more valuable than any other way of providing listening material -- was the second innovation in educational design, namely the incorporation and integration of podcast-creation into both teaching and assessment. In particular, the *Songs* group assignment was changed from an oral presentation delivered in class to the production of a radio program on a music genre that had not been covered in the lectures. This task required small groups of students to research, write, and record their own podcasts. To reduce the risk of groups forming with "hyper-techie" or "technophobe" tendencies, the lecturer took a directive approach to group formation, trying to balance out the inherent technological skills in the different groups. However, as students' feedback suggested that this "engineered" approach to grouping had occurred at the expense of their independence in choosing study-peers, it was not used in subsequent years, when group formation was left up to the students.

Again, to ensure equity of access and opportunity, a laptop computer, professional-standard microphone and digital recorder were provided in a backpack "portable recording studio" for short-term loan. In addition, the innovations grant funded an educational technologist who was available to assist students learn about the technology, especially the use of GarageBand® as the preferred audio recording and editing software; additional class contact time (an hour-long "technology tutorial" each week) was scheduled to allow this to happen. Students were thus helped to move creatively from a "listener" mode into a more comprehensive "producer" mode.

Necessarily, however, this process required much "trial and error", as neither the teacher nor the technologist knew what would prove to be the real difficulties for students. Students were shown how to set up the portable recording studio and were taught a basic range of editing effects to demonstrate what could be done. Technical concerns that became apparent included: (1) making the podcast microphones the audio-in default in GarageBand; (2) putting the microphone into omnidirectional or unidirectional mode according to what the students were going to record; (3) basic audio ripping from CDs; and (4) conversions between different audio file formats. These skills were all discussed and taught in the technology tutorials. The technician also provided help during additional consultation hours outside class.

## Educational Design: Assessment Issues

As a scaffolding exercise to ensure that students had adequate familiarity with the recording software and hardware, each group first prepared a short podcast using a teacher-prepared script and nominated song files. Although this exercise was graded, it had a low weighting in the overall course mark and simple criteria for assessment. In terms of language, the latter focused mainly on pronunciation and intonation; in terms of technology, it focused on how well the group had demonstrated basic editing skills, such as fading out a song or using background music. After this level of achievement had been mastered, groups started on the more heavily-weighted full podcast creation assignment. By asking each group to submit a draft copy of their script before they could borrow the portable recording studio, another layer of learning scaffolding was included.

While all six groups of students were able to successfully record a radio program, three groups produced very sophisticated materials. Again in keeping with the constructive alignment focus, the final examination was based on the student-produced radio programs, as well as on additional songs from the genre submitted by each group. Each student had to choose a song to write about from those proposed by another group, with the outcome being that each person had to listen carefully to at least one program that had been produced by another group, which created new opportunities for peer learning.

## The Lessons from 2006: Improvements in 2008 and 2009

Notably, innovations in education settings often involve risk (Kirkland & Sutch, 2009). Although many lessons were learned during the 2007 APT innovations, and students were overall enthused by the new activities and opportunities, the standardized course evaluations showed a regression in mean ratings when compared to 2006 in all parameters except quality of materials (which is discussed in detail later). The lower ratings reflected students' perceptions that the course was too technical: *I lost a lot of interest when it came to the technological part of the course. I found the technological side of the class too time-consuming and boring!*

In 2008 and 2009, following our action research cycle of "plan, implement, observe, reflect, plan, …", the podcasting innovations continued, with improvements made based on the feedback and experiences of 2007. The first significant change was to enlarge the radio program database. Added to the 2007 resources of radio programs on song genres, the 2008 database was augmented with radio programs dealing with social events or political events that helped explain the social settings discussed in the lectures. This gave 2008 students more opportunities to engage with the contextual information presented in the lectures than the 2006 or 2007 students had had. Clear labelling of the podcasts became crucial as the database grew. Thus, as illustrated in Figure 1 and Table 1, podcasts were coded as 1a, 1b etc. if they were *compulsory* listening for the lecture; 2a, 2b, etc. if they were *compulsory* listening for the tutorial; 3

or 4 if they were *individually compulsory* for those students making oral presentations in the tutorials; and 5 if they were *additional, optional* sources for all students. When students downloaded podcasts from the database, they were able to use this clear pattern of podcast labelling to create their own playlists and prioritize their listening.

The coding allowed students to select which radio programs to listen to, according to whether or not they were making tutorial presentations, or depending upon the class for which they were preparing, while the extra material gave them ample opportunity to expand upon the topics covered. They also had the opportunity to listen for meaning before classes, and to listen more carefully when preparing for exams. Enlarging the database also permitted more Spanish dialects and accents to be included, an emphasis already explained as being central both to the mode of teaching (Table 1) and the satisfaction of students. As one 2009 student noted, this provided "*Great insight into the culture and practices of a range of countries.*"

In 2008, the podcasting production was simplified considerably. Instead of a series of tutorials on how to use GarageBand, an instructional document was produced, showing students all the steps to

*Figure 1. A screenshot showing how playlists were created from the podcast database*

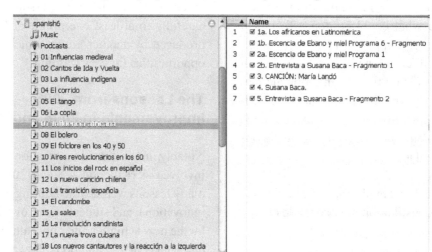

take via screen capture shots. This simplification proved extremely useful in dispelling students' perceptions that the course required a considerable amount of technical knowledge. For instance, instead of teaching students how to record after importing songs into GarageBand, which required them to mute the songs' audio, they were told to record all their readings of the script first, and then import the songs. In general, a "just-in-time" approach was taken: only those who needed to make corrections were instructed on how to do so (for example, only those who needed to learn how to mute the audio were instructed on how to do it).

Another improvement in 2008 was that the composition of groups were discussed on the first day of semester, and the teacher approved students' choices of groups as long as he was satisfied that at least one of the members had appropriate basic technical expertise (such as how to convert audio from CDs to MP3s). Students were also required to use peer evaluation, based on a contract among members of each group, on the distribution of the workload required for the scripting, correction, recording, and final editing of the radio program. The teacher did not intervene in the negotiation of this contract, but students were required to evaluate their peers on how well they performed, according to this agreement.

By the 2009 *Songs* course, the podcast database had grown so large -- tripling in size from 2006 to 2009 (Figure 2) -- and student use of the range of resources had increased so much that more time had to be allocated to discussion of weekly topics in the tutorials. To allow for this, the assignment on producing a podcast radio program was therefore shifted into the other thematic course, *Current Affairs,* where it appeared to sit better contextually (because current affairs are authentically presented as radio programs). Meanwhile, *Songs* saw a reintroduction of the group oral presentation (not in radio program format) that had been a feature of the 2006 course, with a continuing emphasis on APT. Each group's oral presentation was recorded and made available via the streaming server and

as an MP3 file for students to download onto their iPods and use as additional sources for preparing for the examination question on songs put forward by other students. However, the weighting of that question was lower in 2009 than in previous years.

## SIMULATED IMMERSION USING APT: THE OUTCOMES

In one of the few formal evaluations of the educational impact of podcasting in a tertiary setting (in an Italian university), Lazzari (2009) found that students' involvement in podcast production improved performance, promoted cognitive elaboration, and enhanced critical thinking. Students found the experience "challenging, interesting and fruitful*",* and recommended the adoption of this approach in their other subjects, especially in the teaching of foreign languages (Lazzari, 2009, p.33).

Our evaluation of outcomes was based not only on our action research and formative approaches but also on standardized evaluation data and open-ended feedback from students collected independently at the end of each course by the ANU's evaluation center. All these data demonstrate clearly the success of our use of APT as a tool to enhance both audio-lingual and social-communicative language teaching. Students became more actively involved in their learning process, and measurably improved their language acquisition outcomes and their linguistic fluency, as well as their confidence and sheer enjoyment as Spanish-speakers, which was reflected in the kinds of positive and complimentary feedback they gave in the anonymous course evaluation:

*Definitely one of the most interesting courses I have ever done. (2009 student)*

*The content and presentation of the course was amazing. (2009 student)*

*Figure 2. The growth in size of the Songs course podcast database from 2006 to 2009*

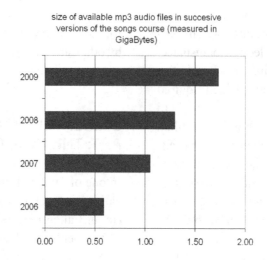

size of available mp3 audio files in succesive versions of the songs course (measured in GigaBytes)

*By far my favourite course has been Dr. Daniel Martín's 'Songs' course. The use of iPods ... was a valuable immersion experience. The course content was fascinating; while a course in Spanish songs might seem trivial and unnecessary, Dr. Martín skilfully managed to link each song with the socio-political context in which it was written, providing us with a deeper understanding of the colourful history of Spain/Latin America. It was also a great way for students to improve their vocabulary. (2008 student)*

By integrating APT fully into the assessment process, we fostered the virtual immersion initially sought. To select audio files appropriate to their language level and that of their peers, students had to do extensive periods of screening through listening; there were no short-cuts. APT also transformed standard oral presentation assignments into technologically-feasible authentic tasks: the student-produced podcasts. Despite the initial concerns raised by the unintended focus on the technology, becoming producers of audio resources as well as consumers increased student motivation significantly. As one 2009 student explained, "*a notable strength of the course was*

*the need for students to be completely involved -- the interactive nature of the course.*"

Working in their small, supportive groups, students could focus on achieving correct pronunciation and intonation in privately-recorded performances of their own scripts, rather than deal with the often-present anxiety of public speaking. Using students' own podcasts as examination material for their peers created yet another tier of authentic listening exercises. As a bonus, making the assessment "products" widely available in the podcast database in the Spanish program showed the extent of language mastery achievable in these thematic courses, a lesson not lost on first- and second-year students.

Undoubtedly it was the innovation funding available in 2006, which made iPods and portable recording studios available to all students and funded a part-time educational technologist, that made possible the groundwork that allowed APT integration to be so successful. During the pilot phase (2007), much work was done on how best to integrate iPod materials into students' existing e-learning environments within the university-wide VLE. Extensive testing of several podcasting production technologies allowed selection of an optimal set of software and hardware that reduced the technological challenges for the students, so that as far as possible they could concentrate on the real task at hand, language learning, rather than on the learning of technology skills.

Nevertheless, despite much thought being given as to how to apply the full technological functionality of APT in ways that did not require the language students to become information technology (IT) students, the 2007 feedback showed that the process of adapting to the new technology had been quite frustrating for some students, as this comment exemplifies: *"Get rid of the audios and heavy technical aspects of this course. It's a Spanish course, not an IT course."*

Even the apparently "obvious" benefits of mobility and accessibility conferred by MALL and APT should not be presumed. Even though students reported that *"the use of iPods made listening ... much easier and more convenient"* (2007 student), the level of concentration needed for this level of language study must not be underestimated:

*I found [the recordings] difficult and need[ed] to listen to them many times taking notes. It was not possible for me to walk around or be doing other things while listening. (2007 student)*

*Listening items (radio interviews etc) in the class materials would have benefitted from transcripts ... listening alone was a challenge. (2008 student)*

Although we discovered that even something as simple as not knowing how to recharge the iPod was enough to impede learning if the student did not feel confident to ask for help, it was generally the more complex podcast production requirements that the 2007 students found difficult, as these required significant learning of new technological expertise (e.g. how to use Garageband, how to record good quality voice production). Interestingly, we wonder whether the availability of the educational technologist in 2007 actually placed a greater emphasis on the technology in students' eyes, as they were constantly having to consult with an expert, whereas the more peer-focused learning approach to podcast production in 2008 seemed more engaging and less threatening. The lessons from this are the importance of structuring technological support mechanisms when introducing APT, as with any other new educational technology, and not making undue assumptions about students' pre-existing knowledge or inclinations towards such technologies.

While our action research model allowed us to make effective changes during and after each iteration of the course, the objective and independent course evaluation ratings of the *Songs* course also tell a story. The 2006 course rated very well. On a scale of 1-7 (with 7 being "excellent"), it earned mean scores ranging between 5.2 (good) and 6 (very good) on all parameters (Figure 3). The mean rating of $5.8\pm1.2$ (n=13) for "overall impact on learning" was higher than the university average. However, as shown by Figure 3, when APT was introduced in 2007, mean ratings across all parameters remained around the 5.0 (good) level, but showed distinct falls compared to 2006 ratings, except for the rating for "quality of materials." This reduction in students' satisfaction was considered largely a response to students' disappointment with the perceived over-emphasis on learning how to use the new technology, especially in terms of having to produce podcasts.

Notably, had we relied on this kind of feedback alone, we could have been discouraged enough to judge the introduction of APT a failure, and simply returned to the previous approaches to teaching. Fortunately, our commitment to an improvement cycle, and our detailed understanding of which elements had been less satisfactory in meeting learning goals, meant that we persisted with a suitably modified approach to APT into the 2008 course. The mean ratings of that iteration reached or surpassed the 2006 levels, across all parameters, with "intellectual challenge" being rated "very good" ($6.2\pm0.6$; n=11) and

*Figure 3. Some parameters from the independent Songs course evaluation data from 2006 to 2009, showing mean ratings (scale of 1-7, 7 being "excellent")*

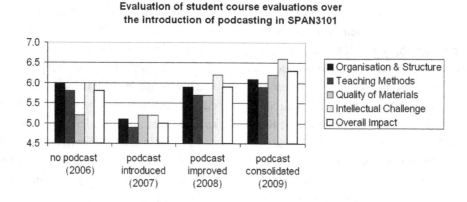

"quality of materials" rating higher than in either of the two previous years. The further consolidation and subtle adjustments to the 2009 course were repaid by even higher mean ratings across all parameters, reaching 6.3±0.8 (n=9) for "overall impact on learning" and 6.6±0.7 (n=9) for "intellectual challenge" (Figure 3).

The success of the APT integration is even more evident when we consider the proportion of students who rated aspects of the course at the maximum value -- "excellent" (7) -- in each iteration of *Songs* (Figure 4). Again there was a fall-off in 2007 compared to 2006, but by 2009 at least half the students rated many of the measured parameters as "excellent."

## FUTURE RESEARCH DIRECTIONS

Although we have focused in this chapter on the details of the *Songs* course, we had similar experiences and outcomes with APT integration into the *Current Affairs* courses over a similar period, and, more recently, with the more limited use of APT in other courses in the program. There is thus no doubt that introducing APT has been a very successful teaching strategy, not only for ANU's Spanish program itself, but also in supporting all

Spanish-related studies at the university. In 2008, there were more than 540 students enrolled in the program, many pursuing combined degrees, which has broadened the impact of our APT work across a wide range of fields and career paths. Moreover, the Spanish APT project has modelled innovative instruction for other language programs at the ANU, and Spanish lecturers have already started training ANU tutors and giving presentations and support to teacher groups outside ANU.

As Victor Hugo noted in *Histoire d'un Crime* (1852), "On résiste à l'invasion des armées; on ne résiste pas à l'invasion des idées" ["One may resist the invasion of armies; one cannot resist the invasion of ideas"]. Without doubt, simulated immersion is an idea whose time has come. In a posting made on the British Council's *TeachingEnglish* website while this chapter was being written, Hayton (2009) described the need for simulated immersion in language teaching, the features of which he describes as:

- "Large amounts of time spent simply hearing the language (several hours per week rather than mere minutes spent in a typical class)
- Maximal exposure to authentic texts

*Figure 4. Some parameters from the independent Songs course evaluation data from 2006 to 2009, showing proportions of students rating parameter as "excellent" (7)*

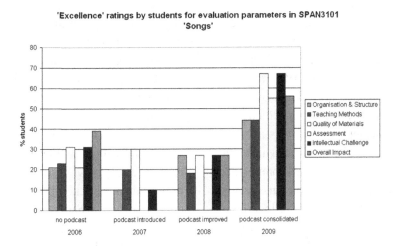

Exposure to a wide range of situations and language forms

Emphasis on bottom-up processing to aid in real-life scenarios. "

All these features are already characteristic of Spanish teaching at ANU, especially facilitated by the use of APT since 2007. Future options that will extend APT further are currently being explored within the Spanish program. One of these is a more detailed investigation of the range of flexible and open learning opportunities created by the extensive podcast database we now have available. In particular, we are working on making at least part of this database available to students enrolled in other courses in the Spanish program. For instance, a specific set of radio program podcasts has been used since 2008 to complement in-class work in a debate module in *Intermediate Level* Spanish. Another future pathway is the blending of APT with text-based technologies such as individual blogging or group wiki creation, approaches we are already trialling within the Spanish program. We are also considering the possibilities for the sharing of podcasts, including those created by students, with universities in Spanish-speaking countries.

Of course, with MALL-related technologies developing so quickly, we are also very conscious of currently unimagined opportunities that may be opening up. Enhancing audio-only podcasting with the visual cues of video technology may improve student understanding. Students with more visual learning styles have asked for additional contextualizing resources that have both visual and audio-visual components: this has encouraged us to investigate the capabilities of using technologies such as iPod Touch® for this purpose, and we are currently trialling the options for maximizing the vodcasting and portability options offered by the new iPod Nano. Like Kaplan-Leiserson (2005), we eagerly await the opportunities that will emerge as MP3 players are increasingly incorporated as standard elements of mobile (cell) phones, and by the 3G network as it brings high-speed connectivity to every mobile device. As Bates (1996) noted, part of the excitement of working with new technologies is that "no-one has yet discovered all [their] interesting uses."

# CONCLUSION

Deal (2007) described educational podcasting as having three formats: (1) as the creation of audio or video archives of classroom lectures; (2) as the delivery of supplemental course materials (e.g. pre-recorded, video reviews of homework problems, or relevant podcasts produced by a third party); and (3) as assignments that require students to produce and submit their own podcasts, a format felt to be most useful in situations in which oral presentation and/or building technical competence in podcasting are closely related to course goals.

In describing the background, educational design, and outcomes of our Spanish podcasting experiences from 2006 to 2009, this chapter illustrates the way in which we have radically reconceptualized these three formats, such that podcasts have become not an adjunct to the course but the very essence of all learning activities. Using APT in this way has thus allowed us to create a simulated immersion experience in language teaching by facilitating highly authentic and individualized learning opportunities. Since 2007, the specific focus on APT in ANU's two Spanish thematic courses has made students fully aware of the opportunities for mobile technologies, especially MP3 players such as iPods, to act as personal and portable language laboratories presenting audio and text resources in highly individualized playlists. Moreover, these students became actively engaged not only in listening to podcasts but also in creating them. It is this fully interactive engagement with APT that currently distinguishes the Spanish program from most of its language program peers at ANU, and, we believe, from Spanish programs elsewhere.

Our approach to integrating APT into language teaching provided students with easy, flexible access to many hours of authentically-sourced listening material that created an immediate and compulsory immersive context. For our students to meet course assessment requirements, there was no option but for them to listen regularly and extensively to the Spanish podcasts. Without transcripts, they could not "skim-listen" in the way they could have skimmed a reading. To be even slightly prepared for the weekly classes, students had no option but to listen to several hours of contemporary and authentic Spanish. Those who had not prepared stood out like sore thumbs: no one came unprepared to class more than once. At the same time, students wanting to excel could choose to listen to additional informative podcasts at will, all freely available on their iPods. This educational strategy was quite deliberately designed to provide a "shock" immersion, simulating in a contained way what happens when a student is suddenly thrust into a native speaker environment in a linguistically different culture. The similarity of this kind of teaching to the exchange program experience, at least from a language perspective, was not lost on our students. One student explained the relevance directly in anonymous feedback:

*The idea of having a thematic subject via iPods is also amazing as it is currently simulating the closest immersion experience I will get without actually going back to South America.*

Like Ragusa, Chan, and Crampton (2009), we have found that using podcasting technology effectively fosters "a more tailored/individualized educational experience" and that it is therefore well-suited to engaging students more deeply in their learning. Our experience also shows, however, that the need for careful planning and high quality educational design is paramount: both the users and the developers of new technologies require new skills and competencies (Chan, Lee, & McLoughlin, 2006) that are "not merely technical, but … also social" (Ragusa et al., 2009). Also, although we have found APT to be a very powerful tool in language teaching, we acknowledge that, to be successful, language teaching must always have a deeper foundation, as one of our students explained:

*[I want] to let you know how much I rate the Spanish program ... not only due to the innovative teaching methods ...like giving you an iPod to listen to Spanish songs and radio, but also because you really feel like the teachers honestly do care about sharing their language and their culture with you.*

# REFERENCES

Abdous, M., Camarena, M. M., & Facer, B. R. (2009). MALL technology: Use of academic podcasting in the foreign language classroom. *ReCALL, 21*, 76–95. doi:10.1017/S0958344009000020

Alexander, S., McKenzie, J., & Geissinger, H. (1998). *An Evaluation of Information Technology Projects for University Learning. Committee for University Teaching and Staff Development. Report to the Department of Employment, Education and Training*. Canberra: Australian Government Publishing Service.

Australian Bureau of Statistics. (2008). 1301.0 Year Book Australia 2008. Cultural diversity: Language. 2006 Census of Population and Housing. Retrieved from http://www.abs.gov.au/AUSSTATS/abs@.nsf/bb8db737e2af84b8ca2571780015701e/636F496B2B943F12CA2573D200109DA9?opendocument

Australian Government. (2008). Study overseas: Experience more. Retrieved from http://www.studyoverseas.gov.au/

Australian Government. (2009). Australian University Mobility in Asia and the Pacific (UMAP) Student exchange program. Department of Education, Employment and Workplace Relations. Retrieved from http://www.endeavour.deewr.gov.au/student_exchanges_new/australian_umap.htm

Australian Learning and Teaching Council. (2009). *New technologies, new pedagogies: Using mobile technologies to develop new ways of teaching and learning*. Retrieved from http://www.altc.edu.au/resource-new-technologies-new-pedagogies-uow-2009

Bates, A. W. (1996). The impact of technological change on open and distant learning, Queensland *Open Learning Conference: Your future depends on it*, 4 - 6 December, 1996, Brisbane, Queensland, Australia. Retrieved from http://bates.cstudies.ubc.ca/brisbane.html

Beldarrain, Y. (2006). Distance education trends: Integrating new technologies to foster student interaction and collaboration. *Distance Education, 27*(2), 139–153. doi:10.1080/01587910600789498

Biggs, J. (1999). *Teaching for quality learning at university*. Buckingham: Society for Research into Higher Education and Open University Press.

Biggs, J. (2003). *Aligning teaching and assessment to curriculum objectives. Imaginative Curriculum Project*. LTSN Generic Centre.

Brown, J. S. (2000). Growing up digital: the web and a new learning ecology. *Change*, March/April: 10-20. Reprinted as "Growing up digital: how the web changes work, education, and the ways people learn" in *USDLA Journal 16(2)*. Retrieved from http://www.usdla.org/html/journal/FEB02_Issue/article01.html

Cain, J. (2007). Podcasting enables 24/7 foreign language study. News Office, Massachusetts Institute of Technology. Retrieved from http://web.mit.edu/newsoffice/2007/podcasting-fll.html

Chan, A., Lee, M. J. W., & McLoughlin, C. (2006). Everyone's learning with podcasting: A Charles Sturt University experience. In *Who's learning? Whose technology? Proceedings ascilite Sydney 2006*. Retrieved from http://www.ascilite.org.au/conferences/sydney06/proceeding/pdf_papers/p171.pdf

Deal, A. (2007). *Podcasting.* A Teaching with Technology White Paper. CarnegieMellon Office of Technology for Education. Retrieved from http://www.cmu.edu/teaching/resources/PublicationsArchives/StudiesWhitepapers/Podcasting_Jun07.pdf

French, D. P. (2006). iPods: Informative or invasive. *Journal of College Science Teaching, 36*(1), 58–59.

Furman, N., Goldberg, D., & Lusin, N. (2007). *Enrollments in languages other than English in United States institutions of higher education, Fall 2006.* New York: Modern Languages Association of America. Retrieved from *Information. Communicatio Socialis, 12*(5), 678–690.

Gilgen, R. (2005). Holding the world in your hand: Creating a mobile language learning environment. *Educase Quarterly, 3*, 30–39.

Godwin-Jones, R. (2005). Skype and podcasting: Disruptive technologies for language learning. *Language Learning & Technology, 9*, 9–12. Retrieved from http://llt.msu.edu/vol9num3/emerging/default.html.

Hayton, T. (2009). Simulated immersion. *TeachingEnglish*, British Council. Retrieved 31 March, 2010 from http://www.teachingenglish.org.uk/think/articles/simulated-immersion

Huntsberger, M., & Stavitsky, A. (2007). The new "podagogy": Incorporating podcasting into journalism education. *Journalism and Mass Communication Educator, 61*(4), 397–410.

Jobbings, D. (2005). *Exploiting the educational potential of podcasting.* Russell Educational Consultancy and Productions. Retrieved from http://www.recap.ltd.uk/articles/podguide.html

Kaplan-Leiserson, E. (2005). Trend: Podcasting in academic and corporate learning. *Learning Circuits.* Retrieved from http://www.astd.org/LC/2005/0605_kaplan.htm

Kemmis, S., & McTaggart, R. (Eds.). (1988). *The action research planner.* Victoria: Deakin University.

Kirkland, K., & Sutch, D. (2009). Overcoming the barriers to educational innovation: A literature review. Futurelab. Retrieved from http://www.futurelab.org.uk/resources/documents/lit_reviews/Barriers_to_Innovation_review.pdf

Lafford, B. A., Lafford, P. A., & Sykes, J. (2007). Entre dicho y hecho ... [Between what is said and done]: An assessment of the application of research from second language acquisition and related fields to the creation of Spanish CALL materials for lexical acquisition. *CALICO Journal, 24*(3).

Lafford, P. A., & Lafford, B. A. (2005). CMC technologies for teaching foreign languages: What's on the horizon? *CALICO Journal, 22*(3), 679–709. Retrieved from https://72.167.96.97/html/article_162.pdf.

Laing, C., Wootton, A., & Irons, A. (2006). iPod! uLearn? *FORMATEX 2006.* Retrieved from http://www.formatex.org/micte2006/Downloadable-files/oral/iPod.pdf

Lazzari, M. (2009). Creative use of podcasting in higher education and its effect on competitive agency. *Computers & Education, 5*, 27–34. doi:10.1016/j.compedu.2008.06.002

Lee, M., & Chan, A. (2007). Pervasive, lifestyle-integrated mobile learning for distance learners: An analysis and unexpected results from a podcasting study. *Open Learning: The Journal of Open and Distance Learning, 22*(3), 201–218.

Martín, M. D. (2005). Permanent crisis, tenuous persistence: Foreign languages in Australian universities. *Arts and Humanities in Higher Education, 4*(1), 53–75. doi:10.1177/1474022205048758

Murphy, B. (2008). Podcasting in higher education. *ITNOW, 50*(3), 22–23. doi:10.1093/itnow/bwn056

Prensky, M. (2001). Digital natives, digital immigrants. *On The Horizon, 9*(5). NCB University Press. Retrieved from www.marcprensky.com/writing/Prensky%20-%20Digital%20Natives,%20Digital%20Immigrants%20-%20Part1.pdf

Ragusa, A., Chan, A., & Crampton, A. (2009). iPods aren't just for tunes. *Information Communication and Society, 12*(5), 678–690. doi:10.1080/13691180802471471

Read, J. (1996). Recent developments in Australian late immersion language education. *Journal of Multilingual and Multicultural Development, 17*(6), 469–484. doi:10.1080/01434639608666296

Thomas, M. (2008). *Handbook of research on Web 2.0 and second language learning*. Hershey, PA: Information Science Reference.

Thorne, S. L., & Payne, J. S. (2005). Evolutionary trajectories, internet-mediated expression, and language education. *CALICO Journal, 22*(3), 371–397. Retrieved from http://language.la.psu.edu/~thorne/thorne_payne_calico2005.pdf.

U.S. Census Bureau. (2009). S1601 Language spoken at home 2006-2008 American Community Survey 3-year estimates. Retrieved from http://factfinder.census.gov/servlet/STTable?geo_id=01000US&ds_name=ACS_2008_3YR_G00_&qr_name=ACS_2008_3YR_G00_S1601

Zuber-Skerritt, O. (1992). *Action research in higher education*. London: Kogan Page.

## ADDITIONAL READING

Biersdorfer, J., & Pogue, D. (2009). *iPod: The missing manual*, 8th edition. Sebastopol, California: O'Reilly Media and Pogue Press.

Dale, C., & Pymm, J. M. (2009). Podagogy: The iPod as a learning technology. *Active Learning in Higher Education, 10*, 84–96. doi:10.1177/1469787408100197

Edirisingha, P., Rizzi, C., Nie, M., & Rothwell, L. (2007). Podcasting to provide teaching and learning support for an undergraduate module on English language and communication. *Turkish Online Journal of Distance Education, 8(3)*, 87-107. Retrieved from http://tojde.anadolu.edu.tr/tojde27/pdf/article_6.pdf

Fose, L., & Mehl, M. (2007). Plugging into students' digital DNA: Five myths prohibiting proper podcasting pedagogy in the new classroom domain. *Journal of Online Learning and Teaching, 3*(3). Retrieved from http://jolt.merlot.org/vol3no3/mehl.pdf.

Kukulska-Hulme, A. (2009). Will mobile learning change language learning? *ReCALL, 21*, 157–165. doi:10.1017/S0958344009000202

Lord, G. (2008). Podcasting Communities and Second Language Pronunciation. *Foreign Language Annals, 41*(2), 364–379. doi:10.1111/j.1944-9720.2008.tb03297.x

McGarr, O. (2009). A review of podcasting in higher education: Its influence on the traditional lecture. *Australasian Journal of Educational Technology, 25(3)*, 309-321. Retrieved from http://www.ascilite.org.au/ajet/ajet25/mcgarr.html

Murphy, B. (2008). Podcasting in higher education. *ITNOW, 50*, 22–23. doi:10.1093/itnow/bwn056

Parson, V., Reddy, P., Wood, J., & Senior, C. (2009). Educating an iPod generation: undergraduate attitudes, experiences and understanding of vodcast and podcast use. *Learning, Media and Technology, 34*(3), 215–228. doi:10.1080/17439880903141497

Pérez, L. I. G. (2006). *El podcasting en España, del uso privado a las grandes emisoras.* ITESM Campus Estado de México: Proyecto Internet.

Rosell-Aguilar, F. (2007). Top of the Pods—In search of a podcasting "Podagogy" for language learning. *Computer Assisted Language Learning, 20*(5), 471–492. doi:10.1080/09588220701746047

Salmon, G. (2005). Flying not flapping: a strategic framework for e-learning and pedagogical innovation in higher education institutions. *ALT-J, 13*(3), 201–218. doi:10.1080/09687760500376439

van Zanten, R. (2008). The value of lecture podcasting for distance and on-campus students. In *Hello! Where are you in the landscape of educational technology? Proceedings ascilite Melbourne 2008.* Retrieved http://www.ascilite.org.au/conferences/melbourne08/procs/vanzanten.pdf

Wagstaff, P. E. (2007). Educational podcasting: Fad or future? *Proceedings of the Australian and New Zealand Marketing Academy Conference, Dunedin December 2007.* Retrieved from http://conferences.anzmac.org/ANZMAC2007/papers/P%20Wagstaff_1a.pdf

Williams, B. (2007). *Educator's podcast guide.* Eugene, Oregon: International Society for Technology in Education.

## KEY TERMS AND DEFINITIONS

**Audio or CD Ripping:** This is the process of converting video and audio from CDs or DVDs to a format storable in a hard drive, and it requires converting material into digital formats suitable for audio- or video-editing software or to be played in portable devices.

**Learning Management System (LMS):** see VLE.

**Omnidirectional Microphone:** This is a type of microphone (or a setting in a pick-up pattern of a microphone) which takes in sound coming from all directions. It allows for the recording of round tables or multiple speakers, but increases the possibility of unwanted noise to be included in the recording.

**Podcast:** This form of audio or video broadcasting using the Internet first became popular in late 2004. The word—a portmanteau of Apple's "iPod" and "broadcast" -- was named "Word of 2005" by the Oxford American Dictionary. Files distributed via podcast do not require the use of an Apple iPod, however, as they can be downloaded and played by a large array of marketed portable audio devices.

**Podcasting:** This is the distribution of multimedia files (audio or video) through the Internet for playback on a mobile device, often in MP3 or mp4 format. The files are released episodically and downloaded via an RSS feed.

**Really Simple Syndication (RSS) Feed:** This system of distributing electronic information allows people to subscribe to obtain an automatically downloaded summary of frequently updated content from websites, including links to the full versions of the content (text or multimedia files) and other metadata, which removes the need to check for revised content manually. RSS is available through specific software (RSS feed readers) or through many commercial browsers.

**Unidirectional Microphone:** This type of microphone (or a setting in a pick-up pattern of a microphone) takes in sound coming from only one particular direction, and is used to record readings rather than group discussions, as it reduces the possibility of unwanted background noise being included in the recording.

**Virtual Learning Environment (VLE):** A VLE comprises a high-end software package designed to support teaching and learning in educational settings by automating administration processes and providing online tools to help lecturers create course websites with a minimum of technical skill, including tools for assessment, discussion, uploading of content, and resource sharing. Although there are significant variations in the proprietary and open-source systems in widespread use across the world, a modern VLE will generally not only provide an e-learning resource platform for simple and rich media formats, with options for RSS feeds and social networking tools such as blogs and wikis, but will also register users, track courses, record data from learners (including access, test results, and assignment input), and provide reports to course teachers and management. Most VLE software is web-based to facilitate access to learning content and administration. While originally created to support distance education, VLEs are also often used in blended learning, that is, course design that uses technology to supplement traditional face-to- face classroom activities. Although there were originally distinct differences in origin and focus between VLEs and learning management systems (LMS), convergent evolution of these systems means that the terms now tend to be used interchangeably, with preferences for one or the other term ending to be country-dependent rather than system-related.

# Section 3
# MALL and Study Abroad

# Chapter 8
# iStudyAbroad

**Kathryn Murphy-Judy**
*Virginia Commonwealth University, USA*

## ABSTRACT

*Students studying abroad already don't leave home without their mobile devices—phones, MP3 players, netbooks, laptops. The potential for m-learning for these device-toting learners holds great promise that can easily be capitalized upon by the savvy teacher. Learners studying abroad who are outfitted with m-learning devices which include well-chosen Web 2.0 resources derive immediate and long range benefits. Furthermore, when organized to communicate with learners back home, the travelers help create a transnational community of practice that shares the wealth of the experiential learning. This chapter takes a tour of mobile learning technologies and techniques that enhance and extend the study abroad experience far beyond the reach of a small group fortunate enough to travel. As has long been the case with CALL (Computer Assisted Language Learning) and TELL (Technology Enhanced Language Learning), and now with MALL (Mobile Assisted Language Learning), experts note that well-chosen resources, along with carefully structured and planned activities, enhance various aspects of language acquisition and social interaction. After the literature review, this chapter considers lessons gleaned from the author's trails, trials, and errors across a range of technologies and borders. It ends with suggestions for ways to optimize iStudyAbroad today and tomorrow.*

## INTRODUCTION

We are poised at the on-ramp for a thrilling m-learning adventure that couples anytime, anywhere mobility with active, experiential learning along individualized, social, or mixed pathways. Mediated learning on the road, whether to local sites

of linguistic and cultural interest or as an integral part of a study abroad (SA) experience, extends and deepens the impact for those who travel and, if well mapped out, for those back home as well. The convergence of Web 2.0 (a.k.a. the social web) with mobile devices affords foreign language learners and teachers exciting opportunities both on and off the planned itinerary.

DOI: 10.4018/978-1-60960-141-6.ch008

The utility of mobile devices for study abroad programs is multiple. Fingertip communication can both minimize risks and create opportunities across the full range of study abroad aspects, including finances, transportation, safety, and, of course, education and communication. For example, timely access to information resources may help defray certain costs: access to restaurant prices, ticket availability, and transportation schedules can provide powerful money- and time-saving opportunities. Safety and health problems, too, are more easily resolved with instantaneous information and access. In this chapter, however, the focus is pedagogical. Already, devices like cell phones connect learners abroad with both L1 and L2 communities also abroad. Families and friends back home make sure that travelers have a cell phone or some option that allows a reasonable amount of communication. Yet, when the experience instantly connects learners abroad with learners back home, the learning advantages for everyone can increase dramatically. By charting these initial inroads of m-learning into the realm of study abroad, this chapter will help instructors learn how to implement iStudyAbroad projects, by providing:

- a review of the literature on study abroad (SA) and mobile devices for second language learning and acquisition while abroad;
- a discussion of possible integrations of iStudyAbroad based mainly on the author's technology-enhanced study abroad programs; and
- solutions and workarounds for some of the issues, as well as future directions.

## REVIEW OF THE LITERATURE

Literature abounds on study abroad (SA) best practices for second language learning and acquisition (SARG, 2005). It is generally agreed that the more learners immerse themselves in the target language and culture, the more they learn about the language, culture and themselves, and the more linguistic and cultural skills they acquire (Dufon & Churchill, 2006). The 'ugly truth' is, as Kinginger (2008) acknowledges, "while SA is certainly a productive context for language learning, its outcomes are neither as dramatic nor as equally distributed among students as one might hope they would be." Addressing the study abroad context, Barron (2003) proposes to increase sociopragmatics, that is, the development of socially appropriate speech strategies (the development of which appears to surpass pragmalinguistics, that is, those structural variations chosen for specific discursive effect) by having learners engage in ethnographic projects while immersed in the target culture. She also prescribes pre-departure and post-return seminars for the mutual benefit of upcoming SA students and returning students. Although she does not mention CALL, TELL, or MALL, both of her interventions -- the ethnographic projects and the student exchanges are ripe for technological mediations, with MALL, perhaps, being most appropriate during a study abroad program.

Students who congregate mainly with fellow travelers speaking L1 advance less in all skills and knowledge than those who have home stays and sustained interaction in the target language (L2). An important study presented by Freed, Segalowicz, and Dewey at the 2001 Congress of the American Council on the Teaching of Foreign Languages (ACTFL) (Freed & al., 2001) gave evidence that time immersed in the target language, regardless of location, is the primary factor in increased acquisition: students attending the Middlebury College on-campus summer school with its L2-only policy demonstrated greater acquisition than those studying abroad during the same period but without an L2-only policy in force. That study culminated in the book-length publication of 2004 (Freed & al.) in which these results among others are explored more fully.

Again, technological mediation received no attention, but research on acquisition and context is critical to the eventual construction of best MALL practices for the study abroad context.

In addition to linguistic immersion, learner reflection on linguistic and cultural differences and experiences adds significantly to the SA learning process. Such reflection is called the "critical common denominator" by some (Cowan et al., 2004). Thus, an emphasis on journaling and/or reflective writing has become de rigueur in many SA programs (Jackson, 2005). Few studies, once again, have brought CALL, TELL, or MALL to bear upon the SA experience, although Hubbs (2000) gives an interesting, personal history on the intersection of new technologies and study abroad. Still, his interest is programmatic rather than pedagogical, targeting the use of electronic media to research and market study abroad programs as a function of international education advising. It is to be hoped that the upcoming special issue of Frontiers, A History of Study Abroad: 1965 to Present, in the chapter titled "The Impact of Telecommunications and other Technologies" will address SLA concerns and best practices (Donatelli 2010, forthcoming).

The literature includes brief references to stand-alone programs that might be used to prepare pre-departure learners on phrase acquisition, basic linguistic notions, cultural norms, or business practices. These only mention SA as part of the broader spectrum of foreign language education (FLE). As such, they do not warrant citation here, except for Godwin-Jones' (1999) quick note in LLT on emerging technologies in which he foresaw almost the full scope of MALL and m-learning years over ten years ago. The first major infusion of computer-mediated communication (CMC) arose with key-pal or email exchanges. Students going abroad who had access to such affordances could interact with host families or peers prior to departure and, once there, could send reports home (Hoffa, 1996). Still, the particularities of a CMC environment on language

learning in the SA environment have not been differentiated from mailing "regular letters", nor have they been optimized for their technological specificity. In the literature, then, even the CMC effect on study abroad has received scant attention, except for what is mentioned in the section on blogging below.

Portable audio and visual recording brought forth a whole new scene of mediated learning and reflection in education. Since the miniaturization of audio in the 1970's and the advent of video recording devices in the 1980's, faculty and students alike have recorded aspects of their travels on tape. Once recording migrated to digital media, it took over the A/V media market. Most of the early user-generated recordings did not integrate immediately into the learning adventures. Rather, they returned home in raw form, awaiting heavy-duty video editing equipment and technical know-how to make them suitable for sharing and dissemination. Digital media and the development of increasingly easy-to-use audio and video editing software—beginning notably with Apple's Quicktime in the early 1990's—led to today's instant "user-produced content." Today, adventures abroad find their way onto web pages and into classrooms readily, as audio and video clips (Brinckwirth, Kissling, Murphy-Judy, & Valencia, 2007; Godwin-Jones, 1999). Still, Web 1.0 was not yet "social"; thus, neither were the posting and circulation of the clips. With ever-improving hardware and software, increasingly sophisticated audio and video are produced instantaneously, with little production expertise needed. Another factor in attaining media mobility and sociability has been the ongoing improvement of compression/decompression (CODEC) routines to decrease file size, thus making files more sharable and transferable online. CODEC improvements added to accelerating network connection speeds and storage capacities, laid the groundwork for social media. QuickTime in particular, once again paved the way for many other consumer routines that now allow us to enjoy things like YouTube® and video podcasts ("vodcasts"), and assure their easy distribution via email and websites.

As Web 2.0 emerged, and as telecommunications gained greater ubiquity and speed, the technology-enhanced language learning scene began changing rapidly, in concert. The arrival of Web 2.0, with its explosion of social networking, introduced greater immediacy and shared learning, thanks to blogs, wikis, social networks (Nings®, FaceBook®, MySpace®, among others), Voice over IP (like Skype®), and podcasts. Importantly, the web, in both its early and current formulations, allows for greater individuation in learning, as well as for greater socialization. Yet, for all the speed and access, educational integrations lag behind.

The scholarly corpus on MALL, as evinced by this volume and the recent ReCALL volume (2008), is small but growing. The inevitable convergence of MALL and study abroad is ripe for new integrations, experimentation, and study. Yet, it was presaged by Godwin-Jones (1999) over ten years ago, as he foresaw the convergence of digital audio, video, and text in transnational exchanges. More recently, he addressed the increased mobility of mobile devices (in the 1999 piece, there was still talk of telephone modems!) and the emergence of smartphone technologies (Godwin-Jones, 2004). The definition of MALL by Shield and Kukulska-Hulme (2008a) applies implicitly to the study abroad context:

*MALL uses a wide range of devices, often with internet connectivity, from ultra-portable laptops and handhelds to mobile phones, digital voice recorders, MP3 and MP4 players, digital cameras and video recorders; in other words, MALL devices are not necessarily computers, although a computer, whether desktop, laptop or handheld is usually involved at some point, if only to connect to the internet. Furthermore, MALL has the potential to assist learners at the exact point of need and in ways that are congruent with learners' increasingly mobile, always-connected lifestyles. (p. 249)*

In their chapter review of the literature in the ReCALL volume mentioned above, Shield and Kukulska-Hulme consider earlier work by Petersen and Divitini (2004) that suggested that m-learning might empower learners during study abroad, perhaps by giving them the ability to capture and share their experiences with other learners in ways appropriate to social media. The ReCALL volume editors compare the more teacher-centric approaches of Dias (2002a, b) and the City College of Southampton (2005). Addressing the SA-MALL interface, however, is left to Petersen and Divitini, with Chabert joining them later in the ReCALL volume. So, finally, there is an article devoted to study abroad and mobile devices (Petersen, Divitini, & Chabert, 2008). Its main thrust is the creation and support of a community of practice using a blog to connect learners abroad with those back home via mobile devices. The pedagogical strategy is to provide more community support for the travelers via CMC (or mobile mediated communication). This strategy, of course, responds to the SA-SLA research that underscores community building and reflection as factors that contribute to foreign language learning in SLA abroad. Nevertheless, the Petersen, Divitini, Chabert project did not yield the anticipated results. The authors surmise that the travelers did not really share a sense of community with the home-campus group. Thus, the authors proposed new strategies to create that sense of community and identity in m-learning.

Whereas studies are few, it should be noted here that blogging and study abroad already have developed a wide usage. Many SA programs include student blogs from abroad on their websites, for both marketing and learning reasons. A quick Google search of "study abroad and blog" resulted in over two million hits in January, 2010. I note here just three blogs of interest:

- MikeT's Random Thoughts, My 2 Cents. Now On Sale! study abroad blogs http://maghrebs. ipower.com/random-thoughts/?p=318

- National Geographic's Glimpse at http://glimpse.org, which, this author believes, is not yet realizing its promise.
- The Middlebury, Haverford, Dickenson project called Blogging the World (from 2005 on).

After facing my own financial difficulties using a BlackBerry® then an iPhone® while directing study abroad programs, I find that this caveat from Shield and Kakulska-Hulmes (2008) regarding the cost of MALL should be a very salient part of our thinking about m-learning in SA, at least until such time as global providers tear down their Berlin walls:

*In the formal contexts, learners often seem to require that their studies be subsidized in order to provide the motivation to use mobile devices to support their learning, while learners in informal contexts appear to be less concerned about cost, accessing learning materials at their own convenience and to suit their own needs. Of course, other factors such as the relative costs of using mobile phone networks in different geographical locations or from different providers must play a role here, but the cost – real or perceived – of participation in m-learning is another area that requires careful exploration and further research by those working in MALL (p.282)*

Maybe in part for financial reasons, podcasting has been one of the more ubiquitous integrations of mobile technologies and SA: it is affordable. At first, MP3 players were mainly content provider driven: music, lectures, podcasts. In short order, the iPod® and other MP3 devices gained the ability to record. From that moment on, they entered the realm of social media. Granted, users could use recording hardware and software to produce podcasts using their computers, but the recording functionality on mp3 players accelerated the driving force of mobility. An important factor in the social aspect, and part of the Apple marketing genius, was the broadcasting feature they dubbed "podcasting." By offering iTunes® as a venue for uploading one's own podcasts, they provided the easy storage and sharing of user-generated content. It is the social factor of social media that underlies the success of YouTube and other participatory sites. The obvious applications of podcasting for interviewing, journaling, and the like have given many programs, SA group leaders, and learners themselves the idea to podcast. iTunes University® hosts several podcasts (from UCLA, the University of Michigan, and Notre Dame, to name but a few). A broad range of university and other study abroad organisms host podcasts for students, parents, and others on their home websites. Research on podcasting is strong in the TELL-MALL circles, albeit less so when its target is study abroad.

In 2006, Marist College won a Campus Technology Innovator Award for its use of podcasts in study abroad (Campus Technology, 2009). In the article that describes the award-winning project, moving away from the podcast qua recorded lecture toward a constructivist, task-based means of learning and sharing is documented. Instead of providing e-learning for General Education courses needed by students while on study abroad, "a remarkable collaboration among faculty, administration, the Office of Academic Technology, and the college's Media Center sought to offer the students an alternative—a "Quest" learning model—that would deepen the study-abroad experience and not allow students to rely on the "crutch" of their home institution's eLearning resources." The article details the technological resources that went into the project and ends with advice for preparing the students who go abroad: "Students need to be trained carefully before they leave their home institution in order to ensure they have mastered the technical skills to complete projects. Working closely with your media center will help enormously to address these challenges." I would add that the faculty, too, have to be completely trained.

Part of the impetus for my own SA project detailed in this chapter arose from hearing Dr. Kevin Gaugler (Marist College) and Mr. Duleep Deosthale (Knowledge Exchange Institute) present "Computer-assisted Study Abroad: Empowering Students with Web 2.0" at the 2008 CALICO-IALLT Symposium (2008). In that presentation, they discussed the mediation of podcasting, blogging, and geotagged photography to enhance in-country experiential learning for students abroad and distance-delivered sharing from host country travelers back to learners at home. Often, Marist's learners abroad function as TAs, delivering up-to-the-minute information, sights, and sounds to those in Poughkeepsie, NY. Many of the podcasts address fields other than foreign languages and cultures, among them journalism, current affairs, and business. Gaugler and his colleagues at Marist College have posted their more recent podcast on cultural identity and study abroad on WAMC news (PBS Kingston NY) here: http://bit.ly/8CD8C1 and describe it in Campus Technology (2006), as well.

Gaugler and his colleagues use podcasting in one fashion. Podcasts, however, are also used routinely to advertise, promote, and prepare students for studying abroad. A quick Google search of "podcasts and study abroad" lists those from a wide variety of colleges and universities. They include ads for various programs, lessons on health and travel issues, and recorded programs from in-country. iTunes offers podcasts by the Fulbright Program, CEA Study Abroad, and Florida Healthspan for medical study overseas, Western Kansas University's Impresiones de España, and San Jose State's 2007 semester in Bath, England, to name but a few.

In summary, then, studies that focus on study abroad in conjunction with CALL, TELL, and/or MALL are limited in number. What this author does see emerging, however, are digital practices that combine forces: YouTube videos, blogs, wikis, Nings, FaceBook groups, podcasts, and the like with learners who are abroad. With the explosion of m-learning possibilities, those of us who integrate them do so based on time-tested SLA theories and practices. We also tweak them for the highly interactive and mobile affordances they offer. It's always been about the pedagogy, not the technology. Moreover, m-learning, like so much other socially mediated learning, is bi-directional. Learners help me as a professor better understand new technologies and their uses. I work with students to build appropriate learning and support routines. Together, (with the emphasis on "together"), we experiment, reflect, and refine what it is that we are learning and doing.

## INTEGRATIONS OF ISTUDYABROAD

### Trails, Trials, and Errors

I led my first VCU summer study abroad program to La Rochelle, France, in 2004. I didn't have an iPod yet, but I did have a digital video camera. The school with which we traditionally partner in La Rochelle, the Institut d'Études Françaises (IEF) of the École Supérieure de Commerce (ESC), offered internet connections on campus to all of us. There were at least two internet cafés in the city. Very few of the students came equipped with iPods® or MP3 players. I do recall one student who maximized his trip, pre-departure and while there, through a variety of chat rooms, making "friends" before he arrived and arranging to meet them in country. Needless to say, he had an amazing variety of linguistic and cultural experiences, far beyond those of his fellow students. The rest of us took lots of digital photos, some of which I eventually used to market the program the next year. The videos, which included interviews with the VCU students and those from the other two universities with whom we travel, also served as marketing tools for the next year. We shared photos but not as much as we could have by using Flickr® (which had just started up in 2004).

By 2006, much had improved. I brought a powerful 17" Apple PowerBook® and an Olympus C-8080® Wide Zoom digital camera (still and motion-with-sound). Although my apartment had neither cabling nor wifi access, I did have access in the common room when it was open and, of course, the school offered us internet connectivity. All of the trip participants exchanged photos. Few of us had cell phones: we mainly used calling cards for local and long distance calling. The big cell phone explosion and ease of cell phone use abroad came the next year.

In 2007, I tried my first Web 2.0 interactions. In the first instance, two local French teachers --one an adjunct professor at VCU, the other a high school teacher pursing a Masters on campus --agreed to work with me on the American side of a transatlantic Ning community: http://vcuenfrance. ning.com/. The VCU professor was supposed to have her class on campus access the Ning: the three faculty members were supposed to build it together from both sides of the Atlantic and then to open it up to all the students. The teacher, a native speaker, was populating the Ning with some of his photos and serving as a resource person for those of us traveling. Even though I held a training session for the two of them prior to my departure, it apparently was not enough. Once I was gone, neither ventured onto the site. In La Rochelle, a firewall at the school was preventing the students and I from accessing the Ning. I ended up being the only one with access by using my own laptop over the school wifi. Lessons learned:

1. Make sure that everyone involved is thoroughly conversant in the affordances.
2. Explicitly detail all roles and time frames.
3. Make certain that students know which aspects are part of their grade.
4. Work with the host institution's IT people before arrival.

In this case, I was still conceptualizing the Ning®, albeit a social network, as more controlled by the teachers, i.e., me and the two others. I was not able to meet with all the student travelers before departure to teach them how to "ning", and once we arrived in La Rochelle, the vagaries of the housing, transportation, and schooling there made it impossible to set up training (I gave up after two weeks). Social networks operate better with less overt authority: by my second attempt, I understood that lesson.

Regarding mobile devices: most of us that year had cell phones and MP3 players. I had a BlackBerry, which, in addition to phone and email (Lotus Notes), offered me weather and web capabilities when and where the French Orange network was accessible. I didn't know the affordances of the BlackBerry well enough to construct any m-learning around it for my students.

In 2008, I tried again to set up a trans-Atlantic community, especially since I had to return halfway through the trip to assume the co-direction of a reverse study abroad (French students from the Rouen ESC coming to my home campus). I had wanted to pair up the VCU students in France with Rouen students in Richmond. Again, the partnering failed. Training the partner(s) should have been assured prior to their departure. Thus, my substitute in France was not versed in the technologies. The other problem was the large number of French students (who outnumbered the Americans in France by ten to one). It would have been logistically difficult to 'pair' the two sets of students, given the lopsided numbers. Without my presence in France to sort out the logistics and to pave the technological way, it simply didn't happen.

Finally, in 2009, I was very familiar with Nings. I thought I had learned the training lesson sufficiently to be able to try again. I simply updated the Ning from 2007 (http://vcuenfrance. ning.com/: you may only access the first page, unless you sign up, for reasons of student privacy). I added a number of effective gadgets, from an event calendar that connects to Google Maps (first is the event calendar on the vcuenfrance Ning and second the linked map):

To a survey administered by Poll Daddy as a gadget:

The students and I had personal blogs. Mine served as a model. Their development of a blog was stipulated as part of their final grade. Those who began the séjour linguistique with little French (novice high ACTFL proficiency scale, A2 CEFR) were only expected to try out new phrases and vocabulary, in a more or less franglais environment at first. As time went on, I expected them to convert to mostly French sentences, using their classroom learning and immersion experiences coupled with help from tutors, peers, and teachers.

The most important aspect of the Ning, this time, was its social network. Once the students started to use the site, adding their own content, and especially inviting their family and friends to participate in it, they took ownership of it. The harder part was getting the group back home involved. I enlisted the adjunct professor from the 2006 attempt and another part-time instructor. I tried to motivate the home classes by attending

their classes prior to my departure. I showed them the Ning and asked them to create 'cool' scavenger hunts of what they would like us to discover in France and share with them (based on our itinerary and the upcoming lessons in their book). In one class, two students got involved. In the other, I believe that the professor confused the study abroad Ning with another one that I co-direct for area K-16 teachers. Eventually, she sent me an email with questions and searches for our group abroad.

Our Ning worked well within our community of practice abroad. By the end of our journey, all of the students were participating, and were even responding to one another. We were all sharing photos, tagging each other on FaceBook, Flickr, and Picasa® accounts (and the like). Then again, they were already using other mobile devices to connect with friends and family. In particular, they were text messaging via cell phones, smart phones, or iPod Touches®. I had limited texting on my international plan because I had failed to realize the extent to which students text (more than call). Two of the learners put invitations to local events

*Figure 1. Premier jour d'excursion au nord de la France: VCU en France*

*Figure 2. Excursion 2 juillet 09 Paris-Giverny-Lisieux: Google Maps*

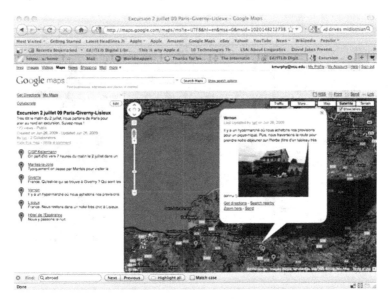

on the Ning. Still, many communications were in English, even the ones they sent me. This is where a target language-only policy (except in cases of danger or potential harm) should be enforced. If I were leading the group this summer, I would probably use Twitter as our texting base since we could form a group and save our tweets. In particular, I would use Twitter or a short text-based platform for either a scavenger hunt or a chasse aux trésors to improve our excursions (to Paris, Giverny, Normandy, Loire Valley, or Cognac).

As part of the MacFac Group at my university (in which Mac users like myself learn and share new applications), I had learned about geomap-

*Figure 3. My Apps: VCU en France*

*Figure 4. VCU en France: connections franco-américaines*

ping, using the iPhone, Trails (an iPhone app), and HoudahGeo software for the photos. Geomapping allows a smartphone with GPS to track the user's meanderings, creating a map into which photos that are time/date/geo-stamped can be inserted (this site explains the process for both Mac and PC platforms: http://multimedia.journalism.berkeley.edu/tutorials/geotagging-photos/tools/). I had planned to incorporate it into the study abroad experience, putting it on the Ning so that our excursions could be followed easily and immediately by our whole community. I also had other wildly innovative ideas for my iPhone. The ugly reality came down to cost. AT&T, as a carrier, does not currently play well with international partners. My students, also, were prohibited from several m-learning experiments that I had wanted to try out, due to cost of their phone plans. I refer the reader back to the Shield and Kukulska-Hulmes comments on the prohibitive costs. Cost is a critical factor, especially for many students. As I will point out below, Google may offer more cost-effective (a.k.a, free) solutions soon.

When I was in wifi areas in France, I was able to use some of the iPhone apps. (Paris is almost entirely a free wifi zone, for example.) Several interesting apps that could assist learners abroad in France and beyond to enjoy their experience even more and to deepen their learning are listed here:

- Map apps like Google Earth that provide mobile mapping often offer users deep information, like that on the Louvre, Ancient Rome, and other Google Earth locales
- Weather information, like Euro Weather and specific sites from one's host country, like TV5 and France24 for France
- Money exchange rate apps, like FX Exchange Rates. Some may have GPS locators for banks and exchanges in one's locale.
- Grocery Lists, like the French Liste d'épicerie mobile. These are lots of fun for creating a picnic on the fly with one's students.
- Voice recording apps, like Voice Memo®, or Dictaphone/AudioMemo®, which can record lectures or guided tours but also singing, conversations, and other great sounds. Newer cameras with video can grab the visuals, too.
- Newspapers and TV sites like LeMonde.fr and TV5 for France
- Radio stations like RadioFrance

- Event applications like Eventful®, an application for cultural events in various cities around France
- FaceBook, the social networking site that all our students use already
- Twitter, a microblogging utility much like texting or SMS that allows for group formations and searching
- Specialty apps, like Cui-Cui! Chants d'oiseaux d'Europe. This one is for bird lovers who would like to identify the birds behind the songs they hear. There are a vast number of these kinds of special interest apps.
- SMS or Skype: is possible to load Skype on one's iPhone, but just not use the phone part. So, it operates essentially like another short message service (or SMS).

Last summer, there were some 50,000 iPhone apps; this March 2010, there are over 175,000. So, the list above is merely the tip of an ever-expanding iceberg.

Perhaps one of the most suitable and useful study abroad m-learning apps is the Trip Journal® with Google Maps and Picasa integration, although some users still prefer Mapper®. The Trip Journal site (http://iqapps.eu/TripJournal/features.php) explains:

*With Trip Journal, you can track your exact travel route. Turn on the track route, and the application will continuously get and record the GPS coordinates of your current position. Our state of the art tracking algorithm processes the GPS entries, before generating the actual travel route that can be seen in real time in the maps screen. The travel route, combined with your recorded trip items and content, can also be shared with friends. It works, too, with Android.*

Trip Journal brings together several of the pieces of Trails®, Astuce®, and MotionX GPS—all geomappers that work like Trails. Google

Latitude® is already available, and offers even greater group independence without lessening cohesion. Apple appears to have its version forthcoming. Both use the GPS function to let users know where others on their network are located. The Apple affordance appears to be related to the video camera of the latest model (http://www.9to5mac.com/apple-google-latitude-functionality-maps-2546345).

A couple of other interesting applications for study abroad exist. For the Director, the Nexonia Expenses app allows on-the-fly expense reporting and budgeting. (Students might be interested in keeping track of their finances, too.) The iPhone like the BlackBerry can tether a computer to the phone as a 3GS modem. Still, cost is a huge problem with all of these. Equally restrictive is battery life. There are cases available for a reasonable cost which include battery extenders that provide four to six more hours of life. As Google enters the mobile phone arena, and as applications are being created for not-quite-smart phones, we will continue to discover many more opportunities to bring phone m-learning projects to study abroad.

## Some New Web 2.0 Directions and Forecasts

As we saw in the literature review above, language-only pacts, journaling, and community support lead to better language acquisition in SA and beyond, and mobile devices can be brought to bear in a variety of effective and motivating interventions. During the excursion phases of SA, battery life can pose too great a problem (although with some bus companies, it might be possible to recharge with travel chargers; battery technologies, too, are evolving). If the program uses housing at a host institution or long-term housing rather than constant touring, many of the mobile devices have greater potential.

Travelers particularly enjoy sharing photos and videos of their experiences. One thing I found most uplifting is that each of my groups studying abroad has been very willing to share their technological resources, too. It might be useful during the pre-departure phase to list who is bringing what, just as an FYI for the whole group. Using FaceBook, YouTube, Twitter, Picasa/Flickr, and/or Ning promotes learner interest in sharing the excitement and wonder of experiencing the L2 country first-hand. Working in the target language, either by blogging or through activities like language-eliciting games (the home team creating a fact-filled scavenger hunt for the travelers, or the travelers challenging the home team to identify recent excursions/events from ill-formed or partial images, for example), students on both sides of the globe will enjoy the playful exchanges.

Already, the cloud-based environment can provide a synchronous/asynchronous environment, in which learners, regardless of locale and time zone, can collaborate and store all their work in a single, highly synergistic work zone. I experimented with the Wave in December 2009, with TAs in a hybrid course, and found that it gave us even greater communicating opportunities than our already considerable assemblage of Google tools (Docs®, Blogger®, Picasa®, Sites®, Calendar®) had been offering. Google Voice®, of course, would be a perfect addition to this suite of tools for a study abroad/back home exchange, but it still only services calls in the US. In addition to Google, Microsoft, Adobe and IBM are developing cloud tools. Even some course management systems (CMS) offer assemblages of tools (for example Blackboard® with Wimba®) which allow learners to go beyond email to communicate among themselves. Unfortunately, family, friends and communities are still barred by some of these proprietary systems. Other CMSs like Moodle®, however, are not as closed.

Currently, the cost factor with certain cell phone providers is prohibitive. Undoubtedly, more affordable plans will eventually be marketed. The Google Voice mentioned above is precisely one of these upcoming options. It is also hoped that new entrants into the smartphone world will bring us better possibilities, greater battery life, lower costs, and more 'cloud' affordances. These will promote social media co-constructions.

## CONCLUSION

We started this chapter by exploring the paths of best practices in study abroad, making our way into the more or less terra incognita of MALL in study abroad. Backtracking to an article on MALL, we find Chinery (2008) reviewing three CALL experts on the accelerating mobile field of language learning:

*Colpaert (2004) emphasizes the importance of developing the language learning environment before deciding on the role of mobile technologies and further emphasizes focusing on the learner ahead of the technology. Salaberry (2001) also argues against "technology-driven pedagogy," suggesting that despite their revolutionary status, it is not clear that any modern technology (e.g., television, radio, the PC) has offered the same pedagogical benefits as traditional second language instruction. Beatty (2003) offers a further caveat that "teachers need to be concerned about investing time and money in unproven technology (p. 72)." (p.9)*

The learners we serve today are so far beyond us in the integration of new mobile technologies into daily life that we need to let go of our attempts to control these unheimliche devices in their learning. Rather, we need to discover which devices already stimulate them to communicate. Students are, at the time of this writing, highly invested in texting (many upwards of 100 texts per day or 3,000 per month) according to Lenhart (2010). We need to motivate them to reflect on their encounters with alterity as well as to interact with each other, with their local communities, and with the folks back home -- because we know that reflection not only increases language acquisition but also improves long term memory, cultural understanding, and student engagement. With their buy-in and access to their media, we can help channel communication flows, suggesting interesting yet instructive strategies that will support and bolster their learning. Yes, we know the languages, the cultures, and the SLA theories and practices, but the students often know and "live" the media better than we do and, most importantly, they are eager to share that knowledge with us. We are all fellow travelers on the m-learning trail. Our willingness to learn from them serves as the best role-modeling of collaborative and constructivist learning that we can provide.

After all, the point of SLA is communication -- not via one-way monologs but rather via dialogs and interaction. These devices are about communication. The learners are motivated by communicating and interacting, which is why they love their mobile devices. It's up to all of us—teachers, learners, institutions and communities—to make win-win communication connections so that iStudyAbroad learning reaches beyond any ego-, ethno-, or techno-centric "I".

# REFERENCES

Barron, A. (2003). Acquisition in Interlanguage Pragmatics (Pragmatics and Beyond New Series 108). Amsterdam, NL: John Benjamins.

Brinckwirth, T., Kissling, E., Murphy-Judy, K., & Valencia, C. (2007). Technology follows technique: Refocusing the observational lens. In Kassen, M., Murphy-Judy, K., Peters, M., & Lavine, R. (Eds.), *Training and Developing Technology Proficient L2 Teachers. CALICO Monograph, vol. #6*. San Marcos, TX: Computer Assisted Language Instruction Consortium.

Campus Technology. (2006). 2006 Campus Technology Innovators: Podcasting in Campus Technology. Retrieved January 1, 2010, from http://campustechnology.com/Articles/2006/07/2006-Campus-Technology-Innovators-Podcasting.aspx?p=1).

Chinnery, G. (2006). Going to the MALL: Mobile Assisted Language Learning. *Language Learning & Technology, 10*(1).

Cowan, D. L., Machacha, R. F., Hausafus, C., & Torrie, M. (2004). Written reflection: The link between study-abroad and service-learning. International Journal of Learning, 9(1). Retrieved January 10, 2010, from www.ijl.cgpublisher.com/home.html.

Dias, J. (2002a) Cell phones in the classroom: boon or bane? C@lling Japan, 10(2), 16-21. Retrieved January 3, 2010 from http://jaltcall.org/cjo/10_2.pdf/.

Dias, J. (2002b). Cell phones in the classroom: boon or bane? Part 2. C@lling Japan, 10(3), 8-13. Retrieved January 3, 2010 from http://jaltcall.org/cjo/10_3.pdf/

Donatelli, L. (in press). The Impact of Telecommunications and other Technologies

Dufon, M., & Churchill, E. (2006). *Language Learners in Study Abroad Contexts*. Clevedon, UK: Multilingual Matters.

EUROCALL. (2008)... *ReCALL, 20*(3).

Freed, B., Segalowitz, N., & Dewey, D. (2001). Second language acquisition in three contexts of learning: Study abroad, intensive immersion, regular classrooms. Paper presented at the American Council for the Teaching of Foreign Languages (ACTFL) conference, Washington D.C.

Gaugler, K., & Deosthale, D. (2008). Computer-assisted Study Abroad: Empowering Students with Web 2.0. Paper presented at the 2008 CALICO-IALLT Symposium in San Francisco, CA.

Godwin-Jones, R. (1999). Emerging Technologies: Mobile Computing and Language Learning. *Language Learning & Technology*, *2*(2), 7–11. Retrieved December 31, 2009.

Godwin-Jones, R. (2004). Emerging Technologies: Language in Action: From Webquests to Virtual Realities. *Language Learning & Technology*, *8*(3), 9–14. Retrieved December 31, 2009.

Hoffa, W. (1996). The Pros and Cons of Travel and Living in Cyberspace. In *Transitions Abroad (January/February 1996)*. E-Mail and Study Abroad.

Hubbs, C. (2000). The Impact of Communications Technology on the Study Abroad Field: A Personal Reflection. Retrieved January, 4, 2010 from http://www.transitionsabroad.com/listings/study/articles/impact_of_technology_on_study_abroad.shtml

In, S. DePaul & W. Hoffa (Eds.), Frontiers 18: A History of Study Abroad: 1965 to Present.

ISC. (2005). Multimedia learning with mobile phones. Innovative Practices with Elearning. Case Studies: Anytime, any place Learning. Retrieved January 3, 2010, from http://www.jisc.ac.uk/uploaded_documents/southampton.pdf.

Jackson, H. (2008, July 9). A "Second" chance to study abroad. Retrieved from http://news.cnet.com/8301-1023_3-9986465-93.html

Kinginger, K. (2008). Language Learning in Study Abroad: Case Studies of Americans in France. The Modern Language Journal Monograph Series (Vol. 1). Summary retrieved January 5, 2010 from http://calper.la.psu.edu/LL_in_Study_Abroad_summary.pdf

Lenhart, A., Ling, R., Campbell, S., & Purcell, K. (2010, April 20). Teens and Mobile Phones. Pew Internet and American Life Project Reports. Retrieved July 9, 2010, from http://www.pewinternet.org/Reports/2010/Teens-and-Mobile-Phones.aspx.

Perry, M. (2010). How to Teach with Google Wave in the Chronicle of Higher Education Wired Blog. Retrieved on January 8, 2010, from http://chronicle.com/blogPost/How-to-Teach-With-Google-Wave/19501/?sid=wc&utm_source=wc&utm_medium=en

Petersen, S., Divitini, M. & Chabert, G. (2008). Identity, sense of community and connectedness in a community of mobile language learners in ReCALL, 20(3), 361-379.

Shield, L., & Kukulska-Hulme, A. (2008)... *ReCALL*, *20*(3), 249–252. doi:10.1017/S095834400800013X

Study Abroad Research Group (SARG). (2010). Website Reference List. Retrieved January 1, 2010 from http://studyabroadresearch.org/ReferenceList.htm

Weintraub, S. (2009, December 31). This is why Apple denied Google Latitude from the App Store...Retrieved from 9-to-5 Mac on January 4, 2010, at http://www.9to5mac.com/apple-google-latitude-functionality-maps-2546345

# Chapter 9

# Crossing Classroom Settings and Academic Disciplines while Crossing Geographical Boundaries

**Giovanna Summerfield**
*Auburn University, USA*

## ABSTRACT

*American universities are exploring new methods for internationalizing their curricula by applying on- and off-campus strategies and by providing their students with opportunities to become global citizens. The number of overseas study programs increases every year (in spite of the brooding economical circumstances), and student enrollments confirm an interest and an awareness of the linguistic as well as the cultural demands of future professional careers. Unfortunately, the traditional curricula used in these abroad programs do not reflect the steady hunger for academic global initiatives. This instrumental case study examines how university learners enrolled in a one-month credited abroad program benefitted from an innovative curriculum which used iPods® as repositories of study materials as well as tools for cultural involvement. This study also suggests that the use of technology was able to extensively engage students in language- and culture-based tasks and was able to cultivate collaboration and creativity while it allowed them a real sense of an abroad classroom, complete with a wealth of information and resources at their fingertips.*

## INTRODUCTION

With a growing recognition of the importance of having international experiences, U.S. students are heading abroad in record numbers. "Many U.S. campuses now include international education as part of their core educational mission,

DOI: 10.4018/978-1-60960-141-6.ch009

recognizing that increasing the global competence among the next generation is a national priority and an academic responsibility," reported IIE (Institute of International Education) President Allan E. Goodman, as cited in Deborah Gardner's article hosted on the IIE pressroom site (2005). According to Open Doors, the annual report on international education published by the Institute of International Education, the increase in

United States students studying abroad over the past decade has been quite impressive: 144%. In 1993/94, approximately 71,150 students studied abroad, as compared to 174,629 in 2002/03, to 190,000 during the 2004-2005 academic year, and to 205,983 students in 2005-2006. These reports also show increased interest in Western European destinations (circa 6%), with the United Kingdom in first place, and Italy in second place (the latter with a very strong increase of 13%). More than 262,000 Americans studied overseas in the 2007-08 academic year -- up 8.5% from the previous year. Moreover, the study abroad experience has moved well beyond the typical "junior year abroad", with students seeking educational experiences of various durations, at different points -- and sometimes more than once -- in their academic careers.

It is true, though, that choosing any program and merely sending students abroad is not the proper academic and personal preparation for our students to comply with the requirements for impending and/or wished-for internationalization, globalization, and cultural diversity awareness. One needs to set the study program within a solid pedagogical frame. In this chapter, I will share the attempts and outcomes of the Department of Foreign Languages and Literatures of Auburn University, not only in selecting a location for a study program in Italy, but also in tailoring the coursework. This case study should serve as a point of reference for learners as well as educators when they are selecting and/or designing abroad curricula.

## BACKGROUND

Several years ago, when I began to research locations for Auburn University's new Italian summer program, my main goals were to find: 1) an area that was off the beaten path, which could still guarantee the possibility for our students to practice Italian with a relative absence of corporate interference and a fairly faithful conservation of values, infrastructures, and popular customs, and 2) an area that could harbor an array of interdisciplinary courses, for an overall educational benefit. The area chosen (maybe not an impartial choice since I was born and raised in Catania, Sicily) was an easy choice, one that made sense. Without undermining any other regional area of Italy, Sicily is a treasure trove of historical, cultural, and artistic legacies, having hosted past guests like the Greeks, the Romans, the Normans, the Arabs, and the Spaniards, to name a few; it is an area with a variety of natural resources, beaches, countryside, a volcano (Mount Etna, the highest and only active volcano in Europe); and it has been, and continues to be, a strategic geographical location.

Together with the director of the host institution, Babilonia, Centro di Lingua and Cultura, in Taormina, Italy, we planned to offer Italian language classes at all levels, with art history, history, and literature courses offered in English and/or Italian, according to the individual linguistic preparation of the participants. Year after year, we have also added courses in geology, music, classic literature in translation, cinema, and creative writing. The backdrop is favorable for students who wish to attain a complete education, one that does not categorize but offers integration: students can easily see how all of the different disciplines relate to one another and how they can benefit from these relations. Students enrolled in these classes experience, first-hand, the material studied, through pertinent local excursions, additional lectures and conferences, and film viewing. Soon after crossing geographical borders, students are, thus, allowed to cross-disciplinary boundaries and classroom settings.

The opportunity which the students are given in Taormina is maximized by culture courses. One of the courses I teach, titled "Images of Sicily", is divided into four main sections: dove siamo (where are we), chi siamo (who are we), come siamo (how are we), and dove andiamo (where are we going). It delves into geographical and historical context, socio-political context, gender roles, Mafia, and economical context, and the future of Sicily (and of the whole Italian peninsula) within the European context. This course is tailored to give students a panoramic view of the society in which they will be living during their summer stay. On their part, the students use Sicily and the Sicilian people as active components of this class, paying particular attention to their gestures, their opinions, their habits, and their visions. The environment in which they will be living during the summer program serves as their own private library and classroom for this course. So where do we actually meet to study and to discuss the interesting issues proposed by the course syllabus? Our meeting room, while in Taormina, can be the Greek Theatre, one of the Sicilian *parchi letterari* (literary parks), a villa or a bar, or even the splendid Isolabella; mostly, though, we meet in a room which fits right into the palm of one's hand. It is, thus, not only mobile, but electronic in nature. Our abroad experience is an "iBroad" experience, one in which the students use iPods for the duration of the program.

After having learned about the experiences of Dr. Hank Edmondson, Professor of Political Science and Public Administration and leader of Georgia College & State University's Summer Study Abroad programs that include "Interdisciplinary Study in Spain, England & Ireland" and "The European Union: Yesterday, Today and Tomorrow" (France, Germany, Belgium, & Luxembourg), I decided to apply for a technological grant offered by my institution. On my grant application, I explained that, first and foremost, the need for technology while abroad was dictated by logistics: an iPod seemed to be the perfect solution to overcome time constraints and cultural overload, not to mention the physical inability to drag along Xeroxed copies of articles and/or essays, literary excerpts, and videocassettes/DVDs. Secondly, and most importantly to me, thanks to this tool, pre-loaded with lectures, slide shows of places to

visit, culture and language tutorials, audiobooks, pertinent podcasts and travelogues, cinematic and music selections, and photo picks, students were able to access cultural and linguistic support on a 24/7 basis. Finally, the addition of a microphone/recorder feature made it suitable for the different individual/group activities which students were to finalize while in Taormina.

Educators who do not have the financial support of their local universities should be aware that there is enormous potential for technology support to academic institutions at all levels, K-20+, through state, national, and private venues. They may want to start by visiting the Ed.Gov website (the U.S. Department of Education site) and then reviewing the eligibility criteria of the Enhancing Education through Technology (Ed-Tech) State Program. Another great source is the National Endowment for the Humanities (either the Materials Development, Curriculum Development and Demonstration, Dissemination and Diffusion program, and/or the Challenge Grant program) which helps academic institutions and cultural organizations to secure long-term support for and improvements to their curricula and/or cultural activities, including the use and applications of technology. Educators should also consider purchasing the USDLA Funding Source Book for Distance Learning and Educational Technology, a 400+ page publication with a variety of references regarding funding sources for technology. Last but not least, they may want to consult with foundations and websites directly linked with their own discipline and focus of research.

Having attained the grant sponsored by Auburn University, I worked closely with our IT staff, during most of my sabbatical leave, from February to the end of May (the date of our departure to Sicily), to prepare and load an iPod for each participant. I needed to make time to collect all of the materials needed (we even brainstormed and created a liability form for all students who were enrolled and assigned an iPod). This was, in a way, the hardest part of the process, for I needed to be selective and deliberate about which material to include. The Apple iTunes® Store offers a wealth of music, films, podcasts, and language tutorials that one can download but, naturally, we wanted to minimize unnecessary expenses and also select material of relevance and effectiveness. As I will show you in this chapter, original material had to be created, uploaded in the proper format, and categorized accordingly, in order to facilitate its availability. Considering that our university learners are quite familiar with technology and, above all, with iPods, it was sometimes more a matter of re-educating myself than of educating the student population of my program. After three years, I can finally say that I have overcome any obstacle and I feel that this is a very successful story to share.

## THE CROSSING

### Pedagogical Tools and Materials

The iPod, one of the most popular Apple products, a portable media player which had already sold more than 37 million units in 2005 (Roney 2005), surpassed 110 million units in 2007, and reached cumulative sales exceeding 220 million in 2009 (World of Apple 2009), is a pedagogical tool that enables learning on the go, meeting the mobile and media-rich learning styles of today's young learners. Even coupled with iTunes, it is not merely a device exclusive for musical tastes and needs; schools and universities have discovered and developed a growing collection of lesson ideas, which extend learning and teaching beyond the classroom. A visit to iTunes U® will reveal more than 300 programs launched by American universities.

Educators, as well as technical experts, have found that iPods offer several unique features for intriguing educational opportunities. Klopfer, Squire, and Jenkins (2002) describe five of these properties:

- **Portability:** the iPod user can take his/her iPod to different sites and move around with ease
- **Social Interactivity:** the user can exchange data and collaborate with other people
- **Context Sensitivity:** the user can gather data unique to his/her current setting and time
- **Connectivity:** the user can connect handhelds to personal computers to create a truly shared environment
- **Individuality:** iPods can provide unique scaffolding that is customized to the individual's path of investigation.

In 2005, the University of Washington and Duke University supported extensive use of iPods within their academic curricula; the University of Washington equipped its language laboratories with iPods to enable untethered access to audio files for language learning, while Duke University provided iPods to all members of its freshman class with the goal of exploring a variety of uses for language instruction (Goodwin-Jones, 2005). Podcasting has been especially popular in several U.S. institutions, and has been used for honing oral language skills, as evidenced by an overwhelming number of articles in the *Language Learning and Technology Journal*. Here, I will share specific examples as they pertain to my study program projects:

- Creation and management of syllabus and calendar of excursions
- Creation and updating of text files, audio recordings, and visual materials
- Selection and management of free podcasts
- Implementation of interactive assignments, such as scavenger hunts and oral interviews.

When loading an iPod for a trip abroad, the first things to work on are the syllabus and the calendar of excursions. Along with the printout of all of the students' events and activities, I added an alarm feature: every cultural activity was announced by a beeping (but not piercing) sound that reminded the students to be at the appropriate place at a specific date and time. The alarm was synchronized with the local time, so, while still in the United States, we had to set the laptop designated for the program (and thus destined to take the trip with me) to the correct time zone for Italy and keep it throughout the duration of the Italian sojourn. The syllabus and the calendar, as any written document, had to be imported in a text (.txt) format under the Note rubric of the iPod. I had to consider the correct font size in order to make it legible, due to the limitations imposed by the width and the length of the iPod screen.

Once this was completed, I started to type the literary passages that I wanted the students to read, as well as a theatrical script in English of a performance which we were scheduled to watch (for all those students who did not possess Italian language fluency). The script was generously given to me by the director of the play, who was obviously interested in capturing the attention of every member of the audience, and who allowed me to translate the piece. I also recorded all of my lectures, to include brief presentations to all the cinematic clips within the learning material. I suggest that readers may want to consider using Audacity®, a free, open source software for recording and editing sounds, although there are others which are also user-friendly. Be aware, though, of the need for an adequate length of recording time and for a format that is compatible with the iPod (that is, either .wav or .mpeg). The purchase of a superior-quality microphone and the use of a noise-free station for recording are mandatory for this kind of assignment. Also, to create a more varied selection, you might want to consider requesting the collaboration of your colleagues, who could record audio versions of the texts in the target language, rather than merely posting the excerpts of a literary work. This is more pleasant for the listener and, for a language

student, is a pedagogically sound tool, as it provides opportunities to adjust to different accents and tones. For Italian educators (and if you can finance the expense), I also suggest Il Narratore audiolibri, in which professional readers read literary texts that are very easy to download (for a fee). There are also websites which offer literary texts which are in the public domain and which can be downloaded in several different formats which are, in turn, easy to convert. For free Italian e-books, consult Antologia (frammentaria) della letteratura italiana (http://www.crs4.it/HTML/Literature.html) or the Manuzio Project (http://www.liberliber.it/).

Although I selected the films and the video clips to upload, I cannot take credit for the transferring of these files on my laptop and iPods. Our IT specialist made sure that this process was smooth and compliant with the copyright regulations, keeping our film clips to a certain length, without compromising the meaning and role of the films within the curriculum. As mentioned above, due to the relative brevity of the film clips, I had to provide students with presentations to the films themselves to cover any technical and/or plot details, as necessary background to better appreciate the films.

And, speaking of presentations, in order to manage our time better, I added some Power-Point® presentations of the different locations to visit during our stay. In our abroad program, the locations are carefully pre-selected from an array of possible excursions offered by the Italian host institution. We generally offer a number of optional excursions, along with the ones that are inherent to the program and are included in the total cost of the study program. The culture course, in turn, has additional excursions offered at no cost for the enrolled students. The itinerary is obviously pertinent to the syllabus, and provides further insight into the local culture and history. The PowerPoints are quick ways to inform the students of the importance of each place to be visited, to provide a list of sites with visual aids to focus on, and to notify students of reference materials to check out prior to and following the visit. Due to the capacities of these devices, when designing the visual presentations, users must keep in mind that the narrative has to be kept short and visible, and that images are also to be within a certain size and quality. To upload the PowerPoints, the designer has to convert them into photos and file them into the appropriate category on the playlist of the iPod. We will revisit this subject later in this chapter, when discussing interactive exercises. For the time being, keep in mind that uploading thumbnail previews of artwork and architecture in their respective locations will allow students an availability that outweighs all the disadvantages of traditional learning (which may include carrying around a ten-pound art history book or even a light but odd-shaped guidebook); instead, students can study, preview, and then review the world's greatest art and be well-prepared while touring, all by carrying a small, hand-held device. The students' interest is piqued before they even leave their campus, and absorption is quicker and easier, producing a richer, and less exhausting, experience. The iPod can also provide additional information to any that a museum guide or an activity director can supply, and can minimize the problem of herding the students around complex museums, the hot valley of the Temples, or busy streets of Catania, shouting to be heard. It gives a better perspective of the places and treasures to be explored, and offers it within a more comprehensive context. While the students visit, they can also listen to the reading of a pertinent poem, fable, or mythological report. (There is nothing better than a wonderful film with a wonderful soundtrack.)

To keep the material entertaining, current, and useful, I added a variety of free Italian podcasts. I must warn the reader that the selection is almost overwhelming. The huge number of possible podcasts calls for a careful selection on the educator's part. Some are very professionally-created language and culture tutorials, with native or near-native participants and/or directors, while others are mere products of uneducated tourists or politically incorrect locals. (Watch out, especially, for free music podcasts. Some contain profanities and discriminatory statements.) Among my selections were some radio broadcasts in English and Italian, some musical selections of pop, classical, and operatic and commercial advertisements, in visual and audio files, to include fashion shows, automotive publicity, and tourist attractions, cooking classes and recipes, Italian language tutorials, and, of course, a series of popular culture tutorials

The selection provided by the iTunes Store, found by typing "language" into the search option, is indeed very rich. But, again, the educator needs to be very careful when choosing the right venues. The podcast series covers all levels of language, from elementary to advanced: there are programs that provide students a very limited number of vocabulary terms per day, and programs in which native speakers discuss cultural issues of a certain importance and relevance. Radio Arlecchino, provided by the College of Liberal Arts of the University of Texas at Austin, illustrates specific Italian grammar concepts. Grammar examples and dialogues are based on the adventures of some of the most famous Italian masks, Arlecchino, Pulcinella, and other characters of the commedia dell'arte, thus marrying culture with structure. Another feature to keep in mind when selecting some of the podcasts offered by the iTunes Store is the "subscribe" option. When you subscribe to specific podcasts, the files within those podcasts will be automatically updated, providing up-to-date material and a growing selection of files in your iPod.

But the students are not the passive receptors of this wealth of material. The most exciting part, for students and instructor, is represented by the weekly activities that the students are required to perform: they are, in fact, required to participate in at least two scavenger hunts and two series of interviews, allocated at different points of time. At the very beginning of the course, since we covered the geographical and historical context, I introduced the pupi siciliani (liberally translated, Sicilian marionettes) and the carretti siciliani (Sicilian carts), as forms of art, but mostly as historical legacies. I had uploaded a slideshow on the pupi, as well as different images of the various protagonists and of a carretto. They were asked to find a life-sized example of each artistic creation in Taormina. Not only did the students text-messaged me with the name and address of the building that hosts them, but some went ahead and snapped a picture and posted it on our Facebook group page, as a proof of their successful scavenger hunt.

We continued with a more complex exercise, after having viewed clips of the film Il Bell'Antonio from the homonymous novel by Sicilian writer Vitaliano Brancati on our iPods. The students had to find all of the major monuments the Italian actor Marcello Mastroianni, in the role of Antonio, passes by, on his way home from Rome, from the Fortino, to Piazza Duomo, and to Via Crociferi in Catania. When in Piazza Armerina, some of the students were also challenged to find some of the gods celebrated through mosaic artworks in the famous Villa del Casale. Together with these images, students had to provide information about the gods they discovered, their location, and the relevance of their presence in this establishment. As with all material independently studied and/or collected, the students were to discuss their findings and responses with their peers and instructor. This became an integral part of their grade in the course.

Though the weekly scavenger hunts were some of the highlights of the course, the personal interviews testify more than any other activity to the benefits of having implemented the use of iPods in our study program. During Weeks Two and Three, the themes discussed were the identity of Sicilians and the gender roles within Sicilian culture. The students were asked to interview at least three persons of different ages, genders, and social backgrounds and to ask them "Chi sono i Siciliani?" ("Who are the Sicilians?"), "What are some of the characteristics that define a Sicilian?" and "What is an image that could represent Sicily to foreigners?" The following week, their assignment was to interview at least one Sicilian woman and one American or foreign woman about the woman's role in each respective society. Students recorded these interviews on their iPods and brought them to our group discussion meeting (at which their input, whether in the form of commentary or opinion, was considered mandatory). The participation of the international student body attending the host institution was vital to the success of the second interview; the students were, in fact, able to interview peers from different countries and cultural backgrounds, adding to the richness and relevance of the exercise.

Students were, thus, forced to interact with their peers in the host institution, but also with the citizens of the host community. The advanced students were able to conduct the interviews in Italian, thus enriching their linguistic experience and practicing the vocabulary and grammar studied prior to and during their sojourn in Italy. Most importantly, these activities recorded with their iPods fostered collaboration within the group of students enrolled in the class. Automatically, they formed pairs and scouted the city to succeed in their assignments; they knew that putting their efforts together would guarantee better outcomes. They also judged it wiser to record these interviews on more than one iPod; some even recorded interviews with the same individual(s) in different formats – different lengths, with and without their questions, and with or without additional comments, either from the speaker him/herself or from the students interviewing the individual. Some included comments to frame the interview, such as the location of the interview, and information about the person interviewed or about the reception of the interviewer. Students also collaborated during film screenings, section reviews, and readings. Often, students would discuss issues learned outside of our class meetings, sharing their personal comments and findings. Furthermore, students attending the culture course were approached by other students to get information pertaining to other classes, such as art history, history, literature, and cinema, which are offered during the program in a more traditional manner. Students attending these classes also borrowed their peers' iPods to review concepts, images, and video clips, in order to be better prepared for their class meetings and/or for their class examinations.

An additional and more in-depth way of sharing the information recorded was presented to all students during the class meetings. I kept a set of speakers, functioning as a unit on its own, operated by batteries or electricity, where the iPod sits. The speakers were foldable and light; I was able to place them inside the front cover of my laptop bag, where they traveled comfortably. The volume was adjustable and sounded excellent within a room of any size. I was delighted, not only to be able to listen to the response of the interviewed person, but also to be able to hear the formulation of the question in Italian by the interviewer(s). The interviews gave us more to discuss than any book or literary passage could have. They appealed to the students because they were practical, real, and the products of their own efforts. The students showed pride in presenting their interlocutors, the way in which they had approached them, and the way in which the students had convinced them to explain some of their points of view based on their life experiences.

For our final discussion on the future of Sicily within the European context (considering multilingualism, emigration/immigration, and globalization), some of these interviews came in quite handy for the students. They were able to refer to them, to contextualize some of their predictions, and to parallel the recent official reporting (statistics about the wave of immigrants, "*gli extracomunitari*," for example) with the word on the street, what they had heard on the street, and what they had been able to record, thanks to the microphone feature in their iPods or to their

digital cameras. They also had the option of posting their visual findings on our Facebook page.

Recording on an iPod is very convenient. Regardless of the iPod model, you can record voice memos using an Apple iPod microphone or a supported third-party iPod-compatible microphone. Using this accessory, you can store voice memos on your iPod and also transfer them to your computer. They are labeled with the date the recording took place, so it is easy to locate the correct one when you are ready to play it. Some of the hardware that has worked for us includes the Belkin Voice Recorder® and the Griffin iTalk®. The Griffin iTalk seems a bit more refined, both in appearance and function. If you wish, you could leave the iTalk permanently mounted on your iPod, adding only a little height to the overall package; you can just press it and talk. The light will let you know when the device is functioning.

The academic value of the iPod is of the greatest importance to me, as an instructor and as director of the summer abroad program. One cannot deny its practical value. The students' ability to watch and/or listen to mandatory and/or optional material during their downtime, whether on the airplane on the way to Sicily, on the bus to/from local excursions while in Taormina, or on the train to/from national excursions during the weekends and holidays, helped us gain much time and flexibility in our choice of meeting places. We were not confined to a classroom, in the midst of a heat wave. We met at the Greek theatre during the preparation stages of the Taormina International Film Festival, for a before-and-after that made us ponder about Sicily's historical role and the time evolution implications; we met at the Wunderbar café, in the main square of Taormina, for a hands-on experience on the identity of the Sicilians, regarding their attitude toward illegal street vendors; we even took our final exam in the gardens of Taormina, near the school, enjoying some shade and the great beauty that the well-to-do British Florence Trevelyan has offered to the illustrious guests of the city.

The iPods allowed me to update files as necessary, once in Taormina. Although, as mentioned above, the iTunes Store automatically updates the podcasts if you have selected this option on your first download, as the instructor tailors the class and the pertinent discussions, s/he can upload new files for all students; finally, if and when the students participate in local lectures, the instructor and/or students can record them (in their entirety or in part, and with permission) and listen to them in class for further discussion. Not surprisingly, some of the students, who were enrolled in the History of Art course, borrowed some of their peers' iPods in order to record the museum guide's presentation of particular works of art that interested them. They could take personal notes during the museum visits organized by their instructor and/or by the host institution. To update all of the iPods was very easy, as students only needed to synchronize their iPods with the instructor's laptop (the hub of all master files). I was also prepared with extra stand-alone plugs in case students wanted to charge their iPods individually, without bothering the instructor and/or worrying about losing the uploaded material.

## Reflecting on Shortcomings and Possible Solutions

As mentioned at the beginning of this chapter, I allocated almost four months to the preparation and uploading of the material. Obviously, year after year, I will need to refresh the library to keep the course content relevant. I will also need to revise the calendar and alarm features, uploading each year's appointments and new slideshows for the local excursions. I do not deny the fact that setting and refreshing the iPods, time after time, can be time-consuming, but we learned that, in the long run, these devices actually helped us manage our time better. In study abroad programs, time and energy are spent traveling from place to place and just trying to keep students together and safe. Having the iPods meant that students could read,

study, and listen to music, literature, and lectures while traveling, and could spend the remainder of their time actually immersing themselves in the culture of the host country. As we saw, it also helped the students with their language acquisition; they were, in fact, able to practice outside of the classroom, to review the material, and even to add resources to the ones offered by the host institution. With the podcasts, they had the ability to learn verbs and idioms, and they could use their portable devices as dictionaries, according to specific needs.

While managing the available material or creating original material, the instructor must have a certain degree of familiarity with computer software, as well as with Apple (or Apple-compatible) hardware. The instructor, in designing and implementing his/her course, needs to be aware of copyright regulations, as well, while keeping up with the academic topics of relevance. All of this knowledge has to be kept fresh, as equipment changes almost as constantly as the topics that will keep the course current. But the instructor is not alone in all of this; the IT specialists at his/her institution should be able to aid the individual who is in need. Throughout the academic year, most IT support staffs also offer collective workshops that cover all demands of technological implementations. You can also count on colleagues who have already gone forward with their educational upgrading. There are many annual conventions held by academic associations which invite papers or which hold group discussions on technology in education. There are also specialized annual conventions offered by the International Society for Technology in Education (ISTE), the International Technology Education Association (ITEA), the Society for Information Technology and Teacher Education (SITTE), The Computer Assisted Language Instruction Consortium (CALICO), and similar organizations. For further inspiration on academic and technological applications, consult specialized journals like *Campus Technology, T.H.E. Journal, IALLT Journal, Language Learn-*

*ing and Technology, CALICO Journal,* and *Journal of Technology Education.*

To prove once more that we are not limited to time and space, while accepting invitations to colloquia and workshops, nationally and internationally, I am also working with our College of Liberal Arts' IT staff to post an informational presentation on Open AU iTunes. At this site, students, faculty, and the whole Internet community are able to download this and other similar pedagogical outcomes. This approach continues to stress the importance of the interdisciplinarity (to include collegiality) and the continuous crossing of geographical boundaries that we wish for in the growing global world in which we educate and entertain our future generations.

## FUTURE DIRECTIONS

In April 2008, Becta, a British governmental agency leading the national drive to ensure the effective and innovative use of technology throughout learning, launched a research program which was carried out to identify and analyze the major trends relating to the use of technology by the new generation of school-aged learners. On page eight of the report, we read that it appears to be increasingly the case that young people have a distinctly multi-tasking relationship with new technologies, and a "multiple consumption" approach to owning them. These technologies include laptop computers, mobile phones, MP3 players, games consoles, and mobile game players. The results are also confirmed by two other recent reports which are cited by Becta: the Ofcom Communications Market Report (Ofcom, 2008) and Trends in Media Use in the USA (Roberts and Foehr, 2008). The Ofcom report gives the following indications of the situation in the UK (as cited in the Becta report, 2008):

- There has been an increase in the use of technologies within the 8–25 age group

since 2005, including an increased popularity of mobile phones, MP3 players and computers. Some 50 per cent of children aged 9 own or use an MP3 player or a mobile phone. By the age of 15, 75% of children own or use an MP3 player or mobile phone. Between the ages of 8 and 11 and again between 12 and 15, a significant increase occurs in the number of media activities carried out, particularly regarding the use of the Internet (26%), mobile phones (39%) and iPods or MP3 players (24%).

- Since 2007, there has been a large increase in specific technological activities within the 15–24 age group (with the highest percentage of activities reported concerning the download of music, films or clips from the Internet (52% increase), playing interactive games online (50% increase), and watching video clips and webcasts (45% increase).

In the United States, Marc Presky (2001) has confirmed that the numbers are overwhelming: over 10,000 hours playing videogames, over 200,000 emails and instant messages sent and received, 20,000 hours watching TV, over 500,000 commercials seen – all before the kids leave college. And, maybe, at the very most, 5,000 hours of book reading. These are today's 'Digital Native' Students.

As new study programs are being developed by the Department of Foreign Languages and Literatures at Auburn University, the implementation of technological components within the academic curriculum of the Taormina study program has served (and continues to serve) as a model, especially in view of the fact that our learners are becoming more and more comfortable with and familiar with technology. The special design of the program has also been a definite reason for the growth in enrollment (since 2007, the year of the iBroad implementation, the number of students enrolled in the program has doubled); in spite of the attractive selection of other courses offered, more than 65% of the students enrolled in the program opt for the culture course which uses the iPods. Due to the success of the course, my department has had to purchase more iPods to lend to the students.

We also invested in the new iPod Nano®, which was released in September of 2009. This fifth generation iPod supports video recording, has a built-in microphone for voice memos and video recording, offers an FM radio with live pause, and has a larger screen than that on the previous models. It is very thin and light, with an attractive anodized aluminum finish. The quality of the video is quite impressive for the size of the device and it allows for a large selection of creative filters to be used for video recording simply by holding down the center button. The only limit to the length of a video seems to be the remaining memory of the device itself, so I recommend (at least) the 8GB memory iPod. Amazingly enough, for the size of the player, there is a built-in speaker in this model. Last but not least, this iPod is currently priced lower than the previous model. My upcoming students and I are ready to assess the pros and cons of this new equipment.

## CONCLUSION

The technological component of the course, combined with the traditional journal entries, with all of the students' personal experiences and opinions (the students' "before" and "after" impressions and daily discoveries), and with recipes, notes about excursions, and final projects, compiled individually throughout the course period, and completed with a diary of personal experiences that I as instructor have helped to create and enhance (thanks to my duties as leader of the program), provides an empowerment that goes beyond geographical boundaries and classroom setting. Thanks to the implementation of iPods

abroad, in fact, I can provide my students with a classroom that not only fits into a pocket but that has far more relevance, convenience, and efficiency than the traditional one.

As noted throughout this chapter, it is imperative for the modern educator to adjust to the demands and talents of the new generations of learners. There is no better place than our overseas sites, as our students explore the world for their personal growth into global and engaged citizens, to launch curricular initiatives which take into consideration new economic and academic trends. The importance of easily accessible, interactive material leaves plenty of time for language and cultural immersion. The eagerness of our students to learn, and the empowerment that educators should afford all of their students, has dictated (and will continue to dictate) these new technologically-tailored curricula.

## REFERENCES

Becta Report. (2008). *Analysis of emerging trends affecting the use of technology in education* (pp. 1–39). Oxford University.

Gardner, D. (2005). *U.S. study abroad increases by 9.6% continuous record growth*. Retrieved October 1, 2007 from http://www.iie.org/Content/ NavigationMenu/Pressroom/PressReleases/U_S__ STUDY_ABROAD_INCREASES_BY_9_6_ CONTINUES_RECORD_GROWTH.htm

Goodwin-Jones, B. (2005). Emerging Technologies. Messages, Gaming, Peer-to-Peer Sharing: Language Learning Strategies and Tools for the Millennial Generation. *LLT, 9*(1), 17–22.

Klopfer, E., Squire, K., & Jenkins, H. (2002). *Environmental detectives PDAs as a window into a virtual simulated world*. Paper presented at International Workshop on Wireless and Mobile Technologies in Education. Retrieved October 16, 2009 from http://www.knowledgejump.com/ technology/ipod/ipod.html

Krebs, A. (1998). *USDLA Funding Source Book for Distance Learning and Educational Technology*. Kendall Publishing.

Narratore Audio Libri. (n.d.). Retrieved August 1, 2009 from www.ilnarratore.com

National Endowment for the Humanities. (n.d.). Retrieved October 1, 2007 from www.neh.gov

Open Doors Report. (n.d.). Retrieved October 1, 2007 and October 10, 2009 from http://www.opendoors.iienetwork.org/

Presky, M. (2001). Digital Natives, Digital Immigrants. Part II. Do They Really Think Differently? *Horizon*, *9*(6).

Roney, M. (2005). Apple could ship more than 37 million iPods in 2005. *Forbes*. Retrieved October 10, 2009 from http://www.forbes.com/2005/11/01/apple-ipod-computer-1101markets13.html

U. S. Department of Education. (n.d.). Retrieved September 15, 2009 from www.ed.gov

World of Apple. (2009, September 9). Apple's "It's Only Rock and Roll" Event. Live Coverage and Press Release. Retrieved March 25, 2010 from http://news.worldofapple.com/?s=Sept%202009.

# Section 4
# MALL and ESL

# Chapter 10

# A Case Study of Using Podcasts in ESL Modules for Hong Kong Pre–Service Teachers and its Impact on their Attitudes toward Podcasting

**Adrian Ting**
*Hong Kong Institute of Education, Hong Kong*

## ABSTRACT

*With the advent of Information and Communication Technologies (ICT), language educators around the world are finding ways to integrate technology into teaching in the hope of improving the quality of teaching and learning (Warschauer & Healey, 1998). In the past few years, as Web 2.0 applications have become so much more user-friendly, academic podcasting in English as a Second Language (ESL) is now widely used by college educators. In particular, many ESL teachers have also started to exploit this technology to help learners acquire better listening skills in English.*

*As English is fast becoming the world's lingua franca, the ownership of the language is no longer exclusive to those of English speaking countries (Crystal, 2003; Hu, 2004; Seidlhofer, 2001). While conventional ESL listening materials have a tendency to be Anglocentric, podcasts allow both teachers and students to create content that is more suitable to the local context, which empowers learners to take charge of their own learning.*

*This chapter reports on a project situated in the theoretical context of the pedagogical value of podcasting in language learning (Facer, Abdous, & Camarena, 2009; King & Gura, 2009) and teacher education (Hockly & Dudeney, 2007), with particular reference to Hong Kong pre-service teachers.*

*The first part of the chapter describes the way in which podcasts are used for instructional, informational, and developmental purposes in two different English language modules for pre-service teachers. The second part of the chapter analyzes a survey conducted at the end of these modules and examines the*

DOI: 10.4018/978-1-60960-141-6.ch010

*quantitative and qualitative feedback collected. The third part of the chapter provides an insight into the attitudes of these prospective teachers toward podcasting in education and its future use in schools.*

*As a result of this project, this chapter concludes that podcasts have a lot of potential, not only as an integrative and supplementary learning tool, but also as a powerful generator of knowledge, which encourages active learning – a view shared by Sturgis (2008).*

## INTRODUCTION

Academic podcasting is now widely used as an educational tool by many universities around the world. As the software for producing podcasts has become increasingly user-friendly, teachers need not be experts in educational technology in order to produce audio podcast files. All that podcasting requires is a computer, a microphone, sound editing software, and space on a server to host the podcasts (King & Gura, 2009). In language education, it is widely accepted that podcasting has enormous benefits. Many studies, such as those by Chinnery (2006) and Stanley (2006), have affirmed its usefulness.

King and Gura (2009) pointed out that ESL professionals are, in fact, the first group of educators to make use of podcasting, as there is "a natural need to consume content that is rich in listening to spoken language and instructional programs designed for them require constant acquisition of new content to satisfy that need" (p. 147). The most obvious use of podcasting in a language module is for listening comprehension. It is a great resource for global listening, as the materials are relevant and authentic (Constantine, 2007). Facer, Abdous, and Camarena (2009) noted that they firmly believe that foreign language learners, especially lower-performing students, can benefit from podcasts that serve as revision materials for oral and aural practice, and that podcasts can enable teachers to make better use of class time for other language learning tasks.

Various studies on the use of podcasting in foreign language courses have shown promise. Chan, Chen, and Döpel (2008) reported positive feedback about a podcasting project in which podcasts were used systematically in foreign language courses. The survey results show that podcasting is popular with students learning foreign languages, as podcasting offers language learning opportunities outside the classroom in the form of supplementary materials. Lord (2008) and Ducate and Lomicka (2009) also revealed the positive impact that podcasts had on pronunciation in foreign language classes (Spanish, French, and German). In both cases, students' attitudes toward the importance of pronunciation in second language learning became more positive through the process of recording podcasts themselves and receiving feedback from peers and teachers alike. Furthermore, the former study also recorded improvement in pronunciation.

In terms of application, podcasting is not limited to providing pronunciation and listening resources for second language learners. Chaka (2009) exemplified many different uses of podcasts in language learning. Apart from conventional uses such as for listening to songs, poems, and news, podcasts can also be used for recording audio journals, creating verbal quizzes, and providing oral feedback to students. Sze (2006) recommended that podcasts be used for speaking tasks such as reading aloud, creating oral diaries, storytelling, giving advice, radio drama, jazz chants, and ELT rap. In addition, O'Bryan and Hegelheimer (2007) proposed that:

*"[I]nstructors can invite guests to speak to their students at any time. The delivery of interviews and tips from guests in a podcast format enables students to easily download the audio or video file,*

*listen to it at their leisure, and keep it for further reference later in the semester or even once they have completed the course." (p.171)*

Moreover, podcasts can also be used for storytelling and for experience sharing. Jenkins and Lonsdale (2008) described a student-generated digital storytelling project which not only encouraged creativity, but also caused students to be more reflective about their own learning. Similarly, King and Gura (2009) documented various case studies in which teachers shared teaching experiences and professional knowledge using podcasting.

## Use of Podcasting in Hong Kong

In Hong Kong, podcasting is growing rapidly. Local media such as *Radio & Television Hong Kong* and the *South China Morning Post* have launched programs in the form of audio or video podcasts (vodcasts) to the public free of charge. Many language educators are encouraging their students to make use of these listening materials. Further, these podcasts are produced in Hong Kong, which makes them more relevant to the students than podcasts produced in other countries. In the higher education sector, universities are also looking into exploiting the potential of podcasting as an educational tool. The Chinese University of Hong Kong recently set up a podcasting platform, offering podcasts in different subject areas such as education, law, and business.

Dr. Paul Sze of the Faculty of Education at the Chinese University of Hong Kong started a podcasting website that shares the real-life teaching experience of teachers who were his former students. The aims of his podcasts are to give teachers a chance to reflect on the meaning of their work through the discussion of a memorable incident in their teaching career, and to offer materials for ESL learners in Hong Kong to practice their listening skills. In his own words, he describes the project in greater detail:

*When I found that an incident retold by them had a more complete storyline (some of these incidents didn't actually have a development so could not be re-presented as stories), I told them about my podcast, and asked if I could turn the incident into an episode. When they consented, I would either write up the story myself, or invite them to write it up themselves. At the beginning, I usually recorded the narration myself, but since the last couple of episodes, I invited the teachers to narrate their stories themselves, because I wanted listeners to hear the teachers' own voices, and also because I thought it would be more meaningful for the teachers concerned. After an episode was posted on the podcast, I would encourage the teacher concerned to ask their students to have a listen. (Of course if the teacher concerned only teaches lower primary grades, this may not be feasible.) My rationale is that students will be excited about listening to a story about, and told by, their own teacher.*

*(Paul Sze, personal communication, November 30, 2009)*

## THE PODCASTING PROJECT

### Background

Podcasting was introduced to two groups of students studying in two different English language enhancement modules: The International English Language Testing System (IELTS) Preparation, and Classroom Language modules. Ethnographically, these two groups of students were homogenous. They fell within the 21-25 age range. They all spoke Chinese as their first language and English as their second language. Of 116 students, four came from mainland China, while the other 112 were from Hong Kong. In terms of their English language ability, although they were not given any diagnostic test to determine their level, they could be described as pre-intermediate to intermediate level English language learners.

In the IELTS Preparation module, the participants were pre-service teachers. They were all studying for the degree of Bachelor of Education, majoring in different subjects such as Chinese, Music, PE, Visual Arts and General Studies. None of the students was an English major. All students were in their final year of study.

In the Classroom Language module, students were pursuing the joint degree of Bachelor of Science and Education, majoring in Information Technology or Mathematics. All students were in their sophomore year.

There were a total of six groups participating in this project.

## Module synopses of IELTS Preparation and Classroom Language

The IELTS Preparation module consisted of 30 hours of face-to-face instruction delivered over 10 weeks. The focus of the course was to help students acquire the relevant knowledge, language proficiency, and the strategies required for the IELTS test. Reading, writing, listening, and speaking skills were covered. Because of the time constraint, greater emphasis was placed on the two productive skills, speaking and writing, as students have performed consistently lower in these two domains. Although reading and listening skills were also dealt with, there was inadequate time to cover them extensively.

The Classroom Language module aimed to help students both to understand different functions of classroom discourse and to acquire a range of classroom language skills and practices (such as asking questions, giving instructions, eliciting ideas, facilitating discussions, and checking for understanding). The overall objective of the module was to prepare students to use English as the language of instruction in teaching their own subjects.

## Reasons for Podcasting in ESL Modules

It has been observed that students often lacked motivation in studying compulsory English language enhancement modules. To start with, even though the modules are mandatory, students' grades were not counted toward their GPAs. Classes met only once a week for two or three hours, which is inadequate for language learning. Both students and teachers believed that there was very little learning taking place beyond the classroom. Although students were encouraged to engage in all kinds of self-access language learning tasks outside of class, many of them still preferred to respond to instructions from teachers, as they seemed to regard the teacher as the authoritative transmitter of knowledge (Salili, 2001).

The rationale for using podcasts in these two ESL modules was primarily an attempt to improve the quality of teaching and learning. In addition, it was hoped that the production of podcasting materials would make the materials more relevant to the local context. As Cheung (2001) and Dörnyei (2001) suggested, using local topics and issues can motivate students to learn English, since these topics and issues are much more relevant to the learners than those commonly found in English language textbooks.

Further, this project sought to explore three specific areas:

- pre-service teachers' own attitudes toward using podcasts in ESL modules,
- pre-service teachers' views on the use of podcasts in Hong Kong primary and secondary schools, and
- ways of using podcasts as instructional tools in predominantly face-to-face ESL modules.

## Making the Podcast Files

In this small-scale study, only teacher-created podcasts were used. As mentioned above, since there was not enough time to cover the module content fully, it was not possible to accommodate a student-led podcasting project. In addition, the official course assessment for the IELTS Preparation module was 100% exam-based, and there was no formal project requirement for the Classroom Language module.

All together, there were eight podcasts produced for the first group of students. The content was instructional and informational, giving information about the IELTS test papers and test procedures, and offering mock speaking interviews of local students taking the speaking test. For the second group of students (those in the Classroom Language module), there were two five-minute podcasts consisting of short interviews from school teachers giving tips on classroom management and ways to give instructions effectively. All of this was related to the topics covered during the course.

These audio podcast files were recorded using Audacity®, a free sound-recording program that allows users to create MP3 files. It was found that the software was extremely user-friendly; there were no reports of technical glitches. The length of the first five IELTS podcasts was kept to under three minutes, with each podcast containing information about the IELTS test procedures and the reading, writing, listening, and speaking paper. The remaining files were recordings of mock oral interviews with a local candidate. Brief analyses of the strengths and weaknesses of the candidates' linguistic abilities were provided. On average, each podcast took approximately half an hour to record and edit (excluding the interviews, which took about an hour to complete).

## Distribution of Podcast Files

Although the project leader had technical know-how about Really Simple Syndication (RSS) and was well aware of the role it played in podcasting, upon an initial survey, it was found that none of the students who participated in the study had heard of podcasts or of iTunes®. None knew how RSS feeds worked. Coupled with other problems (like time constraints and the technical challenges which the students encountered), it was decided that the podcast audio files would be stored on Blackboard® (as seen in Figure 1). Unfortunately, there was no RSS feed function in the current Blackboard version 7 system. Instead, students studying the IELTS Preparation module were informed on a weekly basis as new podcasts became available. For the Classroom Language module, the two podcast interviews were introduced in weeks 4 and 6, right after the respective topics were covered.

Despite the absence of RSS feeds, the podcast files satisfied the working definition of a podcast

*Figure 1. Screenshot of the podcast page on Blackboard 7*

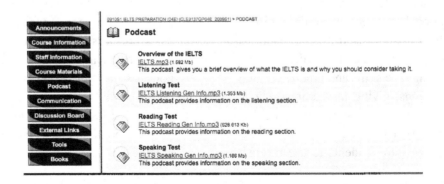

*Table 1. Phase 1: Questionnaire (SA=strongly agree; A=agree; N=neutral; D=disagree; SD=strongly disagree)*

| Section 1 *(IELTS Prep. module; n=62)* | SA | A | N | D | SD |
|---|---|---|---|---|---|
| I find podcasts useful for IELTS preparation. | 43 (69%) | 15 (24%) | 4 (7%) | 0 (0%) | 0 (0%) |
| I find podcasts useful when I miss lecture(s). | 32 (52%) | 21 (33%) | 6 (10%) | 3 (5%) | 0 (0%) |
| I find podcasts helpful in consolidating what I have learned in class. | 37 (60%) | 23 (37%) | 2 (3%) | 0 (0%) | 0 (0%) |
| I find podcasts helpful in helping me with exam- taking skills. | 33 (53%) | 13 (21%) | 11 (18%) | 5 (8%) | 0 (0%) |
| I find podcasts useful in preparing for the IELTS speaking interview. | 35 (56%) | 18 (29%) | 6 (10%) | 3 (5%) | 0 (0%) |
| Section 1 *(Classroom Lang. module; n=21)* | SA | A | N | D | SD |
| I find podcasts useful for acquiring classroom language. | 12 (57%) | 6 (29%) | 3 (14%) | 0 (0%) | 0 (0%) |
| I find podcasts useful when I miss lecture(s). | 9 (42%) | 6 (29%) | 6 (29%) | 0 (0%) | 0 (0%) |
| I find podcasts helpful in consolidating what I have learned in class. | 11 (52%) | 8 (38%) | 2 (10%) | 0 (0%) | 0 (0%) |
| I find podcasts helpful in improving my instruction-giving skills. | 10 (48%) | 4 (19%) | 4 (19%) | 3 (14%) | 0 (0%) |
| I find podcasts useful in improving my question- forming skills. | 8 (38%) | 8 (38%) | 3 (14%) | 2 (10%) | 0 (0%) |

| Section 2 *(n=83)* | | | | | |
|---|---|---|---|---|---|
| Podcasts are easy to use. | Yes = 59 (71%) | | Neutral = 20 (24%) | | No = 4 (5%) |
| I listened to the podcasts directly on Blackboard. | Yes = 83 (100%) | | | No = 0 (0%) | |
| I had used or heard of podcasting before this module. | Yes = 0 (0%) | | | No = 83 (100%) | |
| I downloaded the podcast files on my computer. | Yes = 68 (82%) | | | No = 15 (18%) | |
| I downloaded podcasts onto my MP3 player/iPod. | Yes = 2 (2%) | | | No = 81 (98%) | |

| Section 3 *(n=83)* | |
|---|---|
| Please list the kind of podcasts you would like to see in English Enhancement modules | *News programs, assessments, teaching tips, guest lectures, storytelling, student-led interviews, feedback on assessments, pronunciation, test prep information and strategies, grammar* |

| Section 4 *(n=83)* | | | | | |
|---|---|---|---|---|---|
| Do you think podcasts will be useful for primary/ secondary schools? | Yes = 45 (54%) | | Neutral = 13 (16%) | | No = 25 (30%) |
| If so, which subject(s) do you think podcast will be most useful to? | *English, Chinese, Biology, General Education, Economics, Liberal Studies, Math, IT* | | | | |
| Will you make podcast files for your students in the future? | Yes = 28 (38%) | | Maybe = 24 (29%) | | No = 31 (33%) |
| Other possible uses of podcasts in primary/secondary schools: | *Assembly talks, parents association talks, guest interviews, principal's weekly or monthly address, religious messages, school announcements, clips from open days and other events* | | | | |

as proposed by Salmon, Mobbs, Edirisingha, and Dennett (2008), who defined a podcast as a digital file that:

- plays audio or audio and video
- is made available from a website
- can be opened and /or downloaded and played on a computer and/or
- is downloaded from a website to be played on a small portable player designed to play audio and/or video files

(adapted from Salmon et al, 2008, p.20)

## Research Methodology

The research for this project consisted of a paper-based questionnaire survey and a semi-structured interview. The questionnaire was given to six groups of students in the two English modules at the end of the semester. A total of 83 out of 116 students successfully completed the questionnaire (n = 83; 72%). The questionnaire contained four sections asking about (1) the usefulness of podcast in relation to the course; (2) students' use of the podcasts; (3) suggestions for other uses of podcasts for English enhancement modules; and (4) students' views on the use of podcasting in primary and secondary schools. The focus of the questions in the first section for IELTS Preparation course participants was not the same as those for the Classroom Language group, owing to the different nature of the two modules. To avoid misunderstanding, the questionnaire was piloted on three students chosen at random to make sure that the items were appropriately worded and were appropriate to this research.

In addition, open-ended feedback was also collected. Table 2 are some of the participants' comments:

## Phase 2: In-Depth Interview

A semi-structured in-depth interview was conducted with one member from each group, who was chosen at random. The interview took place a week after the completion of the questionnaire taken during Phase 1. All together, six students were interviewed. They were encouraged to elaborate on their views on podcasts and to brainstorm on the use of podcasts, in both primary and secondary schools and at the college level, in terms of the strengths, weaknesses, opportunities, and threats that podcasts involved (SWOT analysis). Below is a summary of the SWOT Analysis and the comments collected:

*Table 2.*

| | |
|---|---|
| "I really liked the podcasts. They are short and informative and I can listen to them at anytime as long as I have a computer."<br>"The podcasts cover different topics and have different purposes. It's a great source of information. I like the topics covered. They are relevant to Hong Kong learners."<br>"Because the teacher recorded the podcasts, he can slow down the speech rate for us and tailor make the content to suit our needs."<br>"The podcasts are great when I miss a lecture or when I need to study for exams. Sometimes I misplace handouts and notes I made in class. Having the files handy on Blackboard is therefore very convenient. I can also save them on my computer."<br>"Very often when I come to English classes already tired from the previous lectures so it's difficult to concentrate (since listening to English requires more effort). For me it is more productive to listen to these course podcasts when I have more energy." | "I'd like to see podcasts with video – they are more engaging than just listening to the sound clips."<br>"It's OK to post podcasts on Blackboard but when there are many more podcasts, maybe it'd be better to have them posted on a website with RSS function or on iTunes."<br>"In future, the number of podcasts might become overwhelming for students. Perhaps the teacher could recommend which ones to listen to."<br>"The content must be relevant to the course. Otherwise students will not listen to the podcasts. We have many other courses to study and therefore do not have much time to spend on language learning podcasts."<br>"I know my English is poor but don't have the time, motivation or the need to make improvement as I am not going to teach English. Maybe I'll use the podcasts later to improve my English when I finished the degree program."<br>"Perhaps some of our formative speaking assessments presentation could be done or made into podcasts." |

## Discussion and Recommendations

As the survey results revealed, a significant majority of students in this study responded positively toward the use of podcasts in ESL modules. Over 90% of the respondents considered the IELTS Preparation and Classroom Language podcasts to be useful. On the whole, podcasts were considered user-friendly. While all participants listened to the podcasts directly through the Blackboard courseware management system, 82% indicated that they saved the files on their computers for future reference. In spite of the podcasts' popularity, only two out of 83 students downloaded the clips onto their MP3 players or iPods®. This issue was raised during the in-depth interview. The main cause of the problem, apart from the absence of the RSS feeds and the students' lack of prior experience in listening to podcasts, was that many of the students did not have iPods, with the result that they would have to drag and drop the podcasts manually onto their MP3 players. Further, students did not perceive a need for downloading the podcasts and listening to them on their MP3 players, since the podcast files were short enough to be listened to quickly. In fact, this finding is consistent with the results of a survey by Lonn and Teasley (2009), which reported that its participants treated academic podcasts differently from podcasts with other content.

It will be necessary to deal with the issue of RSS feeds. It is envisioned that the problem will be solved once the Blackboard system is upgraded and the podcast option becomes available. Indeed, according to Braun (2007), what differentiates a podcast from other web audio files is that a podcast not only "needs to be produced and published on a somewhat regular schedule [but also] be available for download, be subscription-based, and support an RSS feed with enclosures" (p.6).

As for podcasting's usefulness for primary or secondary school pupils, only 54 percent of the survey respondents thought that podcasting would be useful for pupils at those levels. Overall, they had doubts about pupils' computer skills and their ability to use and produce podcasts themselves.

*Table 3. SWOT analysis on the use of podcasts*

| Strengths | Weaknesses |
|---|---|
| *"Useful local examples of spoken English. Hong Kong accent is more familiar and thus more relevant and realistic, more so than native English audio clips."* <br> *"Podcasting helps students acquire listening skills in language subjects."* <br> *"Most Hong Kong schools are already equipped with computer technologies and are readily available for use."* <br> *"The majority of students already have mobile phones and MP3 players for listening to podcasts."* | *"Sound files alone might not be interesting enough to capture students' attention. They like playing computer games and surf the web but many aren't interesting in e-learning tasks."* <br> *"Not suitable for assessment in schools. If you make the project count, it's hard to assign grades on podcast project. The issue of fairness will be a problematic one."* <br> *"Time consuming – teaching staff may not want to participate."* |
| Opportunities | Threats |
| *"Students listening to podcasts will acquire better language skills in the long run as their exposure to the language increases."* <br><br> *"Student podcast project is an alternative way of assessment. This could motivate students to learn."* <br> *"Collaboration with other parties outside of school such as guests, parents, or even students from other schools to work together on podcast projects. This is a great way to get parents involved in their children's learning."* <br> *"Create new content knowledge for students, not just from text-books."* | *"Motivation can be a problem for some secondary school students especially among underachievers* <br> *"Students in secondary school already have a busy schedule. Many of them have to attend cram school after class to prepare for public exams. They don't have time to listen to podcasts."* <br><br> *"Access to computer and broadband connection is a problem for students coming from low income families."* <br><br> *"Ownership of MP3 player/ iPod – not every student from the low income group has one."* <br> *"If used for assignments, primary school pupils might not know to make podcasts, and teachers might have to help out."* |

The survey respondents were especially doubtful that young learners would produce vodcasts in the near future. (This response is not surprising since nearly half of the pre-service teachers were engaged in the Bachelor of Education Early Childhood Education program.)

It was interesting to observe that students would rely on teachers to choose appropriate podcasts for them. While it is logical that teachers recommend learning resources to students, one of the salient aims of using podcasts (or, indeed, other e-learning tools) in ESL modules is to help students become more independent learners of English, so that students can be in control of choosing, from the wide array of self-access materials available, the kind of resources they deem as appropriate to their own learning and suitable to their interests (Benson, 2009). Teachers can, however, advise learners on how to select podcasts that are suitable for them (Lu, 2009).

The move towards the use of Hong Kong English in producing materials is worth exploring. Some participants in this study expressed a preference for listening to locally produced materials. Indeed, this view is supported by the literature on World Englishes (Matsuda, 2002, 2003; Kirkpatrick, 2007; Hu, 2004). As other variations of English gain equal status as Englishes belonging to what Kachru (2005) refers to as the "inner circle" (i.e. US and British English), it is now becoming more acceptable to use these local Englishes for teaching, rather than the traditional US and British variations.

## FUTURE USE OF PODCASTING IN ESL MODULES

### Teacher-Created Podcasts

With the positive initial results, it is envisioned that the use of podcasting could be extended to other English enhancement modules, including proficiency-based and test preparation courses for English and non-English major students. In the Classroom Language module, for example, more interviews with in-service teachers will be offered, covering a wider range of topics. The survey results indicated that pre-service teachers appreciated this kind of content, since they had little teaching experience yet, themselves. In the IELTS Preparation module, more podcasts will be produced on topics-related issues, similar to student-created podcasts. Instructor-recorded podcasts will offer spoken or audio materials to students in a wide range of contexts.

To address the issue of adding video clips into podcasts, vodcasts will be piloted in the future. As mentioned before, using video helps learners to acquire language, in addition to other skills. For instance, as the interviews for the Classroom Language module become more skills-based, the use of video footage could demonstrate ways in which teachers could give clear instructions about ways in which ideas can be elicited from students. However, file storage can pose a problem. Salmon et al (2008) warned that vodcasts take up much more space than audio podcasts; perhaps enhanced podcasts (e.g. podcasts with slide-shows) might be more feasible.

With regard to making podcasts more interactive, a greater degree of integration with courses will be taken into account. Podcasts that are directly related to course content could be made available for students to listen to, before they attend specific lectures. For content review, unit packages containing quizzes and handouts could be created and stored on the Virtual Learning Environment.

Pronunciation podcasting will be introduced in the future. As Lord (2008) mentioned, pronunciation is an essential (yet often neglected) skill in a second language classroom. Since there are myriad ESL pronunciation podcasts readily available on the Internet, there is no need to create them from scratch – one can simply direct students to them.

## Student-Led Podcasts

In the next phase of podcast integration, students might be asked to create podcasts for their peers. This could be done as a form of theme-based project work (e.g. social issues), or students could interview educators (professors, in-service teachers or principals) on their chosen topics. These podcasts do not necessarily have to be assessed but could be made accessible to the public. What's more, these student-led podcasts could increase student involvement in the course. Therefore, putting learners in charge of these activities could be very empowering for them. As learners begin to take charge of their learning, their motivation will improve (Jonassen, 2006). This is particularly important in language learning. In fact, participants in the Classroom Language module have suggested filming their own teaching practices as a possible podcast project.

## OTHER CONSIDERATIONS

Figure 2 illustrates the formality of various podcast productions proposed by students. From a linguist's point of view, it is important to decide, at the outset, the formality of one's podcasts, since that decision directly affects the diction to be used; formal podcasts require the speaker or the presenter to follow a script written in advance (Braun, 2007). One of the outcomes of these English enhancement modules was to enable students to produce spontaneous spoken English, rather than simply reading off a prepared speech. In order not to deviate from this learning outcome, unless the nature of the podcast itself required reading from a script (e.g. reading aloud or pronunciation), students were encouraged to use natural, unrehearsed, spontaneous speech when recording their podcasts.

In addition, the issue of podcasts' educational and informational value should be considered. Hong Kong students often perceive the MP3 player as being for entertainment, rather than for educational or informational purposes. Awareness of using an MP3 player as a learning tool certainly needs to be raised. In a study, Salmon and Nie (2008) found that the vast majority of students had not used MP3 players to listen to educational podcasts, and that students considered the action of listening to podcasts as entertainment to be different from the action of listening to podcasts for learning. Undoubtedly, it will take time for podcasting to reach what Stephen Bax refers to as the "norminalization stage", a stage at which the use of technology will be "hardly even recognized as technology [but] taken for granted in everyday life" (as cited in O'Bryan and Hegelheimer, 2007, pp.163-164).

*Figure 2. Proposed uses of podcasts: formality and educational/informational value*

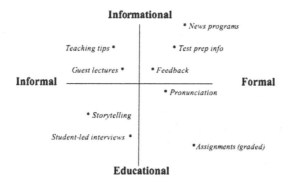

As suggested by Braun (2007), music could be incorporated into podcasts for opening, closing, and making transitions between sections, or as background. There was an attempt to use background music in several of the IELTS preparation podcasts, but this practice will need to be done more systematically and consistently.

## Considerations about Podcasting in Schools

While Cole (2007) recommends that podcasting should be considered by every school as it encourages creativity and opens up a new way of communication, opinions collected from this study as to the use of podcasting in schools varied. Although participants acknowledged the overall benefits of producing podcasts for their students in some subject areas, they showed concern about how much time it would take to produce the podcasts, especially when video was involved (Salmon et al., 2008). Indeed, the benefits of using video as a communication tool are enormous (Gillette, Goettsch, Rowekamp, Salehi, & Tarone, 1999; Sherman, 2003). However, teachers in Hong Kong schools work very long hours and it would be challenging for individual teachers to constantly produce podcasts for their pupils. Nevertheless, the respondents have also remarked that one possible solution is to get all teachers working in their own subject teams to share this workload and to involve students, parents, principals, and even members of the broader community in the production of podcast files (e.g. planning, sharing ideas, file editing, and filming) as suggested by Braun (2007). Once other parties are involved, it will be possible to produce other kinds of podcasts, including school casts and guest interviews, as suggested by the respondents themselves.

Although e-learning in higher education is becoming commonplace, it is perhaps not that well-used at most primary and secondary schools in Hong Kong. It is true that schools are well-equipped with computers and other educational technologies, but most schools lack an e-learning platform like Blackboard that is easy to use and readily available. One solution is to use podcast hosting websites such as PodServe® and PodOmatic®, which are user-friendly and free of charge, to house the podcast files (Braun, 2007).

As a learning tool, the use of student-produced podcasts should be encouraged. In line with project-based learning principles, pupils could engage in meaningful podcast-based project work such as book reports, position papers, debates, news items, dramatic readings, and procedures (King & Gura, 2009). Generally speaking, students try their best in project assignments that are made available to the public, since they have been given an audience (Lu, 2009; Stanley, 2006; Sze, 2006). This indirectly addresses the issue of low motivation for learning in completing projects.

While the benefits of podcasting are overwhelming, it is also important to recognize that one should not use technology for technology's sake, or feel obliged to create podcasts because "podcasting" is the buzzword of the year. Instead of planning learning activities around the learning tool, it is of paramount importance that teachers think about their learning objectives prior to choosing the technology (Morgan, 2008).

## Framework on Podcasting in School

This framework is adapted from the Teachers' Podcast Models for the set up and continuing phases of podcasting (King & Gura, 2009, p.51) and was developed in consideration of the feedback collected from the survey and the interviews in this study. The Hong Kong primary and secondary context was also taken into consideration. It is proposed that podcasting be incorporated in stages, as seen in Figure 3.

*Figure 3. Framework for podcasting in schools*

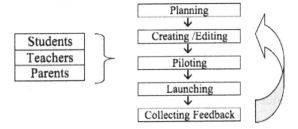

## Stages for Incorporating Podcasting in School

### 1. Planning

At the initial stage, all parties concerned should meet to discuss how to incorporate podcasting in the schools and to identify the key issues of the actual podcasts, such as purpose, audience, content, formality, and format. Participants need to outline everything in a clear plan, including the division of labor. Linda Braun's podcast planning worksheet is a good starting point for planning discussions (Braun, 2007, pp.75-79).

### 2. Creating/ Editing

Once there is a concrete plan, participants can go off and work, either in teams or individually, according to the responsibilities assigned. When the content has been developed, the podcasts can then be recorded. Because the equipment involved for podcasting is generally easy to use, little assistance is required (except for use with young pupils, and with teachers and parents who are not familiar with the technology). Therefore, it might be a good idea to run a training session at the beginning of the project to demonstrate how to use the equipment.

### 3. Piloting

It is important to pilot the podcasts to a small audience before they are made public. At this stage, parents and teachers can provide advice on the appropriateness of content and language. Since English is not the pupils' first language, they will most probably need assistance from teachers with their grammar and vocabulary. The podcasts can then be revised as necessary before being launched.

### 4. Launching

Schools can use web-based podcast hosting sites or their own servers to store the podcast files. If the latter option is preferred, technological assistance may be needed, in order to incorporate the RSS feeds onto the podcast webpage. However, this is not as difficult as one might think; there are many sample RSS feed syntaxes available on the Internet and in the podcasting literature (e.g., Braun, 2007, pp.83-84).

Schools can also promote these podcasts to external parties.

### 5. Collecting Feedback

It is recommended that feedback should be collected from the audience at the end of each term. Feedback and suggestions should be taken into consideration in the revision or creation of new podcasts. Further, if listeners knew that their feedback and suggestions were appreciated, it would help to retain them (Braun, 2007). In order to save time, surveys can be conducted electronically through web applications (such as SurveyMonkey®).

## 6. Recycling (when applicable)

Edirisingha, Salmon, and Nie (2008) encouraged podcasters to reuse their podcasts and to think about this as the podcasts were being planned. The authors point out that, as the technology grows, podcasting may play a more important role in education in the future, which means that the production of podcasts may become costly. With regard to the perpetual problem of heavy workload among Hong Kong school teachers, it would be in their interest to recycle podcast content in order to cut the time needed in creating new learning materials every year.

## FUTURE RESEARCH DIRECTION

Future research into the area of podcasting in schools will focus on Hong Kong school teachers' and students' views on podcasting, its actual implementation, and longitudinal studies on its impact, in order to determine whether there will be any long-term gains in English language proficiency over an extended period of time as a direct result of podcasting. In addition, as Sze (2006) and King and Gura (2009) have reported, the use of podcasting as a professional development resource can be exploited as a conduit to support a professional development network online for Hong Kong teachers of English (Ting & Jones, 2010). It is anticipated that podcasting projects with Hong Kong schools will be initiated in the future, and that a strong network between schools and researchers will be built.

Another area for further research will be the development of Mobile Assisted Language Learning (MALL) in Hong Kong and the role that podcasting plays in the MALL effort. Chaka (2009) and Abdous, Camarena, and Facer (2009) highlighted the value of MALL in shaping the future of language learning and teaching. In particular, as technology progresses, it would be of interest to see how the drawbacks of MALL devices such as small screen sizes, audio and video quality, power and data entry speed might be overcome (Chinnery, 2006).

It is also worth investigating the link between positive student attitudes toward podcasting and language proficiency gains. It is encouraging to see the improvement in students' pronunciation reported in Lord's (2008) podcast study. However, it is often the case that students do not show improvement in language proficiency over a semester (Ducate & Lomicka, 2009). Therefore, more longitudinal studies are required.

## CONCLUSION

This chapter has provided an insight into podcasting in ESL modules at a Hong Kong institute of higher education. The small-scale study revealed that podcasting has many potential benefits to ESL learners taking language courses, so, in the future, more podcasting will be integrated in these college-level English enhancement modules.

This study has also shed light on the possibility of introducing podcasting into Hong Kong primary and secondary schools. It was found that preservice teachers generally had positive attitudes toward the use of podcasting in education. It is hoped that these teachers will help to implement the use of podcasting, not only in English language teaching, but also in the other areas of education which they suggested, which will help to develop the framework for podcasting in schools which has been proposed in this chapter.

As the use of podcasting increases in Hong Kong education, more school-based projects and research will be carried out on MALL, and its impact on language education and students' and teachers' attitudes toward podcasting will shift.

# REFERENCES

Abdous, M., Camarena, M. M., & Facer, B. R. (2009). MALL technology: Use of academic podcasting in the foreign language classroom. *ReCALL*, *21*(1), 76–95. doi:10.1017/S0958344009000020

Benson, P. (2009). Making sense of autonomy in language learning. In Pemberton, R., Toogood, S., & Barfield, A. (Eds.), *Maintaining control: Autonomy and language learning* (pp. 13–26). Hong Kong: Hong Kong University Press.

Braun, L. W. (2007). *Listen up! Podcasting for schools and libraries*. Medford, NJ: Information Today Inc.

Chaka, C. (2009). Portable handheld language learning: From CALL, MALL to PALL. In Marriott, R., & Torres, P. L. (Eds.), *Handbook of research on e-Learning methodologies for language acquisition* (pp. 539–553). Hershey, PA: Information Science Reference.

Chan, W. M., Chen, I. R., & Döpel, M. (2008). Learning on the move: Applying podcasting technologies to foreign language learning. In W.M. Chan, K.N. Chin, P. Martin-Lau, M. Nagami, J. Sew & T. Suthiwan (Eds.), *Proceedings of the Third CLS International Conference CLaSIC 2008* (pp. 36-69). National University of Singapore: Singapore.

Cheung, C. K. (2001). The use of popular culture as a stimulus to motivate secondary students' English learning in Hong Kong. *ELT Journal*, *55*(1), 55–61. doi:10.1093/elt/55.1.55

Chinnery, G. M. (2006). Emerging technologies going to the MALL: Mobile assisted language learning. *Language Learning & Technology*, *10*(1), 9–16.

Cole, G. (2007, September 18). Why every school should be podcasting. *The Guardian*. Retrieved from http://www.guardian.co.uk/education/2007/sep/18/link.link16

Constantine, P. (2007). Podcasts: Another source for listening input. *The Internet TESL Journal*, *8*(1). Retrieved from http://iteslj.org/Techniques/Constantine-PodcastListening.html

Crystal, D. (2003). *English as a global language* (2nd ed.). Cambridge, UK: Cambridge University Press. doi:10.1017/CBO9780511486999

Dörnyei, Z. (2001). *Motivational Strategies in the language classroom*. Cambridge: Cambridge University Press. doi:10.1017/CBO9780511667343

Ducate, L., & Lomicka, L. (2009). Podcasting: an effective tool for honing language students' pronunciation? *Language Learning & Technology*, *13*(3), 66–86.

Edirisingha, P., Salmon, G., & Nie, M. (2008). Developing pedagogical podcasts. In Salmon, G., & Edirisingha, P. (Eds.), *Podcasting for learning in universities* (pp. 153–168). Maidenhead, U.K.: Open University Press.

Facer, B. R., Abdous, M., & Camarena, M. M. (2009). The Impact of podcasting on students' learning outcomes. In Marriott, R., & Torres, P. L. (Eds.), *Handbook of research on e-Learning methodologies for language acquisition* (pp. 339–351). Hershey, PA: Information Science Reference.

Gillette, S., Goettsch, K., Rowekamp, J., Salehi, N., & Tarone, E. (1999). *Connected! Using audio, video, and computer materials in the communicative classroom*. Minneapolis, MN: Master Communications Group, Inc.

Hockley, N., & Dudeney, G. (2007). *How to teach English with technology*. Harlow: Pearson/Longman.

Hu, X. Q. (2004). Why China English should stand alongside British, American and other "World Englishes". *English Today*, *78*, 26–33.

Jenkins, M., & Lonsdale, J. (2008). Podcasts and students' storytelling. In Salmon, G., & Edirisingha, P. (Eds.), *Podcasting for learning in universities*. Maidenhead, U.K.: Open University Press.

Jonassen, D. H. (2006). *Modeling with technology: Mindtools for conceptual change*. Columbus, OH: Merrill/Prentice-Hall.

Kachru, B. B. (2005). *Asian Englishes: Beyond the canon*. Hong Kong: Hong Kong University Press.

King, K., & Gura, M. (2009). *Podcasting for teachers: using a new technology to revolutionize teaching and learning*. Charlotte, NC: IAP.

Kirkpatrick, A. (2007). *World Englishes: implications for international communication and English language teaching*. Cambridge: Cambridge University Press.

Lonn, S., & Teasley, S. D. (2009). Podcasting in higher education: What are the implications for teaching and learning? *The Internet and Higher Education*, *12*, 88–92. doi:10.1016/j.iheduc.2009.06.002

Lord, G. (2008). Podcasting communities and second language pronunciation. *Foreign Language Annals*, *41*(2), 374–389. doi:10.1111/j.1944-9720.2008.tb03297.x

Lu, J. A. (2009). Podcasting as a next generation teaching resource. In Thomas, M. (Ed.), *Handbook of research on Web 2.0 and second language learning* (pp. 350–365). Hershey, PA: Information Science Reference.

Matsuda, A. (2002). "International understanding" through teaching world Englishes. *World Englishes*, *21*(3), 436–440. doi:10.1111/1467-971X.00262

Matsuda, A. (2003). Incorporating world Englishes in teaching English as an international language. *TESOL Quarterly*, *37*(4), 719–729. doi:10.2307/3588220

Morgan, M. (2008). More productive use of technology in the ESL/EFL classroom, *The Internet TESL Journal, 14*(7). Retrieved http://iteslj.org/Articles/Morgan-Technology.html

O'Bryan, A., & Hegelheimer, V. (2007). Integrating CALL into the classroom: The role of podcasting in an ESL listening strategies course. *ReCALL*, *19*(2), 162–180. doi:10.1017/S0958344007000523

Salili, F. (2001). Teacher-student interaction: Attributional implications and effectiveness of teachers' evaluative feedback. In Watkins, D. A., & Biggs, J. B. (Eds.), *Teaching the Chinese learner: Psychological and pedagogical perspectives* (pp. 77–98). Hong Kong: CERC, The University of Hong Kong.

Salmon, G., Mobbs, R., Edirisingha, P., & Dennett, C. (2008). Podcasting technology. In Salmon, G., & Edirisingha, P. (Eds.), *Podcasting for learning in universities*. Maidenhead, U.K.: Open University Press.

Salmon, G., & Nie, M. (2008). Doubling the life of iPods. In Salmon, G., & Edirisingha, P. (Eds.), *Podcasting for learning in universities* (pp. 20–32). Maidenhead, U.K.: Open University Press.

Seidlhofer, B. (2001). Closing a conceptual gap: The case for a description of English as a lingua franca. *International Journal of Applied Linguistics*, *11*, 133–158. doi:10.1111/1473-4192.00011

Sherman, J. (2003). *Using authentic video in the language classroom*. Cambridge: Cambridge University Press.

Stanley, G. (2006). Podcasting: Audio on the internet comes of age, *TESL-EJ, 9*(4). Retrieved from http://www-writing.berkeley.edu/TESL-EJ/ej36/int.html

Sturgis, D. (2008). Today's cheaters, tomorrow's visionaries. In Wittkower, D. E. (Ed.), *iPod and philosophy: iCon of an epoch* (pp. 71–84). Chicago, IL: Open Court.

Sze, P. M. M. (2006). Developing students' listening and speaking skills through ELT podcasts. *Education Journal, 34*(2), 115–134.

Ting, A., & Jones, P. D. (2010). Using free source ePortfolios to empower ESL teachers in collaborative peer reflection. In Kush, J., Lombard, R., Hertzog, J., & Yamamoto, J. (Eds.), *Technology implementation and teacher education: Reflective models*. Hershey, PA: IGI Global. doi:10.4018/978-1-61520-897-5.ch006

Warschauer, M., & Healey, D. (1998). Computers and language learning: An overview. *Language Teaching, 31*, 57–71. doi:10.1017/S0261444800012970

# Chapter 11
# Podcasts in Four Categories:
## Applications to Language Learning

**Ulugbek Nurmukhamedov**
*Northern Arizona University, USA*

**Randall Sadler**
*University of Illinois at Urbana-Champaign, USA*

## ABSTRACT

*Language instructors often struggle to find useful and learner-friendly podcasts to supplement their language instruction. In an attempt to address this issue, we examined a number of podcasts for their applicability for use in teaching vocabulary and language. Based on this analysis, we identified four categories of podcasts that are useful for the learning process: 1) Discrete Category, 2) ESL-Focused, 3) General Audience, and 4) Superpodcasts. In this chapter, we discuss each category of podcast, providing several examples, and then we explore the strengths and weaknesses of each variety. Finally, we offer pedagogical suggestions to demonstrate ways in which language teachers can effectively use the podcasts to organize both in- and out-of-class language learning activities. As a supplement to the chapter, a wiki is also available that includes a number of podcasts covering a variety of languages: http://languagepodcasts.pbworks.com/*

## INTRODUCTION

In January 2007, there were over 105 language-related podcasts available for subscription from the iTunes® store (O'Bryan & Hegelheimer, 2007), and that number increased to over 900 podcasts covering 35 languages by May 2008 (Rith, 2008). In November 2009, the number of podcasts in the *Language Courses* listing in the iTunes store had increased to 1,403, with languages ranging from English to less commonly taught languages such as Armenian and Uzbek; most of the iTunes podcasts were available for free. It is important to note that the 2009 number listed above came from an examination of the *Language Courses* listing from the iTunes store only -- it does not represent the enormous number of podcasts (in

DOI: 10.4018/978-1-60960-141-6.ch011

many different languages) that do not directly address learning those languages, or those podcasts not currently listed on iTunes.

There are a number of ongoing podcast-based projects intended to enhance teacher instruction and learning performance at the university level. For example, *IMPALA (Informal Mobile Podcasting and Learning Adaptation)*, involving leading UK universities, is intended to develop teaching and learning by solidifying classroom instruction through the use of podcasting (see http://www.le.ac.uk/impala/index.html for more information). Duke University is one of the first schools to initiate a project which implements podcasting to enable students to (1) respond to audio quizzes, (2) listen to teacher feedback on their homework assignments, and (3) produce their oral portfolios. Similarly, Yale University and other top-tier American universities have open courses available for free at the learners' disposal on topics such as psychology, history, fine arts, and chemistry via iTunes U® (where one can find over 200,000 free educational podcasts of academic content).

Given the breadth of podcasts available, the questions for educators become: which podcasts they can use to enhance the learning experience for their students, and how they can best use those podcasts. After a discussion of research into podcasting and education, we will show four categories of podcasts relevant to language learning. We will follow this by a discussion of the advantages and disadvantages of each category, and we will discuss ways in which the podcasts in each category may be applied to language teaching.

Although the sample podcasts discussed in this chapter are all aimed at learners of English, the ideas regarding *how* to use them and *why* these specific podcasts are worthwhile apply to the teaching of many different languages. For a list of potential podcasts for English and other languages, check our wiki at http://languagepodcasts.pbworks.com/.

## BACKGROUND

## Podcasting in Education

A number of researchers have claimed that podcasts can be an effective language-learning tool (Thorne & Payne, 2005; Stanley, 2006; O'Bryan & Hegelheimer, 2007; Lacina, 2008; Bird-Soto & Rengel, 2009). Since most students are now coming to class fully equipped with digital devices, podcasting can create a ubiquitous learning opportunity. As long as these students have any sort of MP3 player, they can access classroom homework or extra teacher-recommended materials while "riding the bus or subway, walking across campus or through a shopping mall" (Thorne & Payne, 2005, p. 386). When podcasts are integrated into the existing syllabus or are used to supplement classroom instruction, these efforts can "spice things up in class" (Stanley, 2006, p. 3) because they add variety to classroom instruction by offering myriad additional activities and useful in- and out-of-class resources. In addition, if podcasts are used in the course, either integrated into the classroom curriculum or independently, they are "likely to increase intrinsic motivation by including both authentic texts, such as interviews with guest speakers, as well as by embracing the motivational appeal inherent in many multimedia-based language learning tools" (O'Bryan & Hegelheimer, 2007, p. 175).

## Podcasting for English Language Learners

Podcast episodes can improve listening skills, reinforce speaking strategies, and help to develop students' vocabulary learning (Ducate & Lomicka, 2009). Since many podcasts aimed at English language learners are prepared by native speakers of English, those learners—and particularly those in EFL contexts—will value these authentic speech samples (Fox, 2008). In addition, many podcasts provide digital versions of transcripts, an extra aid for those would like to read the written version of podcasts or vodcasts. Many of the ESL podcasts produced by language experts (e.g. Culips, BBC Learning English, with addresses given later in this chapter) are contextualized, demonstrate interaction between two or more people, include lectures of academic content, and promote the importance of the Academic Word List (Coxhead, 2000) and science vocabulary (Putman, 2008). Many of them also feature authentic conversations among real people (Stanley, 2006).

We now know that teachers and language instructors can apply podcast episodes to develop materials helpful for all of the language skills (reading, writing, listening, speaking). However, language teachers are sometimes not entirely clear which factor should come first: language teaching tasks or using podcasting. In response to this issue, Young (2007) clearly stated that, first, we need to develop activities that are "engaging, problem-solving and task-based, and that encourage authentic self expression for a purpose, [and that] are more appealing than listening to mechanical discrete-point verb conjugations or prefabricated audio files" (p. 45). In addition, Hegelheimer and O'Bryan (2009) believe that podcasts can be tightly integrated into curriculum by doing pre- and post-activities, as well as by making the podcast episodes available after class, since this can "encourage student participation" (p. 341). Plus, depending on the class, its audience, and its purpose and learners' proficiency level, language instructors can apply some of the traditional classroom practices and activities into podcasting.

## PODCASTS AND LANGUAGE LEARNING

In November of 2009, there were over 150,000 podcasts listed on the popular iTunes store (http://www.apple.com/itunes/whats-on/) covering almost any topic imaginable, ranging from *Car*

*Talk* to *Zoology*. While a number of the podcasts listed come from commercial television and radio sites, the majority of them are created by either individuals or small organizations, since "podcast creators have different interests, motivations" (Hegelheimer & O'Bryan, 2009, p. 332). For the purpose of this paper, we will be focusing on four categories of podcasts that are useful for students learning English. The first three, (1) Discrete Category podcasts, (2) ESL-focused podcasts, and (3) General Audience podcasts, all have potential use for learning English. We will finish this section with a fourth category of "Superpodcasts" by focusing on two sites that integrate all three of these categories.

These four categories were created based on an examination of 50 podcasts deemed potentially useful for language learning. It soon became apparent that some of the podcasts had a number of shared characteristics in terms of content, length, narrow versus general focus, delivery (e.g., single versus multiple speakers), and whether or not they included extensive exercises. Based on these shared features, we developed the four categories mentioned above.

For each podcast reviewed below, the reader will find the information shown in Table 1.

In addition, each podcast is further described and analyzed to discuss (1) who produces it, (2) what a typical episode "looks" like, and (3) how the support materials, if any, are structured.

As noted above, there are currently a huge number of podcasts available to anyone interested in using them to practice language. However, it is no exaggeration to say that *not all podcasts are created equal*. The podcasts chosen for this chapter were selected based on the following criteria: first, we chose podcasts that already had many episodes. It is not uncommon for someone to create a podcast and only produce one or two episodes, and then to let it fade away. Most of the podcasts discussed in this article already have hundreds of episodes. Second, we selected podcasts created either by well-known organizations

*Table 1. Podcast Information Guide*

| Title | Title of the podcast | |
|---|---|---|
| URL: | Note: all podcast URLs may also be easily accessed via this address: http://languagepodcasts.pbworks.com/ | |
| # episodes | Total episodes, how often produced | |
| Episode Length | Approximate duration of podcasts | |
| Included: Whether these items are: *Free*, only available to *Paid* members, or *No* if they do not have this type of material. | Audio:<br>Video: | Transcripts:<br>Exercises: |

(e.g., BBC) or based on information provided on podcast websites. We reviewed the information on the podcasts' developers and selected only those podcasts created by people with experience in the language-teaching field, preferably podcasts created by individuals with advanced degrees.

## Discrete Category Podcasts

The first podcast category that we examined consisted of podcasts that focus on discrete categories related to language. Podcasts in this category typically have a narrow focus, and the podcasts are relatively short. The host of the show is usually the only speaker, and the majority of the podcasts in this category are aimed at native speakers of English. The first example, *Grammar Girl*, covers some element of grammar in each episode. The second example, the *Just Vocabulary Podcast*, is aimed at advanced vocabulary learners.

The *Grammar Girl* podcast is hosted by Mignon Fogarty, who has a background in magazine and technical writing. Although this podcast was not created with the needs of ESL students spe-

cifically in mind, the grammar issues covered are those which are a constant source of trouble for both native and nonnative speakers of English. A few recent episodes include discussions of *which* versus *that*; *diffuse* versus *defuse*; and *because, due to, since,* and *as.* (See Table 2)

Each episode of *Grammar Girl* includes a full transcript of the discussion, which takes the reader through an explanation of the point and also provides a number of examples. In the *which* versus *that* discussion this includes an explanation of restrictive versus nonrestrictive clauses, an "advanced" explanation, and a short discussion of relative pronouns. In addition, there are links to related episodes and additional resources. In the *which* explanation, a link is offered to resources on this topic at the Purdue Online Writing Lab. (See Table 3)

This vocabulary podcast is designed for those who are preparing to take standardized tests (particularly the SAT, GRE, and GMAT) that have vocabulary sections. The podcast administrator, Jan Folmer, is originally from the Netherlands, but broadcasts sessions from South Africa and

*Table 2.*

| Title | **Grammar Girl** | |
|---|---|---|
| URL: | http://grammar.quickanddirtytips.com/, *iTunes* | |
| # episodes | 111, ongoing | |
| Episode Length | 2:12 to 10:33 | |
| Included | Audio: Free<br>Video: No | Transcripts: Free<br>Exercises: No |

*Figure 1. Grammar Girl*

*Table 3.*

| Title | **Just Vocabulary Podcast** | |
|---|---|---|
| URL: | http://www.justvocabulary.com, iTunes | |
| # episodes | 558, ongoing daily | |
| Episode Length | 4:00 to 6:00 | |
| Included | Audio: Free<br>Video: No | Transcripts: Free<br>Exercises: Free |

introduces two words a day, five days a week. The formatting of his podcasts is consistent. First, he introduces two new words and gives from two to four example sentences using the target words. This particular podcast also offers supplementary materials such as *Quick Recaps* (a collection of ten words from the previous five days) and *The Power Hours* (20 sessions in one hour).

## ESL-Focused Podcasts

The second category focuses on podcasts that go beyond the word or grammar point level and provide contextualized language for the listeners/ viewers. These podcasts more closely resemble the sorts of listening practice that language learners are familiar with from their schools, in that the podcasts typically offer a listening clip focused on

*Table 4.*

| Title | **Culips ESL Podcast** | |
|---|---|---|
| URL: | http://culips.com/, iTunes | |
| # episodes | 93, ongoing weekly | |
| Episode Length | 5:00 to 12:00 | |
| Included | Audio: Free<br>Video: No | Transcripts: Free<br>Exercises: Free |

some topic of interest (e.g., travel, home, stress, school, etc.). The rate of speech and the choice of language are usually of the "teacher talk" variety. In addition, they may offer a transcript of the podcast, exercises that may include pre-, during, and post-listening activities, and quizzes. While the podcasts themselves are typically free, the supplemental materials are sometimes only available on a paid basis. (See Table 4)

Maura, Robin, Harp, Jessie, and Yoshi are the hosts of the Culips ESL Podcast. On a weekly basis, different episodes from podcasts such as (1) Catch Word Podcast; (2) Curious Questions Podcast; and (3) Chatter Box Podcast are delivered to help learners of English to improve their language proficiency. The *Catch Word Podcast* introduces an idiomatic word or a frequently used expression (e.g., handy, plenty of fish in the sea, when pigs fly) and explains its definition and gives multiple examples. The *Curious Box Podcast* is designed to enable podcast users (mainly ESL students from different parts of the world) to ask cultural questions, as well as vocabulary-related questions, of the hosts. During these sessions, the hosts read the questions (e.g., What phrases (in English) can I use in somebody's wedding anniversary?; In which situations can I use 'no matter what'?) and then talk about the topic. The answers usually include cultural information and topic-specific phrases.

In the *Chatter Box Podcast* episodes, two hosts choose a topic (e.g., April Fool's Day; Facebook; Introducing Vancouver City) provide listeners with background information about the topic, and then present vocabulary. It is important to point out that all of the episodes involve two hosts who, while introducing new words, interact with each other and give a variety of examples about the use of the word by using humor and by commenting on each other's examples. This podcast can be a good tool for ESL learners because the speech rate of the hosts seems to be intentionally slower than the speech rate used among native speakers of English. Both intermediate and advanced learners of English can benefit from the *Culips* podcasts. This podcast includes digital transcripts of the conversation and online quizzes. (See Table 5)

*Breaking News English (BNE)* has been produced by Sean Banville, an EFL teacher currently working in Abu Dhabi, since 2004, and offers hundreds of podcasts for free. New podcasts come out every three days. As mentioned in the title, each podcast focuses on some story that comes from the current "breaking" news, ranging from the election of President Obama to "Rent-a-friend agencies in Japan." The audio file for each podcast may be downloaded, as may the accompanying exercises and online quizzes. The exercises included in a recent podcast focusing on J.K. Rowling illustrate the typical instructional pattern found throughout the site. The 13 page PDF (Portable Document Format) document include a transcript of the podcast, warm-up activities, pre-, during, and after-listening exercises, a survey for listeners, discussion questions designed for students to complete as pair work, a fill-in-the-blank exercise, a writing activity, homework, and answers.

*Table 5.*

| Title | **Breaking News English Podcast** | |
|---|---|---|
| URL: | http://www.breakingnewsenglish.com/, iTunes | |
| # episodes | More than 1,000, ongoing daily | |
| Episode Length | 1:00-3:00 | |
| Included | Audio: Free<br>Video: No | Transcripts: Free<br>Exercises: Free |

The site includes the ability to view the available podcasts by category. Some of the categories include business English, the environment, health, issues, lifestyle, famous people and gossip, technology, and world news. In addition to this site, Banville also offers websites focusing on "ESL Discussions", "Famous People Lessons", and "ESL Holiday Lessons." The depth of the activities provided on Banville's sites, as well of the breadth of topics covered in them, makes them valuable for any ESL/EFL teacher or student, though Banville says that he created the podcasts for students who are "pre-intermediate who like a challenge" (personal communication, November 25, 2009). (See Table 6)

*Podcastsinenglish (PIE)* is produced by Richard Cain and Jackie McAvoy, both of whom are experienced EFL teachers and teacher trainers in Great Britain. Unlike most podcasts with an ESL focus, the PIE site offers podcasts at three levels: elementary, lower-intermediate, and upper-intermediate. Each podcast includes an audio or video file which may be downloaded for free, but which also includes elements which are only available to paid members: transcripts, worksheets (includ-

ing answers), and vocabulary tasks. Many of the podcasts also include a bonus webquest that accesses additional outside web-based materials.

The podcasts themselves typically consist of conversations on a wide range of topics (e.g., from "The Perfect Day" to having a rat as a pet) and a number of different speakers and accents are represented. The accompanying exercises focus on vocabulary used in the podcasts, and often include extensions on that vocabulary not included in the podcast. The worksheets may include pre-, during-, and post-listening exercises.

## General Audience Podcasts

General audience podcasts are those that are definitely not created with language learners in mind and may or may not have a focus on learning at all. The vast majority of podcasts listed in the iTunes directory fall into this area. Given their focus, podcasts in this category typically do not include any exercises, and may or may not include transcripts. Most of these podcasts are free. For language teachers, general audience podcasts offer free access to audio and/or video files on topics

*Table 6.*

| Title | **Podcastsinenglish** | |
|---|---|---|
| URL: | http://www.podcastsinenglish.com/index.shtml, iTunes | |
| # episodes | 168, ongoing weekly | |
| Episode Length | 1:25 to 17:00 | |
| Included | Audio: Free<br>Video: Free | Transcripts: Paid<br>Exercises: Paid |

*Table 7.*

| Title | **TED** | |
|---|---|---|
| Accessed: | http://www.ted.com/talks/browse, *iTunes* | |
| # episodes | 300+, ongoing | |
| Episode Length | 3-30 minutes | |
| Included | Audio: yes<br>Video: yes | Transcripts: yes<br>Exercises: no |

that may be of interest to many of their students. However, the use of these podcasts with lower-level learners will often be problematic, due to the rate of speech and complexity of vocabulary they can present. (See Table 7)

*TED (Technology, Entertainment, and Design)* is a small non-profit group that advertises itself as offering "ideas worth sharing." The TED site offers video podcasts on a wide range of topics, most of which discuss people or issues currently in the international news, ranging from Al Gore on the environment to Ken Robinson discussing whether "schools kill creativity." While *TED* is most definitely not designed specifically with the needs of language learners in mind, it offers podcasts on current topics that would be of interest to a great number of more advanced language learners. (See Table 8)

*PSYC 101 Introduction to Psychology* is a part of the Open Yale Courses project at Yale University. Episodes of this podcast have been directly recorded from a set of lectures delivered by psychologist Dr. Paul Bloom. In his sessions, Dr. Bloom talks about a range of topics that are key to understanding the field of psychology. During the lectures, students ask questions as well as respond to the professor's questions. This authentic interaction within the podcast helps listeners feel like they are a part of class itself. In this podcast, listeners can also enjoy lectures by dynamic invited speakers. Although this podcast is about psychology, no previous knowledge is necessary to understand the content of the course. However, because the podcasts are only available in audio format via iTunes, some images and video excerpts used by the teacher are not accessible.

## ESL Super-Podcasts

The fourth and final category is a much more exclusive group in that the two podcasts discussed below are, to the best of our knowledge, the entire category. Both the BBC (British Broadcasting Corporation) and VoA (Voice of America) offer podcasts aimed at learners of English. However, unlike the discrete category or ESL-focused podcasts discussed above, these two sites offer English learners a variety of podcast options, all of which are entirely free. (See Table 9)

*Table 8.*

| Title | **PSYC 101 Introduction to Psychology** | |
|---|---|---|
| Accessed: | http://oyc.yale.edu/psychology/introduction-to-psychology/, *iTunes* | |
| # episodes | 20, May 25, 2007 | |
| Episode Length | 4:00 to 7:00 | |
| Included | Audio: Free<br>Video: No | Transcripts: No<br>Exercises: No |

*Figure 2. BBC Learning English*

BBC Learning English is a great website filled with diverse activities which range from reading to listening skills. This website also offers some tips rich in content. For example, *General & Business English* teaches useful business-related phrases to improve learners' spoken communication skills in English. In this section, there are also subsections, such as *6 Minute English, Talk About English*, and others, which are intended to help learners of English improve their listening and vocabulary skills. *Grammar, Vocabulary &*

*Pronunciation* is a general section which consists of number of other sections such as *Words in the News* (newspaper vocabulary), *The Teacher* (topical idiomatic expressions), *News About Britain* (current and historical topics about Britain), *Pronunciation Tips* (teaching British English pronunciation), *Ask About English* (mostly grammar and vocabulary tips*), Keep Your English Up To Date* (newly emerging words a.k.a. neologisms), *Face Up To Phrasals* (idioms), *Grammar*

*Table 9.*

| Title | **BBC Learning English** | |
|---|---|---|
| URL: | http://www.bbc.co.uk/worldservice/learningenglish/, *iTunes* | |
| # episodes | Approximately 800, ongoing weekly | |
| Episode Length | 2:00 to 15:00 | |
| Included | Audio: Free<br>Video: Free | Transcripts: Free<br>Exercises: Free |

*Challenge* (grammar tips), and *Funky Phrasals* (more slang, idiomatic expressions).

The significance of the BBC Learning English podcasts is that all of the episodes are free. Free quizzes, as well as recommendations for language teachers, are also included. Since the website has many additional quizzes, digital transcripts of its audio files, and other additional downloads, this podcast could be used as a supplement in any ESL and EFL classroom. (See Table 10)

Voice of America (VoA) also offers podcasts in multiple areas that are specifically aimed at those learning English. The *Special English* audio broadcast has three important elements that make it ideal for ELLs: a restricted core vocabulary of about 1,500 words, simplified sentence structures, and a slower reading pace. Each audio broadcast has an accompanying text version of the story. *Special English TV,* as the name implies, adds video to the broadcast, while the *Wordmaster* podcast explores various elements of language in an interview format. The segments do not typically focus on a single vocabulary term (as in the discrete category podcasts) but all discuss issues related to language or language learning. Once again, the audio files are accompanied by a matching transcript in article format. The *Words and Their Stories* podcast follows the pattern above, but in this case, the accompanying article has key terms highlighted.

While VoA offers a large number of free podcasts that are useful for language learners, one of the glaring omissions on their site is the lack of accompanying exercises. While the *Words and Their Stories* articles highlight key terms, there are no explanations of those terms or exercises to reinforce their introduction. Nevertheless, the wide variety of topics presented and the modifications in language aimed at ELLs make VoA a useful supersite for language teachers and learners.

While all four categories of podcasts described in this section are applicable to language teaching, each has its own strengths, weakness, and audience. The following section will examine each category along these criteria and will offer concrete suggestion for its use.

## ESL VOCABULARY INSTRUCTION AND PODCASTING

In a study by Ducate and Lomicka (2009), learners of French and German created podcasts about their assigned cities, which were designed as advertisements. They were later asked to write blogs about their student-made podcasting experience. Most students spoke positively of this classroom project, noting that they had learned to 1) formulate their thinking before recording their voices, 2) interact with their peers for more ideas, and 3) plan what language to use. A similar study by Abdous, Camarena, and Facer (2009) confirmed that podcast sessions did help students build vocabulary knowledge. Keeping the results of previous research in mind, in the section below we will look at strengths and weaknesses of some of these podcasts, and we will provide specific

*Table 10.*

| Title | **Voice of America** | |
|---|---|---|
| URL: | http://www.voanews.com/specialenglish/, iTunes | |
| # episodes | Hundreds, ongoing | |
| Episode Length | various | |
| Included | Audio. Free<br>Video: Free | Transcripts: Free<br>Exercises: no |

ways that podcasts from each of our categories could be used to enhance language learning.

## Discrete-Category Podcasts

Podcasts in this category contain less frequently used words and are usually introduced by a single person. These characteristics make the podcasts in this category different from those in the other categories we introduced. However, this category can still be integrated into classroom instruction, and advanced learners can benefit from the content of the podcasts. Teachers can recommend that advanced learners of English preparing for standardized tests such as the SAT®, GRE®, and iBT TOEFL® listen to the episodes to develop their vocabulary, out of class.

## In Practice

*Just Vocabulary* introduces two new words in each episode, gives their definitions, and provides listeners with up to four example sentences. In addition, the author touches upon information pertaining to British/American English variations, as well as the usage of the words in context and their connotations. TOEFL instructors who are interested in integrating these podcasts into their class activities can access the digital transcripts and weekly vocabulary quizzes via www.justvocabulary.com or can have RSS feeds linked to a homepage. All of the 599 episodes (accessed November 20, 2009), about 2,000 words' worth of episodes, are available for free.

In addition, TOEFL teachers can set up a blog (or even a traditional blackboard) and can assign students to learn new words from these podcasts and to post the words they do not understand on the blog. Then, other students can be encouraged to explain the definitions of the difficult words to each other. While these explanations would ideally be written in English, it is perfectly acceptable for students to use their L1 to give the definitions, keeping in mind that some of the less-

frequently used words may be extremely difficult to explain in an L2. After defining the unclear words, teachers can encourage their students to give examples on their own, using these words, and can give immediate written or oral feedback during the interaction. By doing so, students can benefit from the comments of their peers, as well as their instructors.

## ESL-Focused Podcasts

Podcasts in this category are designed specifically with the needs of ESL/EFL students in mind, and vary in terms of the English level they address. This capability gives these podcasts a number of advantages -- and disadvantages -- over the other types discussed in this chapter. Because they are typically designed by experienced teachers, one of their greatest advantages is that they usually include not only transcripts, but also a number of exercises. These exercises, as in the case of the *Breaking News English Podcast* described in the previous section, often have multiple pre-, during, and post-listening exercises and could easily be used immediately in a listening classroom. In addition, some of the podcasts (e.g. *Podcastsinenglish*) also include materials for teachers, supplemental materials, and a discussion about who the podcast is intended for. Some also include podcasts and support materials for students at several levels. The exercises provided in the sample podcasts in this section are all of high quality, are pedagogically sound, and include pre-, during and post-listening activities.

Unfortunately, unlike the other three categories of podcasts described in this chapter, the podcasts in this category are not always entirely free (e.g. *Podcastsinenglish*). While all of the ESL-focused podcasts we encountered (either the audio and/or video file) are free, the additional materials, including transcripts, often are not. However, given the quality of the materials and the work that goes into them, most teachers would consider this to be money well spent. It is important to note that, when you pay to access a podcast as a teacher, this does not necessarily mean that you have a right to use those materials for all of your students, as well. However, some podcasts (e.g., podcastinenglish.com) offer the possibility of "school memberships" or something similar, which gives the students access as well.

Another criticism of the podcasts in this category is that they may be less authentic and more modified than general-audience podcasts. However, depending on which students are listening to the episodes, this may also be seen as a significant advantage. The episodes of *Breaking News English*, for example, consist of news stories that are modified by the podcaster, Sean Banville. They are designed to "keep sentence length shorter, …minimize idiomatic language, …use the active rather than the passive and attempt to keep things 'helpfully coherent and cohesive'". In addition, these podcasts use "slower than normal speech, longer pauses to give students time to process things, but keeping intonation as natural as possible" (S. Banville, personal communication, November 25, 2009). All of these elements of *teacher talk* make the podcasts in this category more accessible to language learners and of great potential for language classrooms. This is not to say that all podcasts in this category are scripted. The producers of *Podcastsinenglish* specifically created their site to focus on "conversations [that] are not scripted" in order to be "as natural as possible with the language" (J. McAvoy, personal communication, November 22, 2009).

## In Practice

For many listening teachers, the integration of ESL-focused podcasts into their classrooms should be quite easy. Since many of these are either designed by teachers who *are* using them for their own classes (e.g. *Breaking News English)* or are designed with that in mind (e.g. *Podcast-sinenglish*), they are often structured like lesson plans—or even include explicit lesson plans for

teachers—and may include PDF copies of handouts and exercises. A recent *Podcastsinenglish* episode (http://www.podcastsinenglish.com/pages/freesample.shtml) follows this format, including a 3:33 minute conversation on "Moving Home" in which one of the hosts (Jackie McAvoy) discusses a guest's (Emily's) recent move into a new flat. The podcast can be heard via a web interface on the site or by subscribing to the podcast, or it may be downloaded as an MP3 file. The transcript is also available as a .pdf, as are six exercises (with answers) and vocabulary worksheets (incorporating mostly collocation and word definition activities). Since this podcast also indicates which exercises are pre-, during, and post-listening, the podcasts (with accompanying exercises) could be used for an entire in-class lesson. On the other hand, given the large number of episodes on many of the sites in this category (e.g., 1,000+ in *Breaking News English),* it is highly likely that they could be used as supplemental/homework listening activities for topics currently being covered in a class.

## General Audience Podcasts

As discussed earlier in this chapter, general audience podcasts are not created with language learners in mind and may cover almost any subject imaginable. Due to the former issue, they are not generally suited for lower-level learners. However, for teachers working with intermediate to advanced learners, they may be a valuable resource. The primary advantages of general audience podcasts are threefold. First, as mentioned earlier, they are free. Second, they are authentic; whether the podcast is a speech given for TED, a discussion of a political issue, or an analysis of the latest American football game, the language used in this category of podcast will not be modified with language learners in mind. Finally, there are podcasts in this category that cover any topic a student might imagine, and they range in length from quite short to over an hour long.

The disadvantages for general audience podcasts relate primarily to their authenticity. Because they are authentic, they are likely to be overly challenging for lower-level learners. In addition, just because language is "authentic" does not necessarily mean that it is the sort of language that teachers will want their students to learn. This is not likely to be a problem with TED talks, but there are many podcasts listed in iTunes that carry the *explicit* label, which warns users of potentially offensive language. Teachers must take this into consideration if they assign their students to find podcasts on their own. A third disadvantage related to authenticity is that these podcasts do not typically have exercises, vocabulary sheets, or other support materials other than transcripts and, occasionally, discussion questions. However, an examination of a TED vodcast reveals that these disadvantages do not mean that general audience podcasts are not useful for language teaching.

Each TED vodcast contains two features that are very useful for use in the language classroom. An interactive transcript (see below) provides the viewer with the full text of the talk via a drop-down menu that often provides that full text in multiple languages.

In the Robinson talk, the transcript is available in 32 languages, ranging from Arabic to Ukrainian. In addition, users can click at any point in the transcript to immediately cue the video to that point. For language learners, this feature would allow users to repeat segments of the video as many times as they would like, while either listening or following along on the transcript. In addition, users can have the video subtitled in those same languages.

## In Practice

TED talks can be particularly useful for learners of English with an academic focus. A recent editorial in the journal *Nature* maintained that "those wishing to reveal scientific ideas should learn from the engaging style of TED conference talks" (2009, p. 552). Since the lectures in the podcast are of an academic nature, learners can be exposed to spoken language which is often "temporary and fleeting" (Chapelle & Jamieson, 2008, p. 125). Furthermore, the listeners can learn about register variations between spoken and academic English. These register variations, including the frequency use of lexical items, may be taught using the audio files or the transcripts of the presentations. An analysis of a segment of Robinson's discussion of schools (see Table 11) using the VocabProfiler (http://www.lextutor.

*Figure 3. TED vodcast screen*

*Table 11. VocabProfiler Analysis*

Now our education system is *predicated* on the idea of **academic** ability. And there's a reason. The whole system was invented -- around the world, there were no public systems of education, really, before the 19th century. They all came into being to meet the needs of *industrialism*. So the **hierarchy** is rooted on two ideas. Number one, that the most useful subjects for work are at the top. So you were probably steered *benignly* away from things at school when you were a *kid*, things you liked, on the grounds that you would never get a **job** doing that. Is that right? Don't do music, you're not going to be a musician; don't do art, you won't be an artist. *Benign* advice -- now, *profoundly* mistaken. The whole world is *engulfed* in a **revolution**. And the second is **academic** ability, which has really come to **dominate** our view of **intelligence**, because the universities **designed** the system in their **image**. If you think of it, the whole system of public education around the world is a *protracted* **process** of university entrance. And the **consequence** is that many highly *talented*, *brilliant*, **creative** people think they're not, because the thing they were good at school wasn't valued, or was actually *stigmatized*. And I think we can't afford to go on that way.

ca/vp/eng/) reveals the potential for using these podcasts for advanced ESL students.

Overall, this excerpt includes 221 words. The words in plain text are among the most frequently used 1,000 words in English, and the underlined words are among the 2$^{nd}$ thousand most frequently used. Words from the Academic Word List (AWL) are in **bold**, while less frequently used words are in *italics*. Of these 221 words, 85% (188/211) are among the 1,000 most common words in English, and 90% are among the 2,000 most common English words. In addition, there are 5% (12 words) from the AWL, and only 5% of the terms used in the segment are considered "less frequent." By analyzing transcripts from TED or other general audience podcasts with tools like the VocabProfiler, educators can quickly determine the appropriateness of such podcasts for their students. In addition, the use of this type of tool also serves to point out terms that might be covered in pre-, during, or post-listening exercises created by the teacher.

## Superpodcasts

As discussed in Section II, each superpodcast offers a number of subpodcasts ranging from grammar to vocabulary, to culture and politics, etc. Although podcasts in this category, (particularly VoA), do not typically offer extensive ESL-oriented learner-friendly handouts, the primary advantage of these podcasts is their breadth. Teachers using these podcasts can access texts, listening files, vocabulary exercises,

grammar explanations, YouTube vodcasts, and much more that can easily be integrated into the existing classroom syllabus or that can serve as supplemental activities. In addition, most of the materials from this category can be accessible for both intermediate as well as advanced learners of English. While BBC Learning English overall has a great deal of valuable ESL material available, we will focus on three sections in particular (Words in the News, Grammar Challenge, and Flatmates) to discuss how they can be integrated into teaching.

## Words in the News

This section includes short texts that are usually summaries of current world news. Learners can read the text as well as listen to their audio versions.

## In Practice

To raise the learner's awareness about the important words, some of the key words are in bold (see Figure 4). These types of bolded words (e.g., troubled childhood, key to something) are often "collocations", an aspect of vocabulary that is important for both fluency and accuracy (McCarthy & O'Dell, 2005). These texts can also be used to raise learners' awareness about the differences between dictionary entry meanings and the meanings of the words in context (e.g., Her **empire** also includes magazines…). In addition, teachers might use texts from the *Words in the News* to demonstrate spelling discrepancies between British and American English (e.g., candour and candor). Although *Words in the News* does not include discussion questions, all highlighted words have definitions at the bottom of the article, and links to related BBC articles are also included. Since these related articles are from the main BBC site, the *Words in the News* articles could serve as pre-reading/schema activation exercises for the longer articles.

## Grammar Challenge

This podcast can become a Grammar teacher's best friend, since many of these episodes can be used directly in a grammar class. In addition, teachers can refer their students to some of the podcasts as supplemental materials. Students can listen to the podcasts, which usually include an interaction between a teacher and an ESL student currently living in the UK. Since each podcast starts with a question from a different ESL student, learners in EFL contexts are exposed to differently-accented

English (depending on the ESL students' backgrounds). In addition to listening, students may access the digital transcripts of the conversations, additional explanations of the grammar points, and online quizzes (challenges) on the structure.

## In Practice

Since Grammar and Vocabulary are often intertwined, *Grammar Challenge* can enhance the English learners' lexico-grammatical knowledge. To use *Grammar Challenge*, however, teachers of English need to guide the students so that they know what to look for in order to make the best use of this resource. A teacher can direct a student toward practice in the specific terminology needed. For example, in the Time Prepositions unit, the *Grammar Challenge* hosts had Hiroko (a Japanese student) listen to a short audio clip. Then, Hiroko was asked to answer some of the comprehension and vocabulary questions concerning the audio

*Figure 4. Words in the news*

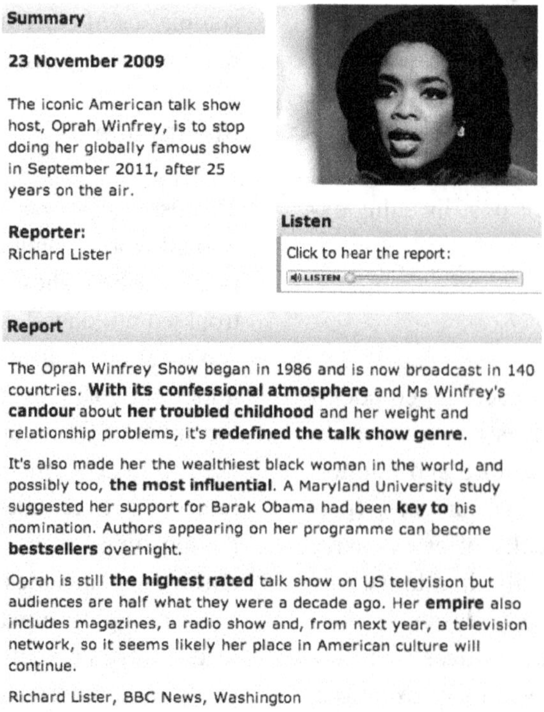

**Summary**

**23 November 2009**

The iconic American talk show host, Oprah Winfrey, is to stop doing her globally famous show in September 2011, after 25 years on the air.

**Reporter:**
Richard Lister

**Listen**

Click to hear the report:

**Report**

The Oprah Winfrey Show began in 1986 and is now broadcast in 140 countries. **With its confessional atmosphere** and Ms Winfrey's **candour** about **her troubled childhood** and her weight and relationship problems, it's **redefined the talk show genre**.

It's also made her the wealthiest black woman in the world, and possibly too, **the most influential**. A Maryland University study suggested her support for Barak Obama had been **key to** his nomination. Authors appearing on her programme can become **bestsellers** overnight.

Oprah is still **the highest rated** talk show on US television but audiences are half what they were a decade ago. Her **empire** also includes magazines, a radio show and, from next year, a television network, so it seems likely her place in American culture will continue.

Richard Lister, BBC News, Washington

clip. Afterwards, the *Grammar Challenge* hosts provided Hiroko with a handout *Find Out More* (a section with useful information about the topic being discussed) which included time prepositions (Figure 5).

Reading the information in Figure 5, examples illustrating the frequently-used time prepositions, learners of English will be able to learn these items in chunks, rather than separately (as many traditional grammar textbooks often teach them).

## Flatmates

This section includes audio versions of the now-completed 184-episode *Flatmates* saga, as well as ongoing YouTube® versions of the episodes being recreated with animation. Each episode is a brief situational conversation (1 to 2 minutes) among four friends. Although the episodes are relatively short, these dialogues manage to teach phrasal verbs, slang (mostly British), and informal phrases in an entertaining manner. Since *Flatmates'* conversations take place in different situations, the vocabulary used also varies. What is more, while conversing, the flatmates use irony, humor, and stylistic devices which are often pragmatically challenging both to teach and to acquire in a second language.

## In Practice

Learners of English can use the *Flatmates* episodes outside of class by accessing digital transcripts, descriptive vocabulary explanations, and additional quizzes based on the episodes. They can also make use of the YouTube vodcasts that show animated *Flatmates* characters, complete with audio and speech bubbles for subtitles. This can be particularly useful for learners with lower listening skills. One particularly learner-friendly element of the YouTube *Flatmates* is that each episode ends with an open-ended question and encourages listeners to answer the question based on conversations that they have just heard. This is particularly good for comprehension check activities. Some of these comprehension questions contain vocabulary items, as well. In addition, learners can post their answers on YouTube and can compare their responses with those of other YouTube members. This type of facility can create interaction among learners. Teachers who would like to integrate *Flatmates* into their teaching might also benefit from a special section designed for language instructors that gives ideas about ways in which the episodes can be effectively used in language teaching.

*Figure 5. Find out more*

**Find Out More**

| | |
|---|---|
| **At** – for times of the day | at half past 7<br>at midnight<br>at sunset<br>at breakfast time |
| **On** - for days and dates | on the 5th of June<br>on Tuesdays,<br>on Saturday morning<br>on Christmas day |
| **In** - for longer periods of time | in April<br>in 1987<br>in the winter of 1976<br>in the 1930s |
| **No preposition** – for some time words | next<br>last<br>tomorrow<br>yesterday |

The four categories of podcasts presented in this chapter have a number of different strengths and weaknesses. If these factors are taken into account, all four categories have the potential to greatly enhance the language learning process.

## SUGGESTIONS AND CONCLUSION

Based on the podcasts that we have analyzed in each of the four categories, we can derive implications in terms of what criteria need to be taken into account when language teachers decide to choose available podcasts to supplement their classroom instruction or to create their own podcasts. Although some issues, among them the overall quality of the podcasts, the inclusion of handouts, the frequency of the broadcast (daily or weekly), and some information in the Discrete or General categories, should play a key role in selecting a podcast to use, there are other important factors that must also be considered. These are discussed below.

### Word Frequency

Podcasts can be developed for any level of student. Although it can often be challenging to develop listening, vocabulary, pronunciation, and grammar podcasts for lower-level learners, this challenge can be overcome by using podcasts that focus on the most frequently used words (a.k.a. the General Word List). In second language vocabulary teaching literature, the 2,000 most frequently used words are important because "these words cover a very large proportion of the running words in spoken and written texts and occur in all kinds of uses of the language" (Nation, 2001, p. 13). In order to know which words are more or less frequently used, teachers can create their own corpus and analyze their data using available concordancing software, or they can use a tool like the VocabProfiler (discussed earlier). In addition, it is often helpful for lower-level students to see the spellings of the new words; thus, it is important to use podcasts that include digital transcripts or that create simultaneous transcript balloons (as seen in the *Flatmates* YouTube vodcasts).

### Interactivity

Some of the podcasts discussed in this chapter were created using a single speaker (e.g., *Vocabulary From Class*, *Just Vocabulary*), while others utilized two or more speakers (e.g., *Podcastsinenglish*, *Culips*). Some episodes involved only the *expert* while others offer interaction between learners and language instructors (e.g., *BBC Grammar Challenge*). While podcasts with a single speaker can be both interesting and informative, episodes that involve more than one speaker tend to be both more authentic and more interesting, due to the interplay between the speakers. Whether choosing podcasts for your students, creating your own podcast, or having your students design podcasts as part of a course, remember that interactivity will enhance the episodes.

### Speech Rate

Speech rate can play a key role in a student's understanding of -- or frustration with -- a podcast. While the ESL-focused podcasts typically use a slower speech rate (in keeping with *teacher talk)*, podcasts from the general audience category do not do so. As mentioned earlier, this is both a strength (authentic speed) and weakness (it can be frustrating) of this category. The speed of these podcasts would seem to make them unusable for classes of lower-level students. However, because almost all of these podcasts can be downloaded as MP3 files, it is important to note that some MP3 players include variable speed control, and that programs such as iTunes on the iPhone® or iPod Touch® also include a speed control. However, even these tools may not be necessary, since a downloaded MP3 can be played directly in QuickTime® or Windows Media Player®, both of which have speed control.

In addition MP3s can be modified by using free programs like Audacity® to change their speed, while keeping the voice sounding natural.

The four categories of podcasts discussed in this chapter have strong potential for language learning, both in classrooms and for independent learning. The sample podcasts provided in this article, while English teaching-focused and relatively few in number, are all pedagogically-sound examples that may serve as stepping-stones to your finding additional podcasts focused on English or any other languages. As you make your own exploration of podcasts, we strongly encourage you to add the strong ones to our podcasting wiki: http://languagepodcasts.pbworks.com

## REFERENCES

Abdous, M., Camarena, M., & Rose Facer, B. (2009). MALL Technology: Use of academic podcasting in the foreign language classroom. *ReCALL, 21*(1), 76–95. doi:10.1017/S0958344009000020

Bird-Soto, N., & Rengel, P. (2009). Podcasting and the intermediate-level Spanish classroom. In Oxford, R., & Oxford, J. (Eds.), *Second language teaching and learning in the Net Generation* (pp. 101–109). Honolulu: University of Hawai'i, National Foreign Language Resource Center.

Chapelle, C., & Jamieson, J. (2008). *Tips for Teaching with CALL: practically approaches to Computer-Assisted Language Learning*. Pearson Longman.

Coxhead, A. (2000). A new academic word list. *TESOL Quarterly, 34*, 213–238. doi:10.2307/3587951

Ducate, L., & Lomicka, L. (2009). Podcasting in the language classroom. Inherently mobile or not? In Oxford, R., & Oxford, J. (Eds.), *Second language teaching and learning in the Net Generation* (pp. 111–125). Honolulu: University of Hawaii, National Foreign Language Resource Center.

Editorials, N. (2009, July). Inspiring non-scientists. *Nature, 460*, 552. doi:10.1038/460552a

Fox, A. (2008). Using Podcasts in the EFL Classroom. *TESL-EJ, 11*(4). Retrieved from http://tesl-ej.org/ej44/a4.html

Hegelheimer, V., & O'Bryan, A. (2009). Mobile technologies and language education: a look at language learning podcasts. In Thomas, M. (Ed.), *Handbook of Research on Web 2.0 and Second Language Learning* (pp. 331–349). Hershey, PA: Information Science Reference.

Lacina, J. (2008). Learning English with iPods. *Childhood Education, 84*(4), 247–249.

McCarthy, M., & O'Dell, F. (2005). *English Collocations in Use*. Cambridge: Cambridge University Press.

Nation, P. (2001). *Learning Vocabulary in Another Language*. Cambridge: Cambridge University Press.

O'Bryan, A., & Hegelheimer, V. (2007). Integrating CALL into the classroom: The role of podcasting in an ESL listening strategies course. *ReCALL, 19*(2), 162–180. doi:10.1017/S0958344007000523

Putman, M. (2008). *Using Podcasts to Enhance Science Vocabulary Development*. Paper presented at the National Educational Computing Conference. Ball State University.

Rith, C. (2008). Learn 35+ Language for Free in iTunes. Life Clover. Retrieved from http://www.lifeclever.com/learn-35-languages-for-free-in-itunes/

Stanley, G. (2006) Podcasting: Audio on the Internet Comes of Age. *TESL-EJ, 9*(4).

Thorne, S. L., & Payne, J. S. (2005). Evolutionary Trajectories, Internet-mediated Expression, and Language Education. *CALICO Journal, 22*(3), 371–397.

Young, D. J. (2007). iPods, MP3 players and podcasts for EFL learning: Current practices and future considerations. *NECTFL Review, 60*, 39–49.

## ADDITIONAL READING

Bongey, S. B., Cizadlo, G., & Kalnbach, L. (2006). Explorations in course-casting: Podcasts in higher education. *Campus-Wide Information Systems, 23*(5), 350–367. doi:10.1108/10650740610714107

Brotherton, J., & Abowd, G. (2004). Lessons learned from eclass: Assessing automated capture and access in the classroom. *ACM Transactions on Computer-Human Interaction, 11*(2), 121–155. doi:10.1145/1005361.1005362

Copley, J. (2007). Audio and video podcasts of lectures for campus-based students: Production and evaluation of student use. *Innovations in Education and Teaching International, 44*(4), 387–399. doi:10.1080/14703290701602805

Coxhead, A. (2000). *The Academic Word List.* Retrieved from http://www.victoria.ac.nz/lals/resources/academicwordlist/default.aspx

Dale, C. (2007). Strategies for using podcasting to support student learning [Electronic Version]. *Journal of Hospitality, Leisure, Sport and Tourism Education, 6.*

De Ridder, I. (2002). Visible or Invisible Links: Does the Highlighting of Hyperlinks Affect Incidental Vocabulary Learning, Text Comprehension and the Reading Process? *Language Learning & Technology, 6*(1), 123–146.

Godwin-Jones, R. (2009). Emerging Technologies: Personal Learning Environments. *Language Learning & Technology, 13*(2), 3–9.

Harmon, J. M. (2002). Teaching independent word learning strategies to struggling readers. *Journal of Adolescent & Adult Literacy, 45*(7), 606–615.

Kiernan, P. J., & Aizawa, K. (2004). Cell phones in task based learning—Are cell phones useful language learning tools? *ReCALL, 16*(1), 71–84. doi:10.1017/S0958344004000618

Listening Podcasts, E. S. L. (2010). Retrieved from http://iteslj.org/links/ESL/Listening/Podcasts/

Maag, M. (2006a). Podcasting and MP3 players: Emerging education technologies. *Computers, Informatics, Nursing, 24*(1), 9–13. doi:10.1097/00024665-200601000-00005

McQuillan, J. (Fall 2006). iPod in Education: The Potential for Language Acquisition. *One in a series of iPod in Education white papers,* 1-13.

Oliver, B. (2005). Mobile blogging, 'Skyping' and podcasting: Targeting undergraduates' communication skills in transnational learning contexts. *Microlearning, 107*(4), 587–600.

Podcasting, E. S. L. (2010). Retrieved from http://www.rong-chang.com/podcast.htm

Podcasts, F. (2010). Retrieved from http://delicious.com/search?p=free+podcasts&chk=&fr=del_icio_us&lc=1&atags=&rtags=&context=all

Podcasts for English Learning and Teaching. (2010). Retrieved from http://esl.about.com/od/podcasts/Podcasts_for_English_Learning_and_Teaching.htm

Rosell-Aguilar, F. (2007). Top of the Pods—In Search of a Podcasting "Podagogy" for Learning. *Computer Assisted Language Learning, 20*(5), 471–492. doi:10.1080/09588220701746047

Segler, T., Pain, H., & Sorace, A. (2002). Second Language Vocabulary Acquisition and Learning Strategies in ICALL Environments. *Computer Assisted Language Learning, 15*(4), 409–422. doi:10.1076/call.15.4.409.8272

Tozcu, A., & Coady, J. (2004). Successful learning of frequent vocabulary through CALL also benefits reading comprehension and speed. *Computer Assisted Language Learning, 17*(5), 473–495. doi:10.1080/0958822042000319674

Travis, P., & Joseph, F. (2009). Improving Learner's Speaking Skills with Podcasts. In Thomas, M. (Ed.), *Handbook of Research on Web 2.0 and Second Language Learning* (pp. 313–330). Hershey, PA: Information Science Reference.

Zimmerman, C. (2009). *Word Knowledge: A Vocabulary Teacher's Handbook*. Oxford: Oxford University Press.

# Afterword

This book has presented a wealth of information, guidance, and suggestions on how to accomplish Academic Podcasting and Mobile Assisted Language Learning, along with well-grounded arguments supporting why one would want to attempt it. There is also good advice about pitfalls to avoid, and reasons one might choose not to pursue an in-house podcasting project. While the book is quite comprehensive, the editors have been kind enough to invite me to contribute this Afterword with a few thoughts on how Apple's iPad might influence MALL.

## IPADS IN THE LANGUAGE CLASSROOM

Turning the metaphorical page from today's podcasting to tomorrow's 'Padcasting (this author's new term for presentations created on the iPad), what will be presented here is a brief look at what one institution is in the process of implementing with a class set of iPads for their Spanish classes. Arizona State University's Downtown Phoenix campus is a rich technological environment, essentially built from the ground up five years ago, with ubiquitous WiFi promoting a 1-to-1 environment where each student is encouraged to have his/her own computing device. All classrooms are mediated, with a teaching station, computer projector, and laptop VGA connection available. While the School of Letters and Sciences has a Language Resource Lab with 24-computer ReLANsign Language Lab system, where the students have half of their class time, the students spend the other half of their class time in a standard (mediated) classroom.

In order to extend individual access to technology to the class time in the standard classroom, (and, granted, provide an attractive, motivational stimulus in class), ASU has purchased twelve (WiFi only) iPads to be checked out for a class session, along with iPads to be checked out to the instructors who will be using them on a semester-by-semester basis. This will allow the instructor to become proficient with the iPad, and when checking out the 12 for the class session, to provide one iPad for every two students, so that in pairs, they can perform various tasks that will help them explore and document the target culture. Making the task relevant can aid learning, so to contextualize the task, the instructor might tell the students to imagine that they will spend the summer in Madrid to study Art History and Spanish, and they need to locate an apartment near the Prado Museum. Starting with a Spanish-language Google search for "Apartmentos Madrid," the students can find an apartment, and then pull up the address in Google Maps. Using Street View, they can see the building, and find a pharmacy nearby. Using the Home button/Sleep button screen capture function, they can snap a picture of the building. Using the two-finger zoom, they can take a close-up picture of the signs in the pharmacy window, and then document the route they would follow to get to the Prado. Using Keynote, the presentation software available for the iPad, they can create a slideshow to present to the class with the VGA adapter connected to the projector for a live presentation. With SonicPics software, they can create a presentation of screen shots or pictures and using the on-board mic, record a narration to be played on the iPad, or exported and uploaded to YouTube.

Many iPad apps have obvious potential for use in the language classroom, including, but not limited to, travel and news apps. Though the list is always expanding, following are a few free or inexpensive apps that have already been identified for potential use. Globe for the iPad links directly to the Wikipedia entries for any fingered (selected) country. InfoBAE.com is a Latin American news website that has an iPad app with text and pictures and videos. A nice feature of InfoBAE is that when the user opts to share an article by e-mail, the app launches an e-mail message with the text and pictures of the article in the body of the e-mail, so without getting involved in DropBox (a cloud-based file-sharing system), students will be able to use a generic Gmail account on each iPad to send pictures and stories to their own e-mail for off-iPad use. Having an audio recording app such as AudioMemos will facilitate the recording of interviews or role-plays. GoodReader provides a .pdf-displaying tool which can also be used to add comments and annotations to the .pdf documents, opening the possibility of worksheet-like activities to be returned to the instructor. Mental Case Classroom Edition provides the ability to create iPad (and iPhone/iPod Touch) flash cards with text or graphic or audio prompts and answers; instructors or students can create flashcard sets to be shared with classmates. (All of the apps mentioned can be found by searching for them by name in the online App Store.)

Does the iPad change the role of podcasting and MALL? To the extent that the iPad is just an iPod Touch in a large form-factor, albeit with all the functionality available (synching audio and video podcasts through iTunes, direct download of podcasts via WiFi, playback of audio podcasts at normal speed, 1/2 speed, or double speed, 30-second replay of video podcasts, etc.), no, it doesn't change that role. To the extent that it embeds the podcasting environment in a hand-held, full-screen, connected device, yes, it does change MALL. With an audio podcast playing in the background, the student can launch another app to be taking notes or dictation, researching related information on a target-language news site, creating an online presentation, or opening up an email-attached .pdf or word processing document with a podcast-based activity. The student can use the on-board mic to record and his/her own interactions, and even test his/her own pronunciation with the free Dragon Dictation app, which takes dictation in English and a growing list of other languages already including French, German, Spanish and Italian. The iPad (and the other competing touch screen devices coming to the market) provide an opportunity for enriching the MALL-scape with creative tools that can always be at hand. The challenge for the language educator is to take advantage of the ever-advancing technology available, without losing sight of the ultimate goal of language acquisition. It is hoped that this discussion has helped stimulate the reader to consider how these technologies can benefit tomorrow's language students.

*Peter Lafford*
*Academic Computing Professional & Computing Director, Specialized Labs*
*Arizona State University at the Downtown Phoenix campus*

# Compilation of References

Abdous, M., Camarena, M. M., & Facer, B. R. (2009). MALL technology: Use of academic podcasting in the foreign language classroom. *ReCALL Journal, 21*, 76–95. doi:10.1017/S0958344009000020

Alexander, S., McKenzie, J., & Geissinger, H. (1998). *An Evaluation of Information Technology Projects for University Learning. Committee for University Teaching and Staff Development. Report to the Department of Employment, Education and Training*. Canberra: Australian Government Publishing Service.

Al-jasser, F. (2008). The effect of teaching English phonotactics on the lexical segmentation of English as a foreign language. *System, 36*, 94–106. doi:10.1016/j.system.2007.12.002

Amemiya, S., Hasegawa, K., Kaneko, K., Miyakoda, H., & Tsukahara, W. (2007). Development and evaluation of a foreign-word learning system by iPods. In *Proceedings of the Sixth IASTED International Conference on WEB-Based Education* (pp. 264-269). Chamonix, France.

Andrew, M. (2008). Student evaluation of video podcasts to augment live lectures in pharmaceutical microbiology. In *Proceedings of the 3rd International Blended Learning Conference: Enhancing the student experience* (pp. 272-282). Hertfordshire, 18-19 April. http://hlsweb.dmu.ac.uk/staff/mhea/blu/Andrew_BLU_conference_paper.pdf

Articlet. (2009, August 4). *Over 57 percent of American homes have access to high-speed internet service.* Retrieved August 28, 2009, from http://articlet.com/article791.html

Attewell, J., Savill-Smith, C., & Douch, R. (2009). *The impact of mobile learning: Examining what it means for teaching and learning.* Retrieved December 21, 2009, from http://www.lsnlearning.org.uk

Augar, N., Raitman, R., & Zhou, W. (2004). Teaching and learning online with wikis. In R. Atkinson, C. McBeath, D. Jonas-Dwyer & R. Phillips (Eds.), *Beyond the comfort zone: Proceedings of the 21st ASCILITE Conference* (pp. 95-104). Perth, 5-8 December. http://www.ascilite.org.au/conferences/perth04/procs/augar.html

Australian Bureau of Statistics. (2008). 1301.0 Year Book Australia 2008. Cultural diversity: Language. 2006 Census of Population and Housing. Retrieved from http://www.abs.gov.au/AUSSTATS/abs@.nsf/bb8db737e2af84b8ca2571780015701e/636F496B2B943F12CA2573D200109DA9?opendocument

Australian Government. (2008). Study overseas: Experience more. Retrieved from http://www.studyoverseas.gov.au/

Australian Government. (2009). Australian University Mobility in Asia and the Pacific (UMAP) Student exchange program. Department of Education, Employment and Workplace Relations. Retrieved from http://www.endeavour.deewr.gov.au/student_exchanges_new/australian_umap.htm

Australian Learning and Teaching Council. (2009). *New technologies, new pedagogies: Using mobile technologies to develop new ways of teaching and learning.* Retrieved from http://www.altc.edu.au/resource-new-technologies-new-pedagogies-uow-2009

Barron, A. (2003). Acquisition in Interlanguage Pragmatics (Pragmatics and Beyond New Series 108). Amsterdam, NL: John Benjamins.

Barsky, E., & Lindstrom, K. (2008). Podcasting the sciences: A practical overview. *Issues in Science and Technology Librarianship*. Retrieved August 4, 2009, from http://www.istl.org/08-fall/article7.html

Bates, A. W. (1996). The impact of technological change on open and distant learning, Queensland *Open Learning Conference: Your future depends on it*, 4 - 6 December, 1996, Brisbane, Queensland, Australia. Retrieved from http://bates.cstudies.ubc.ca/brisbane.html

Becta Report. (2008). *Analysis of emerging trends affecting the use of technology in education* (pp. 1–39). Oxford University.

Beilke, J., Stuve, M., & Williams-Hawkins, M. (2008). "Clubcasting": Educational uses of podcasting in multicultural settings. *Multicultural Education & Technology Journal*, *2*(2), 107–117. doi:10.1108/17504970810883379

Belanger, Y. (2005a, March). *Duke iPod initiative project evaluation update*. Retrieved December 21, 2009, from Duke University Web site: http://cit.duke.edu/pdf/reports/ITAC_iPod_eval_March05.pdf

Belanger, Y. (2005b, June). *Duke University iPod first year experience final evaluation report*. Retrieved December 21, 2009, from Duke University Web site: http://cit.duke.edu/pdf/ipod_initiative_04_05.pdf

Beldarrain, Y. (2006). Distance education trends: Integrating new technologies to foster student interaction and collaboration. *Distance Education*, *27*(2), 139–153. doi:10.1080/01587910600789498

Bennett, E., Maniar, N., Clark, R., & King, T. (2008). Using supplementary podcasts to enhance campus-based courses: Students' perceptions and usage. *Learning Technology Newsletter*, *10*(3), 6–9.

Benson, P. (2009). Making sense of autonomy in language learning. In Pemberton, R., Toogood, S., & Barfield, A. (Eds.), *Maintaining control: Autonomy and language learning* (pp. 13–26). Hong Kong: Hong Kong University Press.

Biggs, J. (1999). *Teaching for quality learning at university*. Buckingham: Society for Research into Higher Education and Open University Press.

Biggs, J. (2003). *Aligning teaching and assessment to curriculum objectives. Imaginative Curriculum Project*. LTSN Generic Centre.

Bird-Soto, N., & Rengel, P. (2009). Podcasting and the intermediate-level Spanish classroom. In Oxford, R., & Oxford, J. (Eds.), *Second language teaching and learning in the Net Generation* (pp. 101–109). Honolulu: University of Hawaii, National Foreign Language Resource Center.

Blaisdell, M. (2006, February 28). *Special double feature! Academic MP3s: Is it iTime yet?* Retrieved March 20, 2010 from Campus Technology website: http://campustechnology.com/articles/2006/02/special-double-feature-academic-mp3s--is-it-itime-yet.aspx

Blake, R. J. (2008). *Brave new digital classroom: Technology and foreign language learning*. Washington, DC: Georgetown University Press.

Blau, E. (1990). The effect of syntax, speed, and pauses on listening comprehension. *TESOL Quarterly*, *16*, 517–528. doi:10.2307/3586469

Blaz, B. (n.d.). *Steps in creating authentic and performance-based assessment tasks*. Retrieved March 20, 2010 from NC Standard Course of Study website: http://www.ncpublicschools.org/curriculum/secondlanguages/resources/orallanguages/05tools?&print=true

Blin, F. (2004). CALL and the development of learner autonomy: Towards an activity-theoretical perspective. *ReCALL*, *16*(2), 377–395. doi:10.1017/S0958344004000928

Boulos, M., Maramba, I., & Wheeler, S. (2006). Wikis, blogs and podcasts: A new generation of web-based tools for virtual collaborative clinical practice and education. *BMC Medical Education*, *6*(41). doi:.doi:10.1186/1472-6920-6-41

Braun, L. W. (2007). *Listen up! Podcasting for schools and libraries*. Medford, NJ: Information Today Inc.

Brinckwirth, T., Kissling, E., Murphy-Judy, K., & Valencia, C. (2007). Technology follows technique: Refocusing the observational lens. In Kassen, M., Murphy-Judy, K., Peters, M., & Lavine, R. (Eds.), *Training and Developing Technology Proficient L2 Teachers. CALICO Monograph, vol. #6*. San Marcos, TX: Computer Assisted Language Instruction Consortium.

Brown, D. (2001). *Teaching by principles: An interactive approach to language pedagogy* (2nd ed.). New York: Addison Wesley Longman.

Brown, J. S. (2000). Growing up digital: the web and a new learning ecology. *Change*, March/April: 10-20. Reprinted as "Growing up digital: how the web changes work, education, and the ways people learn" in *USDLA Journal 16(2)*. Retrieved from http://www.usdla.org/html/journal/FEB02_Issue/article01.html

Bruce, B., & Lin, C. C. (2009). Voices of youth: Podcasting as a means for inquiry-based community engagement. *E-learning, 6*(2), 230–241. doi:10.2304/elea.2009.6.2.230

Burgess, S., & Head, K. (2005). *How to teach for exams*. Essex, UK: Pearson Education Ltd.

Bush, M. (2008). Computer-assisted language learning: From vision to reality? *CALICO Journal, 25*, 443–470.

Byram, M., & Feng, A. (2005). Teaching and researching intercultural competence. In Hinkel, E. (Ed.), *Handbook of Research in Second Language Teaching and Learning* (pp. 911–930). Mahwah, NJ: Earlbaum.

Cain, J. (2007). Podcasting enables 24/7 foreign language study. News Office, Massachusetts Institute of Technology. Retrieved from http://web.mit.edu/newsoffice/2007/podcasting-fll.html

Campus Technology. (2006). 2006 Campus Technology Innovators: Podcasting in Campus Technology. Retrieved January 1, 2010, from http://campustechnology.com/Articles/2006/07/2006-Campus-Technology-Innovators-Podcasting.aspx?p=1).

Carney, N. (2009). Blogging in foreign language education. In Thomas, M. (Ed.), *Web 2.0 and second language learning* (pp. 292–312). Hershey, PA: Information Science Reference.

Cassavoy, L. (n.d.). *How much does an iPhone cost to buy and use*. Retrieved August 28, 2009, from About website: http://smartphones.about.com/od/smartphonebasics/f/iphone_cost.htm

Center for Advanced Research on Language Acquisition. (n.d.). *Process: Types of rubrics*. Retrieved March 20, 2010, from University of Minnesota website: http://www.carla.umn.edu/assessment/VAC/Evaluation/p_6.html

Chaka, C. (2009). Portable handheld language learning: From CALL, MALL to PALL. In Marriott, R., & Torres, P. L. (Eds.), *Handbook of research on e-Learning methodologies for language acquisition* (pp. 539–553). Hershey, PA: Information Science Reference.

Chan, A., Lee, M. J. W., & McLoughlin, C. (2006). Everyone's learning with podcasting: A Charles Sturt University experience. In *Who's learning? Whose technology? Proceedings ascilite Sydney 2006*. Retrieved from http://www.ascilite.org.au/conferences/sydney06/proceeding/pdf_papers/p171.pdf

Chan, W. M., Chen, I. R., & Döpel, M. (2008). Learning on the move: Applying podcasting technologies to foreign language learning. In W.M. Chan, K.N. Chin, P. Martin-Lau, M. Nagami, J. Sew & T. Suthiwan (Eds.), *Proceedings of the Third CLS International Conference CLaSIC 2008* (pp. 36-69). National University of Singapore: Singapore.

Chapelle, C., & Jamieson, J. (2008). *Tips for Teaching with CALL: practically approaches to Computer-Assisted Language Learning*. Pearson Longman.

Chapelle, C. (2005). Computer-assisted language learning. In Hinkel, E. (Ed.), *Handbook of Research in Second Language Teaching and Learning* (pp. 743–755). Mahwah, NJ: Earlbaum.

Cheung, C. K. (2001). The use of popular culture as a stimulus to motivate secondary students' English learning in Hong Kong. *ELT Journal, 55*(1), 55–61. doi:10.1093/elt/55.1.55

Chinnery, G. (2006). Going to the MALL: Mobile assisted language learning. *Language Learning & Technology, 10*(1), 9.

Chinnery, G. M. (2006). Emerging technologies going to the MALL: Mobile assisted language learning. *Language Learning & Technology, 10*(1), 9–16.

Clough, G., Jones, A., McAndrew, G., & Scanlon, E. (2009). Inform learning evidence in online communities of mobile device enthusiasts. In M. Alley (Ed.), *Mobile learning: Transforming the delivery of education and training* (pp. 99-112). Edmonton, AG: Au Press.

Cole, G. (2007, September 18). Why every school should be podcasting. *The Guardian.* Retrieved from http://www.guardian.co.uk/education/2007/sep/18/link.link16

Colpaert, J. (2004). From courseware to coursewear? *Computer Assisted Language Learning, 17*(3-4), 261–266. doi:10.1080/0958822042000319575

Comedy, C. com. (2009). Efficiency expert joke. Retrieved from http://www.clevercomedy.com/joke/j3795j14.html

Constantine, P. (2007). Podcasts: Another source for listening input. *The Internet TESL Journal, 8*(1). Retrieved from http://iteslj.org/Techniques/Constantine-PodcastListening.html

Cooney, G., & Keogh, K. (2007). *Use of mobile phones for language learning and assessment for learning, a pilot project*. Retrieved December 21, 2009 from http://www.learnosity.com/files/learnosity-use-of-mobile-phones-for-language-learning-and-assessment-for-learning.pdf

Copley, J. (2007). Audio and video podcasts of lectures for campus-based students: Production and evaluation of student use. *Innovations in Education and Teaching International, 44*(4), 387–399. doi:10.1080/14703290701602805

Corbeil, J. R., & Valdés-Corbeil, M. E. (2007). Are you ready for mobile learning? *EDUCAUSE Quarterly, 30*(2), 51–58.

Cowan, D. L., Machacha, R. F., Hausafus, C., & Torrie, M. (2004). Written reflection: The link between study-abroad and service-learning. International Journal of Learning, 9(1). Retrieved January 10, 2010, from www.ijl.cgpublisher.com/home.html.

Coxhead, A. (2000). A new academic word list. *TESOL Quarterly, 34*, 213–238. doi:10.2307/3587951

Crystal, D. (2003). *English as a global language* (2nd ed.). Cambridge, UK: Cambridge University Press. doi:10.1017/CBO9780511486999

Dale, C. (2007). Strategies for using podcasting to support student learning. *Journal of Hospitality, Leisure, Sport and Tourism Education, 6*(1), 49–57. .doi:10.3794/johlste.61.155

Daly, D. (2006, May). *Learner evaluation of a ten-session intensive listening programme.* Paper presented at BAAL/CUP conference. University of Warwik, UK.

Danielsson, K., Hedestig, U., Juslin, M., & Orre, C. (2003). Participatory design in development of mobile learning environments. In J. Attewell, & C. Savill-Smith (Eds), *Learning with mobile devices: Research and development* (pp. 47-53). MLEARN 2003: Learning with Mobile Devices; London, UK, May 19-20, 2003.

Davies, A. (2002). Using teacher-generated biography as input material. *ELT Journal, 56*, 368–379. doi:10.1093/elt/56.4.368

Deal, A. (2007). *Podcasting.* A Teaching with Technology White Paper. CarnegieMellon Office of Technology for Education. Retrieved from http://www.cmu.edu/teaching/resources/PublicationsArchives/StudiesWhitepapers/Podcasting_Jun07.pdf

Dervin, F. (2006). Podcasting demystified, *Language Magazine*, 30-31. Retrieved August 4, 2009, from http://www.languagemagazine.com

Dias, J. (2002a) Cell phones in the classroom: boon or bane? C@lling Japan, 10(2), 16-21. Retrieved January 3, 2010 from http://jaltcall.org/cjo/10_2.pdf/.

Dias, J. (2002b). Cell phones in the classroom: boon or bane? Part 2. C@lling Japan, 10(3), 8-13. Retrieved January 3, 2010 from http://jaltcall.org/cjo/10_3.pdf/

Digital Inspiration. (2008, April 24). *Social media survey highlights differences between US and Asia.* Retrieved October 22, 2009, from http://www.labnol.org/internet/blogging/social-media-survey-highlights-differences-between-us-and-asia/3065/

Donatelli, L. (in press). The Impact of Telecommunications and other Technologies

Dörnyei, Z. (2001). *Motivational strategies in the language classroom.* Cambridge, UK: Cambridge University Press. doi:10.1017/CBO9780511667343

Dörnyei, Z. (2001). *Motivational Strategies in the language classroom.* Cambridge: Cambridge University Press. doi:10.1017/CBO9780511667343

Doughty, C., & Williams, J. (1998). *Focus on form in classroom second language acquisition.* Cambridge, UK: Cambridge University Press.

Ducate, L., & Lomicka, L. (2009b). Podcasting: An effective tool for honing language students' pronunciation? *Language Learning & Technology, 13*(3), 66–86.

Ducate, L., & Lomicka, L. (2009). Podcasting: An effective tool for honing language students' pronunciation? *Language Learning & Technology, 13*, 66–86.

Ducate, L., & Lomicka, L. (2009). Podcasting: An effective tool for honing language students' pronunciation? *Language Learning & Technology, 13*(3), 66–86. Retrieved from http://llt.msu.edu/vol13num3/ducatelomicka.pdf.

Ducate, L., & Lomicka, L. (2009). Podcasting in the language classroom. Inherently mobile or not? In Oxford, R., & Oxford, J. (Eds.), *Second language teaching and learning in the Net Generation* (pp. 111–125). Honolulu: University of Hawaii, National Foreign Language Resource Center.

Duffy, P., & Bruns, A. (2006). The use of blogs, wikis and RSS in education: A conversation of possibilities. In *Proceedings of the Online Learning and Teaching Conference 2006.* Retrieved from https://olt.qut.edu.au/udf/OLT2006/gen/static/papers/Duffy_OLT2006_paper.pdf

Dufon, M., & Churchill, E. (2006). *Language Learners in Study Abroad Contexts.* Clevedon, UK: Multilingual Matters.

Edirisingha, P., Rizzi, C., & Rothwell, L. (2007). Podcasting to provide teaching and learning support for an undergraduate module on English language communication. *Turkish Online Journal of Distance Education, 8*(3), 87–107.

Edirisingha, P., Salmon, G., & Nie, M. (2008). Developing pedagogical podcasts. In Salmon, G., & Edirisingha, P. (Eds.), *Podcasting for learning in universities* (pp. 153–168). Maidenhead, U.K.: Open University Press.

Editorials, N. (2009, July). Inspiring non-scientists. *Nature, 460*, 552. doi:10.1038/460552a

Elkhafaifi, H. (2005). The effect of prelistening activities on listening comprehension in Arabic learners. *Foreign Language Annals, 38*(4), 505–513. doi:10.1111/j.1944-9720.2005.tb02517.x

Elliott, A. R. (1995). Foreign language phonology: Field independence, attitude, and the success of formal instruction in Spanish pronunciation. *Modern Language Journal, 79*, 530–542. doi:10.2307/330005

Ellis, R., Basturkmen, H., & Loewen, S. (2001). Preemptive focus on form in the ESL classroom. *TESOL Quarterly, 35*, 407–432. doi:10.2307/3588029

eMarketer. (2009, March 4). *Podcasting goes mainstream.* Retrieved from http://www.emarketer.com/Article.aspx?R=1006937

EUROCALL. (2008)... *ReCALL, 20*(3).

Evans, C. (2008). The effectiveness of m-learning in the form of podcast revision lectures in higher education. *Computers & Education, 50*, 491–498. doi:10.1016/j.compedu.2007.09.016

Facer, B. R., Abdous, M., & Camarena, M. M. (2009). The Impact of podcasting on students' learning outcomes. In Marriott, R., & Torres, P. L. (Eds.), *Handbook of research one-Learning methodologies for language acquisition* (pp. 339–351). Hershey, PA: Information Science Reference.

Ferdig, R. E., Coutts, J., DiPietro, J., Lok, B., & Davis, N. (2007). Innovative technologies for multicultural education needs. *Multicultural Education & Technology Journal*, *1*(1), 47–63. doi:10.1108/17504970710745201

Fernandez, V., Simo, P., & Sallan, J. M. (2009). Podcasting: A new technological tool to facilitate good practice in higher education. *Computers & Education*, *53*(2), 385–392. .doi:10.1016/j.compedu.2009.02.014

Fernández, C. (forthcoming). *Approaches to grammar instruction in teaching materials*: A study in current, beginning-level Spanish textbooks. *Hispania*.

Feyten, C. (1991). The power of listening: An overlooked dimension in language acquisition. *Modern Language Journal*, *75*, 173–180. doi:10.2307/328825

Field, J. (2008a). Bricks or mortar: Which parts of the input does a second language listener rely on? *TESOL Quarterly*, *42*, 411–431.

Field, J. (2008b). *Listening in the language classroom*. Cambridge, UK; New York: Cambridge University Press.

Fox, A. (2008). Using podcasts in the EFL classroom. *TESL-EJ*, *11*(4). Retrieved November 16, 2009, from http://tesl-ej.org/ej44/a4.html

France, D., & Wheeler, A. (2007). Reflections on using podcasting for student feedback. *Planet*, *18*, 10–11.

Freed, B., Segalowitz, N., & Dewey, D. (2001). Second language acquisition in three contexts of learning: Study abroad, intensive immersion, regular classrooms. Paper presented at the American Council for the Teaching of Foreign Languages (ACTFL) conference, Washington D.C.

French, D. P. (2006). iPods: Informative or invasive. *Journal of College Science Teaching*, *36*(1), 58–59.

Furman, N., Goldberg, D., & Lusin, N. (2007). *Enrollments in languages other than English in United States institutions of higher education, Fall 2006*. New York: Modern Languages Association of America. Retrieved from *Information. Communicatio Socialis*, *12*(5), 678–690.

Gardner, D. (2005). *U.S. study abroad increases by 9.6% continuous record growth*. Retrieved October 1, 2007 from http://www.iie.org/Content/NavigationMenu/Pressroom/PressReleases/U_S__STUDY_ABROAD_INCREAS-ES_BY_9_6_CONTINUES_RECORD_GROWTH.htm

Garrison, C., & Ehringhaus, M. (2007). Formative and summative assessments in the classroom. Retrieved from http://www.nmsa.org/Publications/WebExclusive/Assessment/tabid/1120/Default.aspx

Gass, S. (1997). *Input, interaction, and the second language learner*. Mahwah, NJ: Lawrence Erlbaum Associates.

Gaugler, K., & Deosthale, D. (2008). Computer-assisted Study Abroad: Empowering Students with Web 2.0. Paper presented at the 2008 CALICO-IALLT Symposium in San Francisco, CA.

Geoghegan, M., & Klass, D. (2007). *Podcast solutions: The complete guide to audio and video podcasting* (2nd ed.). New York: Friendsof.

Gilgen, R. (2005). Holding the world in your hand: Creating a mobile language learning environment. *Educase Quarterly*, *3*, 30–39.

Gillette, S., Goettsch, K., Rowekamp, J., Salehi, N., & Tarone, E. (1999). *Connected! Using audio, video, and computer materials in the communicative classroom*. Minneapolis, MN: Master Communications Group, Inc.

Gilmore, D. (2004). *We the media: Grassroots journalism by the people, for the people*. Sebastopol, CA: O'Reilly Media, Inc.

Gimeno, A. (2002). Principles in CALL software design and implementation. *International Journal of English Studies*, *2*(1), 109–128.

Godwin-Jones, R. (2005). Skype and podcasting: Disruptive technologies for language learning. *Language Learning & Technology, 9*(3), 9–12.

Godwin-Jones, R. (2003). Emerging technologies: Blogs and wikis environments for on-line collaboration. *Language Learning & Technology, 7*(2), 12–16.

Godwin-Jones, R. (1999). Emerging Technologies: Mobile Computing and Language Learning. *Language Learning & Technology, 2*(2), 7–11. Retrieved December 31, 2009.

Godwin-Jones, R. (2004). Emerging Technologies: Language in Action: From Webquests to Virtual Realities. *Language Learning & Technology, 8*(3), 9–14. Retrieved December 31, 2009.

Goodwin-Jones, B. (2005). Emerging Technologies. Messages, Gaming, Peer-to-Peer Sharing: Language Learning Strategies and Tools for the Millennial Generation. *LLT, 9*(1), 17–22.

Grammar Girl. (2009). Retrieved on November 20, 2009 from http://grammar.quickanddirtytips.com/

Graves, K. (2000). *Designing language courses: A guide for teachers.* New York: Heinle & Heinle Thomson Learning.

Gruba, P. (2006). Playing the video-text: A media-literacy perspective on video-mediated L2 listening. *Language Learning & Technology, 10*, 77–92.

Gruba, P., Clark, C., Ng, K., & Wells, M. (2009). Blending technologies in second language courses: A reflexive enquiry. In *Same places, different spaces. Proceedings ascilite Auckland 2009.* http://www.ascilite.org.au/conferences/auckland09/procs/gruba.pdf

Guichon, N., & McLornan, S. (2008). The effects of multimodality on L2 learners: Implications for CALL resource design. *System, 36*, 85–93. doi:10.1016/j.system.2007.11.005

Guy, T. (2009, August). *Research shows Asians use PDA/Smartphone for online communication more than Americans/Europeans.* Retrieved October 22, 2009, from Bloggersbase website: http://www.bloggersbase.com/internet/research-shows-asians-use-pdasmartphone-for-online-communication-than-americanseuropeans/

Harris, H., & Park, S. (2008). Education usages of podcasting. *British Journal of Educational Technology, 39*(3), 548–551. .doi:10.1111/j.1467-8535.2007.00788.x

Hartigan, T., Hill, J., Lewis-Faupel, S., & Springsteen, A. (2006). iPods and podcasting: Too cool for school? Retrieved November 30, 2009, from http://www.educause.edu/ir/library/pdf/NCP0664A.pdf

Hayton, T. (2009). Simulated immersion. *TeachingEnglish*, British Council. Retrieved 31 March, 2010 from http://www.teachingenglish.org.uk/think/articles/simulated-immersion

Hegelheimer, V., & O'Bryan, A. (2009). Mobile technologies and language education: a look at language learning podcasts. In Thomas, M. (Ed.), *Handbook of Research on Web 2.0 and Second Language Learning* (pp. 331–349). Hershey, PA: Information Science Reference.

Herrington, J., & Kervin, L. (2007). Authentic learning supported by technology: Ten suggestions and cases of integration in classroom. *Educational Media International, 44*(3), 219–236. doi:10.1080/09523980701491666

Herron, C., Dubreil, B., Corrie, C., & Cole, S. P. (2002). A classroom investigation: Can video improve intermediate-level french language students' ability to learn about a foreign culture? *Modern Language Journal, 86*, 36–53. doi:10.1111/1540-4781.00135

Hew, K. F. (2008). Use of audio podcast in K-12 and higher education: A review of research topics and methodologies. *Educational Technology Research and Development.*

History—Creative Commons. (n.d.). Retrieved November 30, 2009, from http://creativecommons.org/about/history/

Hockley, N., & Dudeney, G. (2007). *How to teach English with technology.* Harlow: Pearson/Longman.

Hoffa, W. (1996). The Pros and Cons of Travel and Living in Cyberspace. In *Transitions Abroad (January/February 1996)*. E-Mail and Study Abroad.

Hoffler, T. N., & Leutner, D. (2007). Instructional animation versus static pictures: A meta-analysis. *Learning and Instruction, 17*(6), 722–738. doi:10.1016/j.learninstruc.2007.09.013

Hu, X. Q. (2004). Why China English should stand alongside British, American and other "World Englishes". *English Today, 78*, 26–33.

Huann, T. Y., & Thong, M. K. (2006). *Audioblogging and podcasting in education*. Retrieved October 18, 2009, from Education Ministry: Government of Singapore website: http://iresearch.edumall.sg/iresearch/slot/u110/litreviews/audioblogg_podcast.pdf

Hubbs, C. (2000). The Impact of Communications Technology on the Study Abroad Field: A Personal Reflection. Retrieved January, 4, 2010 from http://www.transitionsabroad.com/listings/study/articles/impact_of_technology_on_study_abroad.shtml

Huffaker, D. (2005). The educated blogger: Using weblogs to promote literacy in the classroom. *AACE Journal, 13*(2), 91–98.

Huizenga, J., Admiraal, W., Akkerman, S., & ten Dam, G. (2009). Mobile game-based learning in secondary education: Engagement, motivation and learning in a mobile city game. *Journal of Computer Assisted Learning, 25*(4), 332–344. doi:10.1111/j.1365-2729.2009.00316.x

Huntsberger, M., & Stavitsky, A. (2007). The new "podagogy": Incorporating podcasting into journalism education. *Journalism and Mass Communication Educator, 61*(4), 397–410.

In, S. DePaul & W. Hoffa (Eds.), Frontiers 18: A History of Study Abroad: 1965 to Present.

ISC. (2005). Multimedia learning with mobile phones. Innovative Practices with Elearning. Case Studies: Anytime, any place Learning. Retrieved January 3, 2010, from http://www.jisc.ac.uk/uploaded_documents/southampton.pdf.

Jackson, H. (2008, July 9). A "Second" chance to study abroad. Retrieved from http://news.cnet.com/8301-1023_3-9986465-93.html

Jamet, E., Gavota, M., & Quaireau, C. (2008). Attention guiding in multimedia learning. *Learning and Instruction, 18*(2), 135–145. doi:10.1016/j.learninstruc.2007.01.011

Jaokar, A. (2006). *Ajit Jaokar's mobile Web 2.0 blog: What is "Mobile Web 2.0"?* Retrieved October 18, 2009, from Web2journal website: http://web2.sys-con.com/node/251673

Jenkins, M., & Lonsdale, J. (2008). Podcasts and students' storytelling. In Salmon, G., & Edirisingha, P. (Eds.), *Podcasting for learning in universities*. Maidenhead, U.K.: Open University Press.

Jobbings, D. (2005). *Exploiting the educational potential of podcasting*. Russell Educational Consultancy and Productions. Retrieved from http://www.recap.ltd.uk/articles/podguide.html

Johnson, K. (2001). *An introduction to foreign language learning and teaching*. London: Pearson Education Limited.

Jonassen, D. H. (2006). *Modeling with technology: Mindtools for conceptual change*. Columbus, OH: Merrill/Prentice-Hall.

Jones, Jeremy. (2001). CALL and the Teacher's Role in Promoting Learner Autonomy. *CALL-EJ Online 3*(1).

Jung, U. (1997). *Encyclopedia of language and education, Volume 4: Second language education* (G.R. Tucker & D. Corson, eds.). Springer.

Just, M., & Carpenter, M. A. (1992). A capacity theory of comprehension: Individual differences in working memory. *Psychological Review, 99*, 122–149. doi:10.1037/0033-295X.99.1.122

Kachru, B. B. (2005). *Asian Englishes: Beyond the canon*. Hong Kong: Hong Kong University Press.

Kadyte, V. (2003). Learning can happen anywhere: A mobile system for language learning. In J. Attewell, & C. Savill-Smith (Eds.), *Learning with mobile devices: Research and development* (pp. 73-78). MLEARN 2003: Learning with Mobile Devices; London, UK, May 19-20, 2003.

Kaplan-Leiserson, E. (2005). Trend: Podcasting in academic and corporate learning. *Learning Circuits.* Retrieved from http://www.astd.org/LC/2005/0605_kaplan.htm

Katz, S., & Blyth, C. (2009). What is grammar? In Katz, S., & Blyth, C. (Eds.), *AAUSC 2008 Volume, Conceptions of L2 grammar: Theoretical approaches and their application in the L2 classroom* (pp. 2–14). Boston, MA: Heinle Cengage Learning.

Kemmis, S., & McTaggart, R. (Eds.). (1988). *The action research planner*. Victoria: Deakin University.

King, K., & Gura, M. (2009). *Podcasting for teachers: using a new technology to revolutionize teaching and learning*. Charlotte, NC: IAP.

Kinginger, K. (2008). Language Learning in Study Abroad: Case Studies of Americans in France. The Modern Language Journal Monograph Series (Vol. 1). Summary retrieved January 5, 2010 from http://calper.la.psu.edu/LL_in_Study_Abroad_summary.pdf

Kirkland, K., & Sutch, D. (2009). Overcoming the barriers to educational innovation: A literature review. Futurelab. Retrieved from http://www.futurelab.org.uk/resources/documents/lit_reviews/Barriers_to_Innovation_review.pdf

Kirkpatrick, A. (2007). *World Englishes: implications for international communication and English language teaching*. Cambridge: Cambridge University Press.

Klopfer, E., Squire, K., & Jenkins, H. (2002). *Environmental detectives PDAs as a window into a virtual simulated world*. Paper presented at International Workshop on Wireless and Mobile Technologies in Education. Retrieved October 16, 2009 from http://www.knowledgejump.com/technology/ipod/ipod.html

Krashen, S. (1985). *The input hypothesis*. London: Longman.

Krebs, A. (1998). *USDLA Funding Source Book for Distance Learning and Educational Technology*. Kendall Publishing.

Kukulska-Hulme, A., & Traxler, J. (2005). Mobile teaching and learning. In Kukulska-Hulme, A., & Traxler, J. (Eds.), *Mobile learning: A handbook for educators and trainers* (pp. 25–44). New York: Routledge.

Kukulska-Hulme, A. (2006). Mobile language learning now and in the future (pp. 119-134). Retrieved from http://www.groupe-compas.net/wp-content/uploads/2009/08/kukulska-hulme.pdf

Lacina, J. (2008). Learning English with iPods. *Childhood Education, 84*(4), 247–249.

Lafford, B. A., Lafford, P. A., & Sykes, J. (2007). Entre dicho y hecho ... [Between what is said and done]: An assessment of the application of research from second language acquisition and related fields to the creation of Spanish CALL materials for lexical acquisition. *CALICO Journal, 24*(3).

Lafford, P. A., & Lafford, B. A. (2005). CMC technologies for teaching foreign languages: What's on the horizon? *CALICO Journal, 22*(3), 679–709. Retrieved from https://72.167.96.97/html/article_162.pdf.

Laing, C., Wootton, A., & Irons, A. (2006). iPod! uLearn? *FORMATEX 2006.* Retrieved from http://www.formatex.org/micte2006/Downloadable-files/oral/iPod.pdf

Larsen-Freeman, D., & Long, M. (1991). *An introduction to second language acquisition research*. New York: Longman.

Lazzari, M. (2008). Creative use of podcasting in higher education and its effect on competitive agency. *Computers & Education, 52*(1), 27–34. doi:10.1016/j.compedu.2008.06.002

Lazzari, M. (2009). Creative use of podcasting in higher education and its effect on competitive agency. *Computers & Education, 5,* 27–34. doi:10.1016/j.compedu.2008.06.002

Lee, M. J. W., Miller, C., & Newnham, L. (2008). Podcasting syndication services and university students: Why don't they subscribe? *The Internet and Higher Education*, *12*, 53–59. doi:10.1016/j.iheduc.2008.10.001

Lee, J., & VanPatten, B. (2003). *Making communicative language teaching happen*. New York: McGraw-Hill.

Lee, M., & Chan, A. (2007). Pervasive, lifestyle-integrated mobile learning for distance learners: An analysis and unexpected results from a podcasting study. *Open Learning: The Journal of Open and Distance Learning*, *22*(3), 201–218.

Lee, M. J. W., & Chan, A. (2007). Reducing the effects of isolation and promoting inclusivity for distance learners through podcasting. *Turkish Online Journal of Distance Education, 8*(1). Retrieved from http://tojde.anadolu.edu.tr/tojde25/pdf/article_7.pdf

Lenhart, A., Ling, R., Campbell, S., & Purcell, K. (2010, April 20). Teens and Mobile Phones. Pew Internet and American Life Project Reports. Retrieved July 9, 2010, from http://www.pewinternet.org/Reports/2010/Teens-and-Mobile-Phones.aspx.

Leow, R. P. (2009). Input enhancement and L2 grammatical development: What the research reveals. In Katz, S., & Blyth, C. (Eds.), *AAUSC 2008 Volume, Conceptions of L2 grammar: Theoretical approaches and their application in the L2 classroom* (pp. 16–34). Boston, MA: Heinle Cengage Learning.

Leung, C., & Chan, Y. (2003). Mobile learning: A new paradigm in electronic learning. In *Proceeding of 3rd IEEE International Conference on Advanced Learning Technology* (pp. 76-80).

Levy, M., & Kennedy, C. (2005). Learning Italian via mobile SMS. In Kukulska-Hulme, A., & Traxler, J. (Eds.), *Mobile learning: A handbook for educators and trainers* (pp. 76–83). New York: Routledge.

Lim, D. H. (2004). Cross cultural differences in online learning motivation. *Educational Media International*, *41*(2), 163–175. doi:10.1080/09523980410001685784

Liu, T. C., Wang, H. Y., Liang, J. K., Chan, T. W., Ko, H. W., & Yang, J. C. (2003). Wireless and mobile technologies to enhance teaching and learning. *Journal of Computer Assisted Learning*, *19*, 371–382. doi:10.1046/j.0266-4909.2003.00038.x

Lonn, S., & Teasley, S. D. (2009). Podcasting in higher education: What are the implications for teaching and learning? *The Internet and Higher Education*, *12*, 88–92. doi:10.1016/j.iheduc.2009.06.002

Lord, G. (2008). Podcasting communities and second language pronunciation. *Foreign Language Annals*, *41*, 364–379. doi:10.1111/j.1944-9720.2008.tb03297.x

Lu, J. A. (2009). Podcasting as a next generation teaching resource. In Thomas, M. (Ed.), *Handbook of research on Web 2.0 and second language learning* (pp. 350–365). Hershey, PA: Information Science Reference.

Luckin, R., du Boulay, B., Smith, H., Underwood, J., Fitzpatrick, G., & Holmberg, J. (2005). Using mobile technology to create flexible learning contexts. *Journal of Interactive Media in Education*, *22*, 1–21.

Luckin, R., Brewster, D., Pearce, R. S., & du Boulay, B. (2003). SMILE: The creation of space for interaction through technology. In J. Attewell, & C. Savill-Smith (Eds), *Learning with mobile devices: Research and development* (pp. 87-93). MLEARN 2003: Learning with Mobile Devices; London, UK, May 19-20, 2003.

Lys, F. (2008, March 18-22). *In touch with the iPod Touch*. Paper presented at CALICO 2008, University of San Francisco, San Francisco, CA.

Maltby, A., & Mackie, S. (2009). Virtual learning environments—Help or hindrance for the "disengaged" student? *ALT-J: Research in Learning Technology*, *17*(1), 49–62.

Mandernach, B. J. (2009). Effect of instructor-personalized multimedia in the online classroom. *International Review of Research in Open and Distance Learning*, *10*(3).

Martín, M. D. (2005). Permanent crisis, tenuous persistence: Foreign languages in Australian universities. *Arts and Humanities in Higher Education*, *4*(1), 53–75. doi:10.1177/1474022205048758

Matsuda, A. (2002). "International understanding" through teaching world Englishes. *World Englishes, 21*(3), 436–440. doi:10.1111/1467-971X.00262

Matsuda, A. (2003). Incorporating world Englishes in teaching English as an international language. *TESOL Quarterly, 37*(4), 719–729. doi:10.2307/3588220

Mattison, D. (2003). Quickiwiki, swiki, twiki, zwiki and the plone wars: Wiki as a PIM and collaborative content tool. *Searcher, 11*(4), 32–48.

McBride, K. (2009). Podcasts and second language learning: Promoting listening comprehension and intercultural competence. In Abraham, L. B., & Williams, L. (Eds.), *Electronic discourse in language learning and language teaching* (pp. 153–167). Amsterdam: John Benjamins.

McCarthy, M., & O'Dell, F. (2005). *English Collocations in Use*. Cambridge: Cambridge University Press.

McCarty, S. (2005). Spoken Internet to go: Popularization through podcasting. *JALT CALL, 1*(2), 67-74. Retrieved November 16, 2009, from http://www.waoe.org/president/podcasting_article.html

McCloskey, P. (2007, July 9). Consensus: Podcasting has no 'inherent' pedagogic value. Campus Technology. Retrieved November 4, 2009, from http://campustechnology.com/articles/49018

McCombs, S., & Liu, Y. (2007). The efficacy of podcasting technology in instructional delivery. *International Journal of Technology in Teaching and Learning, 3*(2), 123–134.

McLoughlin, C., & Lee, M. (2007). Listen and learn: A systematic review of the evidence that podcasting supports learning in higher education. In C. Montgomerie & J. Seale (Eds.), *Proceedings of World Conference on Educational Multimedia, Hypermedia and Telecommunications 2007* (pp. 1669-1677). Chesapeake, VA: AACE.

McQuillan, J. (2006b). Language on the go: Tuning into podcasting. *The International Journal of Foreign Language Teaching, 2*, 16–18.

McQuillan, J. (2006a). *iPod in Education: The potential for language acquisition*. One in a series of iPod in education white papers. Cupertino, CA: Apple Inc.

Mendelsohn, D. J. (2006). Learning how to listen using learning strategies. In Usó-Juan, E., & Martínez-Flor, A. (Eds.), *Current trends in the development and teaching of the four language skills* (pp. 75–89). Berlin: Mouton de Gruyter. doi:10.1515/9783110197778.2.75

Meng, P. (2005). Podcasting and vodcasting: A white paper. Retrieved November 16, 2009, from http://edmarketing.apple.com/adcinstitute/wpcontent/Missouri_Podcasting_White_Paper.pdf

Meng, P. (2005). Podcasting and vodcasting: A white paper. IAT Services, University of Missouri (pp. 1-13). Retrieved from http://www.tfaoi.com/cm/3cm/3cm310.pdf

Mifsud, L. (2003). Learning 2go: Making reality of the scenarios? In J. Attewell, & C. Savill-Smith (Eds.), *Learning with mobile devices: Research and development* (pp. 99-104). MLEARN 2003: Learning with Mobile Devices; London, May 19-20, 2003.

*Mobile phone adoption in developing countries.* (n.d.). Retrieved November 25, 2009, from wikiinvest website: http://www.wikinvest.com/concept/Mobile_Phone_Adoption_in_Developing_Countries

Mooij, M. K. (2004). *Consumer behavior and culture: Consequences for global marketing and advertising*. Thousand Oaks, CA: Sage Publications Inc.

Morgan, M. (2008). More productive use of technology in the ESL/EFL classroom, *The Internet TESL Journal, 14*(7). Retrieved http://iteslj.org/Articles/Morgan-Technology.html

Mueller, G. A. (1980). Visual contextual cues and listening comprehension: An experiment. *Modern Language Journal, 64*(3), 335–340. doi:10.2307/324500

Murphy, B. (2008). Podcasting in higher education. *IT-NOW, 50*(3), 22–23. doi:10.1093/itnow/bwn056

Murray, D. (2005). Technologies for second language. *Annual Review of Applied Linguistics*, *25*, 188–201. doi:10.1017/S0267190505000103

Murray, L., Hourigan, T., & Jeanneau, C. (2007). Blog writing integration for academic language learning purposes: Towards an assessment framework. *IBÉRICA*, *14*, 9–32.

Nakatani, Y. (2005). The effects of awareness-raising training on oral communication strategy use. *Modern Language Journal*, *89*, 76–91. doi:10.1111/j.0026-7902.2005.00266.x

Narratore Audio Libri. (n.d.). Retrieved August 1, 2009 from www.ilnarratore.com

Nathan, P., & Chan, A. (2007). Engaging undergraduates with podcasting in a business subject. In *ICT: Providing choices for learners and learning. Proceedings ascilite Singapore 2007*. Retrieved from http://www.ascilite.org.au/conferences/singapore07/procs/nathan.pdf

Nation, P. (2001). *Learning Vocabulary in Another Language*. Cambridge: Cambridge University Press.

National Endowment for the Humanities. (n.d.). Retrieved October 1, 2007 from www.neh.gov

National Standards in Foreign Language Education Project (NSFLEP). (1999). *National Standards for foreign language learning: Preparing for the 21st century*. Lawrence, KS: Allen Pres.

O'Bryan, A., & Hegelheimer, V. (2007). Integrating CALL into the classroom: The role of podcasting in an ESL listening strategies course. *ReCALL*, *19*(2), 162–180. doi:10.1017/S0958344007000523

O'Connor di Vito, N. (1991). Incorporating native speaker norms in second language teaching materials. *Applied Linguistics*, *12*, 383–395. doi:10.1093/applin/12.4.383

O'Hare, D. (2001). The future is already happening: Training aeronautical skills in virtual environments. *Pacific Wings Magazine*. Retrieved from http://psy.otago.ac.nz/cogerg/The%20Future%20is%20Already %20Happening.pdf

O'Reilly, T. (2005). *What is Web 2.0: Design patterns and business models for the next generation of software*. Retrieved September 28, 2009, from O'Reilly Media website: http://oreilly.com/web2/archive/what-is-web-20.html

O'Bryan, A., & Hegelheimer, V. (2007). Integrating CALL into the classroom: The role of podcasting in an ESL listening strategies course. *ReCALL*, *19*(2), 162–180. doi:10.1017/S0958344007000523

Open Doors Report. (n.d.). Retrieved October 1, 2007 and October 10, 2009 from http://www.opendoors.iienetwork.org/

Oppenheimer, T. (2003). *The flickering mind*. New York: Random House.

Park, C. (2006). Learning style preferences of Asian American (Chinese, Filipino, Korean, and Vietnamese) students in secondary schools. In Park, C., Endo, R., & Goodwin, A. L. (Eds.), *Asian and Pacific American education: Learning, socialization, and identity* (pp. 77–97). Scottsdale, AZ: Information Age Publishing.

Parker, K., & Chao, J. (2007). Wiki as a teaching tool, interdisciplinary. *Journal of Knowledge and Learning Objects*, *3*, 57–72.

Parson, V., Reddy, P., Wood, J., & Senior, C. (2009). Educating an "iPod" generation: Undergraduate attitudes, experiences and understanding of vodcast and podcast use. *Learning, Media and Technology*, *34*(3), 215–228. doi:10.1080/17439880903141497

Peng, S. S., & Wright, D. (1994). Explanation of academic achievement of Asian American students. *The Journal of Educational Research*, *87*(6), 346–352. doi:10.1080/00220671.1994.9941265

Perry, M. (2010). How to Teach with Google Wave in the Chronicle of Higher Education Wired Blog. Retrieved on January 8, 2010, from http://chronicle.com/blogPost/How-to-Teach-With-Google-Wave/19501/?sid=wc&utm_source=wc&utm_medium=en

Petersen, S., Divitini, M. & Chabert, G. (2008). Identity, sense of community and connectedness in a community of mobile language learners in ReCALL, 20(3), 361-379.

Pettes Guikema, J. (2009). Discourse analysis of podcasts in French: Implications for foreign language listening development. In Abraham, L. B., & Williams, L. (Eds.), *Electronic discourse in language learning and language teaching* (pp. 169–189). Amsterdam: John Benjamins.

Pettit, J., & Kukulska-Hulme, A. (2006). Going with the grain: Mobile devices in practice. In *Proceedings of the 23rd Annual Ascilite Conference* (pp. 647-656). Retrieved from http://www.ascilite.org.au/conferences/sydney06/proceeding/pdf_papers/p91.pdf

Phifer, L. (2009, August 10). *3G*. Retrieved October 18, 2009, from Search Telecom website: http://searchtelecom.techtarget.com/sDefinition/0,sid103_gci214486,00.html

Pieri, M., & Diamantini, D. (2009). From e-learning to mobile learning: New opportunities. In M. Alley (Ed.), *Mobile learning: Transforming the delivery of education and training* (pp. 99-112). Edmonton, AG: Au Press.

Plass, J. L., Chun, D. M., Mayer, R. E., & Leutner, D. (2003). Cognitive load in reading a foreign language text with multimedia aids and the influence of verbal and spatial abilities. *Computers in Human Behavior, 19*(2), 221–243. .doi:10.1016/S0747-5632(02)00015-8

*Podcast*. (n.d.). Retrieved October 28, 2009, from PC Magazine Encyclopedia website: http://www.pcmag.com/encyclopedia_term/0,2542,t=podcast&i=49433,00.asp

*podscope*. (2007). Retrieved November 30, 2009, from http://podscope.com/

Prensky, M. (2001). Digital Natives, Digital Immigrants: A New Way to Look At Ourselves and Our Kids. *Horizon, 9*(5), 1–6. doi:10.1108/10748120110424816

Prensky, M. (2001). Digital natives, digital immigrants. *On The Horizon, 9*(5). NCB University Press. Retrieved from www.marcprensky.com/writing/Prensky%20-%20Digital%20Natives,%20Digital%20Immigrants%20-%20Part1.pdf

Prensky, M. (2009). H. sapiens digital: From digital immigrants and digital natives to digital wisdom. *INNOVATE Journal of Online Education, 5*(3). Retrieved November 16, 2009, from http://innovateonline.info/pdf/vol5_issue3/H._Sapiens_Digital-__From_Digital_Immigrants_and_Digital_Natives_to_Digital_Wisdom.pdf

Presky, M. (2001). Digital Natives, Digital Immigrants. Part II. Do They Really Think Differently? *Horizon, 9*(6).

Project-based learning. (n.d.). In *Wikipedia*. Retrieved November 27, 2009, from http://en.wikipedia.org/wiki/Project-based_learning

Pulverness, A. (2003). Materials for cultural awareness. In Tomlinson, B. (Ed.), *Developing materials for language teaching* (pp. 426–438). London: Continuum.

Purdie, N., & Hattie, J. (1996). Cultural differences in the use of strategies for self-regulated learning. *American Educational Research Journal, 33*(4), 845–871.

Putman, M. (2008). *Using Podcasts to Enhance Science Vocabulary Development*. Paper presented at the National Educational Computing Conference. Ball State University.

Ractham, P., & Zhang, X. (2006). Podcasting in academia: A new knowledge management paradigm within academic settings. In K. Keiser et al. (Eds.), *Proceedings of the 44th Annual Computer Personnel Research Conference (ACM SIGMIS/CPR) 2006.* (pp. 314-317). New York.

Ragusa, A., Chan, A., & Crampton, A. (2009). iPods aren't just for tunes. *Information Communication and Society, 12*(5), 678–690. doi:10.1080/13691180802471471

Ramasubbu, S., & Wilcox, B. (2009, January 8). *Mobile learning in classrooms of the future*. Retrieved November 25, 2009, from Converge website: http://www.convergemag.com/edtech/Mobile-Learning-in-Classrooms-of-the-Future.html.

*Ramp*. (2007). Retrieved November 30, 2009, from http://www.ramp.com/

Read, J. (1996). Recent developments in Australian late immersion language education. *Journal of Multilingual and Multicultural Development, 17*(6), 469–484. doi:10.1080/01434639608666296

Reynolds, C., & Bennett, L. (2008, July). A social constructivist approach to the use of podcasts. *ALT Newsletter,* (July). Retrieved from http://newsweaver.co.uk/alt/e_article001142653.cfm

Richards, J. C. (1983). Listening comprehension: Approach, design, procedure. *TESOL Quarterly, 17,* 219–239. doi:10.2307/3586651

Rifkin, B. (2005). A ceiling effect in traditional classroom foreign language instruction: Data from Russian. *Modern Language Journal, 89,* 3–18. doi:10.1111/j.0026-7902.2005.00262.x

Rith, C. (2008). Learn 35+ Language for Free in iTunes. Life Clover. Retrieved from http://www.lifeclever.com/learn-35-languages-for-free-in-itunes/

Robinson, J. L., & Dodd, J. E. (2006). Case study: Use of handheld computers by university communications students. *MERLOT Journal of Online Learning and Teaching, 2*(1), 49–61.

Roney, M. (2005). Apple could ship more than 37 million iPods in 2005. *Forbes.* Retrieved October 10, 2009 from http://www.forbes.com/2005/11/01/apple-ipod-computer-1101markets13.html

Rosell-Aguilar, F. (2007). Top of the pods: In search of a podcasting 'podagogy' for language learning. *Computer Assisted Language Learning, 20,* 471–492. doi:10.1080/09588220701746047

Rosell-Aguilar, F. (2007). Top of the Pods –In search of a podcasting "podagogy" for language learning. *Computer Assisted Language Learning, 5,* 471–492. doi:10.1080/09588220701746047

Rosell-Aguilar, F. (2007). Top of the pods: In search of a podcasting "podagogy" for language learning. *Computer Assisted Language Learning, 20*(5), 471–492. doi:10.1080/09588220701746047

Rosell-Aguilar, F. (2009). Podcasting for language learning: Re-examining the potential. In Lomicka, L., & Lord, G. (Eds.), *The next generation: Social networking and online collaboration in foreign language learning* (pp. 13–34). San Marcos, TX: CALICO.

Rosell-Aguilar, F. (2009). Podcasting for language learning: Re-examining the potential. In L. Lomicka and G. Lord (Eds.), *The next generation: Social networking and online collaboration in foreign language learning* (pp. 13-34). San Mateo, TX: CALICO.

Rost, M. (2002). *Teaching and researching listening.* Essex, UK: Pearson Education Ltd.

Rost, M. (2001). Listening. In Ronald, R., & Nunan, D. (Eds.), *Guide to teaching English to speakers of other languages* (pp. 7–13). Cambridge, UK: Cambridge University Press. doi:10.1017/CBO9780511667206.002

Rost, M. (2006). Areas of research that influence L2 listening instruction. In Usó-Juan, E., & Martínez-Flor, A. (Eds.), *Current trends in the development and teaching of the four language skills* (pp. 47–74). Berlin: Mouton de Gruyter. doi:10.1515/9783110197778.2.47

Rost, M. (1991). *Listening in action.* Englewood Cliffs, NJ: Prentice Hall International (UK) Ltd.

Rumelhart, D. (1980). Schemata: The building blocks of cognition. In Spiro, R., Bruce, B., & Brewer, W. (Eds.), *Theoretical issues in reading comprehension* (pp. 33–35). Hillsdale, NJ: Earlbaum.

Rüschoff, B., & Ritter, M. (2001). Technology-enhanced language learning: Construction of knowledge and template-based learning in the foreign language classroom. *Computer Assisted Language Learning, 14,* 219–232. doi:10.1076/call.14.3.219.5789

Salili, F. (2001). Teacher-student interaction: Attributional implications and effectiveness of teachers' evaluative feedback. In Watkins, D. A., & Biggs, J. B. (Eds.), *Teaching the Chinese learner: Psychological and pedagogical perspectives* (pp. 77–98). Hong Kong: CERC, The University of Hong Kong.

Salmon, G., Mobbs, R., Edirisingha, P., & Dennett, C. (2008). Podcasting technology. In Salmon, G., & Edirisingha, P. (Eds.), *Podcasting for learning in universities*. Maidenhead, U.K.: Open University Press.

Salmon, G., & Nie, M. (2008). Doubling the life of iPods. In Salmon, G., & Edirisingha, P. (Eds.), *Podcasting for learning in universities* (pp. 20–32). Maidenhead, U.K.: Open University Press.

Sathe, N., & Waltje, J. (2008). The iPod project: A mobile mini-lab. *Journal of the Research Centre for Educational Technology, 4*, 32–56.

Schlosser, C. A., & Burmeister, M. L. (2006). *Audio in online courses: Beyond podcasting.* Retrieved from http://www.nova.edu/~burmeist/audio_online.html

Schmidt, J. (2008). Podcasting as a learning tool: German language and culture every day. *Unterrichtspraxis, 41*, 186–194. doi:10.1111/j.1756-1221.2008.00023.x

Schütz, R. (2005). *Stephen Krashen's theory of second language acquisition.* Retrieved March 12, 2010, from http://perso.univ-lyon2.fr/~giled/050801Stephen%20Krashen's%20Theory.htm

Schwartz, B. D. (1993). On explicit and negative data affecting competence and linguistic behavior. *Studies in Second Language Acquisition, 15*, 147–163. doi:10.1017/S0272263100011931

Schwartz, L., Sharon Clark, S., Cossarin, M., & Rudolph, J. (2003). Educational wikis: Features and selection criteria. *Language Learning & Technology, 7*(2), 12–16.

Secules, T., Herron, C., & Tomasello, M. (1992). The effect of video context on foreign language learning. *Modern Language Journal, 76*, 480–490. doi:10.2307/330049

Seidlhofer, B. (2001). Closing a conceptual gap: The case for a description of English as a lingua franca. *International Journal of Applied Linguistics, 11*, 133–158. doi:10.1111/1473-4192.00011

Seitzinger, J. (2006). Be constructive: Blogs, podcasts, and wikis as constructivist learning tools. *Learning Solutions.* July, 2006.

Seufert, T., Schutze, M., & Brunken, R. (2009). Memory characteristics and modality in multimedia learning: An aptitude-treatment-interaction study. *Learning and Instruction, 19*(1), 28–42. doi:10.1016/j.learninstruc.2008.01.002

Sharples, M. (2003). Disruptive devices: Mobile technology for conversational learning. *International Journal of Continuing Engineering Education and Lifelong Learning, 12*(5/6), 504–520. doi:10.1504/IJCEELL.2002.002148

Sharples, M., Taylor, J., & Vavoula, G. (2005). Towards a theory of mobile learning. Paper presented at *mLearn* 2005, Capetown South Africa. Retrieved from http://www.mlearn.org.za/CD/papers/Sharples-Theory of Mobile.pdf

Sharwood-Smith, M. (1993). Input enhancement in instructed SLA: Theoretical bases. *Studies in Second Language Acquisition, 15*, 165–179. doi:10.1017/S0272263100011943

Sherman, J. (2003). *Using authentic video in the language classroom.* Cambridge: Cambridge University Press.

Shield, L., & Kukulska-Hulme, A. (2008)... *ReCALL, 20*(3), 249–252. doi:10.1017/S095834400800013X

Shrum, J., & Glisan, E. (2005). *Teacher's handbook: Contextualized language instruction.* Boston, MA: Thomson-Heinle.

Simon, E. (2008). Foreign language faculty in the age of web 2.0. *EDUCAUSE Quarterly, 3*, 6–7.

Simpson, J. (Ed.). (2009). *Oxford English Dictionary* (3rd ed.). New York: Oxford University Press. Retrieved March 30, 2010, from http://dictionary.oed.com

Stanley, G. (2006) Podcasting: Audio on the Internet Comes of Age. *TESL-EJ, 9*(4).

Stanley, G. (2006). Podcasting: Audio on the internet comes of age. *TESL-EJ 9*(4), 1-7. http://tesl-ej.org/ej36/int.html

Stanley, G. (2006). Podcasting: Audio on the internet comes of age, *TESL-EJ, 9*(4). Retrieved from http://www-writing.berkeley.edu/TESL-EJ/ej36/int.html

Stevick, E. W. (1989). *Success with Foreign Languages: Seven who achieved it and what worked for them*. New York: Prentice Hall.

Stolovitch, H. D., & Keeps, E. J. (2003). *Telling ain't training*. Alexandria, VA: ASTD.

Study Abroad Research Group (SARG). (2010). Website Reference List. Retrieved January 1, 2010 from http://studyabroadresearch.org/ReferenceList.htm

Sturgis, D. (2008). Today's cheaters, tomorrow's visionaries. In Wittkower, D. E. (Ed.), *iPod and philosophy: iCon of an epoch* (pp. 71–84). Chicago, IL: Open Court.

Sturm, M., Kennell, T., McBride, R., & Kelly, M. (2009). The pedagogical implications of Web 2.0. In Thomas, M. (Ed.), *Web 2.0 and second language learning* (pp. 367–384). Hershey, PA: Information Science Reference.

Swain, M., & Lapkin, S. (1995). Problems in output and the cognitive processes they generate: A step towards second language learning. *Applied Linguistics*, *16*, 371–391. doi:10.1093/applin/16.3.371

Swain, M., & Lapkin, S. (1989). Canadian immersion and adult second language teaching –What's the connection. *Modern Language Journal*, *73*, 150–159. doi:10.2307/326570

Swartz, J. (2009, October 21). *Marketers salivating over smartphone potential*. Retrieved October 31, 2009, from USA Today website: http://www.usatoday.com/tech/news/2009-10-20-social-network-smartphone_N.htm

Sze, P. M.-M. (2006). Developing students' listening and speaking skills through ELT podcasts. *Education Journal*, *34*, 115–134.

Sze, P. M. M. (2006). Developing students' listening and speaking skills through ELT podcasts. *Education Journal*, *34*(2), 115–134.

Takenoya, M. (1995). Acquisition of pragmatic rules: The gap between what the language textbooks present and how learners perform. In Haggstrom, M. A., Morgan, L. Z., & Wieczorek, J. A. (Eds.), *The foreign language classroom: Bridging theory and practice* (pp. 149–164). New York: Garland.

Taylor, G. (2005). Perceived processing strategies of students watching captioned video. *Foreign Language Annals*, *38*(3), 422–427. doi:10.1111/j.1944-9720.2005.tb02228.x

The Center for Educational Development. Retrieved April 21, 2010 from http://www.eslpod.com/website/index_new.html

The New Media Consortium & EDUCAUSE Learning Initiative. (2008). *Horizon report*. Retrieved from http://www.nmc.org/pdf/2008-Horizon-Report.pdf

The University of Wisconsin Language Institute Website. Retrieved November 16, 2009, from http://languageinstitute.wisc.edu/

Thomas, M. (2008). *Handbook of research on Web 2.0 and second language learning*. Hershey, PA: Information Science Reference.

Thorne, S. L., & Payne, J. S. (2005). Evolutionary trajectories, internet-mediated expression, and language education. *CALICO Journal*, *22*(3), 371–397.

Thorne, S. L., & Payne, J. S. (2005). Evolutionary trajectories, internet mediated expression, and language education. *CALICO Journal*, *22*, 371–397.

Thornton, P., & Houser, C. (2005). Using mobile phones in English education in Japan. *Journal of Computer Assisted Learning*, *21*, 217–228. doi:10.1111/j.1365-2729.2005.00129.x

Ting, A., & Jones, P. D. (2010). Using free source ePortfolios to empower ESL teachers in collaborative peer reflection. In Kush, J., Lombard, R., Hertzog, J., & Yamamoto, J. (Eds.), *Technology implementation and teacher education: Reflective models*. Hershey, PA: IGI Global. doi:10.4018/978-1-61520-897-5.ch006

Tiwari, B. (2010, March 2). *Exciting time for WiMAX and LTE in Japan*. Retrieved March 12, 2010, from WiMax 360 website: http://wimaxcommunity.ning.com/profiles/blogs/exciting-time-for-wimax-and

Toma, T. (2000). Cognition and courseware design by teachers: The concept of multimediatizing. *Society for Information Technology & Teacher Education International Conference: Proceedings of SITE 2000, 1*-3.

Trahey, M., & White, L. (1993). Positive evidence and preemption in the second language classroom. *Studies in Second Language Acquisition, 15,* 181–204. doi:10.1017/S0272263100011955

U. S. Department of Education. (n.d.). Retrieved September 15, 2009 from www.ed.gov

U.S. Census Bureau. (2009). S1601 Language spoken at home 2006-2008 American Community Survey 3-year estimates. Retrieved from http://factfinder.census.gov/servlet/STTable?geo_id=01000US&ds_name=ACS_2008_3YR_G00_&qr_name=ACS_2008_3YR_G00_S1601

VanPatten, B. (2003). *From input to output: A teacher's guide to second language acquisition.* New York: McGraw-Hill.

Vincent, T. (2009, October 6). *Create it in your hand, share it with the world.* Retrieved November 25, 2009, from Learning in Hand website: http://learninginhand.com/blog/2009/10/create-it-in-your-hand-share-it-with.html

Viswanathan, R. (2009). Using mobile technology and podcasts to teach soft skills. In Thomas, M. (Ed.), *Web 2.0 and second language learning* (pp. 223–235). Hershey, PA: Information Science Reference.

Waele, R. D. (2006). *Understanding Mobile 2.0.* Retrieved October 18, 2009, from Read Write Web website: http://www.readwriteweb.com/archives/understanding_mobile_2.php

Wang, S., & Heffernan, N. (2009). Mobile 2.0 and mobile language learning. In Thomas, M. (Ed.), *Web 2.0 and second language learning* (pp. 472–490). Hershey, PA: Information Science Reference.

Warschauer, M., & Healey, D. (1998). Computers and language learning: An overview. *Language Teaching, 31,* 57–71. doi:10.1017/S0261444800012970

*Web 3.0 and beyond: The next 20 years of the internet.* (2007, October 24). Retrieved March 12, 2010, from Times Online website: http://technology.timesonline.co.uk/tol/news/tech_and_web/the_web/article2726190.ece

Weintraub, S. (2009, December 31). This is why Apple denied Google Latitude from the App Store...Retrieved from 9-to-5 Mac on January 4, 2010, at http://www.9to5mac.com/apple-google-latitude-functionality-maps-2546345

*What is WiMax?* (n.d.). Retrieved November 27, 2009, from WiMax website: http://www.wimax.com/education

White, C., Easton, P., & Anderson, C. (2000). Students' perceived value of video in a multimedia language course. *Educational Media International, 37*(3), 167–175. doi:10.1080/09523980050184736

White, G. (2006). Teaching listening: Time for a change in methodology. In Usó-Juan, E., & Martínez-Flor, A. (Eds.), *Current trends in the development and teaching of the four language skills* (pp. 111–135). Berlin: Mouton de Gruyter. doi:10.1515/9783110197778.2.111

William, S., & McMinn, J. (2008). *Podcasting possibilities: Increasing time and motivation in the language classroom.* European Institute for E-Learning (EIfEL) (pp. 212-215). Retrieved from http://www.eife-l.org/publications/proceedings/ilf08/contributions/improving-quality-of-learning-with-technologies/McMinn.pdf

Williams, J. (2004). *Teaching writing in second and foreign language classrooms.* New York: McGraw-Hill.

Window on State Government. (2010). *Texas in focus: South Texas demographics.* Retrieved from http://www.window.state.tx.us/specialrpt/tif/southtexas/demographics.html

World of Apple. (2009, September 9). Apple's "It's Only Rock and Roll" Event. Live Coverage and Press Release. Retrieved March 25, 2010 from http://news.worldofapple.com/?s=Sept%202009.

Young, D. J. (2007). iPods, MP3 players and podcasts for FL learning: Current practices and future considerations. *NECTFL Review, 60,* 39–49.

Young, D. (2007). iPods, MP3 players and podcasts for FL learning: Current practices and future considerations. *The NECTFL Review, 60*, 39–49.

Young, D. J. (2007). iPods, MP3 players and podcasts for EFL learning: Current practices and future considerations. *NECTFL Review, 60*, 39–49.

Young, J. (n.d.). *Mobile Phone Adoption in Developing Countries.* Retrieved March 12, 2010, from Wikinvest website: http://www.wikinvest.com/concept/Mobile_Phone_Adoption_in_Developing_Countries

Zuber-Skerritt, O. (1992). *Action research in higher education.* London: Kogan Page.

Zurita, G., & Nussbaumw, M. (2004). A constructivist mobile learning environment supported by a wireless handheld network. *Journal of Computer Assisted Learning, 20*, 235–243. doi:10.1111/j.1365-2729.2004.00089.x

# About the Contributors

**Betty Rose Facer** is Senior Lecturer of French and the Director of the Language Learning Center in the Department of Foreign Languages and Literatures at Old Dominion University in Norfolk, Virginia. She received her Master of Arts degree from Syracuse University in French Language and Literatures. Her research interests include computer-assisted language learning and instruction, and the impact of new media on foreign language pedagogy. She is the recipient of numerous grants, including one from the National Endowment for the Humanities (NEH) to focus on the use of technology in language learning and teaching. She has made presentations at the International Association for Language Learning Technology, the Computer Assisted Language Instruction Consortium, the Mid Atlantic Association for Language Learning Technology, and the American Council on the Teaching of Foreign Languages. She serves as an Official Delegate to the Joint National Committee for Languages (JNCL) in Washington, DC to identify national needs and to plan national language policies.

**Mohammed Abdous** is the Assistant Vice-President for Teaching and Learning with Technology and the Director of the Center for Learning Technologies at Old Dominion University in Norfolk, Virginia, where he provides leadership and assistance to the Provost's Office and to the Distance Learning office to (1) conceive, implement, and evaluate processes for effectively integrating technology into teaching and learning practices, and (2) manage and produce quality online programs and courses. His responsibilities include, among other things, the development of institution-wide faculty development programs and the management of online program/course production projects. Dr. Abdous' research interests include emerging technologies, process re-engineering, and quality assurance for online courses. Dr. Abdous works also as a UNICEF consultant for the Tunisian and Syrian Ministries of Education, where he has conducted a series of workshops on program and project evaluation, textbooks and curriculum design, and evaluation and project review.

\* \* \*

**Elizabeth Beckmann** teaches in the Centre for Educational Development and Academic Methods at the Australian National University, where she supports academics who are introducing innovations into their teaching. A highly experienced educator, communicator, and evaluator, Elizabeth has worked in fields as diverse as environmental management, museums studies, and public communication. She is particularly interested in the ways in which new technologies can be used to support learning in a range of fields, including languages.

**Daryl Beres** (MA ESL, University of Minnesota) is Director of the Language Resource Center at Mount Holyoke College, where she also teaches English for Speakers of Other Languages. Her research interests include computer- and mobile-assisted language learning, English for academic purposes, and Generation 1.5 and the transition to college.

**Joseph Rene Corbeil** is an Associate Professor at The University of Texas at Brownsville/Texas Southmost College. He earned his doctoral degree in Education-Curriculum and Instruction with an emphasis on Instructional Technology from the University of Houston, and his Master of Education degree in Educational Technology from The University of Texas at Brownsville. Currently, he teaches fully web-based undergraduate and graduate courses in Educational Technology. His research interests include best practices in synchronous and asynchronous communication and enhancing social presence and teacher immediacy in e-Learning environments through the use of Web 2.0 and social networking tools like blogs, wikis, and podcasts. He is also interested in exploring the potential of portable communication/computing technologies for mobile learning (m-Leaning) in adult education programs.

**Maria Elena Corbeil** is an Associate Professor at The University of Texas at Brownsville/Texas Southmost College. She currently develops and teaches fully online technology education and corporate training courses. She earned her doctoral degree in Education-Curriculum and Instruction; a Masters degree in Education with a specialization in English as a Second Language; and a Bachelors degree in English. She began her career at UTB/TSC as an English as a Second Language instructor, after which she became the ESL Learning Instructional Specialist, and later, director, of the learning center. Maria Elena has also taught in Foreign Language Teacher Certification and English as a Foreign Language programs in Mexico City. Previously, she worked for Miami Book Fair International and served as a volunteer in community literacy programs. She has published and presented in numerous journals and conferences on her research interests, which include innovations in distance learning.

**Claudia Fernández** is Assistant Professor of Modern Languages-Spanish at Knox College. Her research focuses on the acquisition of grammar in classroom contexts, the effectiveness of L2 instructional techniques, and the development of both traditional and technology-based materials. Her work has been published in the 2007 AAUSC volume and in Studies in Second Language Acquisition, and she has co-authored several book chapters. She is the writer, producer and host of SPOD, a series of podcasts for beginning Spanish learners that can be found on iTunesU.

**Robert Fischer** is Professor of French and Chair of the Department of Modern Languages at Texas State University. He has served as the Executive Director of the Computer Assisted Language Instruction Consortium (CALICO) for 12 years. He has published, presented papers, and consulted widely in the field of computer-assisted language learning and has directed several grant-funded projects in the development and use of multimedia authoring tools for foreign language listening and reading comprehension.

**Tony Gonzalez** is a Ph.D. student in Learning, Design, and Technology at the University of Georgia, where he also teaches Japanese. Before beginning a career in education, he worked for fifteen years as a translator, software localization engineer, and software developer in Tokyo, Japan and in Mountain View, California. He is the producer of the "Genkier" series of podcasts for learning Japanese, and he also develops mobile applications and online materials for foreign language learning. He was President of the Georgia Association of Teachers of Japanese from 2008 to 2009. In 2010, he was awarded the UGA Graduate School's Excellence in Teaching Award for his contributions to teaching and learning. His research interests are related to independent foreign language study in digital contexts.

**Su-Ling Hsueh** obtained both Master and Ph.D. degrees in Instructional Psychology and Technology from Brigham Young University. She currently serves in the Defense Language Institute Foreign Language Center as Assistant Dean to oversee and develop language technology. Dr. Hsueh's research focuses on technology integration, faculty technology training, and technology assisted 2nd language learning and teaching, and related topics. Some of her publications include An Investigation of the Technological, Pedagogical and Content Knowledge Framework in Successful Chinese Language Classrooms, and American and Chinese Culture: Conceptions of individualism, competition, authority, and time with their implications for distance learning. She has also presented numerous topics at professional and academic gatherings (e.g., "Integrate TPCK in Successful Language Classrooms," "Effectively Integrating the iPod in Language Teaching") in various conferences such as ACTFL, IALLT, and FLANC.

**Peter A. Lafford** is Academic Computing Professional and Computing Director for the Specialized Labs in the School of Letters and Sciences, University College, Arizona State University. He has an MA in French from Middlebury College, an MA in English/ESL from Arizona State University, and a BA in French Linguistics from Cornell University. A member of ASU's University Technology Office since moving to the new Downtown Phoenix campus in 2006, he has been promoting academic technology and its application to language teaching at Arizona State University for over twenty years. Prior to joining ASU, he taught French, Spanish, and English as a Second Language.

**Lara Lomicka** (Ph.D. Pennsylvania State University) is Associate Professor of French at the University of South Caroli¬na, where she is the Director of Basic Courses and the Assistant Director of Teacher Education. She serves as the AATF (American Association of Teachers of French) Chair for the Telematics and New Technologies Commission and is the Software Editor for the CALICO (Computer Assisted Language Instruction Consortium) journal. She was the recipient of the 2008 ACTFL/Cengage Award in Technology and Language Teaching. Her work has appeared in journals such as Computer Assisted Language Instruction Consortium (CALICO), System, The French Review, Language Learning & Technology, and Foreign Language Annals, and she and Gillian Lord co-edited the 2009 CALICO monograph The Next Generation: Social Networking and Online Collaboration in Foreign Language Learning. She regularly publishes in the areas of teacher education and technology with specific interests in blogs, wikis, podcasting, and intercultural learning.

**Gillian Lord** (Ph.D. Pennsylvania State University) is Associate Professor of Spanish and Linguistics at the University of Florida, and she currently serves on the executive board of CALICO. She teaches courses on Hispanic Linguistics and on second language acquisition and teacher education, including technology in language education. Her research focuses on different aspects of language acquisition, such as study abroad, technology, and teacher training. Her work has appeared in journals such as Computer Assisted Language Instruction Consortium (CALICO), System, Hispania, and Foreign Language Annals, and she and Lara Lomicka co-edited the 2009 CALICO monograph The Next Generation: Social Networking and Online Collaboration in Foreign Language Learning. Her current projects involve directing the lower division Spanish program at the University of Florida and writing a Handbook for

Language Program Directors, as well as ongoing projects investigating podcasting, wikis, and twitter in the classroom.

**Mario Daniel Martín** was born in Salta, Argentina. He is currently the convener of the Spanish Program at the Australian National University, where he pursues his passion to include technology in the foreign language classroom. Dr Martín's research interests include the Spanish-speaking community in Australia and the history and politics of language teaching in Australia. As a creative writer, Dr. Martín has won international and national literary prizes. He has published three poetry books, two theatre books, and two books of short stories, and written the scripts for three films and four theatre plays, all published and produced in Argentina. His research and creative interests have found their way into his teaching. He designed the first university course for Spanish native speakers in Australia, and he created modules in Spanish courses based on theatre, visual materials (comics), biography, and radio production. He has also been active in disseminating his teaching developments through teachers' forums and workshops,

**Kathryn Murphy-Judy**, Ph.D., is Associate Professor of French at Virginia Commonwealth University in the School of World Studies. She has been working in media and mediated learning, second language acquisition, and teacher education for over thirty-five years. She can be contacted at kmurphy@vcu.edu.

**Ulugbek Nurmukhamedov** is currently a first-year Ph.D. student in Applied Linguistics at Northern Arizona University. He came to the U.S. with an MA in Translation Theory and Practice from Uzbek State World Languages University (Uzbekistan) and earned his MA in TESOL from the University of Illinois at Urbana-Champaign (UIUC). He has also worked as an ESL Instructor at the Intensive English Institute at UIUC. His current research interests include L2 writing and L2 vocabulary. He is also interested in exploring effective ways to apply technology to improve writing instruction, especially teacher-written feedback. Ulugbek is passionate about using research from corpus linguistics to promote creativity in language use and to enhance vocabulary and grammar accuracy among L2 writers.

**Susanne Rott** is Associate Professor of German and Second Language Acquisition. She directs the Sandy Port Errant Language and Culture Learning Center as well as the Basic German Language Program at the University of Illinois at Chicago. In her research she focuses on the lexical development of second language learners, in particular the partial acquisition of individual word aspects, collocational units, and lexico-grammatical constructions, as well as the impact of instructional interventions on learning. As the director of the Language and Culture Learning Center she works with faculty to develop computer-based learning units to effectively blend foreign language and culture instruction.

**Randall Sadler** is an Assistant Professor of Linguistics at the University of Illinois. His research areas include CMC (computer-mediated communication) and language teaching, particularly focusing on Virtual Worlds like Second Life™ and the ways in which they can play a role in the language learning and teaching process. He is the co-author of A Student's Guide to First-Year Composition and will soon have a book published by Peter Lang titled Virtual Worlds and Language Learning: From Theory to Practice.

**Alison Schoew** (MA, Applied Linguistics, Old Dominion University) is the Technical Writer at ODU's Center for Learning Technologies and is an adjunct English instructor for ODU's teacher candidates, teaching students across the nation via satellite. She holds a certificate in teaching English as a Second Language, and has had extensive experience working one-to-one with scientists and researchers, assisting them in explaining their work for presentation and publication in English. She has a passion for comparing varieties of English.

**Giovanna Summerfield** is Associate Professor of Italian and French at Auburn University. Her research focuses on the long eighteenth-century (1660-1830) French and Italian literature (with an emphasis on Sicilian writers), religious and philosophical movements, women's studies, European and Mediterranean history/civilization, and material culture. Among some of her publications are New Perspectives on the European Bildungsroman (co-authored). London, UK: Continuum, 2010, Remembering Sicily. Mineola, NY: Legas Publishing, 2009, Credere aude: Mystifying Enlightenment. Tübingen: Gunter Narr Verlag, 2008, Patois and Linguistic Pastiche in Modern Literature. Cambridge Scholars Publishing, 2007, and "Contes de fées by Women of the Seventeenth-Century: New Discourses of Sexuality and Gender." Les femmes au Grand Siècle. Tübingen: Gunter Narr Verlag, 2002 (reprinted in Literature Criticism From 1400-1800, Vol. 153 by Gale, Oct 2008). Dr. Summerfield created and implemented Auburn University's summer and semester Study Abroad programs in Taormina, Italy in 2006.

**Adrian Ting** has extensive experience in teaching English as a second language to Hong Kong learners. Currently, he works for the Centre for Language in Education, and at The Hong Kong Institute of Education, and he is responsible for teaching English language courses to both pre-service undergraduates and in-service teaching professionals. One of his major areas of research looks into the impact of the increased use of new technologies on the learning styles of Hong Kong digital natives and their abilities to acquire proficiency in a second language. He is also interested in computer-assisted language learning, e-learning syllabus design, teacher training, and learner motivation.

# Index

## Symbols

3G  85, 86, 89, 91
3GS modem  143
4G  71, 85, 91
4G cellular networks  38

## A

academic backgrounds  4
academic podcasting  1, 14, 15, 22, 33, 50, 66, 67, 94, 109, 111, 127, 160, 173, 193
Academic Podcasting Technology (APT)  111, 112, 116, 117, 118, 119, 121, 122, 123, 124, 125, 126
academic podcasts  71, 73, 82, 167
Academic Word List (AWL)  189
Adobe Premiere Pro®  44
Advanced Audio Coding (AAC)  41, 42, 43, 44, 45
American Council on the Teaching of Foreign Languages (ACTFL)  134, 140, 145
application-specific file formats  47
application-specific file types  47
Astuce®  143
Audacity  69
audio content  37, 48, 53, 72
audio-only MP3  43
audio-only podcast  38, 43
audio tools  8
aural enhancement  26
aural practice  161
aural text  24, 25, 26, 27, 28, 31, 36
Australian National University (ANU)  111, 112, 113, 114, 117, 121, 124, 125, 126
authentic language  28, 29

authentic learning experiences  66
authentic linguistic models  66

## B

Bachelor of Applied Arts and Science (BAAS)  60
Bachelor of Applied Technology (BAT)  60
BBC Learning English  178, 184, 185, 189
Belkin Voice Recorder  154
BlackBerry  139, 143
Blackboard  144, 164, 165, 166, 167
Blogger®  144
blogs  70, 71, 72, 74, 75, 76, 77, 78, 80, 82, 83, 84, 85, 86, 87, 88, 90, 131
Breaking News English (BNE)  181
British Broadcasting Corporation (BBC)  178, 179, 183, 184, 185, 189, 190, 192

## C

Calendar®  144
CD ripping  130
chapter marker  52
chatter box podcast  181
ChinesePod  72, 82
classroom-based learning  81
classroom language  162, 163, 164, 166, 167, 168, 169
cloud-based environment  144
collaborative webs  66
collective intelligence-data  66
communicative function  27
community of practice (COP)  75, 91
community service project  11
compression/decompression (CODEC)  135
Computer Assisted Language Instruction Consortium (CALICO)  155, 156

computer assisted language learning (CALL) 22, 25, 34, 35, 112, 128, 133, 134, 135, 138, 144

computer-generated static images 45

computer-mediated communication (CMC) 135, 136

course management systems (CMS) 144

creative commons (CC) 48, 49

Creative Commons Licenses 53

Creative Zen® 41

cultural aspects 37, 40, 48

cultural context 108

cultural information 31, 32, 181

culture 21, 24, 31, 32, 33, 34, 36

**D**

dailyfrenchpod 72

data mashups 66

Defense Language Institute Foreign Language Center (DLIFLC) 80

Delicious® 71

derivative work 53

device-toting learners 133

digital audio file 55

digital skills 10

Docs® 144

**E**

easily-accessible tools 66

École Supérieure de Commerce (ESC) 138, 139

editing/publishing software 66

EFL contexts 177, 190

EFL learner 24

e-learning 80, 81, 89, 122, 130, 131, 137, 167, 168, 170

ELT rap 161

email-to-mobile phone method 98

English as a Second Language (ESL) 160, 161, 162, 163, 167, 168, 172, 174, 175

English Language Teaching (ELT) 3, 16

Enhanced podcasts 53

enhancing education through technology (Ed-Tech) 149

episode 177, 178, 179, 180, 181, 182, 183, 184, 185, 186, 187, 190, 191, 192

ESL learners 181

ESLpod 26

ESL podcasts 178, 181

ESL student 190

explicit information (EI) 29, 30, 31

**F**

Facebook® 70

face-to-face 54, 56, 81, 94, 97, 98, 106, 113, 114, 163

face-to-face classrooms 81

fair use 48, 53

file transfer protocol (FTP) 59

Final Cut Studio® 44

Flash® 44

Flash Video 44, 45

Flatmates 189, 191, 192

Flickr® 71, 138

foreign language education (FLE) 135

format 23, 26, 36

**G**

GarageBand® 42, 43, 44, 52, 53, 119, 120, 121

genre-based podcasts 9

global listening 161

Google® 71

Google Earth 142

Google Reader® 47

Grammar Challenge 184, 189, 190, 191, 192

Grammar Girl 30, 34, 179, 180

Griffin iTalk 154

**H**

host 23, 26, 29, 30, 36

human communication 45

human interaction component 81

**I**

iLife® 42

iLife package 42

iMandarin 72

iMovie® 44

imparfait 26

implicit linguistic system 24, 26, 30, 36

informal mobile podcasting and learning adaptation (IMPALA) 177

information and communication technologies (ICT) 160, 162, 163, 164, 165, 166, 167, 170
information technology (IT) 123
input-enhancement 26
Institut d'Études Françaises (IEF) 138
Institute of International Education (IIE) 147
instructional content 72
instructor-learner 39
International Society for Technology in Education (ISTE) 155
International Technology Education Association (ITEA) 155
iPad 37
iPhone 43, 45, 53, 79, 87, 102, 142, 143
iPod lab 5
iPod Nano® 117, 125, 157
iPods® 1, 5, 14, 15, 16, 37, 41, 42, 43, 44, 45, 51, 53, 72, 74, 76, 78, 79, 80, 81, 96, 100, 102, 103, 104, 106, 107, 109, 110, 117, 118, 121, 122, 123, 126, 128, 129, 149, 150, 151, 152, 153, 154, 155, 156, 157, 158
iPod Touch® 4, 41, 74, 102, 125, 192
iTunes 22, 29, 41, 42, 43, 44, 72, 93, 112, 137, 138, 150, 152, 155, 156, 176, 177, 178, 179, 180, 181, 182, 183, 184, 185, 188, 192, 193
iTunes U 44, 177

**J**

JapanesePod101 72
Just Vocabulary Podcast 179, 180

**K**

Keynote® 42
knowledge management 81

**L**

L2 acquisition 21, 22, 24, 25, 26, 29, 30, 33
L2 development 23
L2 input 23
L2 instruction 23, 29
L2 instructors 22
L2 learner 21

L2 learning 21, 22, 23, 24, 33
L2 learning materials 21
L2 learning tools 21
L2 listening 22, 29, 34, 35
L2 teaching practices 23
L2 teaching techniques 26
language learning 1, 2, 4, 5, 9, 12, 13, 14, 15, 16, 21, 22, 23, 24, 31, 33, 34, 35, 36, 39, 47, 48, 50, 51, 52, 54, 55, 56, 65, 66, 67, 68, 70, 72, 128, 129, 130, 134, 135, 136, 144, 150, 160, 161, 163, 166, 167, 172, 173, 174, 175, 176, 177, 178, 185, 186, 192, 193, 194
language learning objectives 21
language resource center (LRC) 100, 102
learner-centered design principles 107, 109
learner-friendly devices 71
learner-instructor interaction 39
learner-learner interaction 39
Learner skepticism 108
learning approach 123
learning community 108
learning management system (LMS) 60, 114, 115, 117, 130, 131
learning outcomes 22, 23, 56, 69, 112, 117, 173
linguistics 5, 16
linguistic system 24, 26, 30, 36
listening skills 26, 27, 28, 29, 30, 31
listening tools 21

**M**

Macintosh® 42
main text 25, 26, 28, 36
MALL-scape 197
MALL technologies 23, 112
Marcos 54, 55, 145
meaning-bearing input 24, 25
meta-cognitive fashion 81
Microsoft Word® 47
m-learning 71, 80, 81, 93, 94, 95, 96, 97, 98, 100, 101, 102, 106, 107, 108, 133, 134, 135, 136, 137, 138, 139, 142, 143, 145
mobile 2.0 70, 71, 72, 78, 84, 85, 86, 90
mobile assisted 21, 22, 54, 111, 133, 145, 172

mobile assisted language learning (MALL) 14, 16, 22, 23, 26, 33, 55, 93, 94, 96, 99, 100, 101, 102, 103, 104, 105, 106, 107, 108, 109, 111, 112, 116, 123, 125, 127, 133, 134, 135, 136, 137, 138, 144, 145, 172, 173

mobile assisted language learning resources 55, 66

Mobile broadband 66

mobile devices 56, 71, 72, 74, 78, 83, 93, 94, 95, 96, 97, 100, 101, 102, 103, 107, 108, 109, 110, 133, 134, 136, 137, 139, 140, 143, 145

mobile handsets 71

mobile learning 71, 78, 81, 89, 90, 91, 95, 107, 108, 109, 128, 129, 133

mobile technologies 55, 65, 68, 88, 94, 95, 97, 99, 126, 127, 137, 144

mobile technology 71, 85, 86, 90, 108, 110

Moodle 144

morpho-syntactic 23, 25, 30

motion video 44, 45, 46

Movie Maker® 44

MP3 55, 59, 65, 69, 74, 94, 100, 101, 102, 104, 105, 106, 110, 112, 114, 115, 116, 117, 118, 121, 125, 126, 130, 133, 136, 137, 138, 139, 156, 164, 165, 166, 167, 169, 177, 187, 192, 194

MP3 files 41, 43, 115, 118, 164, 192

MP3 players 1, 4, 11, 13, 16, 94, 100, 101, 102, 104, 105, 106, 110, 116, 117, 118, 125, 126, 133, 137, 138, 139, 165, 167, 169, 177

MPEG4 44, 45

m-teachers 107, 109

m-teaching 93, 95, 107, 108

multimedia content 37, 38, 39, 40, 43, 48, 49, 50

multimedia development software 38

multimedia podcast 38, 40, 43, 50, 53

multimedia podcasting project 37, 38, 50

mutually-beneficial cycle 86

mutually-supportive connection 80

MySpace® 76, 136

**N**

National Standards for Foreign Language Education Project (NSFLEP) 31, 35

Nings® 136

nonverbal aspects 45

**O**

omnidirectional microphone 130

online mobile-assisted language learning courses 56

open doors 147, 158

organisation for economic co-operation and development (OECD) 115

out of the box 38

**P**

paper-based activity 80

passé composé 26

pdf (Portable Document Format) 47

pedagogical applications 1

pedagogical content 37, 38, 49

pedagogic know-how 22

peer-evaluation checklist 81

peer review 1

personal digital assistant (PDA) 71

personal mobile 108

Picasa® 140, 144

PlayStation Portable® 37

podcast-based activity 197

podcast design 21, 22, 23, 24, 25, 26, 33

podcasting 1, 2, 3, 4, 5, 6, 7, 8, 9, 10, 11, 12, 13, 14, 15, 16, 17, 19, 20, 22, 23, 32, 33, 34, 35, 37, 38, 39, 40, 42, 43, 49, 50, 51, 52, 54, 55, 163, 164, 165, 166, 167, 168, 169, 170, 171, 172, 173, 174, 176, 177, 178, 185, 193, 194

podcasting project 9, 10, 19, 37, 38, 50, 161, 164

podcasting research 1, 2

podcast project 28, 32, 33, 36

podcasts 1, 2, 3, 4, 5, 6, 7, 8, 9, 10, 11, 12, 13, 15, 16, 17, 20, 21, 22, 23, 24, 25, 26, 27, 28, 29, 30, 181, 182, 183, 184, 185, 186, 187, 188, 189, 190, 192, 193, 194

Podcastsinenglish (PIE) 182, 186, 187, 192
podcast software 56, 58, 59
portable document format (PDF) 181, 187
portable media player (PMP) 44, 45, 53
PowerPoint® 42, 151, 152
project-based learning (PjBL) 80, 89
project-oriented perspective 9

**Q**

QuickTime 135

**R**

Really Simple Syndication (RSS) 59, 65, 72,
       74, 86, 87, 112, 130, 131, 164, 166, 167,
       171
Really Simple Syndication (RSS) function 72
ReCALL 136, 145, 146
RSS aggregators 47
RSS feed 43, 44, 46, 47, 48, 65, 130, 164, 167,
       171
RSS subscription 23
rtf (formatted text) 47
RussianPod101 72, 82

**S**

SA environment 135
scholastic aptitude test (SAT) 85
Second Language 112, 129
Second Language Acquisition (SLA) 2, 14
second language (L2) 21
silver bullet 38
Sites® 144
situation-centered 77
skill-based approach 27
Skype® 136
SLA theories 23, 138, 145
smartphones 53, 70, 71, 75, 76, 79, 80, 87
social network 139, 140
social networking 55, 56, 66, 70, 71, 74, 77,
       85, 131, 136, 143
social networking activities 56
Social operating systems 66
Social Presence 69
Society for Information Technology and

Teacher Education (SITTE) 155
socio-cultural contexts 111
socio-linguistic skills 56
Spanish 111, 112, 113, 114, 117, 120, 121, 122,
       123, 124, 125, 126, 127, 128
speech-to-text conversion 11
strategy-based perspective 27
student-teacher interactions 54
study abroad (SA) 133, 134, 135, 136, 137,
       138, 143

**T**

tablet PC 71, 75, 76, 80
target culture 21, 24, 31, 32, 33
target language 134, 141, 144
teacher immediacy 69
technology-assisted language instruction 9
technology-based activities 80
technology enhanced language learning (TELL)
       133, 134, 135, 137, 138
technology, entertainment, and design (TED)
       183, 187, 188, 189
text-based platform 141
textual enhancement 26
trails 138, 142, 143
Twitter® 70, 107
txt (text only) 47

**U**

unidirectional microphone 130
user-created tools 66
user-generated recordings 135
user-led services 71

**V**

video podcasts (vodcasts) 136
video production 40, 44, 45, 46
virtual learning environment (VLE) 114, 117,
       118, 122, 130, 131, 168
visual cues 66, 125
visual input 8
visual recording 135
Voice of America (VoA) 183, 185, 189

**W**

Walkman® 37
Web 2.0  2, 13, 70, 71, 72, 76, 77, 78, 84, 85,
        87, 88, 89, 90, 133, 136, 138, 139, 143,
        145, 160, 174
Web 2.0 resources  133
Web 3.0  70, 85, 90
web-based external resources  53
Web society  70
WiFi  91, 196, 197
wikis  70, 71, 72, 75, 76, 77, 78, 80, 82, 83, 84,
        85, 87, 88, 89, 90, 131
WiMAX  71, 85, 90, 91
Wimba  144
Windows®  42
Windows 7®  44

Windows Live Movie Maker®  44, 52, 53
Windows XP®  44
Wireless Broadband  71
wireless learning environment  81
wireless networks  38
WordPress®  47
world-wide audience  55
World Wide Web  70, 85

**Y**

YouTube®  70, 76, 135, 137, 138, 144, 189,
        191, 192

**Z**

Zune  37, 41, 42, 43, 45, 53